Youth and Popular Culture in Africa

Rochester Studies in African History and the Diaspora

Toyin Falola, Series Editor
The Jacob and Frances Sanger Mossiker Chair in the Humanities
and University Distinguished Teaching Professor
University of Texas at Austin

Recent Titles

African Migration Narratives: Politics, Race, and Space
Edited by Cajetan Iheka and Jack Taylor

Ethics and Society in Nigeria: Identity, History, Political Theory
Nimi Wariboko

African Islands: Leading Edges of Empire and Globalization
Edited by Toyin Falola, R. Joseph Parrott, and Danielle Porter-Sanchez

Catholicism and the Making of Politics in Central Mozambique, 1940–1986
Eric Morier-Genoud

Liberated Africans and the Abolition of the Slave Trade, 1807–1896
Edited by Richard Anderson and Henry B. Lovejoy

The Other Abyssinians: The Northern Oromo and the Creation of Modern Ethiopia, 1855–1913
Brian J. Yates

Nigeria's Digital Diaspora: Citizen Media, Democracy, and Participation
Farooq A. Kperogi

West African Masking Traditions: History, Memory, and Transnationalism
Raphael Chijioke Njoku

Cultivating Their Own: Agriculture in Western Kenya during the "Development" Era
Muey C. Saeteurn

Disability in Africa: Inclusion, Care, and the Ethics of Humanity
Edited by Toyin Falola and Nic Hamel

A complete list of titles in the Rochester Studies in African History and the Diaspora series may be found on our website, www.urpress.com.

Youth and Popular Culture in Africa

Media, Music, and Politics

Edited by Paul Ugor

UNIVERSITY OF ROCHESTER PRESS

Copyright © 2021 by the Editor and Contributors

All rights reserved. Except as permitted under current legislation, no part of this work may be photocopied, stored in a retrieval system, published, performed in public, adapted, broadcast, transmitted, recorded, or reproduced in any form or by any means, without the prior permission of the copyright owner.

First published 2021

University of Rochester Press
668 Mt. Hope Avenue, Rochester, NY 14620, USA
www.urpress.com
and Boydell & Brewer Limited
PO Box 9, Woodbridge, Suffolk IP12 3DF, UK
www.boydellandbrewer.com

ISBN-13: 978-1-64825-024-8
ISSN: 1092-5228

Library of Congress Cataloging-in-Publication Data

Names: Ugor, Paul, editor.
Title: Youth and popular culture in Africa : media, music, and politics / edited by Paul Ugor.
Other titles: Rochester studies in African history and the diaspora ; 92. 1092-5228
Description: Rochester : University of Rochester Press, 2021. | Series: Rochester studies in African history and the diaspora, 1092-5228 ; 92 | Includes bibliographical references and index.
Identifiers: LCCN 2020056203 | ISBN 9781648250248 (hardback)
Subjects: LCSH: Mass media and youth–Africa. | Youth–Africa–Social conditions. | Popular culture–Africa. | Arts and youth–Africa.
Classification: LCC HQ799.2.M352 A359 2021 | DDC 302.23083096–dc23
LC record available at https://lccn.loc.gov/2020056203

This publication is printed on acid-free paper.

Printed in the United States of America.

Chapter 2, "Rapping, Imagination, and Urban Space in Dar es Salaam," previously appeared as "From the margins to the mainstream: making and remaking an alternative music economy in Dar es Salaam," by David Kerr, *Journal of African Cultural Studies* 30, 1 (2018). Reprinted by permission of Taylor & Francis Ltd, http://www.tandfonline.com.

To my uncle, Michael Ugbong Abuadiye. And to my former teacher and friend, Victor Adugba Agwu. Two men who taught me by their actions that to invest in young people is not a waste.

Contents

Preface ix

Introduction: Youth, Media, and Popular Arts Culture in
    Contemporary Africa 1
    Paul Ugor

Part One: Media Globalization, Popular Afro Hip-Hop, and Postcolonial Political Critique

1. Hip-Hop, Civic Awareness, and Antiestablishment Politics in
Senegal: The Rise of the *Y en a Marre* Movement 37
Bamba Ndiaye

2. Rapping, Imagination, and Urban Space in Dar es Salaam 63
David Kerr

3. Entertainers and Breadwinners: Music in the Lives of Street
Children in Abidjan, Côte d'Ivoire 88
Ty-Juana Taylor

4. Young People, Music, and Sociopolitical Change in Postwar
Sierra Leone 111
Ibrahim Bangura

5. The Politics of Pleasure in Nigerian Afrobeats 132
Paul Ugor

Part Two: Popular Online Media and Democratic Participation and Engagement

6. The Regeneration of Play: Popular Culture as Infrapolitics
on Instagram 163
James Yeku

7. "This Is Very Embarrassing and Insulting": *Flash Fiction Ghana* and Transgressive Writing 188
   Kwabena Opoku-Agyemang

8. Capitalizing on Transgression: Popular Homophobia and Popular Culture in Uganda 208
   Austin Bryan

9. Twitter, Youth Agency, and New Narratives of Power in #RhodesMustFall 235
   Jendele Hungbo

10. Resisting Political Oppression: Youth and Social Media in Zimbabwe 255
    Godfrey Maringira and Simbarashe Gukurume

Part Three: Popular Arts, Everyday Life, and the Politicization of Culture

11. Dressing *en Style*: Fashion and Fandom in Niger 279
    Adeline Masquelier

12. The Revolution Lost: Generational Change and Urban Youth Logics in Conakry's Dance Scene 307
    Adrienne Cohen

13. Culture Players and Poly-Ticks: Botswana Youth and Popular Culture Practices 327
    Connie Rapoo

14. #FeesMustFall and Youth Deconstruction of South Africa's Liberation Narrative 352
    Kristi Heather Kenyon, Juliana Coughlin, and David Bosc

    Afterword: Young People and the Future of African Worlds 385
    Nadine Dolby

    Notes on Contributors 391

    Index 395

Preface

When I won a prestigious postdoctoral fellowship at the University of Birmingham in 2010, I thought of it as an extraordinary opportunity to revise my doctoral thesis for publication, hone my research skills, and prepare for a tenure-track position. I had no idea how profoundly impactful that opportunity would be on my career trajectory as an academic. The work I did at the University of Birmingham ten years ago continues to shape my current scholarship, including this edited volume. I am particularly grateful to Professor Karin Barber, my postdoc advisor, who not only gave me a free hand to explore whatever wild ideas I had but invited me to codirect a graduate seminar on Media and Popular Arts in Africa. The idea for this edited volume was inspired by that seminar. It was in that seminar that I was struck by the centrality of youth in the production, consumption, and circulation of popular arts and culture in Africa.

This volume examines some of the contemporary popular arts, media, and everyday signifying practices of marginalized African youth as well as how these expressive forms function as important social platforms for popular expressivity and consciousness. What the collection demonstrates is that not only are young people in Africa the key producers, promoters, and consumers of popular culture, they are the new drivers of everyday culture in general, functioning as the new mediators and gatekeepers of mainstream culture, as powerful purveyors of new cultural codes and tastes, as prescribers of new moral values and mentalities, as the mobilizers and agitators bringing about revolutionary social change, and as innovators and modernizers who excavate, refurbish, and reintegrate local expressive forms into the global popular cultural imagination.

Like most research projects, this one has been ongoing for a few years, and all the contributors have been extremely patient and committed the entire time. From the bottom of my heart, I thank all of you for trusting me with your precious research projects and for standing with me throughout the long and difficult journey of bringing the project to fruition. I am particularly proud of the graduate students and junior scholars in the collection who signed up at short notice to join the project and submitted incredibly insightful contributions. Professor Adeline Masquelier, a "Big Masquerade" in the field of African youth studies, responded quickly to my request for a contribution and sent me her chapter soon after returning from a long trip to Europe. Many, many thanks, Adeline! We have lots more to do together in the future.

Many colleagues and friends have helped me with this project. I'd like to thank Dr. Esther De Bruijn, who joined the project at the beginning but had to leave to complete work on her monograph. The discussions we had about the project have shaped some of the ideas in the introduction to this volume. Cajetan Iheka not only read the first and second drafts of the introduction but also helped sharpen my rejoinder to the external reviewers' reports. Thanks for all your support and encouragement, Nna! Sylvia Morris also read both drafts of the intro and weeded our minor edits. You are an eagle-eyed editor indeed, and I cannot wait to see how you blossom in your new research adventure. Thank you so much for being such a great friend and "mother"!

Some of my friends and colleagues have been incredible fans and cheerleaders. Professors Rebecca Saunders, Bonny Ibhawoh, Daniel Coleman, Susan Kim, Chris De Santis, Chielozona Eze, Chris Brue, Brian Rejack, Mike Thuene, Chris Iklaki and Drs. Amber Dean, Amatoritsero Ede, Nduka Otiono, Liwhu Betiang, Peter Betiang, Lord Yevugah-Mawuko, Jasper Ayelazuno, Amy Niang, as well as Pastor Paulo Ogbeche: thank you all for the endless encouragement and support. Your friendship, mentorship, and reassurances have been immensely helpful in the sometimes difficult moments of work.

I dedicate this book to my uncle, Mike Abuadiye, and to my former teacher and friend, Victor Agwu. Soon after high school (I was seventeen years old), my uncle drove me around town on his motorbike looking for a place to borrow money to enable me to buy the Joint Admissions and Matriculations Board (JAMB) form so I could go to college in the next academic year. I have no idea how he repaid that loan. (I should probably ask!) Many years later, my uncle's colleague Victor Agwu, who was actually my teacher at Government Secondary School, Obudu, became my friend. When I was leaving for graduate studies in Canada in 2004, he covered the huge cost of my medical screening at the Canadian High Commission in Lagos and gave me half of the money for my flight ticket. Their incredible sacrifices changed my life! If I have dedicated my life to studying the experiences, struggles, ingenuity, and creativity of the millions of young men and women in Africa, it is because these two men showed me that investing in young people is not a waste! I have since learned how to extend a hand of support to vulnerable young people in dire need of help, guidance, and mentorship. Our collective future depends on them.

Dr. Paul Ugor
August 14, 2020
Bloomington-Normal, Illinois, USA

Introduction

Youth, Media, and Popular Arts Culture in Contemporary Africa

Paul Ugor

> In many places, and especially outside relatively privileged urban centres, young people are finding creative means of articulating their aspirations—and their alternatives to established social and political orders—using cultural idioms and establishing modes of association that may be invisible and obscure to national policy-maker
> —Alex de Waal, "Realizing Child Rights in Africa."

Since the late 1980s, the lives of young people in Africa have become a major subject of interest in African cultural studies. Currently estimated to be about four hundred million of the world's total youth population of 1.2 billion,[1] and according to the African Union, approximately 77 percent of the continent's total inhabitants under the age of thirty-five,[2] young people and children in Africa have taken center stage in African studies in recent years, not just because of their sheer numbers but primarily because of the multiple ways in which they have exploded as powerful social actors in the continent's public domain and on the world stage. Across the continent and beyond, African youth have become key players and influencers in the realms of politics, economy, the culture industry, religious movements, and all kinds

---

1 The African Union report estimates the continent's youth population using the fifteen to thirty-five age range. For a full report see, https://au.int/en/youth-development.
2 Hajjar, "The Children's Continent," World Economic Forum, January 2020, https://www.weforum.org/agenda/2020/01/the-children-s-continent/.

of activist endeavors for social justice and change. But as Mamadou Diouf has rightly observed, "The dramatic eruption of young people in both the public and domestic spheres seems to have resulted in the construction of African youth as a threat, and to have provoked, within society as a whole, a panic that is simultaneously moral and civic."[3]

The dread and anxieties about the outburst and prominence of African youth in both local and transnational public spaces have prompted several studies that have documented and analyzed the social experiences of their lives, especially the numerous ways in which young people in Africa have been impacted adversely by global and local political-economic forces. These studies demonstrate clearly how the enduring legacies of colonial domination, compounded by failed postcolonial governance and the harsh social conditions triggered by aggressive liberalization and privatization, have left many young people and children in Africa in dire situations.[4] Most young people in Africa live amidst social crises marked by chronic economic decline, joblessness, limited access to quality education and training, poor health-care services, lack of social amenities, and a general social climate of privation, insecurity, and uncertainty. What the thriving industry of critique about African youth in the past three decades shows is that while young people and children are the majority in Africa, their lives and futures are hardly prioritized in the social agendas in the continent. Although youth and children are at the core of the continent's sociocultural imaginary, they are "often placed at the margins of the public sphere and major political, socio-economic, and cultural processes."[5]

African youth have responded in varied ways to the myriad forces shaping their lives and the mistreatments, indifference, and exploitation they have experienced. The first wave of Africanist youth ethnographies in the 1990s demonstrated how pervasive inclement conditions forced young people to embrace violence and criminality, especially as a way of navigating and

---

3   Diouf, "Engaging Postcolonial Cultures," 3.
4   See Durham, *Youth and Social Imagination in Africa*; De Waal and Argenti, *Young Africa*; Christiansen, Utas, and Vigh, *Navigating Youth, Generating Adulthood*; Phillips, "A Global Generation? Youth Studies in a Postcolonial World"; and Van Gyampo and Anyidoho, "Youth Politics in Africa."
5   De Boeck and Honwana, "Introduction," 1. Also see de Waal, "Realizing Child Rights in Africa," 13.

surviving the harsh social environments surrounding their lives.[6] If vulnerable and despondent youth and children are not being weaponized by the political elite and their allies against the opposition in the fierce struggles for control over the postcolonial state, they are unconscionably exploited and instrumentalized in the illegitimate exploration and extraction of abundant mineral resources by underhanded entrepreneurs operating in the informal sector across the continent. On account of the infinite challenges confronting youth and their social trajectories in Africa, they have been infamously perceived as either being "lost," "stuck," or in "waithood," a form of social limbo and immobilization in which young people are firmly trapped in that precarious intermediate zone between adolescence and adulthood.[7] Instead of being a transitory stage in which young people transition to being fully functioning, independent members of society, they are locked in a vicious cycle of social immobility with very limited opportunities of guaranteed futures. Given their varied responses to the perilous conditions surrounding and defining their lives, there are now debates as to whether African youth are innovative creators who act as agents of positive social change, or miscreants acting as destructive agents of the continent's sociocultural fabric.[8]

But recent Africanist youth studies show that African youth are not just hapless and passive victims whose lives have been completely mangled by powerful postcolonial forces beyond their control. While difficult political, economic, and social conditions persist across the entire continent, Africa's youth, like their global counterparts facing enormous social challenges, are creating new and resourceful avenues to make sense of their own lives.[9]

---

6   Richards, *Fighting for the Rain Forest*; Abdullah, et al., *Lumpen Youth Culture and Political Violence*; Gay and Donham, "States of Violence: Politics, Youth, and Memory in Contemporary Africa"; Sommers, *The Outcast Majority: War, Development, and Youth in Africa*; Argenti, "Air Youth"; Gore and Pratten, "The Politics of Plunder"; Leach, "Introduction"; Honwana, *Child Soldiers in Africa*; Hoffman, *War Machines*; Krijn, *War and the Crisis of Youth in Sierra Leone*.

7   O'Brien, "A Lost Generation"; Sommers, *Stuck*; Honwana, *The Time of Work*; Masquelier, "Teatime: Boredom and the Temporalities of Young Men in Niger"; and Honwana, "Waithood: Youth Transitions and Social Change."

8   Honwana and De Boeck, *Makers & Breakers*; Abbink and van Kessek, *Vandals or Vanguards*; and Mutongi, "Thugs or Entrepreneurs?"

9   See, for example, Evers et al., *Not Just Victims*; Sommers, *Rwandan Youth and the Struggle for Adulthood*; Hoffman, *War Machines*; Honwana, *The Time of Work: Work, Social Change and Politics in Africa*; Ugor, "Introduction:

One specific area in which young people have shown extraordinary signs of resourcefulness, agency, and influence is in the creative industries. In various places across the continent, in both rural and urban areas (but mostly in the latter), "young people are finding creative means of articulating their aspirations—and their alternatives to established social and political orders—using cultural idioms and establishing modes of association that may be invisible or obscure to national policy-makers."[10] Almost completely sidelined in the local and global dynamics of political-economic power and the abundant wealth now associated with neoliberal globalization, African youth have turned to the new cultural resources made available by cultural globalization to create new and sometimes avant-garde expressive imageries and iconographies that not only herald their irrefutable presence but also convey their everyday struggles, fears, and aspirations.

These cultural idioms and spatial iconographies created by youth not only serve to create safe spaces, forceful avenues of public expression and advocacy, economic opportunities, and social mobility for young people but also ensure escape from the intolerable suffering and restrictive containment by the dominant powers. Now impacted and defined by forces beyond their national borders, African youth "appropriate new technologies (digital and audiovisual) in such a way as to recreate the dynamics of the oral and the spectacular, along with the literary and iconographic imagination."[11] This edited volume examines the fascinating, lively, and dynamic cultural field of the diverse imaginative work done by Africa's young men and women as musicians, writers, dancers, artists, fashion icons, comedians, users and consumers of new media, and social activists. The contributors document and analyze multiple performative and textual practices in everyday life that have made the continent's youth influential culture creators (i.e., powerful social players in the theater of globalization) who have stubbornly "resolved to make their way into the world market's economy of desires and consumption."[12]

Examining a variety of popular literary, visual, and performance arts by young people and their contextual and aesthetic dimensions, the volume reveals how Africa's youth, despite being in some senses defined by forces beyond their control, also shape global and local cultural developments,

---

    Extenuating Circumstances"; and Ugor and Mawuko-Yevigah, *Globalizing African Youth*.
10 de Waal, "Realizing Child Rights in Africa," 19.
11 Diouf, 6.
12 Diouf, 5.

especially through the active production and politicization of popular culture. Mostly contextualized within the continuing devastating effects of structural adjustment or neoliberal globalization, the essays provide examples of how young people instrumentalize popular culture to create spaces of control and self-representation, address corrupt political elites and their transnational allies, fashion identities that enable them to survive and navigate the precarious postcolonial urban space, and engage in activism for social justice and change after decades of white supremacist domination. Contributors focus on popular cultural forms produced by youth because popular culture, as David Coplan notes in his social history of black popular music and theater in urban South Africa, functions as "an important means of understanding the experience, attitudes, and reactions of the vast numbers of otherwise inarticulate people, those who vitally affect the course of urban development but who do not read or write about it."[13] These are mostly the marginalized youth. This edited volume thus is not only a record of but also an analysis of some of the contemporary cultural work done by marginalized young people in their efforts to make sense of circumstances around them and to regain some form of control and autonomy over their lives.

The Idea of the "Popular" in African Cultural Production

Africa has always been noted for the vitality, innovativeness, and profoundness of its people's creativity, and it has been mostly ordinary people at the center of that bustling, imaginative work. For centuries commonplace people—those outside of the elite classes and the highest echelons of the royal establishment—have created diverse and innovative cultural representations in the form of oral, visual, performative, and written texts to record and interpret contemporaneous social events and experiences.[14] These popular expressive forms, which have often emerged out of the urban informal sector, have now become important sites of scholarly engagement and theoretical reflection in African cultural studies, especially because of their historical value as sources of collective experience and memory. The term "popular arts" has been used to capture a vast array of popular expressive forms that include popular fiction, theater, dance, music, poetry, paintings, cartoons, magazines, electronic media (film, television, radio, and the internet), everyday

---

13   Coplan, *In Township Tonight*.
14   Barber, *A History of African Popular Culture*.

life practices, and other kinds of cultural repertoires produced by the urban masses to capture and respond to the shifting political-economic, social, and cultural changes taking place around them. Popular culture encompasses all the varied representational genres mostly produced by the working and intermediate classes to express their everyday struggles, hopes, dreams, and anxieties.[15] Largely produced by local artisans in the informal sector, these examples of popular expressivity are generated out of specific localities and social conditions, and their meanings derive from local histories, idioms, aesthetic values, and political-economic issues (although at times with universal themes). It is for this reason that Karin Barber insists that African popular arts "cannot be understood by a vague general explanatory appeal to colonialism and social change. The new consciousness they articulate is highly specific and their meanings must be read through the details of local social, political, and economic experience which is continually undergoing historical change."[16]

Highly syncretic, improvisational, and experimental in form and content, African popular arts help formulate locally situated narratives that constitute the knowledge(s) that continue to shape how ordinary people live and see the world in contemporary postcolonial Africa.[17] These popular expressions function as ongoing imaginative and philosophical ponderings of seismic political-economic and social changes, as autochthonous diaries of the impact of social transformations on ordinary people, as social maps of the meaning-making processes of common people, and as cultural documents that embody the desperate and relentless attempts at survival that go unnoticed in the quiet, unremarkable spaces outside of the epicenters of global cosmopolitan cultures. According to Newell and Okome, popular arts offer invaluable insights into what they call Africa's "popular neighborhoods."[18] If we are to get a realistic sense of life in contemporary Africa outside of the facade of formal history that the postcolonial state formulates for itself and the world—a life far removed from the commonplace success stories often peddled by neoliberal technocrats with an eye for profit from Africa's natural resources—it is to popular arts that we must turn to for such penetrating

---

15   Barber, "Introduction," *Readings in African Popular Culture*.
16   Barber, *Readings in African Popular Culture*, 53.
17   Fabian, "Popular Arts in Africa: Findings and Conjectures"; Barber, "Popular Arts in Africa"; Newell and Okome, *Measuring Time & Popular Culture in Africa*.
18   Newell and Okome, *Popular Culture in Africa*, 15.

insights. Popular arts in Africa continue to be the most powerful cultural spaces where ordinary people document their lives, talk to each other and the wider world about the issues that matter to and affect them, and offer their unique and insightful interpretations of both local and global events and how these events impact their lives.[19] It is the unrestricted space where ordinary locals formulate creative disputations about contemporary modernity and its disjunctures: its opportunities, privileges, and possibilities but also its contradictions, stifling limitations, and self-negations.

In one of his earliest disquisitions on African popular culture, Johannes Fabian noted that popular expressivity by urban masses in Africa "did not come about merely as a response to questions and conditions; it asks questions and create conditions."[20] While popular arts serve to document the life experiences of ordinary people and the social forces shaping their lives in both urban and rural spaces, they also interrogate and interpret contemporaneous happenings. In doing so, they come to define urban cultural practices and meanings, and thus not only shape what people think about local and global events but also how they act and constitute urban identities. In their survey of popular culture in Francophone Central Africa, for example, Bogumil Jewsiewicki and Katrien Pype observe how popular music and dance in bars have become "important tools of urban identification and political resistance."[21] In positing popular culture as a discursive force in the urban space, therefore, Fabian was pointing to the taut relations between popular expressivity and power, especially how these relations mirror social contestations and renegotiations between powerful forces and marginalized groups. For Fabian, then, marginality and survival take center stage in the politics of popular culture. Popular culture becomes the signifying practices of disempowered groups seeking to insert and assert their voices in social processes that overwhelm them (i.e., popular culture becomes the practice of creativity and freedom).[22]

---

19   Barber, *A History of African Popular Culture* & *Readings in African Popular Culture*; Simone, "Some Reflections on Making Popular Culture in Africa," 2008; Ode, "Popular Literature in Africa"; Newell and Okome, *Popular Culture in Africa*; Agwuele and Falola (eds.), *Africans and the Politics of Popular Culture*.
20   Fabian, "Popular Culture in Africa: Finding and Conjectures."
21   See Jewsiewicki and Pype, "Popular Culture in Francophone Central Africa," 4.
22   Fabian, *Moments of Freedom*.

It is no wonder then that the mass of sidelined youth in Africa who have been mistreated by their own leaders and ignored by the world have been the major producers and consumers of popular arts. The scholarly literature on African popular culture indicates innumerable examples of young people as the heartbeat of popular cultural production on the continent. In his work on Onitsha Market literature, for example, Emmanuel Obiechina noted how the popular pamphlets "were widely read and discussed, especially among young grammar schoolboys and girls" because they "served to interpret the aspirations of young men and women in the [emerging] modern world."[23] These popular fictions "provided advice for young men and women on how to cope with the problems of modern life."[24] In her own work on popular Yoruba traveling theater, Barber observed how the Oyin Adejobi troupe, although led by an authoritative Yoruba elder, often played to audiences that were predominantly "low-class, youthful, and male."[25] Stephanie Newell further points to the preponderance of youth authorship and readership of popular fiction in Ghana. She notes that the authors were often young people between the ages of seventeen and thirty-five, representing those who "have not yet achieved the social and economic status of full adult men. Many pamphlet-writers were recent school leavers in the 1950s and 1960s: in fact, some Nigerian authors had not yet left secondary school."[26]

In her astute examination of the popular TV show *Big Brother Africa*, Nadine Dolby has powerful insights into the multiple ways in which popular television offered a new public sphere for young people in the continent to actively engage in citizenship practices and contestations that come to shape how they experience the world.[27] There are also several other examples that show the intersection between youth and popular culture in Africa such as Malick Sidibe's documentary photographs of Malian youth culture from the late 1950s to the mid-1970s; the everyday signifying practices of young Matatu bus drivers in Nairobi, Kenya; Clyde Mitchell's account of the Kalela dance, a popular ethnic dance staged on Sundays by groups of young male dancers mostly employed in lowly positions in the mines in the Copperbelt region's urban spaces; as well as the popular *ngoma* dance (called Beni) whose origins is traced to "young Swahili Moslems" in Mombasa and Lamu in East

---

23   Obiechina, *An African Popular Literature*, 4 and 9.
24   Obiechina, 10.
25   Barber, *Yorùbá Popular Theatre*, 8.
26   Newell, *Ghanaian Popular Fiction*, 11
27   Dolby, "Popular Culture and Public Space in Africa."

Africa and represented a form of vibrant popular culture whose participants were primarily "concerned with the survival, success, and reputation of their members, acting as welfare societies, as sources of prestige, and suppliers of skills."[28] These numerous examples do not suggest that young people are solely responsible for producing and consuming popular arts in Africa but simply point to how African youth, especially as a disregarded generation seeking to voice their struggles and frustrations, have been central actors in the creation, organization, circulation, promotion, and consumption of popular arts and culture in the continent and beyond. This vital position that voiceless and disenfranchised youth occupy in the continent's culture industry certainly requires thoughtful reflection and continued examination because as Alex De Wall has observed in the chapter epigraph, most of the creative genres and alternative networks and modes of association formulated by youth are often poorly understood by national culture critics and policymakers.

Since the post–World War II years especially, whether in relation to popular music and dance, fiction, theater, language, movies, fashion, television, sports, photography, magazines, the internet, or everyday culture and practices, the young men and women in Africa, like their contemporaries worldwide who are insatiable consumers of modern-day culture, are the main drivers of these popular cultural forms. Yet there has been limited intellectual work invested in examining the different ways in which young people are key actors in producing, circulating, and consuming much of popular culture in Africa. Although African youth are often casually referenced in scholarly works on African popular culture, it seems that Africanists have struggled to come to terms with the powerful role they play in the vibrant scene of popular arts production. A small body of scholarly work specifically examining the links between youth, popular culture, and identity politics in Africa already exists, but this limited research output is insufficient to capture the thriving and relentless creativity, innovation, and cultural activism of African youth in the continent and beyond, especially in the age of cultural globalization. It is this gap in the field of African popular arts that this book seeks to address. Addressing this scholarly void in African studies is crucial because the insights to be gained from studying young people as active producers and consumers of popular culture has the potential to tell us a lot about the

---

28 See Diawara et al., *Malick Sidibe: Photographs*; Mungai, *Nairobi Matatu Men*; Mitchell, *Kalela Dance, 1956*; Ranger, *Dance and Society in Eastern Africa, 1975*.

lives of more than 75 percent of Africans and the changing nature of cultural life in the continent today. Young people are constantly staging actions and making public comments through their cultural work, and the popular cultural texts they produce have the potential to tell us not just about the young people themselves but also about the state of things in the continent and the world in general.

In the current era of media globalization, some of the remarkable cultural innovations and creativity in the production, circulation, and commercialization of popular culture in Africa come from young people. There is a rapidly expanding African youth population that is now media literate and savvy, flooded daily with excess infotainment and culture in the era of neoliberal globalization and its associated social inequities, and existing as part of a massive global youth market prone to the manipulation of consumer industries through the ingenious "aestheticization of consumer goods and services."[29] This means that new cultural and media resources are now at the very center of the social lives of young people in Africa. As several studies have shown, a rapidly changing world marked by huge cultural shifts, the aggressive politicization of culture, neoliberal deregulation, and the emergence of a new media culture marked by the ubiquity of popular culture and entertainment, have all animated a new and different topography of socialization and civic culture: one quite different from the traditional forms of acculturation and civic engagement associated with young people in previous eras.[30]

Processes of technological innovation—aggregation, convergence, miniaturization, interactivity, interoperability, digitization—in fact, the wholesale *technologization* of culture and everyday life now means that young people experience the world on a more global scale than their peers three decades earlier. Seismic changes in the media ecology have also energized fundamental changes in the ecologies of politics, economy, and culture. These transformations have huge implications for how young people experience the world, how they embody and respond to these changes, and how they document such massive changes and their effects on their personal life experiences in different forms of popular expression. This edited collection thus examines the current global cultural landscape characterized by the explosion and

---

29   Osgerby, *Youth Media*, 3.
30   See Ruddock, *Youth & Media*; Subrahmanyam and Smahel, *Digital Youth*; Dahlgren, *Young Citizens and New Media*; von Feilitzen and Carlsson, *Children, Young People & Media Globalization*; Ralph, Jo Brown and Lees, *Youth and the Global Media*; Schultze et al., *Dancing in the Dark*.

Figure I.1. A young YouTube video blogger exploring traditional African hairstyles in Lagos, Nigeria. Photos and montage created by Nowell Behakong Ugor (age twelve).

expansion of new media, the abundance of novel communications resources, and other meaning-making cultural objects that nowadays serve as new artistic and everyday existential tools for ordinary people, especially young people in Africa. The contributors explore and demonstrate the multifarious ways in which African youth, in the midst of the international flow of technological resources, have reinvented and recontextualized superfluous media and cultural apparatuses and paraphernalia in different local settings to (re)formulate new repertoires of meaning making in the public and private domains.

All the contributors in this edited volume are thus primarily concerned with popular arts produced and consumed by young people in contemporary

Africa. By "arts," we mean all kinds of cultural texts, representations, and practices—visual, oral, written, performative, fictional, and social—created by African youth, mostly about their lives and their immediate societies and cultures for themselves but also consumed by the larger public and shared locally and globally to mass audiences. We proceed from the premise that popular cultural texts not only function as "social facts" but also double as "commentaries upon, and interpretations of, social facts. They are part of social reality, but they also take up an attitude to social reality."[31] Popular cultural texts in general not only embody social data but also function as interpretative acts of that sociohistorical data. Popular arts by young people in Africa not only provide insights into their lives and their immediate societies but also operate as ongoing modes of interpretation of modernity that seek to make sense of both local and global events and experiences.

So, we are interested in thinking about what African youth produce as popular arts, how, why, and under what conditions or contexts they produce those texts, the aesthetic dimensions of these texts as cultural artifacts, and why these textual practices matter as social facts, interpretive acts, and cultural symbols of the general cultural activism of young people in a rapidly changing world where the global cultural economy is the site for relentless struggles over the meanings that come to shape political-economic and social systems. If young people are the main gauge of social change, perhaps the popular cultural texts African youth produce can tell us something about their lives and the societies and cultures they inhabit. The contributors also examine how these youth texts are interpellated in existing local and global power relations. For, as Andy Ruddock eloquently argued, "The way that young people use media in everyday life settings is an important measure for the depth of social inclusion."[32] Between the creative texts they produce for themselves and the wider society lie layers of multiple social codes and meanings that reflect political-economic and cultural negotiations that have huge implications not just for African youth themselves but for the broader global culture at large. If popular culture, as Stuart Hall argued, is "the arena of consent and resistance . . . where hegemony arises, and where it is secured" and contested,[33] we show how popular culture has become a poignant site of endless struggles for young people grappling with the meanings that shape their collective social experiences. And what we demonstrate is that African

---

31 Barber, *Anthropology of Texts, Persons and Publics*, 4.
32 Ruddock, *Youth and Media*, 2.
33 Hall, "Notes on Deconstructing the Popular," 79.

popular culture is a dynamic field of creativity, innovation, and agency for young people. In spite of the severe odds against African youth, the essays collected here show varied instances of how young people have "attained high visibility, thereby reclaiming their voice that had been previously denied to them through popular culture."[34] If popular culture is the site of pleasure and play for young Africans, it is also their platform for transformational politics.

Globalization and Youth Cultures in Africa

Steven Miles has noted that "if we are to understand the local nature of our lives, including the local expressions of youth lifestyles, we have also to consider the global context within which the local operates."[35] To make sense of popular arts by African youth as cultural enactments that convey crucial insights into local social struggles and cultural meanings, we ought to situate them within a broader global cultural order in which young people operate as significant cultural players in the mediation of social meanings. That unique historical context is the era of multiple globalizations, which are economic, technological, political, and cultural. Major scientific and technological innovations, especially in global communications and transportation, have led to the radicalization of economic production, the mass movement of people and material goods, and the relentless sharing of information. Increased interconnectedness has also meant that local economies, cultures, governments—in fact, our collective fates—are all intertwined.[36] These social transformations have come with their own benefits and drawbacks. For example, while the transnationalization of production, marked by privatization, deregulation, and the prioritization of profits, has created excess wealth and opportunities for some, it has drained and eliminated social opportunities and the possibility of economic independence for others. African youth especially have been at the receiving end of economic globalization: a place where liberalization, deregulation, and privatization have led to neoliberal economic policies that have left them with no access to social services and economic opportunities. According to Francis Nyamnjoh, "If globalization is

---

34 Yenika-Agbaw and Mhando, "African Youth: Cultural Identity in Literature, Media and Imagines Spaces," 7.
35 Miles, *Youth Lifestyles in a Changing World*, 60.
36 Giddens, *Modernity and Self-Identity*, 64.

a process of accelerated flow of media content, to most African cultures and children it is also a process of accelerated exclusion."[37] The increased uncertainties, risks, and general hazards associated with a rapidly globalized world have pushed the backs of many African youth against the wall, hemmed in between an aggressive and callous global neoliberal economic order, one the one hand, and a rampaging ruling elite driven by unending greed, primitive accumulation, and hence pervasive and incurable corruption, on the other.

But there is a somewhat happy side to the sad story. As the essays in this collection show, if economic globalization has led to huge imbalances in global wealth, cultural globalization has opened up opportunities for many people, especially disenfranchised youth who constitute the bulk of the world's precariat and occupy the perilous margins of the global economy. The globalization of culture, especially communications and media technologies, has not only translated to excess information in the global public domain but has also enabled the profusion of alternative creative resources that have led to the crystallization of new cultural repertoires and spaces for many people all over the world. As great consumers of culture in a late-capitalist economy and postmodern world, youth globally have reinvented themselves, appropriating proliferating technological and cultural resources for their own use. Bill Osgerby has noted how particular attention is now being given to "the local 'inflection' of global media," especially a focused scrutiny on how young people in different cultural spaces are "appropriating and giving new meanings to globally circulating cultural forms and media texts."[38] African youth are also beginning to take advantage of the wave of cultural globalization. Vivian Yenika-Agbaw and Lindah Mhando have noted how the young men and women they encountered in formal and informal spaces while traveling in Africa seemed savvier than the previous generation. "They were knowledgeable about global events and cultures. Most had Facebook friends from all over the world and were familiar with trendy youth culture, including fashion, slang, lingo, television shows, movies, and music."[39] Matthias Krings and Tom Simmert have recently observed that African popular culture has entered the global mainstream culture industry,[40] but I would argue that that

---

37   Nyanmjoh, "Children, Media and Globalization," 4.
38   Osgerby, *Youth Media*, 14.
39   Yenika-Agbaw and Mhando, "African Youth: Cultural Identity in Literature, Media and Imagines Spaces," 2.
40   Krings and Simmert, "African Popular Culture Enters the Global Mainstream."

shift has been made possible mostly by the creative urban youth who have become media literate and extremely savvy in the use of new media.

The essays by Ndiaye Bamba, David Kerr, Ty-Juana Taylor, Ibrahim Bangura, and Paul Ugor in this volume show how creative young African men and women in forgotten spaces have become global celebrities and influential cultural icons by simply working with local music labels run by other youth entrepreneurs, using second-hand laptops, free online software, and other powerful media apps in creating a popular musical genre that appeals to their peers locally and globally. Through popular Afro hip-hop, young people not only challenge and resist local and global hegemonic forces but also create their own spaces of pleasure and comfort where they interact with each other on their own terms and in their own unique language(s). The essays by James Yeku, Opoku-Agyemang, Austin Bryan, Jendele Hungbo, and Godfrey Maringira and Simbarashe Gukurume all show how young people with cheap cell phones made in Asia and free social media apps downloaded from the internet engage in activist politics by mocking and shaming corrupt political leaders in Nigeria and Zimbabwe and deep-rooted white supremacist hegemonies in South Africa; challenging pervasive homophobia and toxic patriarchy and social exclusion in Ghana, Uganda, and Botswana; and generally participate in a global culture of image making and self-promotion on Instagram, Twitter, Facebook, or other social media platforms. Talented young artists socially trapped in Africa's most dangerous neighborhoods, with extremely high rates of poverty and crime, may become award-winning photographers, filmmakers, or choreographers, simply by documenting the everyday life of their decrepit neighborhoods using a single digital still or video camera. In March 2019, for example, the I-rep Documentary Film Festival in Lagos, Nigeria, featured *Awon Boyz*, a thirty-eight-minute documentary by a young and gifted film director, Tolu Itegboje, which takes the audience on an arduous journey into the adventure-filled life of the stranded young men, popularly known as "area boys," who lead treacherous lives in decrepit slums in Lagos. It is a riveting visual portrait with fascinating insights into the charged vortex of the multidimensional life led by a vulnerable and exploited youth generation whose complex existence has become coterminous with postcolonial violence.

The chapters in Part 3 by Adeline Masquelier, Adrienne Cohen, Connie Rapoo, and Kristi Kenyon, Juliana Coughlin, and David Bosc reiterate the bustling creativity and resilience of African youth. These youth ethnographies show that although their subjects have been at the receiving end of transnationalism and economic globalization, the materialism and consumption associated with a global late-capitalist economy have also engendered imagination, innovation, consumerist desires, and new ways of being, not to mention an acerbic criticality among young people in place like Niger, South Africa, Botswana, and Guinea. The essays triangulate the powerful links between popular culture, youth, and globalization, affirming the view that marginalized youth all over the world "seem to think that the things that kill can also cure, as they appropriate the raw materials of globalization—its commodities, mass mediated messages, and displacements—and turn them into tools for building community and critique."[41] What most of the contributors in our volume show is that for the marginalized youth in Africa, globalization is like medicine; it can kill, and has killed African youth in the millions, but it now also helps them heal and redeem themselves from voicelessness, invisibility, disenfranchisement, and an endless cycle of poverty. Despite the harsh conditions brought by neoliberalism and brutish postcolonial governmentality, African youth continue to find alternative but effective ways of making meaningful lives, eking out a living, and having fun in harsh, unsafe, and uncertain conditions.[42] The explosion of popular culture among young people in Africa is thus a cultural response to unfavorable local-global conditions, but the popular genres they produce also serve as their unique tools for bypassing the limitations imposed on their lives by society, functioning both as resources of everyday survival and frank commentaries on the inclement conditions that have made their lives miserable and filled with drama and trauma.

Youth and Popular Arts in Africa: Aesthetic and Thematic Patterns

While we have traced the explosion of popular arts by African youth in recent years to economic and cultural globalization, especially chronic economic decline due to structural adjustment on the one hand and the transnational flow of new cultural resources such as computers, the internet, cell phones, digital video cameras, social media, and other newer forms of communication technologies, on the other, these new communication technologies and other cultural resources themselves do not simply generate popular art forms.

---

41 Lipsitz, "Forward: Midnight's Children," xi.
42 See Ugor, "Introduction," *Globalizing African Youth* and "Introduction," *Postcolonial Texts*.

Reflecting on the links between technology and social change in Africa, Sokari Ekine notes, "People decide why and how a particular technology will be used and, depending on the political and socio-economic environment in which they live, adapt it accordingly."[43] Andy Ruddock makes a similar point, arguing that "Media technologies are . . . important not because of what they can do, technically, but because of how these capacities are used to create spaces where people can contemplate their situation."[44]

All the contributors in this edited collection demonstrate how young people reinvent, recontextualize, and repurpose the enormous communication technologies available to them in different cultural spaces and under different socioeconomic and political conditions. Liesbeth de Block and David Buckingham have noted this unique use of media technologies by youth, asserting that "access to media technology is only the starting point in a much longer process of learning [and cultural productivity]. What children [and youth] do—and indeed what they want to do—with these media depends very much on their social circumstances and on the social contexts in which they gain that access."[45] With regard to African popular arts culture, several scholars have noted how different cultural contexts will not only shape the content and types of popular genres and practices, but their structural forms will be different from each other.[46] Mary Jo Arnoldi thus warns against imposing external categories on African popular arts and to evaluate them within "the participants' own definitions of the contexts and carefully analyze their actions and responses within these events."[47] But differences in the operationalization and consumption of popular arts do not eliminate occasional parallels. There are clear lines of creative differences, but there are also similarities between traditional and urban popular arts and even canonical Western genres. So, in this segment, I examine some of the common aesthetic and thematic elements associated with popular arts and culture by African youth. In noting these commonalities, however, I am attentive to the fact that sociocultural, political, and economic contexts wield a powerful influence on the aesthetic dimensions of these popular youth texts. The

---

43   Ekine, "Introduction." *SMS Uprising*, xi.
44   Ruddock, *Youth and Media*, 51.
45   De Block and Buckingham, *Global Children, Global Media*, ix.
46   See Arnoldi, "Rethinking Definitions of African Traditional and Popular Arts"; Becker, "Anthropology and the Study of Popular Culture"; and Barber, "Popular Arts in Africa" and *A History of African Popular Culture*.
47   Arnoldi, "Rethinking Definitions of African Traditional and Popular Arts," 82.

unique contexts that might shape particular aesthetic attributes of a specific popular youth genre—say its form, language, theme, spatial politics, or other structural elements—may not necessarily be similar to the same structural form in another popular youth repertoire in another place and time. What I am sketching, therefore, are broad trends/patterns, not unique aesthetic conventions.

Popular arts by African youth are by nature highly improvisational and hybrid. To be clear, improvisation and syncretism are not novel features of African popular arts. Karin Barber has already shown how African cultural workers and their various popular art forms have been influenced and shaped by interactions with global arts and media since the seventeenth century. According to Barber, "Media in much of Africa are not experienced as a recent and external force, but as a constitutive element in the formation of African popular culture from the early twentieth century onwards."[48] The prolonged interactions between global media and indigenous entertainment forms in various parts of Africa over several centuries have led to the reinvention of existing local entertainment genres; new ways of learning and retaining local cultural forms; the merging of disparate performance and entertainment traditions; the opening up of new social spaces in which new classes of performers can emerge; the bringing of novel texts and performances to new audiences both within and outside the continent; and even expansive publicity, unparalleled glamor, and new genre conventions for most types of popular entertainment across the continent.[49] This relentless inherent syncretism and improvisation in African popular culture is, however, now a boon for youth involved in popular arts and culture. And what is now different is the degree or intensity of borrowing, mixing, and improvisation.

Young artists might draw on established art forms, both modern and traditional, foreign and indigenous, which are traceable to earlier aesthetic traditions from even five centuries ago and combine such elements with Afro hip-hop (see Part 1 in this volume); they might straddle different expressive platforms—print, electronic, stage, the streets, and internet (Parts 2 and 3 in this volume); and may combine geographical and cultural settings that stretch across Africa, Europe, North America, South and Central America, and Southeast Asia; as they may address crowds that are simultaneously conservative and progressive, feminist and masculinist, African and non-African, old and young. What is new in these popular representations by youth is not

---

48 Barber, "Orality, the Media, and New Popular Cultures in Africa," 4.
49 Barber, 3–18.

the borrowing and hybridity but the intensity of iconoclasm and cultural borderlessness. Adrienne Cohen, for example, demonstrates how young choreographers in Conakry, Guinea, borrow and radically transmute entrenched aesthetic conventions idolized by the socialist-trained artists between 1958 and 1984 and rework those conventions into their dance and musical creations driven by pure capitalist aspirations. In the Nigerian Afrobeats scene, Olamide's 2015 song "Melo-Melo" features ballet dance scenes, saxophone-based instrumentation, and traditional Yoruba romance songs, while Flavour (in "Ijele") combines ritual scenes, traditional Igbo war drumming, and dance with contemporary Nigerian Afro hip-hop.[50] These young artists innovate in popular arts culture by reinventing traditional or folk repertoires into modern popular art forms that combine multiple genres—old and new—in producing distinct popular artistic categories that draw from but also subvert and undermine the conventions of older creative traditions that may be traditional, popular or elite, and they do so in playful, dynamic, and ironic ways.

This dimension of hypersyncretism and hybridity of popular arts by African youth is profound, for these popular cultural repertoires gesture not only to the increasingly deethnicized and hybrid identities of urban African youth, but also their cosmopolitanist and globalist perceptions of world citizenship. In the face of an ongoing brazen rejection of globalization and the international cultural heterogeneity it has engendered, expressed in the form of nativist and white supremacy movements in the West, African youth are voicing and fostering cross-cultural integration through the aesthetics of de-differentiation (see essays by Kerr, Taylor, Bryan, and Masquelier in this volume). As Ellen Hurst-Harosh and Fridah K. Erastus have noted in their work on youth language practices in social media, advertising, and creative arts, the varied creative language practices by youth in "African communities have come to represent new generations of Africans intersected by global culture but with their own cultural practices and creativity woven into the fabric of their language use."[51] While the young artisans and audiences of African popular arts are proud to be African, they see themselves as citizens of the world who are free and entitled to borrow and share in the privileges and benefits of economic and cultural globalization, and in fact, in the richness, vitality, and fluidity of world culture.

---

50   Olamide, "Melo-Melo"; Flavour, "Ijele."
51   Hurst-Harosh and Erastus, "An Overview of African Youth Language Practices and Their Use in Social Media, Advertising and Creative Arts," 1.

Another important feature of popular arts produced by African youth is innovation. African youth, like their counterparts all over the world, live in a moment of excess information and rapid social change. Not only are these youth by-products of fundamental transformations in global politics, economy, and culture, they are witnesses to some of the major transformations taking shape locally and globally. They may not be at the center of the global transnational processes that have witnessed increased movements in people and material goods but from their different peripheral locations are able to recognize and receive the materials goods and symbols associated with a postmodern world. As Brad Weiss and Jesse Weaver Shipley have shown in their respective studies on popular culture and consumerism among urban youth in Tanzania and Ghana, African youth might be far removed from the metropolitan centers of cultural power, but incorporation, which is a characteristic of a global cosmopolitan world, is at the very center of their lives.[52] My chapter examining the images of pleasure and consumption in popular Afrobeats addresses this same cultural dynamic among urban youth in Nigeria. In their popular artworks and everyday life, young people strive constantly to incorporate the new symbols of global prestige and power. As Adeline Masquelier shows in this volume, a young man wearing a locally designed T-shirt in Niamey, Niger, might also wear his latest denim jeans, thus maintaining a hybridized identity that combines local cultural tastes with distant aesthetic trends traceable to wider metropolitan cultural spaces in Africa and the Western world. A young dapper Sapeur fashionista in Côte d'Ivoire might combine the latest blazer trending in Paris with a used flat cap or bowler hat bought from a local store in Abidjan, as Ty-Juana Taylor shows in this volume. A young and upcoming hip-hop musician in Nigeria might shoot his music video in Lagos but will also feature images from New York showing the latest Ferrari, Jaguar, or Tesla not available in the local cultural scene, as Paul Ugor demonstrates. So, young people always innovate by not only creating new genres, practices, and tastes but also by incorporating the latest symbols of cultural power and prestige circulating in local and transnational circles. The innovations are not just in terms of production styles but newness in terms of contemporaneous events. Contemporaneity and spontaneity go hand in hand. The latest scandal in the local political or cultural scene will find its way into a short comedy skit or meme(s) on Facebook and Twitter as James Yeku, Jendele Hungbo, Godfrey Maringira, and Simbarashe Gukurume demonstrate in this volume, just as the most egregious utterance

---

52   Weiss, *Street Dreams and Hip-Hop Barbershop*; and Shipley, *Living the Hiplife*.

by Donald Trump (about Africa being a "shithole," for example) will be integrated into the performance of a young comedian featured at the popular AY show in Lagos, Nigeria. The young artists and entertainers do not simply innovate by doing something new with the genre but also engage in ongoing social discourses by taking on the up-to-the-minute issues and debates in town and around the world. In so doing, the young artists are not only engaged in the freedom and creativity intrinsic to popular culture as Johannes Fabian avers but also renegotiate and transform power in the public and private domains.

Popular arts and cultures by African youth are also highly countercultural or postmodern, not only in terms of the unique ways in which they transcend or undermine established aesthetic boundaries and conventions but also in the ways they aestheticize spectacle, hyperbole, and fragmentation (see essays by Bamba, Taylor, Masquelier, Cohen, and Brian in this volume). While the idea of the postmodern itself remains contentious, there's a degree of consensus about its key aesthetic features: a rejection of meta-narratives (i.e., its denunciation of sweeping aesthetic and theoretical interpretations ostensibly of universal application).[53] The imposing narratives and epistemological formulations that underpinned and sustained global political-economic and cultural powers—empires, nations, civilizations, canonical texts and their aesthetic conventions, and other old powers—have now crumbled due to intense scrutiny. This is what Lyotard meant by postmodernism's "incredulity towards meta-narratives."[54] It discards a universal vision of the world in favor of localities, specificities, fragmentations, and differences. Postmodern cultural artifacts are therefore playful, self-ironizing, self-reflexive, and schizoid. They detest the austere autonomy associated with modernist aesthetics in favor of exaggeration, spectacle, and commercialism. We see some of these postmodern aesthetic elements in popular arts and culture by African youth, especially the element of spectacularism. Whether it is the radical *Y en a Marre* Movement in Senegal (Ndiaye); nonnormative sexualities and gender identity politics in Uganda (Bryan); the bustling and innovative dance/choreographers troupes in Conakry (Cohen); the young Afro hip-hop musicians in Senegal, Tanzania, Sierra Leone, Cote d'Ivoire and Nigeria (Taylor, Kerr, Bangura, and Ugor); or popular dress and fashion styles in Côte d'Ivoire and Niger (Taylor and Masquelier), there's a sense in which spectacle, mostly in the form of exaggeration, becomes an inherent aesthetic

---

53   Harvey, *Condition of Postmodernity*, 7–9.
54   Lyotard, "Answering the Question: What is Postmodernism?," 357–63.

element. But I want to note that sensationalism in these popular genres and creative practices functions as a compensatory aesthetic. Operating within a postcolonial field of cultural production devoid of the superfluous technical resources available to their peers elsewhere in the world, spectacle, mostly in the form of exaggeration, primarily functions to fill in the technical weaknesses of the text but also works to bolster its visibility and ensures recognition and acceptability in a global materialist culture obsessed with spectacle: a society, Guy Debord argues, that lives in fantasy, not reality. According to Debord, "The spectacle proclaims the predominance of appearances and asserts that all human life, which is to say all social life, is mere appearance . . . a visible negation of life . . . a negation of life that has invented a visual form for itself." "It turns reality on its head."[55]

But there's another sense in which popular cultures by African youth are postmodern. There is a sense in which culture is self-consciously understood as an economic activity. If the young authors of popular fiction in Nigeria and Ghana in the 1960s and 1970s wrote for the sheer satisfaction of the cultural prestige of being an author, the contemporary young creators of popular arts have an unblinking eye for high profits. Popular arts culture is thus heavily driven by commercial instincts and neoliberal logics. Here, we are thinking about the postmodern in the sense in which Frederic Jameson argues that it is nothing more than the systemic modification of capitalism,[56] especially the ways in which capitalism has permeated the realm of cultural production (i.e., postmodernism as the makeover of capitalism).[57] Living and working under harrowing postcolonial conditions in which few opportunities exist for young people, the young African artists who produce popular culture are interested in generating huge profits from their creative endeavors. Their representations and texts may engage in interpretive and critical work, holding the thieving elites in their various countries responsible for the unending struggles with falling education standards, high unemployment rates, poor health-care services, endless housing crises, and other social problems; nevertheless one of the primary aims of these young artists is for their work to appeal to a vast global audience in order to generate massive profits.

This aspect of African popular arts culture is especially common among the Afro hip-hop musicians, as David Kerr, Bamba Ndiaye, Ty-Juana Taylor, Ibrahim Bangura, and Paul Ugor show in this collection. Their albums or

---

55 Debord, *Society of the Spectacle*, 14–18. Also see Key, *Age of Manipulation*.
56 Jameson, "Periodizing the 60's," 376–90.
57 Jameson, *Postmodernism, Or the Cultural Logic of Late Capitalism*, 4.

single tracks might invoke specific local events, histories and idioms, and appeal to specific local audiences, but their handlers always aim to strike performance deals with promotion agencies worldwide, where they play to mammoth crowds in metropolitan cities in the continent and beyond while earning millions of dollars.[58] Given the roles of popular arts producers and influencers as firsthand witnesses to the endless suffering of their local peers and immediate communities, their newfound wealth makes its way into local neighborhoods and economies as payments for work done by other young artists in the culture and entertainment industry but also as handouts to family members, friends, and neighbors. For the contemporary young producers of popular culture in Africa, the idea is to produce art not just for art's sake but to gross substantial earnings from cultural work to provide for the self, to participate in the global culture of material consumption of goods and services, and to provide for extended family and other dependents. This commodification of popular culture by African youth is itself reflective, as Maira Sunaina and Elisabeth Soep have shown, of a broader cultural pattern of the intersection between global markets, popular culture practices, and global youth cultures in the era of the commodification of culture.[59]

Stardom and celebrity culture have also become important aspects of popular culture by African youth (see Bryan, Taylor, Kerr, Masquelier, and Ugor in this volume). In *Consumers and Citizens*, Garcia Canclini notes how consumption in late-modern society constitutes a new means of thinking that offers new avenues for citizenship. According to Canclini, for "many men and women, especially youth, the questions specific to citizenship . . . are answered more often than not through consumption of commodities and media offerings than through the abstract rules of democracy or through participation in discredited political organizations."[60] At a moment of huge cultural changes that fundamentally alter the relations between private lives and the broader social reality, Canclini argues that "the main terrains where mass tastes and citizenship are shaped" are those of the cultural sector, such as social media, film, video, and television.[61] With the weakening of the influences of normative authority and socialization institutions such as the

---

58 As I write this introduction, there's a huge social media uproar on the stunning performance of popular Nigerian hip-hop musician Davido in Paris: https://www.youtube.com/watch?v=x-Khfa39bk0.
59 See Sunaina and Soep, eds., *Youthscapes: The Popular, the National, the Global*.
60 Canclini, *Consumers and Citizens*, 5.
61 Canclini, 32–33.

nation-state, schools, family, church, class, community, and so on, the crucial existential questions of who young people are, and where they are in society are today largely answered through the consumption of consumer goods and lifestyles. The cultural sector now doubly shapes emerging cultural formations of identity and citizenship. According to Furlong and Cartmel, the general decline in labor markets worldwide has created a cultural scenario where "young people are increasingly turning to the marketplace to purchase props for their identity, which can make them more confident in their relationship with their peers."[62]

And in contemporary Africa, where the active engagement with online social media has become part of mainstream culture for young people, image and perception have become quite central to popular youth cultures. While new media, especially online social media, have become important sources of popular resistance and dissent by young people, as James Yeku, Godfrey Maringira, Simbarashe Gukurume, Christi Kenyon, and Jendele Hungbo demonstrate in this collection, they now also function as new resources of enselfment in which young people fabricate idealized identities they circulate on social media and other everyday social spaces inhabited by their peers (see Austin Bryan, Adeline Masquelier, and Paul Ugor in this volume). Realizing that we now live in a postmodern world of spectacle in which the appearance of wealth is all-important, African youth have now taken to popular arts and media such as hip-hop, Facebook, Instagram, Twitter, and other social spaces to create "appearances" of the lives they wish to lead, rather than the actual ones they really live. The appearances and invented images of themselves they create on social media and local spaces provide vicarious inroads into the exclusive world of consumption they witness from the margins of the global economy and culture. So popular culture now not only functions as a new political instrument as some studies here show but also as the main resource of enselfment and identity formation in everyday popular culture by youth both in rural and urban spaces.

An Overview of Contributions

The first five essays in the collection demonstrate how Afro hip-hop as a popular youth genre is both a by-product of and a critical response to local power structures and neoliberal globalization. David Kerr's chapter on underground

---

62 Furlong and Cartmel, eds., *Young People and Social Change*, 62.

rap and hip-hop culture in marginalized neighborhoods in Dar es Salaam, Tanzania, is an astute example in this regard. Excluded from the mainstream Tanzanian music industry, young hip-hop artists with extraordinary rapping skills have created their own local spaces, *Maskani*, in which they stage discourses and critiques of postcolonial power relations through varied "repertoire of performance forms, including rapping, dancing, joking and storytelling." Kerr reveals how *Uswahilini/Maskani* and youth-led cultural activities such as *Kampu* function not only as popular sites of everyday life for marginalized youth but also as critical sites of sociocultural engagement with skewed local-global dynamics of power. Bamba Ndiaye's chapter on the *Y en a Marre* is another compelling testimony to the local-global dynamic that has come to define the unique character of contemporary popular culture in Africa. *Y en a Marre*, "a non-partisan youth movement co-founded by two hip hop artists" in Senegal as a response to egregious state violation of the constitution and recurrent electric power outages in 2011 inaugurated an impressive revolutionary art movement among rap and hip-hop musicians in West Africa that redefined the region's political landscape in fundamental ways. In a thoughtful and detailed fashion, Ndiaye demonstrates how the *Y en a Marre* rappers-activists organized "what can be termed 'lyrical attacks' on the government through various artistic and rhetorical conduits including bus tours, social media, music videos, graffiti, radio shows, and flyer etc." Combining a range of aesthetic strategies that include "urban guerrilla poetry," "social movement diatribes," and "letter-writing rap," the young Senegalese rap and hip-hop musicians created a formidable genre of popular urban expression that not only resonated powerfully with young people but attracted a mass public following. As these brave rap musicians challenged powerful politicians on the unconstitutionality of their actions, primitive accumulation, and corruption—not to mention their treacherous collusion with French multinational corporations whose interests have left the nation in dire economic straits—the Yenamarristes became popular entertainers that galvanized a new public consciousness among ordinary citizens. These rap artists were no longer just popular performers experimenting with hip-hop as a global genre but essentially "guardians" of the public interest and the conscience of the nation.

Ty-Juana Taylor's contribution reveals the interesting intersections between popular music, youth culture, identity performance, and labor in the city of Abidjan, Côte d'Ivoire. Her chapter is a captivating cultural account of the ways in which coupé décalé, a transnational popular genre created in Paris, and its associated culture of ostentation, materialism, and musicking, "allowed youth to escape daunting realities at home, including war, lack of jobs, national instability, and economic decline." Her chapter shows a deep understanding of how Afro hip-hop and dance function as important cultural tools that help marginalized homeless youth in Africa's treacherous urban spaces to cope with and navigate the vicissitudes of postcolonial life. Ibrahim Bangura's own contribution is another thoughtful piece that provides useful inroads into the ways in which popular rap and hip-hop function as an influential tool of political critique in the context of postwar political-economic and social crises in Sierra Leone. Now war weary, after more than a decade of a bloody civil war in which young people were the major protagonists, Bangura shows how disaffected and disenfranchised Sierra Leonean youth have turned to Afro hip-hop as the main cultural instrument to engage with its indifferent political elites. Just like Kerr, Taylor, and Masquelier, Bangura provides a rich ethnography that demonstrates how youth carved out local spaces, the "Ataya Bases," from which they mobilized and engaged the failures of postwar political-economic and social crises in Sierra Leone. The five essays in the first segment of the collection are compelling examples of the multiple ways in which Afro hip-hop, especially as a form of popular culture among young people, has become a veritable tool of social navigation, conscientization, identity formation, and a bold engagement with perverse local power regimes and the intrinsic inequities, opportunities, and complexities of globalization. Through their analyses of Afro hip-hop, all five contributors show how the fringe cultural spaces created by African youth in conditions of marginality, marked by their own inherent power hierarchies, might function not only as popular sites of creativity and peer/generational networking and engagement but also double as vintage social podiums from which to renegotiate power relations both with local power structures and neoliberal globalization.

In Part 2, the contributors show concrete instances of the ways in which online media have become the new site of popular culture and civic engagement for African youth. James Yeku's chapter is a powerful demonstration of how the interconnectivity and interoperability associated with new media have animated new and alternative cultural spaces from where ordinary people, especially marginalized youth, engage the powerful forces that shape their lives. In a persuasive manner, Yeku triangulates the links between online social media, Nigerian youth and cultural activism. His use of the notion of "infra-politics" to frame the counter-discourses of youth on social media is reminiscent of Bayart's idea of the "quiet encroachment of the ordinary." It is a form of subversive acquiescence in which supposedly disempowered youth subvert the power structures that create misery in their lives. Similarly, Kwabena Opoku-Agyemang's chapter maps out the complex links between youth, popular fiction, and discourses about culture and social change in the public domain in Ghana. What is clear from his insightful analysis is that young amateur writers are beginning to use the flash fiction genre to unsettle established cultural norms.

Austin Bryan's rich ethnography of the cultural activism of youth with non-normative sexualities in Uganda is another moving account of the new ways in which African youth are deploying online media as new cultural resources to challenge dominant discourses of sexual and gender identity in Africa. Bold, controversial, and sensationalist, the young queer artists Bryan profiles have reinvented their supposed aberrant sexualities into cultural capital, creating alternate personas, brands, and social gravitas that allow them to circulate locally and internationally through all kinds of imageries on social media. Through sensationalist rhetoric on social media—Facebook, Twitter, YouTube, blogs, online magazines, and popular television—youth with non-conventional gender and sex identities reinvent widespread homophobia into a rewarding cultural capital that grants them thriving careers, sustained livelihoods and cultural legitimacy that opens up international spaces of refuge and solace. Jendele Hungbo provides a riveting account of the mass protest led by students against colonial legacies in South Africa's educational institutions. Focusing specifically on the maximization of Twitter as a mobilizing tool for the #RhodesMustFall campaign, he reveals how social media have become a functional site of both socialization and civic discourse for disgruntled youth. His chapter is a strong testimony to the many ways in which new cultural tools in the form of online media have become effective avenues for young people to redefine power relations between old forms of repressive power in the context of racial capitalism and their reincarnation in a neoliberal context.

Analogous to the political and cultural activism of Nigerian and South African youth in online media that Yeku and Hungbo anatomize, Godfrey Maringira and Simbarashe Gukurume show how new cultural repertoires such as memes, video clips, political poems, and songs created by youth as part of popular entertainment in Zimbabwe take on a political motive (i.e., how they aim to "engage with a devious state that is driven by the desire to decimate its citizens through military authority and power"). In making a compelling case for the ways in which online media is now both a source of popular entertainment and a site of political activism for Zimbabwean youth, they note that while ordinary citizens may "laugh about the memes, the Facebook wall postings, and the hilarious comments on Twitter handles" posted by youth, they insist that the people's "reflection and understanding of these messages are rooted in their political undertones and meanings."

Part 3 of the volume links popular arts and everyday life to the cultural politics of young people in Africa. Adeline Masquelier begins that part with an exciting example of the politicization of culture by African youth. She shows how urban Nigerian youth obsessed with formulating cosmopolitan urban identities through celebrity culture mimic the sartorial styles of a popular Nigerien Afro hip-hop artist, Wizkid. Unsurprisingly, this politics of sartorial mimicry by urban youth is happening in the context of chronic economic deterioration and general social hardship brought about by liberalization from the late 1980s. Unable to access the welfare packages that came with national capitalism, and now cut off from the benefits of privatization and liberation that accrue to a tiny elite class, Nigerien youth, like most of their peers in the continent, lead precarious lives without any assurances of a secured future. It is within this context of precarity, Masquelier notes, that Nigerien youth have created their own social spaces, the *fadas*, where youth "forge new modes of sociability and new expressions of self-esteem in the absence of direct avenues to sustainable livelihoods." Nigerien youth do so, mostly through the creative and experimental use of dress and fashion. Masquelier argues that these popular sartorial pursuits by disenfranchised youth in Niger function as "pragmatic performances through which individuals position themselves on a competitive social landscape, enabling them to project an image of prosperity against all odds." Acutely aware of the power of images/imageries in a postmodern world obsessed with appearances, young people turn to dress and style as a way of fashioning out urban identities that doubly mask and contest their marginality.

Adrienne Cohen shows how the shift from a socialist welfare state to a neoliberal postcolony has sparked a new regime of aesthetics among a younger generation of ballet dancers and musicians whose structure of performance has changed from an earlier statist and Pan-Africanist approach to cultural production to a new era marked by experimentation, innovation, and commercialism. Through her examination of the work of a younger cohort of dancers, musicians, and ballet directors in Guinea's capital city of Conakry, she argues that in an "era in which troupes operate privately and young artists must find creative ways to support themselves financially in a global market economy, Conakry dancers and musicians cultivate new practices and logics that both evidence their struggles and uncertainties and that celebrate their sense of global connection and potential." The entrenched aesthetic forms embraced by the socialist-trained artists from 1958–84 who emphasized "national culture" have now been replaced by a more postmodern and economically pragmatic approach to creativity that simultaneously recognizes dance and music as socially conscious art and economic activity. Connie Rapoo addresses a similar political-economic dynamic in Botswana, showing how the deepening social and economic crises brought about by neoliberal policies led to the rise of activist popular arts, which now serve as powerful creative platforms for youth to comment on the harsh social realities around them. Through her exploration of a solo performance by Moduduetso Lecoge and urban hip-hop music in Gaborone, Rapoo underscores "young people's significant role in using the power of culture and performance to document, interpret, and change the social, political and economic challenges" confronting Botswana. What her essay exposes is the ways in which the formation of urban identities by youth in Botswana transpires at the intersections of politics and popular culture.

Kristi Kenyon, Juliana Coughlin, and David Bosc conclude the volume by examining the sensational #FeesMustFall movement led by students across universities in South Africa from October 2015 to April 2016. Like Jendele Hungbo, they track the ways in which the intrinsic protest culture associated with antiapartheid struggles laid a foundation for a strong culture of youth activism, which reinvented itself in the context of postapartheid neoliberal capitalism. By focusing on a mass student-led campaign that is representative of a popular protest culture among South African youth, Kenyon, Coughlin, and Bosc demonstrate how the generation born after apartheid, the so-called born frees, have been "labelled, and the unique ways in which they are redefining themselves and building an alternate identity at odds with a national narrative that has celebrated them without listening to their stories." The cultural insights the three authors offer into protest culture in South Africa is fascinating because what they reveal is a generational rift between the past and the present, where, as the generation born after apartheid attain adulthood, the "assumed connections, allegiances, and the narrative of progress in which they are embedded are increasingly called into question." They argue that as the *born-frees* draw on old techniques of antiapartheid struggles from the past and combine them with new cultural repertoires such as tweets, blogs, songs, and literature, South African youth are enacting the potential of popular culture to deconstruct and reconstruct "meaning from available and created cultural artefacts" and thus "forming, articulating and communicating a new consciousness."

Highly interdisciplinary and drawing contributions from different scholarly traditions within the humanities, social sciences, and education, the contributors combine grounded ethnographic insights resulting from long years of painstaking on-the-field research and high-power theory. The result is an incisive collection of essays that reveals fascinating insights into the evolving cultural ecology of young people in Africa. What the collection demonstrates is that not only are young people in Africa the key producers, promoters, and consumers of popular culture, they are the new drivers of everyday culture in general, functioning as the new mediators and gatekeepers of mainstream culture, as powerful purveyors of new cultural codes and tastes, as prescribers of new moral values and mentalities, as the mobilizers and agitators bringing about revolutionary social change, as innovators and modernizers who excavate, refurbish, and reintegrate indigenous forms into the global popular cultural imagination, and the new miners of global wealth who have mastered the tools of modernity in reinventing, mainstreaming, and commercializing autochthonous cultural texts and practices into the international cultural economy. All of these mediating social roles by African youth are played primarily through popular culture and media.

Bibliography

Abbink, Jon, and Ineke Van Kessel, eds. *Vanguards or Vandals: Youth, Politics and Conflict in Africa*. Leiden, The Netherlands, and Boston: Brill, 2005.

Agwuele, Austine, and Toyin Falola, eds. *Africans and the Politics of Popular Culture*. Rochester, NY: University of Rochester Press, 2009.

Arnoldi, Mary Jo. "Rethinking Definitions of African Traditional and Popular Arts." *African Studies Review* 30, no. 3 (September 1987): 79–83.

Barber, Karin. *The Anthropology of Texts, Persons and Publics: Oral and Witten Culture in Africa and Beyond*. Cambridge: Cambridge University Press, 2007.

———. *A History of African Popular Culture*. Cambridge: Cambridge University Press, 2018.

———. "Orality, the Media, and New Popular Cultures in Africa." In *Media and Identity in Africa*, edited by Kimani Njogu and John Middleton, 3–18. Bloomington: Indiana University Press, 2010.

———. *Yorùbá Popular Theatre: Three Plays by The Oyin Adéjobí Company (with Báyọ̀ Ògúndíjọ)*. Atlanta: African Historical Sources Series no. 9, ASA, 1994.

———. "Popular Arts in Africa." *African Studies Review* 30, no. 3 (September 1987): 1–78.

Becker, Hieke. "Anthropology and the Study of African Popular Culture: A Perspective from the Southern Tip of Africa." *Research in African Literatures* 43, no. 4 (Winter 2012): 17–37.

Charry, Eric, ed. *Hip Hop Africa: New African Music in a Globalizing World.* Bloomington: Indiana University Press, 2012.

Christiansen, Catrine, Mats Utas, and Henrik E. Vigh, eds. *Navigating Youth, Generating Adulthood: Social Belonging in an African Context.* Uppsala, Sweden: Nordiska Afrikainstitute, 2006.

Coplan, David. *In Township Tonight: South Africa's Black City Music and Theatre.* 2nd ed. Chicago: University of Chicago Press, 2008.

Dahlgren, Peter, ed. *Young Citizens and New Media: Learning Democratic Participation.* New York: Routledge, 2007.

De Block, Liesbeth, and David Buckingham. *Global Children, Global Media: Migration, Media and Childhood.* New York: Palgrave Macmillan, 2007.

Debord, Guy. *The Society of the Spectacle.* New York: Zone, 1995.

De Waal, Alex. "Realizing Child Rights in Africa: Children, Young People and Leadership." *Young Africa: Realizing the Rights of Children and Youth.* Trenton, NJ: Africa World, 2002.

De Waal, Alex, and Nicolas Argenti, eds. *Young Africa: Realizing the Rights of Children and Youth.* Trenton, NJ: Africa World, 2002.

Diawara, Manthia, Gunilla Knape, and Andre Magnin. *Malick Sidibe: Photographs.* Hasselblad Center: Steidl, 2004.

Diouf, Mamadou. "Engaging Postcolonial Cultures: African Youth and Public Space." *African Studies Review* 46, no. 2 (September 2003): 1–12.

Dolby, Nadie. *Constructing Racialized Selves: Youth, Identity, and Popular Culture in South Africa.* Albany: State University of New York Press, 2001.

———. "Popular Culture and Public Space in Africa: The Possibility of Cultural Citizenship." *African Studies Review* 49, no. 3 (2006): 31–47.

Durham, Deborah, ed. "Youth and the Social Imagination in Africa: Introduction to Parts 1 and 2." *Anthological Quarterly* 73, no. 3 (July 2000): 113–20.

Ekine, Sokari. "Introduction." *SMS Uprising: Mobile Activism in Africa.* Cape Town: Pambazuka, 2010.

Evers, Sandra, Carline Seagle, and Froukje Krijtenburg, eds. *Not Just a Victim: The Child as Catalyst and Witness of Contemporary Africa.* Leiden, The Netherlands: Brill, 2011.

Fabian, Johannes. *Moments of Freedom: Anthropology and Popular Culture.* Charlottesville: University Virginia Press, 1998.

———. "Popular Culture in Africa: Finding and Conjectures." *Africa: Journal of the International African Institute* 8, no. 4 (1978), 315–34.

Furlong, A., and F. Cartmel, eds. *Young People and Social Change: Individualization and Risk in Late Modernity.* London: SAGE, 1997.

Garcia Canclini, Nestor. *Consumers and Citizens: Globalization and Multi-cultural Conflicts*. Trans and Introduction by George Yudice. Minneapolis: University of Minnesota Press, 2001.

Gay, G., Edna Donham, and Donald L. Donham. *States of Violence: Politics, Youth, and Memory in Contemporary Africa*. Charlottesville: University of Virginia Press, 2006.

Giddens, Anthony. *Modernity and Self-Identity: Self and Society in Late Modern Age*. Cambridge: Polity, 1991.

Gore, Charles, and David Pratten. "The Politics of Plunder: The Rhetorics of Order and Disorder in Southeastern Nigeria." *African Affairs* 102 (2003): 211–40.

Hall, Stuart. "Notes on Deconstructing the Popular." In *Cultural Theory: An Anthology*, edited by Imre Szeman and Timothy Kaposy, 72–80. Chichester, UK: Wiley-Blackwell, 2011.

Harvey, David. *The Condition of Postmodernity: An Inquiry into the Origins of Cultural Change*. Cambridge, MA: Basil Blackwell, 1989.

Hoffman, Danny. *The War Machines: Young Men and Violence in Sierra Leone and Liberia*. Durham, NC, and London: Duke University Press, 2011.

Honwana, Alcinda. *Child Soldiers in Africa*. Philadelphia: University of Pennsylvania Press, 2006.

———. *The Time of Work: Work, Social Change and Politics in Africa*. Sterling, VA: Kumarian, 2012.

———. "Waithood: Youth Transitions and Social Change." *Development and Equity: An Interdisciplinary Exploration by Ten Scholars from Africa, Asia and Latin America*, edited by Dick Foeken, Ton Dietz, Leo de Haan, and Linda Johnson. Leiden, The Netherlands: Brill, 2014.

Honwana, Alcinda, and Filip De Boeck, eds. *Makers and Breakers: Children and Youth in Postcolonial Africa*. Trenton, NJ: Africa World, 2005.

Hurst-Harosh, Ellen, and Fridah Kanana Erastus, eds. *African Youth Languages: New Media, Performing Arts and Sociolinguistic Development*. Cham, Switzerland: Palgrave Macmillan, 2018.

Jameson, Frederic. "Periodizing the 60's." (1984). *Cultural Theory*. Edited by Imre Szeman and Timothy Kaposy. Chichester, UK: Wiley-Blackwell, 2011 376–90.

———. *Postmodernism, Or the Cultural Logic of Late Capitalism*. Durham, NC: Duke University Press, 1991.

Jewsiewicki, Bogumil, and Katrien Pype. "Popular Culture in Francophone Central Africa." *Oxford Research Encyclopedia, African History* (oxfordre.com/africanhistory). Oxford: Oxford University Press, 2020.

Lyotard, Jean-François. "Answering the Question: What is Postmodernism." *Cultural Theory*, 357–63.

Key, Wilson Brian. *The Age of Manipulation*. New York: Henry Holt, 1989.

Krings, Mathias, and Tom Simmert. "African Popular Culture Enters the Global Mainstream." *Current History: Journal of Contemporary World Affairs*, 119, no. 817 (May 2020): 182–87. https://doi.org/10.1525/curh.2020.119.817.182.

Leach, Melissa. "Introduction to Special Issue: Security, Socioecology, Polity: Mande Hunters, Civil Society, and Nation-States in Contemporary Africa." *Africa Today* 50, no. 4 (Summer 2004), vii–xvi.

Lipsitz, George. "Forward: Midnight's Children: Youth Culture in the Age of Globalization." *Youthscapes: The Popular, the National, the Global*, ed. Sunaina Maira and Elisabeth Soep. Philadelphia: University of Pennsylvania Press, 2005.

Maira, Sunaina, and Elisabeth Soep, eds. *Youthscapes: The Popular, the National, the Global*. Philadelphia: University of Pennsylvania Press, 2005.

Masquelier, Adeline. "Teatime: Boredom and the Temporalities of Young Men in Niger." *Africa* 83, no, 3 (2013: 385–402.

Miles, Steven. *Youth Lifestyles in a Changing World*. Buckingham: Open University Press, 2000.

Mitchell, Clyde. J. *The Kalela Dance*. Rhodes-Livingstone Paper no. 27. Manchester: Manchester University Press, 1956.

Mutongi, Kenda. "Thugs or Entrepreneurs? Perceptions of Matatu Operators in Nairobi, 1970 to the Present." *Africa* 74, no. 4 (2006): 549–68.

Newell, Stephanie. *Ghanaian Popular Fiction: Thrilling Discoveries in Conjugal Life and other Tales*. Oxford: James Curry, 2000.

Newell, Stephanie, and Onookome Okome, eds. *Popular Culture in Africa: The Episteme of the Everyday*. New York: Routledge, 2013.

Nassenstein, Nico, and Andrea Hollington, eds. *Youth Language Practices in Africa and Beyond*. Berlin: De Gruyter Mouton, 2015.

Nyamnjoh, Francis. "Children, Media and Globalization: A Research Agenda for Africa." In *Children, Young People & Media Globalization*, ed. Cecilia von Feilitzen and Ulla Carlsson. Nordicom, Sweden: The UNESCO International Clearinghouse on Children, Youth and Media. 2002.

Obiechina, Emmanuel. *An African Popular Literature: A Study of Onitsha Market Pamphlets*. Cambridge: Cambridge University Press, 1973.

———. ed. *Onitsha Market Literature*. Ibadan: Heinemann, 1972.

Ode, S. Ogede. "Popular Literature in Africa." *The Cambridge History of African and Caribbean Literature*. Eds. Irele, Abiola and Simon Gikandi. Cambridge: Cambridge University Press, 2003.

Onookome, Okome and Stephanie Newell, eds. "Measuring Time: Karin Barber and the Study of Everyday Africa." *Research in African Literatures* 43, no. 4 (2012): vii–xvii.

Osgerby, Bill. *Youth Media*. London: Routledge, 2004.

Peters, Krijn. *War and the Crisis of Youth in Sierra Leone*. Cambridge: Cambridge University Press, 2011.

Phillips, Joschka, "A Global Generation? Youth Studies in Africa." *Societies* 8, no. 14 (2018): 1–18.

Ranger, Terence O. *Dance and Society in Eastern Africa, 1890–1970: The Beni Ngoma*. Berkeley and Los Angeles: University of California Press, 1975.

Ralph, Sue, Jo Langham Brown, and Tim Lees, eds. *Youth and the Global Media*. Bedfordshire, UK: University of Luton Press, 1998.

Richard, Paul. *Fighting for the Rainforest: War, Youth and Resources in Sierra Leone*. Oxford: James Currey, 1996.

Rudduck, Andy. *Youth and Media*. Los Angeles: Sage, 2013.

Shipley, Jesse Weaver. *Living the Hiplife: Celebrity and Entrepreneurship in Ghanaian Popular Music*. Durham, NC: Duke University Press, 2013.

Schultze, J. Quentin, et al. *Youth, Popular Culture and the Electronic Media*. Grand Rapids, Michigan: W. B. Eerdmans, 1991.

Simone, Abdoumaliq. "Some Reflections on Making Popular Culture in Africa." *African Studies Review* 51, no. 3 (December 2008): 75–89.

Sommers, Marc. *The Outcast Majority: War, Development, and Youth in Africa*. Athens, Georgia: University of Georgia Press, 2015.

———. *Rwandan Youth and the Struggle for Adulthood*. Athens: University of Georgia Press, 2015.

Subrahmanyam, Kaveri, and David Smahel. *Digital Youth: The Role of Media in Development*. New York: Springer, 2011.

Tsika, Noah. *Nollywood Stars: Media and Migration in West Africa and the Diaspora*. Indianapolis: Indiana University Press, 2016.

Ugor, Paul. "Introduction: Extenuating Circumstances, African Youth, and Social Agency in a Late-modern World." *Postcolonial Text* 8, nos. 3–4 (2013): 1–12.

———. *Nollywood: Popular Culture and Narratives of Youth Struggles in Nigeria*. Durham, NC: Carolina Academic Press, 2016.

Ugor, Paul, and Lord Mawuko-Yevugah, eds. *Globalizing African Youth: Challenges, Agency and Resistance*. Aldershot, UK: Ashgate, 2015.

United Nations. "Population Facts." *Department of Economic and Social Affairs* 1 (May 2015).

Weiss, Brad. *Street Dreams and Hip Hop Barbershop: Global Fantasy in Urban Tanzania*. Bloomington: Indiana University Press, 2009.

von Feilitzen, Cecilia, and Ulla Carlsson, eds. *Children, Young People & Media Globalization*. Nordicom, Sweden: the UNESCO International Clearinghouse on Children, Youth and Media, 2002.

Van Gyampo, Ransford Edward, and Nna Akua Anyidoho. "Youth Politics in Africa." *The Oxford Research Encyclopedia, Politics* (oxfordre.com/politics). Oxford: Oxford University Press, 2019.

Wa Mungia, Mbugwa. *Narobi's Matatu Men: Portrait of a Subculture*. Goethe-Institut Kenya: Native Intelligence and the Jomo Kenyatta Foundation, 2013.

Yenika-Agbaw, Vivian, and Lindah Mhando, eds. *African Youth in Contemporary Literature and Popular Culture: Identity Quest*. New York: Routledge, 2014.

Part One

Media Globalization, Popular Afro Hip-Hop, and Postcolonial Political Critique

Chapter One

Hip-Hop, Civic Awareness, and Antiestablishment Politics in Senegal

The Rise of the *Y en a Marre* Movement

Bamba Ndiaye

Introduction

In the introduction to Carlos Moore's book *Fela: This Bitch of a Life*, Margaret Bushy recalls that "on the day of [Fela Kuti's] funeral, the streets of Lagos were brought to a standstill, with more than a million people defying the Nigerian government ban on public gatherings that had been imposed by the military dictator General Sani Abacha."[1] This statement epitomizes the contentious relationship that the popular Nigerian artist had vis-à-vis the political establishment that always viewed his art as subversive and, therefore, a threat to the Nigerian government. More importantly, the feud between Fela Kuti and the Nigerian government mirrors the disdain as well as the fear that African governments hold toward politically engaged artistic productions. In fact, for the longest time, popular music has functioned as a trenchant political site of social activism in Africa primarily because it is the most

---

1   Bushy, "Introduction," xii.

widely appreciated art form on the continent.[2] From Fela Kuti to Franco Luambo via Miriam Makeba and, more recently, the *Y en a marre* movement, popular music on the continent has remained a major site for challenging the sociopolitical status quo.[3] As Allen notes, "In many ways, and on different registers, artists are engaging their political circumstances through music"[4]. This essay argues that African musicians have always used their art to challenge or influence the political status quo or specific cultural values. Following in the steps of previous generations, contemporary Francophone West African youth activists are fostering sociopolitical change through art, especially popular rap music, which in recent years has gained wide popularity and visibility among young people. In this regard, this chapter takes a retrospective analysis of the "politicization" of African popular music as a weapon of protest by young artists in Senegal. It examines how the *Y en a marre* movement has succeeded in occupying the political space in Senegal, especially through the intersection of rap music and sociopolitical activism. Finally, it accords attention to concepts of "musical diatribe" and "musical open letter" as well as the counternarratives emanating from the power structure to discredit and stall these radical artistic movements by youth.

Insurgent Music: Following in the Footsteps of the Previous Generations

Y en a marre was founded in 2011 to protest recurring electrical power outages in Senegal. Shortly thereafter, the movement morphed into a powerful watchdog vis-à-vis the Senegalese political establishment and began challenging many of the country's most powerful and entrenched political leaders. *Y en a marre* quickly inspired other youth insurgent movements across the continent, including *Balai Citoyen* in Burkina Faso. The movement is divided into chapters called "Esprit," which are scattered all over Senegal and overseas. The movement defines itself as "apolitical," meaning they are neither affiliated with any political party nor do they adhere to any political party's ideology. Since its inception, *Y en a marre* has been a powerful oppositional force in Senegal, distinguishing itself from the traditional political opposition parties through their mass mobilization capacity and community projects,

---

2   Allen, "Music and Politics," 1.
3   *Y en a marre* can be translated as "enough is enough" or "fed up."
4   Allen, "Music and Politics," 5.

although they worked with political formations in the past to oppose policies and bring about sociopolitical change in Senegal. As the movement was cofounded by two well-established hip-hop artists, its activism is infused with a strong dose of artistry that seeks to foster deep social changes and address corruption and poor governance. Artistic creation and contemporary social activism go hand in hand in Africa.

The new generation of African popular artists engage the political scene with a militant musical discourse, most of the time antithetical to the interests of their respective governments. In fact, this activist tradition of African music has gained ground with the advent of popular radio, TV, newspaper, and more recently, social media. Contemporary young African artists benefit from more accessible and flexible media platforms, which allow them to share politically charged messages with a national as well as a transnational audience. Young hip-hop artists are certainly more vocal and at the forefront of the battle against poor governance, corruption, and lack of democracy in Africa. Their rap music epitomizes the virulence of the antiestablishment narratives that young people have been directing at their governments since the late 1980s. The confrontation between the Tunisian rapper El General and Ben Ali's government is a prime example of the use of contemporary art form as a political weapon. In December 2010, El General released "Head of State," the first overt musical diatribe against the autocratic leader. The song went viral on social media and subsequently provoked a police investigation against the rapper followed by a prison sentence. "Head of State" inspired the participants of the Arab Spring who used it as a rallying cry and also paved the way for other Tunisian hip-hop artists to openly criticize their political leaders.

On December 31, 2018, while the Senegalese nation was patiently waiting for the traditional New Year's Eve Presidential Address to the nation, Thiat and Kilifeu of Keur Gui Crew, who were cofounders of *Y en a marre*, released "Saï saï au Coeur" on YouTube. This politically charged rap song represents a frontal attack against President Macky Sall and his government. The young artists deliberately chose to release the song on a symbolic day when the president traditionally gives the annual report of the state of the nation and announces the achievements of the government. They chose the same day to provide a report of their own assessment that entirely contradicted the narrative of the Sall regime. This song is part of a larger insurgent musical repertoire that aims to denounce incompetent governments. It also functions as a burlesque, parodying President Sall's book, *Le Sénégal au Coeur (2018)*. West African hip-hop artists in general, and the Senegalese artists in particular, have succeeded in incorporating derision and irony in their musical productions. This confrontation is reminiscent of Fela Kuti's Yabis subgenre, which deliberately ridiculed the government. Derision and irony in the West African context are forms of political critique that effectively negate the political discourse of the government in power.

Due to its provocative nature, the song "Saï saï au Coeur" made the headlines of all the major news websites and newspapers in the country. In a matter of one week, "Saï saï au Coeur" recorded one million views on YouTube, making the song one of the most-viewed rap songs in Senegalese hip-hop history. The Wolof term "saï-saï" has different meanings depending on the context. The term can be pejorative, referring to a person who is mischievous, sneaky, and dishonest. While it can be used as a euphemism to describe illegitimate sexual intercourse, Wolof speakers also use it to reference lizards and/or evildoers. Thus, calling someone "saï-saï," especially a public figure, is a covert insult insinuating they have acted wrongfully. A few weeks prior to the release of "Saï saï au Coeur," Amy Colé Dieng, a singer and vocal critic of the Sall government, called Macky "saï-saï" in a widely shared WhatsApp vocal message. Subsequently, Amy Colé got arrested and taken into police custody, thus triggering an unprecedented public outcry. Fans, fellow artists, politicians, and activists defended the Senegalese singer and denounced the violation of her freedom of speech and opinion by the state. By releasing the song "Saï saï au Coeur" a few weeks after the Amy Colé incident, the young hip-hop activists (Thiat and Kelifeu) sought to reignite the controversies surrounding the use of the term "saï-saï." Conscious that music constitutes one of the most accessible form of transmitting messages to African masses, the release of the rap song was part of a strategic move employed by *Y en a marre* and Keur Gui Crew to confront political leaders with the use of strong symbolism in the music video. "Saï saï au Coeur" functions as an antithesis to the presidential discourse of national success and growth. It paints a grim picture of Senegal's socioeconomic situation in contrast to what President Sall depicted in his address: a gleaming Senegal on the right track to a prospering economy. The *Y en a marre* artists used taunting and revealing images in their videos to depict the hardships faced by the masses that the president and his government omitted in their address to the nation.

The beginning of the "Saï saï au Coeur" video features a young man sitting at a street corner and putting crackers (what Senegalese people call "biscuits") on a small table for sale. Next to him is Thiat reading a newspaper and wearing a Cabral-style hat that has become a staple among contemporary African activists. While the young man is organizing the merchandise on the table, a young woman stops by and astonishedly asks: "Now you own a table? What happened to your corner-store?" To this he responds: "You see, Westerners are selling us everything these days. They are selling us dry fish, they are selling us yeet and even netetu."[5] The symbolism here is very powerful. The same young man who now owns a small table full of goods played the role of a shopkeeper in a previous music video that Thiat and Kilifeu released in 2014 called *Diogoufi*, two years after Macky Sall came to power. The message the rappers transmit is that in a span of two years, the Senegalese economy has drastically regressed to a point where a regular Senegalese who used to own a corner store has now been downgraded to a mere tabletop of merchandise in a street corner.

The response the young man provides in the video when asked what happened to his corner store represents the local response to the arrival in Senegal of the French chain of supermarkets named Auchan. The latter is a multinational corporation headquartered in Croix, France, and it specializes in retailing. Auchan's presence and the exponential growth of multinational grocery chain stores in Senegal are worrisome for many local retailers and shopkeepers who accuse the French retailer of threatening the local job market and the livelihood of thousands of Senegalese through unfair neoliberal competition. The Senegalese trade union, *UNACOIS*, vehemently opposed the French retailer's expansion in Senegal, arguing that "Auchan would be a danger to Senegalese industry, agriculture, livestock and transport." Its presence threatens many Senegalese with unemployment and jeopardizes the Senegalese economy's autonomy.[6] Thiat and Kilifeu made sure that these local responses to neoliberal globalization, which is aggressively aided by the postcolonial ruling elite, are amplified through their musical and video productions. The rappers/activists embody the voice of the masses who are demanding jobs, access to medical care, and better economic opportunities. Although President Sall and his regime responded to some of these demands by instituting programs such as the *Bourse familiale* (Family aid) to provide financial resources to the country's most economically deprived families, and the *Couverture Maladie Universelle* (Universal health coverage) to provide health insurance and free medical care to the most vulnerable segments of

---

5   Yeet is fermented sea snail, and Netetu is fermented African locust bean used as seasoning in many Senegalese and other West African dishes. Both "yeet" and "netetu" are staples in Senegalese cuisine, see https://www.youtube.com/watch?v=kiiJME7wsV4.

6   Seneweb, "Auchan Dans Le Viseur De L'unacois Jappo."

the population, the popular demand for a better social safety network has not died down.

While World Bank figures show that the Senegalese economy has made steady progress since 2012 (6.8 percent growth in 2017 and 2018), many segments of Senegalese society do not see/feel the effects of this astonishing economic growth recorded by neoliberal technocrats in their daily lives. Their daily struggles and misfortunes remain unchanged, which means that only a small elite group and foreign multinationals are reaping the benefit of the purported economic growth. The 2017 UNDP (United Nations Development Program) report shows that the poverty level in Senegal remained extremely high at 46.7 percent. Despite steady economic growth since 2012, the welfare of an important segment of the population has left much to be desired. Ousmane Sonko, among other opposition leaders, contends that only foreign multinationals benefit from the economic growth as 84 percent of the Senegalese economy is in the hands of foreign companies.[7] *Y en a marre* and other civil society organizations have echoed Sonko's preoccupations on multiple occasions. In a thought-provoking monologue called *10 cours à la nation* (Ten lessons to the nation) in reference to the French phrase *discours à la nation* (address to the nation), Thiat elaborates on these social difficulties in the prelude to the song "Saï saï au Coeur" when he says:

> As we are delivering the final report, nothing has changed!
> Nothing to put in our mouths!
> Seven years of our existence have been wasted
> By unprecedented state-sponsored crimes
> The same crooks, the same incompetent people, the same old folks are still in place.
> How many apes [sic] switched political parties (to join the presidential party)?
> How many media company owners have been corrupted?
> How many judges without dignity?
> How many instances of police brutality?
> How many instances of land litigation?
> How many incompetent ministers?
> How many scandals?
> How many people have medical coverage?
> And you are giving away social aids
> Only to people who belong to your party and forget about the rest of the country.
> Your brother manages the oil, while your in-laws manage the contracts

---

7   Ousmane Sonko's speech in Montreal, November 14, 2018.

The French [companies] control all public [infrastructure] projects
While Senegalese people are still struggling.
The same cats, the same dogs
They have no self-dignity.
They improve their lives with the sorrow of the people
Give us our voter IDs, you are incompetent
You know that we are going to get rid of you.[8]

These lyrics constitute an outburst by a despondent youth generation, a bitter complaint against a regime that has failed to satisfy the basic needs of its population. They are also a criticism against a political class evidently more preoccupied with the personal welfare of the elite rather than with the well-being of the general population. Moreover, his lyrics represent a diatribe against the "cannibalization" of the Senegalese economy by French multinationals that have accentuated their presence in the country since the arrival of President Sall to power.

To a large extent, "Saï saï au Coeur" is a castigation of neoliberalism and its postcolonial political facilitators at the local level. It provoked noticeable reactions among the Senegalese political class. Opposition parties welcomed the song with enthusiasm while the governing coalition castigated *Y en a marre* and Keur Gui Crew, calling them "rude," "disrespectful," and "insulting." President Sall's reaction to the song was undoubtedly the most prominent when he stated during the *Conférence internationale sur l'emergence de l'Afrique* (International conference on Africa's emergence) that "we need to educate/train the youth. [We do not want] young people who insult everyone, young people who insult Presidents. We are not going to progress like that."[9] Although President Sall did not explicitly name Keur Gui Crew, it was clear that the president's words targeted them, as all the major newspapers and online news websites noted the veiled reference.

Qualifying hip-hop artists' lyrics as rude, disrespectful, and insulting is not a new phenomenon in Senegal. Since the emergence of the popular musical genre in the country during the 1980s, hip-hop artists have often been the target of critics who believe that the music is "antithetical" to Senegalese values and norms of respect and discipline. This argument has been a way

---

8   Thiat, "Saï saï au coeur."
9   "Il faut former la jeunesse. Pas une jeunesse qui insulte tout le monde, une jeunesse qui insulte les Présidents. Nous n'allons pas nous développer avec ça" (my translation). Macky Sall's speech during the *Conférence sur l'émergence de l'Afrique,* January 17, 2019.

for a small elite group to defend the status quo they were responsible for and now being pressured to change it. Hence such phrases as "antithetical to Senegalese cultures" were now being perceived as calls for passivity. This was a widespread phenomenon in Africa where "immovable" politicians try to repress informative art and political transitions. In the 1980s Africa's conservative politics reached an uneasy peak as opposition to authoritarian and nonprogressive leadership started to gather momentum in many African countries such as Kenya, Uganda, and Central African Republic. It's the same wind of opposition that brought Mugabe to power in Southern Rhodesia before turning undemocratic himself in the following decade and being ousted by the masses yearning for democracy and good governance. These are the same winds of change that even Senegalese leaders could no longer shield themselves from.

Musical Diatribe and "Musical Open Letter" as Rhetoric of Social Protest

With rap firmly anchored in Senegalese youth culture, the genre began to replicate the expression of civil discontent at the origin of the hip-hop movement in America. Music, like all art forms, has always been used as a tool or a vehicle for social commentary, whether songs are about one's immediate surroundings or the world at large. However, hip-hop, more so than other forms of music, constitutes a platform for exposing the misery of the rapper's surroundings and valorizing the disenfranchised masses.[10] Rap in Senegal quickly joined this revolutionary charge starting in 2000. Jesse Shipley has noted how "during the 2000 presidential elections, hip-hop artists helped sway young voters bringing Abdoulaye Wade to power with a referendum tied to generational change."[11] In the same vein, *Y en a marre* employed rap music to transition from the musical scene to the political opposition. Along with protests and advocacy, members of the movement have used rap as a primary tool for sociopolitical contestation. As in many other parts of the continent, *Y en a marre* has weaponized and maximized the globalized art form of hip-hop as a medium for constructing a political identity and a language of resistance against the political power establishment.

---

10   Shipley, *Living the Hiplife*, 16.
11   Shipley, 16.

During the 2012 presidential election, Senegalese hip-hop artists who rallied behind *Y en a marre* used their music and murals painted in high traffic areas to remind their fellow citizens of the sanctity of the constitution, as well as the necessity of respecting political promises. Rosalind Fredericks captures this innovative type of political engagement by hip-hop artists when she states: "Through activating their networks in virtual, audio, and urban space, rappers catapulted themselves to the center of the political stage in not only the wave of protest leading up to the elections but through inspiring a deeper public reflection on citizenship and democratic practice."[12] The movement is strongly grounded in the verbal art form in which lyrics are part of an arsenal of contention to create a popular uproar against the political establishment, which generally regards their songs as seditious and threatening to their political interests and fortunes. The powerful and antagonizing message that *Y en a marre* artists conveyed in their rap songs and their verbal attacks through media outlets resulted in multiple police interrogations, arrests, and physical attacks against the movement's members. To point out the insurgent character of the movement's discourse and its confrontational methods, the *New York Times* reporter Adam Nossiter writes:

> It is not that Senegal lacks established politicians, political parties or even newspapers opposing Mr. Wade, often with torrents of incendiary if not wide-of-the-mark verbiage, a Senegalese tradition. The rappers, however, have struck a nerve because they cut to the chase. Their language is direct, sometimes crude and quite unambiguous.[13]

Nossiter's comment highlights not only the discursive turmoil *Y en a marre* ushered into the political atmosphere but also the defiance that characterizes almost every major campaign of the movement. Rap artists who belong to the movement produced provocative music, which constitutes an integral part of a political tactic that Malal Talla, one of the leading figures of the movement, calls "Urban Guerrilla Poetry."

"Urban Guerrilla Poetry" is a recitation of short poems where the audience is often not prepared for the crude content of the verses. According to Malal Talla, the term "Urban Guerilla Poetry" is derived from the name of a combat tactic that was prevalent during socialist revolutionary activities where they used nonconventional fighting tactics in attacking government officials

---

12   Fredericks, "Old Man Is Dead," 130–48.
13   Nossiter, "In Blunt and Sometimes Crude Rap, a Strong Political Voice Emerges."

and installations or interests in dense cities under camouflage or by surprise hits. Therefore, urban guerrilla poetry can be understood as "the use of rap lyrics to attack government officials throughout cities and getting away with it."[14] With this tactic, members of *Y en a marre* frequently organize what can be termed "lyrical attacks" on the government through various artistic and rhetorical conduits including bus tours, social media, music videos, graffiti, radio shows, and flyer. Marame Guèye underscores some of the ways the movement antagonized the Senegalese government: "When Wade's government prohibited peaceful demonstrations, rap musicians hopped on buses singing and distributing flyers. These texts served as hideouts from the riot police and constituted 'unruly' places beyond Wade's reach".[15] This assessment shows the ingenuity and variety in *Y en a marre's* urban guerrilla tactics, some of which proved occasionally more efficient than street protests or riots. In this respect, the "Urban Guerrilla Poetry" represented a social movement diatribe, which serves as a rhetorical response to a political discourse. Social activists enter into a dialogue with citizens to expose the injustices the masses have been enduring.

Social Movement Diatribe or the Rhetoric of Provocation

Contrary to mainstream political discourse, which generally aims at convincing political subjects to adhere to an ideology or a political program or philosophical disquisitions, social movement diatribe in the West African context seeks to engage the power structures in a verbal altercation to expose their political flaws. It also attempts, by means of oral performance, to open citizens' eyes to sociopolitical injustices in order to provoke a public outcry against elected officials. The diatribe has a short- as well as long-term goal. On the one hand, it tries to unmask the fallacies and insufficiencies of the power structure in order to provoke a mass reaction against corruption, disenfranchisement, embezzlement of public funds as well as to denounce water or power outages, to name a few. On the other hand, the diatribe ultimately seeks a regime change through the ballot by trying to sway votes away from (and to the detriment of) the regime. Contemporary social activists in Francophone West Africa incorporate the diatribe in their arsenal of contention/protest as a tactical response to demagogy and political falsehood.

---

14 Guèye, "Urban Guerrilla Poetry," 27.
15 Guèye, 23.

Furthermore, the oral nature of diatribe ensures a more inclusive activism by making information easily understandable to the general public. The *Bailai Citoyen* in Burkina Faso uses this method to diffuse information among its followers:

> The dissemination of the movement's ideas passes essentially by oral means, taking into consideration all literacy levels. Messages are relayed by artists during concerts which also serve as rallies, by audiovisual animators but also directly in the neighborhood and localities by the *cibals* (*members of Balai Citoyen*). Social media has also played a crucial role, especially during the two insurrections.[16]

Not only does this statement reinforce the efficiency of social movement diatribe, it also signposts the importance of information accessibility in the sense that illiteracy should not handicap equal access to information, especially regarding the political affairs of a given country. Social movement diatribe accords significance to orality, which is historically the primary way of ingurgitating knowledge and information in many African cultures. This shows a level of social movement inclusivity, which embraces people regardless of their level of academic education. In addition, it symbolizes an interesting contrast to the elitism of traditional political parties.

In the Senegalese and Burkinabé context, social movement diatribe has been civically informative and politically denunciative, thus turning activists in the process into "conscientious objectors." As a method of social protest, social activists use diatribe in rap songs, oral performances (rap concerts), and TV and radio debates. We can talk about hip-hop diatribe when a politically charged rap song is designed to expose and raise awareness about the injustices of a corrupt and predatory regime/system and nominally target government officials (and other people in positions of power, like judges and religious leaders) by use of virulent lyrics sometimes including overt invectives and other derogatory name-calling. Many of the songs produced by *Y en a marre* founding members Thiat and Kilifeu fit the description of hip-hop diatribe, which is also partially consistent with James Braxton Peterson's conception of diatribe in his work entitled *Hip-Hop Headphones* (2016).

Analyzing Lauryn Hill's song, "The Mystery of Inequality" (which deals with criminalization, mass incarceration, and militarization of the police in America), Peterson argues: "Through Lauryn Hill's lyrics, the absurd depths of injustice in our criminal justice systems are poetically exposed. The song stands (even now) as a diatribe that dismantles the myths of justice in our

---

16 Ritimo.org. "Au Burkina Faso: Le Balai citoyen" (my translation).

systems and deconstructs the 'mystery' of the 'inequality' that plagues our systems."[17] Peterson's characterization invokes the denunciative and belligerent tone of Hill's song, which launches a "violent" attack on the American criminal justice system by calling out "corrupt" lawyers and judges, "political prostitution," and the clergy all working hand in hand to unjustly incarcerate more black bodies. Similarly, by using diatribe as a rhetorical act in the musical production, *Y en a marre* activists assume a provocative/belligerent stand vis-à-vis the political and judicial system. However, their belligerence sometimes comes with harmful physical or judicial repercussions. In many instances, Senegalese activists expect backlash from being overtly critical of their regimes. They know that they can be targets of physical violence or judicial action at any time and plan accordingly.

Y en a marre artists like Thiat and Kilifeu were placed in police custody and interrogated for verbally attacking and antagonizing the regime. These two artists have made it clear since the beginning of their hip-hop careers that they would not be soft on elected officials. They have used deliberately offensive lyrics and sometimes invectives in their rap songs to provoke a reaction from authorities. They reiterate the vexing nature of their lyrics in their song "*Lalake*":

> Vocal, senseless and fake people will never challenge us.
> We ruined your musical career and snatched your fanbase.
> We overcame the obstacles you put in our path and we perform way better on stage.
> Your first prize in hip-hop was a girlfriend, ours was jailtime.
> We are way more daring than you are, we cause troubles and trigger controversies.[18]

The last two verses of the stanza not only underscore the artists' commitment to instigate unrest through their musical discourse but also their readiness to endure the severe consequences of their actions. While some people might find this attitude irresponsible, it should be acknowledged that expressions of temerity fit in well with social movement activism because the moment an individual declares oneself a social activist, they consciously or unconsciously "subscribe" to the risks associated with activism. Therefore, knowing that they are potential government targets, it is in the (second) nature of social activists like Thiat and Kilifeu to shock their interlocutors and prepare for

---

17   Peterson, *Hip-Hop Headphones: A Scholar's Critical Playlist*, 4.
18   Keur Gui Crew, "Lalake."

the resulting consequences. This is the essence of diatribe as understood by social movement theorist Theodore Windt.

In his article "Diatribe: Last Resort for Protest," Windt argues that the diatribe is an endeavor to concomitantly chastise, captivate, shock, and transmit unfavorable impressions of public officials.[19] His conception of social movement diatribe corresponds to *Y en a marre* activists' resort to Urban Guerrilla Poetry as a means of denouncing public figures and connecting with the masses. From the use of social movement diatribe emerges an unapologetic discourse that defies societal rules of respect (from the perspectives of their targets). In other words, Senegalese youth activists engaged in this form of protest to trample all rules of political correctness, as the terms they use to address politicians in their oral performances and music videos are often deemed by politicians to be disrespectful and inappropriate for young Senegalese. In this respect, social movement diatribe provokes a reaction from politicians who ground their critiques of the rhetorical form on the social and moral values of African/Senegalese societies, namely respect toward elders and persons in positions of authority. At the same time, it engenders a counterattack on behalf of activists based on those same values, thus providing two conflicting perspectives on morality. In more concrete terms, a politician may say that Thiat is being disrespectful by calling fellow politicians older than himself "liars" in his songs or TV interviews. Thiat would respond to this comment by saying that "embezzling tax-payers' money is theft, which is punished by society and religion." Both arguments are premised on societal values and morality as interpreted by both sides. However, by using diatribe in the first place, social movement participants challenge moral norms.

Windt contends that a diatribe serves basically two main functions in contrast to traditional speech forms: to primarily attract attention and gather an audience, and then uses "shock" to rearrange perspectives. Windt also adds that people rarely become concerned about issues until they are shocked. To make the shock effect potent, the obscene language becomes part of social activists' lexicons. Their diatribe becomes a way to both satirize basic values and expectations by dramatizing the discrepancy between language and actions, between illusions and realities.[20] This is reminiscent of *Y en a marre* activists' use of provocative rap lyrics to constantly challenge the traditional form of rhetoric and cultural transactions that expect younger people to

---

19   Windt, "The Diatribe: Last Resort for Protest," 1–14.
20   Windt, 5.

address their elders and leaders with respect and reverence. During a rally in July 2011, at the Obélisque Square near downtown Dakar, Thiat used the shocking function of diatribe when he unequivocally declared: "An old man can be useful to a country when he works towards the right direction. But a 90-year-old man who says things and then backs out of his words and lies [to the people] is not a model."[21] Thiat's declaration shocked many people, including supporters of his own movement. The activist's words were in sharp contrast to Amadou Hampaté Ba's famous phrase in *Amkoullel L'enfant Peul* (1991): "The death of an elder is like a burning library." Thiat's declaration was unambiguously directed at President Wade, who had just turned eighty-six in May 2012. However, the statements stood as an oxymoron that acknowledged the importance given to elders in African society, particularly Senegalese, but also destroyed the integrity of President Wade who, in Thiat's own perspective, did not fit the description of the "model elder" that Hampaté Ba referenced in his work. Not only did calling President Wade a "liar" represent an offense to social norms, it was also a violation of the Senegalese penal code whose Article 80 considers offensive words directed at the president to be a crime. For this reason, the *Y en a marre* activists got arrested, interrogated, and placed in police custody.

Although Thiat's words and his subsequent arrest raised outrage on both sides of the sociopolitical spectrum, support for Thiat came from the movement's membership as well as from political opposition leaders. The newspaper *Le Populaire* provided a detailed coverage of the whole incidence and described the commotion that occurred at the police station and in court when Thiat got arrested:

> Supporters of the Y en a marre movement besieged the police station, Thiat was indeed not alone in his face-to-face with the police. Supporters of the movement were waiting outside of the DIC [Criminal Investigation Division] building and the courthouse while Thiat was being interrogated and tried. Kilifeu, Fou Malade, Fadel Barro were on the front line among other leaders of the movement. We also noted the presence of politicians who came to show their support. Their determination to spend the night was such that many of them had brought mattresses, gas bottles and tea equipment, basically everything needed to camp in front of the courthouse and maintained the pressure. And when, at 00:40, Thiat was taken to the Central Police Station of Dakar, the young people went and waited outside of the police station. This started to an-

---

21   Thiat's speech during a rally against the candidacy of President Wade for a third term, July 23, 2011.

noy police officers on the spot who insisted that the young people should leave the premises. Y en a marre supporters did not want to leave Thiat alone in the hands of the police.[22]

This episode epitomizes some of the consequences that can arise from the use of "harsh" language as a means of protest. Using diatribe has often resulted in the condemnation of activists. Although in the case Thiat was released the next day, Wade's government used the incident to send a strong signal to Thiat's fellow activists, reminding them that their paroles have consequences. However, this did not intimidate *Y en a marre* activists, who kept using more shocking terms to describe Senegalese politicians, especially during televised debates.

In several televised debates, the activists continued to use diatribe to confront politicians. The most recent instance occurred in January 2019 when Thiat was invited to a debate with Farba Senghor, a former Wade's protégé and minister in the Wade regime. Thiat refused to shake Senghor's hand. He then argued that Farba Senghor was a mediocre person and a thief who embezzled public funds. Thiat's action not only shocked Mr. Senghor but also disturbed the TV show hosts as well as many people in the general public. The interaction between Thiat, Farba Senghor, and the hosting journalists during this debate epitomizes the shock function and moral reactions to social movement diatribe. In his defense, Thiat argued that Farba Senghor was the outcome of a cult of mediocrity that exists in Senegal when it comes to appointing people to positions of high responsibility. He also added that since Senegal does not have laws that sanction people like Farba Senghor, it becomes imperative for the people to openly show them how angry they are with them.[23] *Y en a marre* activists such as Thiat know that this kind of rhetoric always engenders angry reactions from their interlocutor, especially during a nationally broadcast debate like theirs. He is also aware that based on the Senegalese notions of *worma* (respect of the individual) and *yar* (discipline), his attitude towards Fabar Senghor would provoke a backlash.

The TV host's response to Thiat's argument for why he did not shake his opponent's hand marks the societal/moral response to diatribe when he asserted: "Thiat, don't you think that despite your disagreements (with Farba

---

22 "Thiat de Y en a marre arrêté." *Le Populaire,* July 25, 2011.
23 Thiat's argument during the TV program, *Kër Jaraaf,* January 25, 2019, https://senego.com/video-traite-de-singe-et-de-voleur-de-la-republique-par-thiat-farba-senghor-boude-lemission_833959.html.

Senghor), you should be able to shake his hand and then tell him the truth? Because that is more respectful and that is how we do it in our culture here in Senegal."[24] The journalist's words reaffirm the argument made earlier in this section; namely that morality and social norms are always used as an attempt to counteract social movement diatribe. Social activists countered this by also making their own use of morality and social norms. In response, Thiat disagreed with the journalist's argument:

> There is not anything more disrespectful than embezzling public funds and not be held accountable for it. It is not sensible that Karim (President Wade's son) was imprisoned while he (Farba Senghor) remained free. We don't know if he benefitted from arbitration, we still do not know what happened with his case, and he never enlightened the Senegalese population about that. So, do not talk to me about respect. The lack of respect that has been existing in Senegal since 2000 comes from these politicians who steal public funds, who are arrogant and, on top of that, switch political parties (to join the presidential coalition). They must respect the Senegalese people, and I do not want to deal with these kinds of people, and I advise all Senegalese people to not deal with them either.[25]

The social activist's rebuttal partially challenges Senegalese notions of respect and morality. In other words, Thiat's underlying assumption is that if refusing to greet someone on TV is not culturally acceptable, embezzling public money should also be reprehensible. If calling a politician a "liar" is wrong, society should also condemn those politicians who do not respect their promises to do right by ordinary citizens. In other words, diatribe is antithetical to political correctness and is borderline humiliation in certain contexts.

Due to the humiliating treatment he received from activists, Farba Senghor ended up quitting the TV show, provoking mixed reactions from internet users, including *Y en a marre* supporters. While many people praised Thiat for openly antagonizing and humiliating Wade's former minister of agriculture, others argued that *the Y en a marre* activist owed Farba Senghor respect regardless of how the latter handled his previous governmental responsibilities. Mandiaye Thiam, a Facebook user, commented on the incident as follows: "Even if Farba Senghor was the worst of humankind, he deserves respect. Greetings in Islam represents a symbolic gesture of great

---

24 The TV host's argument when Thiat refused to shake Mr. Senghor's hand on the TV show, *Kër Jaraaf*, January 25, 2019.
25 Thiat during the TV program, *Kër Jaraaf*, January 25, 2019.

value. By refusing to shake his hand, Thiat goes lower than him."[26] Another user added: "The debate could have been done with respect. I did not appreciate Thiat's attitude. I find it unacceptable regardless of Farba's virtues or flaws".[27] These comments show that although some people may support the overall struggle of *Y en a marre*, they do not always condone confrontational methods or tactics.

In light of Y *en a marre's* cantankerous activist interactions with politicians, we can conclude that diatribe in the Francophone West African context constitutes an invitation to a verbal confrontation as well as to judicial action. In this respect, the more elements of the state apparatus that engage with activists in this strategic "mind game," the more the activists gain the sympathy and support of the public, as the state appears intimidating in the eyes of the population. Counterattacking activists verbally weakens the charisma/integrity of public authorities, making them look "petty" in the process whereas attacking them in court appears as if the state wants to curtail freedom of expression, which makes their authority questionable in the eyes of the international community. In this context, African governments generally find themselves in a quandary and would certainly be better off ignoring activists' verbal attacks. In some cases, authorities sponsor lower-level party members to respond to these attacks and to confront social activists through various platforms including social media. In more extreme cases, we see physical attacks against activists. Thiat was physically attacked by a Macky Sall supporter a week before the 2019 presidential election during a live TV show on 2STV (a private TV station in Dakar). The supporter argued that the activist had been disrespectful to the president. This shows that though diatribe remains an efficient aggressive tactic that turns social movement activists into forces to be reckoned with, but it also can be a threat to their safety.

Beyond the shock effect it produces among public opinion and political leaders, diatribe occasionally proves to be highly offensive toward activists' targets. In Francophone West Africa, the usage of diatribe also involves

---

26 Même si Farba Senghor est le pire des hommes, il mérite le respect. La salutation est en Islam un geste symbolique d'une énorme valeur. En refusant de lui serrer la main, Thiat tombe plus bas que lui (my translation). Sokhna BeentOuh IBraahiim's Facebook page, January 26, 2019. Yes, it is the correct spelling.
27 Le débat pouvait se faire dans le respect. J'apprécie pas du tt! Ak nou Farba meunti mel, je trouve que li rafetoul. (My translation) Ma Taye Beugue Karim's Facebook page, January 26, 2019.

coining phrases to denounce certain political practices and certain types of politicians. For instance, Thiat and Kilifeu popularized the phrase *singes de la république* (monkeys of the republic) to describe any politician who left the opposition to join forces with the presidential coalition. The term symbolically refers to a monkey jumping from one tree branch to another, much like certain Senegalese career politicians jump from one presidential coalition to another. Farba Senghor is a prime example. He used to be one of Wade's closest collaborators and a prominent member of the Senegalese Democratic Party (PDS). He assumed multiple appointments in the Wade regime, including minister of agriculture, and minister of transportation. Although Farba Senghor and other PDS members had been expelled from the party for an act of rebellion and insubordination to the party's rule, the Senegalese public expressed disappointment following his political alliance with President Macky Sall, whose regime he had previously been critical of. This practice called *transhumance politique* (switching political parties) in Senegal evokes public disdain toward politicians who indulge in it. During the last decade, the Senegalese civil society has been pushing in vain for the passage of a law to ban this phenomenon. In the meantime, *Y en a marre* activists continue to use the term *singes de la république* to designate and shame these politicians who they believe do not deserve to speak in public any longer since they represent antirepublican values.[28]

Ultimately, social movement diatribes remain powerful rhetorical tools for political contention. It enables activists to use the power of the spoken word to shock, antagonize, and sometimes shame their opponents. In the case of *Y en a marre*, diatribe transpires through their music and public addresses urging certain people, including politicians, to call them "rude," "disrespectful," and "inconsiderate." Following the incident between Thiat and Farba Senghor, the journalist Bassirou Dieng attacked Thiat in a virulent article entitled "*Thiat de Y en a marre . . . Un impoli qui humilie ses aînés*" (Thiat from Y en a marre . . . a disrespectful person who humiliates his elders). Dieng wrote "a Muslim must not refuse to shake the hand of his neighbor, as prescribed by the Quran. I could not be silent about the hateful behavior of indiscipline and arrogance of the young rapper and member of Keur Gui, Thiat, on the set of 7TV. Who do you think you are to dare 'humiliate' someone who could be your father?"[29] Dieng's article mirrors the reaction of

---

28 Thiat on the TV program *Kër Jaraaf*, January 25, 2019.
29 Un musulman ne doit pas refuser de serrer la main de son prochain, conformément aux prescriptions. Je ne pouvais, à vrai dire, rester muet face au

many Senegalese who in reality also support *Y en a marre* activism. Even if the diatribe has proven to be effective so far, it also has shortcomings, given that it can alienate segments of civil society who also value respect for elders, humility, and discipline. Beyond the usage of diatribe, social activists have at their disposal other oratory tools such as the "musical open letter" to fight against the political establishment.

"The Letter-Writing": Rap Music as a Rhetorical Act

In their 2011 article entitled "'Mr. President': Musical Open Letters as Political Commentary in Africa," Daniel Künzler and Uta Teuster-Jahn define the musical open letter as "a new genre of popular music since 2000, in the context of democratization and a certain postdemocratization disillusionment. Through those letters, young urban musicians publicly and directly address political leaders protesting against a lack of accountability and demanding a fair dialogue about the representation of voters' interests."[30] This musical genre is not actually a new phenomenon in African music, particularly Senegalese music. As early as 1990, the famous Senegalese singer and proclaimed, "King of Mbalax," Youssou N'Dour adopted this musical genre in his song called *Bataaxal* (Letter). Prior to the 2000s, however, this musical genre did not have a predilection for addressing political issues. Youssou N'Dour's song *"Bataaxal,"* for instance, deals with love and friendship, but the rise to prominence of urban hip-hop in the early 2000s, coupled with multiple political transitions in many Francophone West African countries including Benin, Mali, Mauritania, and Senegal, the open letter has become the preferred musical form among African hip-hop artists for enter into a dialogue with political leaders.

Similar to the diatribe, the musical open letter "speak[s] out in plain language and often defy etiquette rules, in contrast to more traditional, veiled forms of musically expressed criticism".[31] Targets of this musical genre are

---

    comportement troué d'indiscipline et d'arrogance du jeune rappeur Thiat du groupe Keur Gui de Kaolack sur le plateau de la télévision 7TV de notre consœur Maïmouna Ndour Faye. Pour qui te prends-tu pour oser « humilier » publiquement quelqu'un qui peut, pourtant être ton père? (My translation). Dieng, *"Thiat de Y en a marre . . . Un impoli qui humilie ses aînés."*

30 Künzler and Teuster-Jahn, "Mr. President," 1.
31 Künzler and Teuster-Jahn, 1.

often national political leaders, but the genre also has a transnational impact on the continent, especially when used to critique foreign interventions into African politics. Didier Awadi's song *"J'Accuse"* remains a prime example of how the open letter form tackles foreign political meddling. Sworn Pan-Africanist and self-proclaimed Sankarist, Didier Awadi criticizes and condemns the interventionist policies of certain Western countries as well as their support of African dictatorships:

> I accuse the USA of conspiracy against humanity, of non-compliance with the resolutions of the UN Security Council.
> I accuse America of interference in private matters, when they attack Somalia, where is respect for dignity?
> [. . .] Truman should be tried for crimes against humanity.
> How can we accept such atrocity?
> Hiroshima Nagasaki the after-effects are still there.
> I accuse Georges Bush of being a real butcher. Lying about chemical weapons in Iraq, where is morality?
> [. . .] I also accuse France of crime against humanity. Too many deaths in Central Africa I could not forget them. [. . .] I accuse France of irresponsibility before history. Too many coups in Africa are sponsored by them in the dark.
> Dahomey, Congo, Rwanda I stop there but France is causing too much damage that's why I accuse Giscard of being an accomplice of Bokassa.
> Bokassa paid his debt, Giscard was free why is that? [. . .]
> I accuse Africa of chronic irresponsibility, I accuse our presidents, our leaders of being selfish and cynical.
> They want power, all the power, but once in power, they promise things without the power to accomplish them.
> They sold Africa, its wealth, even its beaches . . . When you walk into a bank, and it looks nice, it's because it's foreign owned.
> Do you consider yourself independent?
> You can dream because it is the former colonizer who still manages everything. They manage our currency and gold in the Bank of France's coffers.[32]

---

32 J'accuse les USA de complot contre l'humanité, de non-respect des résolutions du conseil de sécurité. J'accuse l'Amérique d'ingérence sur les affaires privées, quand ils vont en Somalie, où est le respect de la dignité ? Moi j'étais très content de voir les Somaliens les jeter. On devrait juger Truman pour crime contre l'humanité. Comment peut-on accepter de telles atrocités ? Hiroshima Nagasaki les séquelles sont toujours là. J'accuse Georges Bush d'être un véritable boucher. Mentir sur les armes chimiques où est donc la moralité ? /
[. . .] J'accuse aussi la France de crime contre l'humanité. Trop de morts en

HIP-HOP, CIVIC AWARENESS, AND ANTIESTABLISHMENT POLITICS · 57

Awadi's song stands out as one of the first instances of musical open letters in Francophone West African rap music. His aforementioned lyrics are reminiscent of the famous letter French writer Emile Zola sent to French President Félix Faure in defense of General Albert Dreyfus who had been wrongfully convicted for espionage. Not only does the rapper blame Western leaders of crimes against humanity by fueling conflicts around the world, he also directly calls out African leaders on their involvement in the socioeconomic issues that plague the continent. Other rappers in the region also made use of this tool to address political issues in their countries or request better socioeconomic policies from their presidents.

In Mali, the rap group Tata Pound released *Cikan-le message* (2004) in which they reminded President Amadou Toumani Touré that the country belonged to all Malians, and that the law should apply to everyone including lawmakers themselves. In the same vein, the Beninois rapper Noir et Blanc (Black and White) produced in 2004 *Monsieur le President* (Mister President) while the Burkinabé rap group *Yeleen* released in 2006 *Dar es Salam* (House of Peace) a musical letter they requested the then President Blaise Compaoré to transmit to his fellow African and Western leaders. In keeping with this innovative musical tradition, *Y en a marre* also adopted the method to convey messages to Senegalese leaders. Simon Kouka, a member of the movement and rapper, incarnates the role of a letter sender/transmitter in his song *Lettre au Président* (Letter to the President). This

---

> Centre-Afrique je ne pourrais pas les oublier. Vous oubliez un peu trop vite tous les tirailleurs Sénégalais, de force en relais, déportés, aujourd'hui expulsés. Ils sont venus, ils se sont battus, ils ont vaincu, votre pays détruit, ils sont revenus et ils ont reconstruit. J'accuse aussi la France d'irresponsabilité devant l'histoire. Trop de coup d'états en Afrique sont commandités par eux dans le noir, au Dahomey, au Congo, au Rwanda je m'arrête là mais la France fait trop de dégâts c'est pourquoi j'accuse Giscard d'être un complice de Bokassa. Bokassa paye sa dette, Giscard libre pourquoi ça? Je dis que la France est ingrate quand elle parle de visa. Quand nos pères sont partis mourir pour elle y'avait pas de visa . . . J'accuse toute l'Afrique d'irresponsabilité chronique, nos présidents, nos dirigeants d'être égoïstes et cyniques. Ils veulent du pouvoir encore du pouvoir, tout le pouvoir, une fois au pouvoir promettent des choses sans le pouvoir. Ils ont vendu l'Afrique, ses richesses mêmes ses plages . . .
> Quand tu vas dans une banque, si elle est bien, c'est parce qu'elle est étrangère. Tu te crois indépendant ? Rêves parce que c'est le colon qui gère. Gère même la monnaie dans les coffres de la Banque de France. Gère même notre or dans les coffres de la Banque de France. (My translation). See Awadi, "J'accuse."

song translates the daily hardships that many Senegalese suffer/face under President Sall's regime.

Simon preludes his artistic product with the chorus "*sonnu nanu, sonnu nanu*" Mr. President (we are tired, we are tired Mister President) which echoes the clamor of millions of Senegalese who had hoped for better days under the Sall regime. Simon melodiously emphasizes the despair of many Senegalese by using a musical instrument that not only inspires sadness and anguish but also nostalgia and sentimentality. Simon makes sure to clarify that his message emanates from a *Y en a marre* activist anxious about the destiny of his people:

> Prezi, it is a Yenamarriste who is sending you this letter, which comes from the bottom of his heart.
> A Yenamarriste who will undermine the fervor of fallacious people.
> The one who will be the protector of equal rights for haves and have-nots.
> Because of our love for Senegal, we have accepted to support Bukki (hyena).
> We accepted the criticism [from family members], the insults and decided to stay home instead of migrating abroad. Prezi, your load is more than heavy however, you are the one who is supposed to find solutions to our problems. If you listen, you will hear, do not ignore us we are begging you. Do not mess up like Laye (Abdoulaye Wade) who pretended to know but ended up being vengeful. He was surrounded by ogres who poisoned his mind. He still cannot fathom how he lost the power. Prezi be-careful of the people around you.[33]

Simon's lyrics, on the one hand, epitomize the hope *Y en a marre* initially placed in Macky Sall's regime following his presidential victory in 2012. In addition, the rapper's verse "protector of equal rights for haves and have-nots" confirms the role of sentinel the *Y en a marre* activists have been playing since 2011. On the other hand, the use of the metaphor "*Bukki*" (Hyena), reflects activists' distrust vis-à-vis the political establishment embodied by Abdoulaye Wade and his close allies. The metaphor additionally serves as an invitation to President Sall to beware of those same "*Hyenas*" who caused Wade's downfall. In Senegalese folktale tradition, *Bukki* (Hyena) is the quintessential embodiment of malice and antipathy. The carnivore epitomizes threat, greed, injustice, and betrayal in contrast to *Leuk* (hare), which exemplifies ruse. In Senegalese folktales, *Bukki* and *Leuk* are always depicted as companions with a conflicted relationship trying to outsmart each other. They possess opposite values and different abilities. However, *Leuk* always comes out victorious in their confrontations.

---

33   Kouka, "Lettre au Président."

The metaphor *Bukki* designates politicians who stand for Senegalese countervalues. Thus, by comparing Wade's entourage to *Bukki* and inviting President Sall to distance himself from them, Simon attributes to these politicians, all *Bukki's* flaws. However, not only does Simon send President Sall and his regime a strong message of hope through his musical letter, but he also warns him against co-opting these potential untrustworthy politicians (*Bukki*) for his cabinet given the fact that switching political parties remains a common practice in Senegal. Interestingly, "Letter to the President" does not reflect the usual *Y en a marre* musical register.

Grounded in denunciation and awareness raising, *Y en a marre's* musical production remains overwhelmingly hostile toward the political establishment; but in this instance, "Letter to the President" seems more like *une main tendue* (a helping hand) accompanied with an advisory note to President Sall. The song is a departure from the strident lyrical norm of *Y en a marre* marked by the strong bass drumbeat. "Letter to the President" is melodious and known for its keyboard-dominated musical flourishes that evoke a sentimentality that one generally hears in a love song. Instead of vigorously criticizing the president as he did in other *Y en a marre* rap songs, Simon reminds the president that they are not his enemies in reality:

> Let's make it clear, we are not your enemy
> But expect a clear shock if you ever decide to betray your friends.
> Excellency, when you came to seek our support,
> The Senegalese people saw the share we gave you.
> While people were asking you to appoint them as minister,
> We told you to prioritize the demands of the masses.
> While other people were asking to be added to your legislative lists
> We told you to prioritize the demands of the masses.[34]

These verses resonate as an "amicable reminder" that *Y en a marre* supported the candidacy of President Sall during the 2012 presidential election, and for this reason, the Senegalese president should not see them as adversaries. Finally, the leitmotif, "We told you to prioritize the demands of the masses," emphasizes the primacy of national interests over individual benefits. President Sall himself seemed to acquiesce to this when he popularized the phrase *La patrie avant le parti* (the homeland before the party) to stress national interests over political priorities of his party. Nine years into his presidency, however, the phrase seems more like an empty slogan given the blatant nepotism in his government. Additionally, the phrase reinforces the activists' watchdog role

---

34 Kouka, "Lettre au Président."

vis-à-vis governmental actions. Nevertheless, from the outset, Simon and his fellow activists seemed to be aware that the task of Macky's regime was not going to be easy and that it would take a few months to undo the negative deeds of the previous regime. In this respect, Simon asserts:

> We are all aware of it the situation in which you found the country.
> We are aware of the domestic debts Wade left behind.
> Standing straight is not going to be easy since you chose to mitigate a big issue,
> The people chose you, so you knew it was not going to be easy. When you said prioritize the interests of the country before the party's interests, we applauded.
> When you talked about subsidizing peanut farmers, *I swear* we applauded. When you talked about getting rid of 50 government agencies to reduce public spending, we applauded. However, when is the cost of living going to decrease?[35]

Not only do the aforementioned lyrics acknowledge the challenge awaiting President Sall and his regime, but they also highlight that the activists were willing to allow the government a grace period to overcome these challenges as well. Coincidentally, *Y en a marre* lost its activist momentum following the 2012 presidential election. In the postelection period, the Senegalese activists focused more on community service, capacity building, and project implementation until 2016 when they actively resumed opposition of President Sall's constitutional referendum (in 2016, the regime organized a referendum to change the constitution), thus exacerbating the fallout between the regime and the social movement. Nevertheless, it should be pointed out that in contrast to other rap songs that *Y en a marre* produced, "Letter to the President" maintains a respectful tone and lyrics pleading for constructive sociopolitical change in Senegal. Though still critical and inspiring, this musical open letter pales in comparison to the movement's 2012 song released before the presidential election: characterized as it was by explicit language and the harshness of the musical instrumentation, among other elements.

---

35 Kouka, "Lettre au Président."

Conclusion

Ultimately, the power of popular music, especially rap music, has transcended the barriers of entertainment and folklore to infiltrate African politics as an agent of change. Hip-hop artists in Francophone West Africa carry the legacies of musicians such as Miriam Makeba, and Fela Kuti, who used their art as a weapon of protest against hostile governments that tried to demonize them and deny them basic rights. The rise of Senegalese hip-hop in the 1990s meant the emergence of a new political force that predominantly appealed to the younger generations. Emanating from the middle class of Dakar with a strong American influence, hip-hop quickly spread to the suburbs of Dakar and the other regions of Senegal where groups like Keur Gui Crew gave the music its particular "Senegaleseness" and used it as a means of social and political activism. In addition to this oral art form, West African social movements include the diatribe in the arsenal of contentious art forms to influence the traditional political discourse. Although the diatribe is a somewhat unconventional weapon of protest due to its shock value, it has proved useful for the *Y en a marre* movement. By same token, these activists use the "musical open letter" to convey messages to a political power structure that seems unreceptive to their calls. Thus, given the lack of access to funding and traditional media outlets, social activists in contemporary Francophone West Africa have made rap music the cornerstone of their activism. It provides them access to a large and relatively young international audience. In the same vein, social activists have capitalized on the accessibility of social media to mobilize human as well as media and financial resources.

Bibliography

Actunet, A. Z. "Traité De "Voleur De La Republique" Par Thiat: Farba Senghor Boude Le Pateau De Ker Jaraaf." 2019.
Allen, Lara. "Music and Politics in Africa." *Social Dynamics* 30, no. 2 (2004): 1–19.
Appert, C.M. *In Hip Hop Time: Music, Memory, and Social Change in Urban Senegal.* Oxford University Press, 2018.
Awadi, Didier. "J'accuse." In *Un Autre monde est possible* 2004.
Bâ, A.H. *Amkoullel, L'enfant Peul: Mémoires.* Eighty-four Editions, 1991.
Charry, Eric S. *Hip Hop Africa: New African Music in a Globalizing World.* African Expressive Cultures. Bloomington: Indiana University Press, 2012.
Clark, Msia Kibona, and Mickie Mwanzia Koster. *Hip Hop and Social Change in Africa: Ni Wakati.* Lanham, MD: Lexington, 2018.

Fredericks, Rosalind. "'The Old Man Is Dead': Hip Hop and the Arts of Citizenship of Senegalese Youth." *Antipode* 46, no. 1 (2014): 130–48.
Gueye, Marame. "Urban Guerrilla Poetry: The Movement Y' En a Marre and the Socio-Political Influences of Hip Hop in Senegal." *Journal of Pan African Studies* 6, no. 3 (2013).
Keur Gui Crew. "Diogoufi." *Encyclopédie. Produced by Penku Side, 2014.* 2016.
———. "Lalake." Single. Produced by Penku Side, 2009.
Kouka, Simon. "Lettre Au Président", 2014.
Künzler, Daniel, and Uta Reuster-Jahn. "Mr. Presidents: Musical Open Letters as Political Commentary in Africa." *Africa Today* 59, no. 1 (2012): 89–113.
Lo, Sheba. "Building Our Nation: Senegalese Hip-Hop Artists as Agents of Social and Political Change." In *Hip Hop and Social Change in Africa: Ni Wakati,* edited by Msia Kibona Clark and Mickie Mwanzia Koster. Lanham, MD: Lexington, 2014.
Mamphilly, Zach. "Senegal's Rappers Continue to 'Cry from the Heart' for a More Just Society." *The Conversation*, 2018.
Mine, Daouda. "Thiat De Y En a Marre Arrêté." *Le Populaire*, 2011.
Moore, C. *Fela: This Bitch of a Life*. London: Omnibus, 2011.
Nossiter, Adam. "In Blunt and Sometimes Crude Rap, a Strong Political Voice Emerges." *New York Times*, September 18, 2011.
Peterson, J. B. *Hip Hop Headphones: A Scholar's Critical Playlist*. London: Bloomsbury, 2016.
Ritimo.org. "Au Burkina Faso: Le Balai citoyen." March 27th, 2018. https://www.ritimo.org/Au-Burkina-Faso-Le-Balai-citoyen.
Seneweb. "Auchan Dans Le Viseur De L'unacois Jappo." *Seneweb*, June 23, 2018. https://seneweb.com/news/Societe/auchan-dans-le-viseur-de-l-rsquo-unacois_n_250444.html.
Shipley, J. W. *Living the Hiplife: Celebrity and Entrepreneurship in Ghanaian Popular Music*. Durham, NC: Duke University Press, 2012.
Smockey. "Opération Mana Mana." *Pré-volution*. Out Here Records, 2015.
Windt, Theodore Otto. "The Diatribe: Last Resort for Protest." *Quarterly Journal of Speech* 58, no. 1 (1972): 1–14.
"Y En a Marre: Documentaire 'Dox Ak Sa Gox.'" YouTube, 2015. https://www.youtube.com/watch?v=9s9r7vZUIDQ.

Chapter Two

Rapping, Imagination, and Urban Space in Dar es Salaam

David Kerr

The first hip-hop recordings arrived in Dar es Salaam in the mid-1980s when films like *Wild Style* and *Breakin'*, which featured early hip-hop recordings in their soundtracks, were being shown in the city. High import duties ensured that hip-hop recordings were scarce and principally available to wealthier Tanzanians, who consequently formed many of the early rap groups. Following the liberalization of the media in the early 1990s, there has been a proliferation of new musical genres collectively defined as *muziki wa kizazi kipya* (music of the new generation). This loose set of genres such as hip-hop, bongo flava, R'n'B, reggae, and zouk are mostly associated with youth. The new generation that performs these genres entered adulthood during structural adjustment reforms and is marked by their appropriation of style, form, and fashion from the transnational circulation of popular musical forms.

As these genres have become popular, rapping has become a widespread cultural practice among young people. It has produced musical stars as well as unrecorded *maandagraundi* (or underground) rappers. The most popular rappers have become not only national or regional stars but also continent-wide celebrities regularly performing on TV channels such as Channel O and MTV Africa and at TV spectacles such as the *Big Brother Africa*. By contrast, underground rappers define themselves through their exclusion from these transnational circuits of commercial musical production, distribution, and dissemination. Central to the practice of underground rapping are unplanned settlements commonly referred to as *uswahilini,* which provide space for underground rapping practice and performance. Informal spaces of sociality referred to as *maskani* (dwelling or abode) or *kijiweni* (little stone) act as the primary informal performance spaces for aspiring underground rappers. The young men who spend time at maskani in uswahilini are largely underemployed (popularly referred to as *daywaka*) or engaged in *mishe-mishe* (looking for money).

In this chapter I will argue that underground rapping provides a space for young people in Tanzania to engage with the world conceptually, philosophically, and discursively. Underground rappers draw on both the transnational signs and symbols of hip-hop as well as local creative, political, and imaginative discourses to empower themselves as social actors. Exploring the productive creative practices of young people can offer insights into the imaginative response of young people in Dar es Salaam to their difficult economic and social conditions. I argue that rapping acts as a means for creating value and meaning in young people's life worlds. I will explore the ways in which underground rappers use the urban space of uswahilini to engage in practices of creatively and imaginatively shaping both their present and future.

Research Context and Methodology

In the first week of my extended fieldwork visit to Dar es Salaam in 2009 I was introduced to the rapper Mwinjaka ally Mwinjakaw, more commonly known by his stage name, Mbaya Wao (or bad man).[1] He invited me to visit him at his family home in Kijitonyama, where a collective of rappers would congregate each Monday. Seated on breeze blocks and wooden benches propped up against the side of a family compound, these meetings would typically last from morning until nightfall. The meeting place was situated next to a barbershop where one of the collective's members, Majivu (ashes), worked. Graffiti marking the walls of the compound where the group met declared this as a space of hip-hop. Coffee and cigarettes purchased from passing *wamachinga,* or street traders, sustained the long meetings. Meetings were mainly taken up by members of the collective reciting their lyrics and receiving both praise and critique from the collective. The intense

---

[1] This article is based on three fieldwork trips to Dar es Salaam in 2006, 2009, and 2011, with follow-up research conducted through electronic communication.

Fig. 2.1. The wall at Mbaya Wao's maskani in Kijitonyama.

performances, sharing of lyrics, and discussion of rapping characterized these meetings. It was the rapping that brought the members together. This was the sole space within which the rappers in the collective were able to regularly perform. The rappers that formed the collective had not recorded in studios, did not perform in bars or at nightclubs and gained no financial reward from their rapping. Despite the lack of opportunities for commercial success or financial reward, these rappers devoted a great deal of time and intellectual energy to the practice of rapping.

Groups of predominantly young men who invested a significant amount of time in rapping and referred to themselves as *maandagraundi* (underground rappers) can be found across the residential neighborhoods of Dar es Salaam.[2] These rappers have little chance of entering the networks of com-

---

2   While a practice predominantly associated with men, there are a number of notable female rappers in Tanzania, such as Witnesz, Zay B, Sista P, and Stosh.

mercial sale, distribution, and performance of music. Yet rapping continues to play a significant role in their lives. Underground rapping can offer us insights into the response of young people in Dar es Salaam to the difficult economic and social conditions that adversely affect their lives. In the last decade or so, a lively academic debate about African youth and their role in contemporary African societies has developed. At the center of debates about the role of African youth has often been a concern with their marginalization in the public and political spheres.[3] This literature has frequently focused on notions of crisis and the role of young people in outbreaks of violence.[4] Complicating the notion of African youth as simply marginal, Honwana and De Boeck describe them as experiencing a double dynamic in which their perceived marginality and liminality places them both in the margins and squarely at the center of contemporary African life.[5] I will build upon this observation, demonstrating how young people in informal settlements, through contesting their marginality from the commercial realm of music production and circulation, come to dominate space socially, sonically, and physically, moving their older competitors temporarily to the margins. In particular, I wish to highlight the manifold ways in which the dynamics of marginality could be read through the production and circulation of rap music.

Recently, scholars have taken up the challenge of engaging with a variety of new forms of "marginal" socialities created by young people in African cities.[6] A further field of research has engaged with issues of the neoliberal economic changes to African economies, the relentless retreat of the state

---

      To both the male and female rappers, the act of *kuchana* (to rap) was associated with hard, serious masculinity as opposed to *kuimba* (to sing), which was perceived as soft, frivolous, and feminine. Borrowing the notion of gender performativity from Butler, we can see how rapping acts as a means of performing masculinity for the young men involved. The association of rapping with masculinity is destablized by female rappers (see Butler, *Gender Trouble*).

3   Diouf, "Engaging Postcolonial Cultures"; and Jua, "Differential Responses to Disappearing Transitional Pathways."

4   Chritstiansen, Utas, and Vigh et al., *Navigating Youth, Generating Adulthood*, 2006; and Abbink and Van Kessel, *Vanguard or Vandals*, 2005.

5   Honwana and De Boeck, *Makers and Breakers*, 10.

6   Masquelier, *Teatime*; Weiss, *Street Dreams and Hip-Hop Barbershops*; Geenen, "Sleep Occupies No Space"; Heinonen, *Youth Gangs and Street Children*; Biaya, "Youth and Street Culture in Urban Africa"; Di Nunzio, "We Are Good at Surviving"; and Ugor, "Survival Strategies and Citizenship Claims."

in the face of aggressive neoliberalism, and the distance between the aspirations and possibilities for attainment of these dreams for African youth. The prevention of African youth from full participation in the global imaginary, with its associated circulation of goods and symbols, has also engendered much discussion.[7] In his work on young men and barbershops in Arusha, Weiss explores the ways in which young men are "marginal to, and so *subjected* by, the global order of signs and values they intensely desire."[8] As such, Weiss reads this gap between this global order of signs and local constrained experience as pain. Pain for young men in Arusha is a mode of being in the world, which connects the subjugated individual to the world of signs that serves to subjugate them.

The development of underground rapping in Dar es Salaam is, as I shall explain in greater detail in this article, intimately linked to "neoliberal" changes in the Tanzanian musical economy. As scholars have indicated, acts of consumption and production can no longer be viewed as entirely separate dynamics but rather "appear as moments in a cycle."[9] However, I wish to shift the analytical frame slightly from the consumption of the signs and symbols of hip-hop and the global imaginary to the uses of rapping by young men as a means of producing events, texts, forms of sociality, and themselves. Drawing on the distinction between consumers and users offered by De Certeau,[10] this chapter will focus on the creativity of underground rapping. Focusing on rapping as production lends itself to an analysis that focuses less on the distance between desire and attainment than as a means for the "mutual creation of human beings."[11] Das and Poole's research on the margins of the state draws on Agamben's work on bare life and the state of exception to conceive of the margins as a necessary entailment of the state in the same way that Agamben conceptualizes the exception as "neither external nor internal" to the rule.[12] That which is excluded is also constitutive of the state. Das and Poole use this focus to rethink the ways in which the boundaries of the state are remade in everyday life. I will use this analysis to argue

---

7   Comaroff and Comaroff, *Millennial Capitalism*; Weiss, *Street Dreams and Hip-Hop Barbershops*; Mains, "Neoliberal Times."
8   Weiss, *Street Dreams and Hip-Hop Barbershops*, 116.
9   Barber, "Preliminary Notes on Audiences in Africa," 358.
10   De Certeau, *Practice of Everyday Life*.
11   Graebner, "Whose Music?," 502.
12   Agamben, *State of Exception*, 23.

that the margins do not so much lie outside the commercial world of music making but "like rivers, run through it."[13]

A Brief History of Rap Music in Tanzania

Before describing the practice of underground rapping, it is important to situate it within a wider economy of music making. Following independence, culture, as the "essence and spirit" of the nation,[14] was placed at the center of the project of nation building. The role of the state and the notion of developing a "national culture" have been significant to the development of popular music in Tanzania since independence. Following independence, state and parastate organizations became the largest patrons of musicians. Radio Tanzania Dar es Salaam (RTD) was both the country's only radio station and sole recording studio. Recording and broadcasting practices were heavily influenced by the policies of the state.[15] The state largely governed what was played on Tanzanian radio, and RTD was tasked with broadcasting mostly Tanzanian music.[16] Through BASATA (the Tanzanian Arts Council) musical genres were decreed by the state as either national (and therefore eligible for state support and broadcasting on the radio) or foreign (and thus ineligible for support). *Kwaya, ngoma, dansi* and *taarab* were considered national, while others, such as funk and soul, were considered foreign.[17]

Following state cultural guidelines, hip-hop was not broadcast on the national radio. It was breakdancing films in the mid-1980s such as *Wild Style* and *Breakin'*—which included hip-hop in their soundtracks—that hip-hop first arrived in Dar es Salaam.[18] High duties on imported goods meant that hip-hop recordings were principally available to wealthier Tanzanians or those with connections abroad. Consequently, many of Dar es Salaam's first generation of rappers came from the wealthier parts of the city such as Upanga and Oyster Bay. Rapping during the 1980s was principally practiced in secondary schools, and aspiring rappers would typically recite verses in

---

13   Das and Poole, "State and Its Margins,"13.
14   Nyerere, *Freedom and Unity*, 186.
15   Perullo, "Hooligans and Heroes," 74.
16   Perullo, 252.
17   Ivaska, *Cultured States*, 78; and Askew, "Musical Images and Imaginations," 276.
18   Perullo, "Hooligans and Heroes," 254.

English copied from recordings they had heard.[19] Recordings by Tanzania's first rap groups were in English. In 1991 the first large rap competition 'Yo Rap Bonanza' was held in Dar es Salaam (Lemelle 2006, 235), and it was in the same year that Saleh Jabir released what is commonly cited as the first Tanzanian rap recording in Swahili, "Ice Ice Baby: King of Swahili Rap" (Englert 2003, 77; Charry 2012, 15). The move to rapping in Swahili made hip-hop music accessible to a much wider audience.

Liberalization of the Tanzanian media, following the Broadcasting Services Act of 1993, allowed private individuals and businesses to purchase licenses to broadcast on radio or TV. The consequent proliferation of radio stations played an important role in the growing popularity of rap music in Tanzania. In 2001 there were ten private radio stations operating in Dar es Salaam,[20] by 2009 this number had risen to an estimated fifty-two private radio stations.[21] A range of music genres, collectively defined as *muziki wa kizazi kipya*, which to a greater or lesser degree incorporate rapping, have since become widely popular in Tanzania. In 2001 one of these genres, Bongo Flava, was designated by BASATA an officially state-recognized Tanzanian genre of music. As rap music in Tanzania has turned from an elite to a popular form of music, rappers have moved from being marginal figures to respected cultural icons. Professor Jay's 2002 album *Machozi, Jasho na Damu*"[22] was cited by many of the rappers and audience members I interviewed as a watershed moment in the increased respectability of rappers. The sociopolitical commentary of the album, which focuses on the difficulties experienced by the Dar es Salaam resident, is credited with expanding the audience for rap music in Tanzania. In particular, the song "*Bongo Dar es Salaam*," with its sometimes comic narrative of the strategies employed by the city's residents to get ahead, could be recognized and appreciated by both young and old. The adoption of Swahili as the language for hip-hop performance, and the growth of FM radio stations that were no longer constrained by state policies, led to rap music becoming a ubiquitous form of popular culture in Dar es Salaam.

---

19   Haas and Gesthuizen, "Ndani ya Bongo," 281.
20   Brennan and Burton, "Emerging Metropolis," 65.
21   Perullo, "Hooligans and Heroes," 5–6.
22   Blood, Sweat, and Tears.

Rappers as Celebrities

The liberalization of media in the region from the mid-1990s[23] enabled circuits of live performance and collaboration (in which artists from neighboring countries performed on each other's songs). Popular rappers became not only national but also regional celebrities.[24] By the early 2000s, magazines, tabloid newspapers, and TV programs in Dar es Salaam began to carry regular stories about the careers and personal lives of the most famous artists in what was termed a "Bongo Explosion."[25] During the last decade, global networks for performance have been created, and Tanzania's most successful rappers regularly perform in Europe, the United States, and Asia to largely expatriate East African audiences. Tanzanian rappers have been nominated for awards on Africa-wide TV channels such as Channel O and MTV Africa (both based in South Africa) and have performed at continental spectacles such as the launch of *Big Brother Africa*.[26] Tanzanian artists have begun to establish networks of collaboration that span the continent. Notably, rapper AY has collaborated with several Nigerian artists on his recordings.[27] Successful Tanzanian rappers have become stars across Africa, with the attendant media interest. Rapping has transformed from its beginning as a cultural form largely practiced in English to small audiences in schoolyards to a popular and ubiquitous form of Swahili popular culture. While rappers themselves may still be perceived as liminoid and transgressive figures associated with unsuitable behavior[28], rapping has moved to the cultural

---

23   Ogola, "The Political Economy of the Media in Kenya," 85.
24   On my first fieldwork trip to Dar es Salaam in 2006 a number of rappers I interviewed including AY, Afande Sele, and Joseph Mbilinyi / Mr 2 / Sugu discussed the possibilities for performing on regional circuits including Kenya, Uganda, Rwanda, and Burundi.
25   Reuster-Jahn and Hacke, "Bongo Flava Industry in Tanzania," 8.
26   For example, in 2009 AY performed at the finale of *Big Brother Africa* and was nominated for the award of best male hip-hop vocalist by MTV Africa.
27   In 2008 AY collaborated on a recording with the Nigerian brothers P-Square, followed in 2013 by a collaboration with Nigerian singer J. Martins.
28   Musicians have long been associated with asocial traits and perceived as "*wahuni* i.e. vagabonds, drunkards, drugtakers" (Graebner, "Whose Music?," 110) and many rappers continued to be perceived in this way (Perullo, 76; Suriano, 208).

mainstream.[29] Popular music occupies a central space in moral, social, and political discourses in Dar es Salaam.

The Music Economy: How Do You Become a Rapper?

The ability of rappers in Dar es Salaam to achieve success is circumscribed by access to networks and institutions. Contact with studios in which music can be recorded, and the media through which music can be disseminated, is essential to the process of becoming a commercially successful artist. Following the liberalization of the economy, a number of private institutions have become major players in the recording, broadcasting, and distribution of music. Liberalization of the economy not only enabled the import of music but also of recording equipment. As Tanzania liberalized its economy from the late 1980s, imported goods dropped in price, which enabled individuals to import studio equipment. A few independent studios established in the early 1990s were crucial to the development of rapped music. The Don Bosco studio opened in 1991 and was followed in the early 1990s by Mawingu, P Funk's, and MJ Productions studios.[30] These four studios are where many of the seminal early rap records in Tanzania were recorded. Groups such as Kwanza Unit, GWM, the Villains, Hardblasters, and solo rappers KBC and Mr II were recorded here. The producers who worked on these sessions, especially P. Funk, Master J, and Bonnie Luv (who recorded at Mawingu), are cited by many Tanzanians today as the founders of the Bongo Flava genre. As digital musical production and recording technologies have developed, establishing a studio requires less capital investment; consequently, there has been a proliferation of studios. While the relationships between studios and artists vary, in many cases rappers or singers pay a studio to produce the backing track and recording of the vocals. Studios charge between two hundred thousand and half a million Tanzanian shillings per recorded song.[31]

---

29   One of Tanzania's most well-known rappers, Joseph Mbilinyi, known as Mr 2 or Sugu, has been the member of parliament for Mbeya since 2010. In 2015 another well-known rapper, Joseph Haule (Professor Jay), stood for and won the Mikumi-Morogoro seat, which he subsequently lost in 2020.
30   Perullo, "Hooligans and Heroes," 250.
31   The equivalent of between $200 and $500.

Radio remains the preeminent medium through which music is consumed in Dar es Salaam[32] and a vital means for artists achieving commercial success.[33] Founded in 1994, Radio One was the first radio station in Dar es Salaam to dedicate itself exclusively to entertainment and was shortly followed by Clouds FM. As rapper Gwamaka Kaihura King GK said of radio in Dar es Salaam:

> The young had no place, had no radio, had no TV, before the youngsters had no voice. The only radio which was there was radio Tanzania and that radio Tanzania was centred on the age between 40 and 50, the young who are many who had voice had no place to express themselves. But when Radio 1 came in that was a voice, it acted like a voice of young so they had a chance to speak out.[34]

Clouds FM, Radio One, and East Africa Radio are currently the predominant radio stations operating in Dar es Salaam. Despite the limited geographical reach of its broadcasts, Clouds FM has come to occupy a preeminent role in the dissemination of rap music in Dar es Salaam. As the rapper D-Knob says of Clouds FM:

> Before anyone believed in Tanzanian music, Clouds was there, Clouds was promoting Tanzanian music before they had a radio or a media house. They were the ones with sound system going everywhere playing local music, nobody was doing that. When the music started to pay everyone jumped into music but Clouds was a monopoly in the music. . . Founder of Clouds FM or what do they call it MD, he was an MC, those guys used to sing and dance they know everything about street talent.

Airplay on the private FM stations is essential to an artist's success in the contemporary music economy of Dar es Salaam. It is primarily through radio play that audiences are able to hear rappers' songs. Songs are sent to

---

32 Askew, 211.
33 Perullo, "Hooligans and Heroes," 264.
34 Performers of older Tanzanian popular music genres and older audience members have an ambiguous relationship with contemporary Tanzanian popular music. The growing popularity of *muziki wa kizazi kipya* has diminished the radio play given to and demand for performances of older music styles, moving older styles to more marginal spaces in the music economy of the city. *Muziki wa kizazi* is also a source of pride for many older performers and audience members as its popularity regionally and across the continent has enabled Tanzanians to become stars.

the radio stations prior to being made commercially available for sale on tape cassettes or CDs and many songs played on the radio are never made commercially available for sale. Radio presenters and DJs act as cultural intermediaries, mediating between rappers, studios, and the airwaves. They play a crucial role in deciding which songs are broadcast, thereby given national visibility. There are widespread rumors of a Payola, or pay for play, system operating at radio and TV stations in Dar es Salaam,[35] with suggestions that payment of over 1 million shillings is required by a cartel of influential DJs. It is also widely thought by artists that the companies who reproduce and distribute music are influenced in their decisions about which albums should be accepted by prominent radio executives.

While they have been central to the development of rap music, the private institutions of studios and radio stations have also engendered anxiety about how, and by whom, control is exerted over music. The connections that exist between powerful individuals within the institutions of recording, broadcasting, and distributing music are thought to influence the careers of aspiring musicians. Liberalization of the media has moved, rather than removed, control over who is included or excluded in the circuits of producing and broadcasting music in Tanzania. Social capital is unevenly distributed between radio DJs, studio producers, and rappers, who, depending on their standing, financial capability, and connections, are able to exert varying degrees of control over their own recordings. The liberalization of the media has both constrained and enabled musical production, creating opportunities for some while excluding others.

Underground Rappers

Rappers who lack the social and financial capital to record and broadcast music have developed their own spaces for practicing and performing rap. While it may be tempting to view underground rapping as a "subaltern" practice, rappers are socially and economically heterogeneous. Those that I interviewed varied from lifelong residents of Dar es Salaam to recent migrants to the city. Some were in formal, salaried employment at supermarkets, gardeners, or barbers, while the majority were either underemployed (popularly referred to as *deiwaka*) or unemployed. They had attained varying degrees of

---

35   Perullo, "Hooligans and Heroes," 233; and Kibona Clark, "Struggle for Hip Hop Authenticity," 16.

educational qualification, from those that had only completed part of their primary schooling to some who had finished secondary school. Underground rapping is predominantly the activity of "young men." I use the term *youth* here not to denote a fixed age group but a category informed by its relations to markers of adulthood. The young men that engage in underground rap struggle to gain the social and financial capital necessary to achieve the standing that would mark their entry into adulthood, such as marriage or living independently. Underground rappers are in what Honwana and others have defined as a "state of waithood."[36]

In Western discourse on popular culture, the term *underground* is associated with the notion of subculture[37] popularized by the work of the Centre for Contemporary Cultural Studies in Birmingham. A subculture is at odds with hegemonic culture[38] and is frequently associated with social, political, and spatial marginality. More recently, scholarship has sought to challenge the notion of subculture by reconceptualizing music, style, and identity as lifestyles, styles, or neotribes.[39] The notion of belonging to a subculture, lifestyle or neotribe does not correspond closely to the practice of popular music in Tanzania. Being underground in the Tanzanian context does not imply a rejection of the norms and styles of mainstream Tanzanian musical practice. *Maandagraundi* is a somewhat loose category referring to those rappers who have yet to achieve widespread fame or renown. Reuster-Jahn defines "underground" rappers as "rappers who have not yet released an album"[40] while Englert defines *maandagraundi* as "those who have not yet experienced success on a larger scale."[41] It is their exclusion from participation in the institutions (studios, radio stations, and distribution of music) that determine a rapper's underground status in Dar es Salaam. A rapper's ability to become famous depends upon their access to studios to record in and media that will broadcast their music. These resources are mediated by social capital, personal networks, and financial resources. Underground rapping is not recorded or made available for broadcast and sale so consequently

---

36   Dhillon and Yousef, *Generation in Waiting*; and Honwana, "Waithood: Youth Transitions and Social Change."
37   Hebdige, *Subculture: The Meaning of Style*.
38   Fikentscher, *You Better Work*; Harrison, "Cheaper than a CD, Plus We Really Mean It"; and Szemere, "Subcultural Politics and Social Change."
39   Bennett, "Subcultures or Neo-Tribes?"
40   Reuster-Jahn, *Bongo Flava and the Electoral Campaign*, 56.
41   Englert, "Bongo Flava (Still) Hidden," 75.

does not become a commodity. While in many ways a socially heterogeneous group, underground rappers all lack significant financial resources or well-established networks within the music industry.

Uswahilini

As a practice characterized by exclusion from the mainstream music industry, alternative spaces outside of commercial control have been central to the development of underground rapping. Informally occupied neighbourhoods known as *uswahilini*, and the possibilities for sociality and performance enabled by these spaces, have been essential to the development of underground rapping. *Uswahilini* exist, to a certain extent, outside the purview of the offices of the state. Largely hidden from view by the taller buildings that line the boundaries of *uswahilini*, they are, in some senses, invisible. As we shall see, it is the very absence of state services that, in part, affords new possibilities for modes of creativity within these neighborhoods. Since its foundation by the Sultan Majid of Zanzibar, Dar es Salaam had been divided into different zones reflecting class and racial divisions. The 1924 township rules formalized these racial and social divisions, and the different areas of Dar es Salaam came to be referred to by the racial origin of their occupants, thus *uzungun*i (for the European-occupied areas), *uhindini* (for areas occupied by Asians) and *uswahilini* (for areas occupied by the Swahili people, i.e., Africans).[42] While these racial categorizations no longer hold true, the term *uswahilini* is still used in contemporary Dar es Salaam to describe unplanned settlements. During the 1930s, as Dar es Salaam's population expanded, the colonial administration was unable to provide sufficient housing, and informal settlements in Buguruni, Keko and Gerezani developed.[43] Following independence, the Tanzanian government expanded planned settlements in Sinza, Mikocheni, Kijitonyama, and Mbagala,[44] but the city's population and unplanned settlements in Kinondoni Hanna Nasif and Mwananyamala swelled. As Dar es Salaam's population has continued to increase so have the populations in *uswahilini* areas, and these currently cover 35 percent of the city and house the majority of Dar es Salaam's citizens. It is estimated that between 60 percent and 70 percent of the housing in Dar es Salaam is in

---

42   Smiley, *City of Three Colors*, 180.
43   Burton, "Townsmen in the Making," 335.
44   Nguluma, *Housing Themselves*, 23.

uswahilini areas.[45] *Uswahilini* areas are typically built upon marginal land, either on the edge of the city or on land that is undesirable to property developers. For example, the area of Kinondoni Hanna Nasifu located close to the Msimbazi Creek is subject to occasional flooding. *Uswahilini* are marginal to the provision of services by the state, the presence of state agencies, and its legal protections. For instance, in Kinondoni Hanna Nasif, 71 percent of homes have no electricity, and 77 percent were made of temporary building material.[46]

Maskani: Youth Spaces of Sociality and Recognition

Uswahilini is not a space simply defined by the absence of state services but also by its enabling of creative possibilities. These are places that embody what Moyer has characterized as the "carnivalesque."[47] Across *uswahilini* the predominant sites of male socializing are spaces referred to as *kijiweni* (little stone) or *maskani* (dwelling or abode). The occupation of *maskani* by mostly young men, and the enactment of rituals such as the shaking of members' hands on entering and leaving the *maskani*, resignify these as spaces distinct from *mitaa* (the street). While some *maskani* acquire their own markings of permanence, such as plastic chairs and wooden benches, others have a more temporary quality, moving between sites in the neighborhood, their only marking being the bodies of the men who occupy them. *Maskani* form part of a wide range of resignification practices in African urban space including gang use of public space to create *salle* (living rooms) in Kinshasa,[48] the practice of *fadas* (tea) ceremonies in Niger,[49] and *kijiweni* centered on barber shops in Arusha.[50] One means through which space is resignified by young men in Dar es Salaam is that of performance. *Maskani* act as informal performance spaces for those excluded from commercial leisure spaces such as bars and nightclubs. A repertoire of performance forms, including rapping, dancing, joking and storytelling, are part of the activities at *maskani*. It is at their *maskani* that underground rappers are able to perform, practice,

---

45 Ngware, "Welfare through Civic Participation," 301.
46 Brenan and Burton, "The Emerging Metropolis," 65.
47 Moyer, "Not Quiet the Comforts of Home," 171.
48 Geenen, "Sleep Occupies No Space."
49 Masquelier, *Teatime*.
50 Weiss, *Street Dreams and Hip-Hop Barbershops*.

Fig. 2.2. Mbaya Wao drinking coffee at his *maskani* in Kijitonyama.

and discuss rapping. Mbaya Wao met with his *maskani* every Monday, the only day he had free from work. At the *maskani* members recited their lyrics, with each rapper taking turns and receiving praise and critique from their peers. This *maskani* was a space of intense discussion of rapping, sharing of lyrics and ideas. Through the process of creating and discussing their lyrics, rappers engage with the world creatively and intellectually. Demonstrating command over the skills and knowledge that enable the creation of innovative rap texts is essential in gaining peer recognition. Underground rappers have created their own regimes of knowledge and skill through which they contest their marginalization from official orders of knowledge, such as secondary schooling or university education.

At other *maskani*, such as underground rapper Salim Muba's in Kiwalani, the members were a mixture of rappers and nonrappers. As Salim describes, the *maskani* offered an important space for both performance and critique:

Sometimes we can be five of us, or sometimes my friends they can be there, and I can be rapping and they can be listening to me; that's what we are doing. Even if they are not hip hop artists, they can listen to me. So that they can give me their comments.

Competitive performance formed an important element of the repertoire of Sizoh Wamichano's *maskani* in Mikocheni. Each week, members of Sizoh's *maskani* would go to the local beaches where they met other rappers to both share their lyrics and compete against each other. At these meetings, rappers took turns reciting their lyrics. Rappers who ran out of lyrics or who did not sufficiently impress the other members of the *maskani* fell silent. Sizoh revealed,

Maybe we are going to make an exercise in the beach, maybe Coco beach or Msasani beach. We meet with other artists and make competition. No beat it is live, one verse, one verse, one verse, for everyone. If you are not strong, maybe after three rounds you are keep quiet.

Maskani are spaces of both exclusion and inclusion, in which the ingenuity, creativity, and skill of a rapper are recognized by peers. Spaces in which certain performers are deemed not to have sufficient skill, or do not seem to take rapping seriously, are excluded or silenced. Through practice and performance, collaboration and competition, rappers command attention, claiming control over physical, sonic, and social space.

Kampu: the Politics of Presence

Events held in *uswahilini* called *kampu* (from the English *camp*) or *vigodoro*[51] (small mattress) seek to engage a wider audience than the *maskani*. *Kampu* necessitate both greater temporal and financial contributions from their organizers while addressing a far larger audience than *maskani*. Organized by a committee made up of young people from a particular *uswahilini* neighborhood, *kampu* are held in an open area, often a street or athletic field. Each member of the organizing committee contributes financially to the arrangements of the event, financing the building of a stage, renting of sound equipment, and supplying drinks for the performers. Contributions are from

---

51 This name *vigodoro* makes reference to the impossibility of sleeping while the event is ongoing.

five thousand Tanzanian shillings per person and up. Two members of the *madini* (diamond) *kampu* in Kindondoni, Hanna Nasifu Seif Nunduma (Ze Boy One Dar) and Bakhari Mahadhara (Gazar B), described that in addition to organizing two events, members of *madini kampu* had continued to contribute to a fund following the events. These additional funds could then be called on by its members in times of celebration or adversity, for example, to pay for a funeral or wedding. Bakhari explained that before the organization of the *kampu* had begun they had decided that "the aim of the *kampu* was helping each other." *Kampu* generate city-wide networks of young people excluded from the mainstream commercial networks of music production.

As *kampu* are set up, the narrow streets of *uswahilini* are blocked by a stage at one end and speakers at the other, thus marking out the performance and dance space for both audience members and performers. The use of equipment to amplify sound distinguishes *kampu* from *maskani* and enables these events to address a far larger audience. Performers from other *kampu* and *maskanis* are invited by handwritten letters or text messages from the organizing committee. Kampu start at nine or ten o'clock in the evening and end, electricity permitting, in the early morning. While they are held, *kampu* dominate *uswahilini*, both spatially and sonically. Loudspeakers transmit the sound of performance across *uswahilini*. No charge is made for attending *kampu*, and no remuneration is offered to performers. Each *kampu* begins with the organizing committee being invited to the stage, where they receive a piece of cake in recognition of their contribution to the event's organization. This is followed by a series of dance and musical performances accompanied by music from a DJ. The event is presided over by members of the organizing committee who maintain a roster of artists wishing to perform and announce each performer as they take the stage. The genres associated with *muziki wa kizazi kipya* of reggae, R&B, hip-hop and Bongo Flava dominate both singing and dance performances. Rapping is a key element of *kampu*.

Held mainly outside the control of state, entrepreneurial, and communal interests, *kampu* are transgressive and liminoid spaces. While permission for the event is sought from the local political leader of the *mtaa* urban area or police chief there is no police presence at *kampu*. Kampu dominate *uswahilini* through the occupation of a street with sound equipment, stages, and the congregation of large numbers of young people transcending the customary uses and control of space. Music booms from the speakers set up at either end of the street and can be heard for a substantial distance, making sleep difficult for those living in the vicinity. Marijuana and *gongo* (a form of locally distilled spirit) are openly consumed. Performers and members of the audience engage in more openly sexually explicit dialogue than is usually publicly acceptable. It is the young people organizing the event who are in charge of who is able to speak, thus inverting conventions over control of public speech. Young people become the sole voices heard. Older people attend *kampu*, perhaps in large part because the volume of the music makes sleep difficult for those who live near the event. Young people are the most active and engaged members of the audience, dominating the dance area in large boisterous groups, while the older members of the audience usually stand on the sidelines of the performance and dance area looking on. On occasion, the charged, transgressive, and competitive atmosphere of *kampu* leads to physical violence. At a *kampu* I attended in Chang'ombe in 2011, fighting broke out in the early hours of the morning. The level of violence slowly escalated from pushing and shoving between some young men to the throwing of large rocks, which eventually led to the canceling of the event. During this episode of violence, control of the event had ceded entirely from the committee that had organized the event to a section of the audience.

While underground rappers are excluded from the commercial avenues for performance in bars and nightclubs, *kampu* provide an alternative economy of celebrity and renown. Rappers and their reputations are mobile, traveling through the networks of *maskani* and *kampu* in Dar es Salaam's *uswahilini* neighborhoods. In some cases, this economy of reputation enables rappers to travel as far as Arusha and Dodoma, approximately 650 kilometres and 520 kilometres, respectively, from Dar es Salaam to perform. To a certain extent they mirror the mobility enabled by the commercial musical economy. *Kampu* and *maskani* form an alternative economy of music performance and of local fame and reputation. Performances by underground rappers at both *maskani* and *kampu* afford opportunities for recognition. These are spaces in which the linguistic ingenuity, skill as performer, and swagger[52] of rappers are tested and confirmed. Performing regularly at *kampu* grants underground rappers' status and allows them to become local celebrities. *Kampu* enable a local reputation-based economy, in which an individual rapper's importance can be recognized within a "community of sentiment," [53]). Through their creation of an alternative economy of musical performance, underground rappers remake the boundaries of the local musical economy. To return here

---

52 Swagger is defined by Bradley as "confidence and even brashness" (180) or by Mose as "*braggadocio, lyrical and performance skill*" (112).
53 Appadurai, *Modernity at Large*, 8.

to Honwana, and De Boeck's observation that African youth exist both at the margins and squarely at the center of contemporary life, *kampu* can be read as both at the margins and the heart of contemporary rap music practice in Dar es Salaam.

Underground rapping performances at *kampu* are both corporeal and imaginative practices. Performances are accompanied by a repertoire of gestures that draws on global and local models of embodied behavior. The act of rapping is physical and draws on a set of mimetic movements and gestures. Underground rapping is accompanied by bodily gestures, such as the use of hand movement or the nodding of the head to emphasise the rhythm. Public performances at *kampu*, or in well-attended *maskani*, frequently include the bending of knees and a hand grabbing the crotch of the trousers by rappers.[54] Movement helps the rapper to dominate space around him. Through the corporeal and verbal practices of performance, underground rappers embody the subjectivity of a rapper. Underground rappers frequently described the feeling of performance with the word *mzuka* translated by Reuster-Jahn and Kiebling as "'sudden apparition, pop-up, spirit, ghost'" (Reuster-Jahn and Kiebling 2006, 160) or more commonly by underground rappers as "to be possessed." *Mzuka* was a term used commonly in street Swahili as a greeting to denote well-being. We should, therefore, be wary of reading the use of this term by rappers literally. However, the image of possession is instructive. Possession is both a transformative and liminoid moment, a space between one world and the next, a moment of "expansion of consciousness, sense, and self" (Stroeken 2006, 787). The rapper Omari Muba described the experience of rapping as

> being a rapper OK I feel great, I feel that I am complete now. Before being a rapper, I was not complete, I was not a rapper. . . . You do just like a man, a soldier.

Rapping is, here, an experience that transforms the very subjectivity of the rapper. Moral discourses on the occult are common in contemporary Dar es Salaam (Sanders 2008), and we should be cautious in reading this expression too literally. Rather, being *mzuka* describes the centrality of the rapper and his being more than himself. Rapping is a technology of the self through which rappers seek to resignify space and to remake themselves.

---

54   This is a posture commonly associated with rappers during performances in Tanzania.

The Margins

The liberalization of the Tanzanian economy and media has enabled the growth in popularity of rap music, creating both new opportunities and new uncertainties. In particular, the liberalization of the media has enabled and excluded aspiring artists from opportunities for celebrity and success. Displays of wealth, eschewed by Tanzanians under Ujamaa, have become a feature of rap music videos, as has the exclusion of aspiring artists without either money or networks to participate in the musical economy. One lens through which we could seek to explore the practice of underground rapping would be to borrow from Weiss's work on young men in Arusha whose aspiration "to participate in the imagined horizon apprehended as a truly fantastical reality is thus fundamentally predicted on one's absence and exclusion from that world" (Weiss 2009, 89). For young men in Arusha this marginalization from the global order of signs is experienced as pain, which Weiss describes not merely as an absence but an active subject a mode of being-in-the-world. Young men in Dar es Salaam who engage in rapping experience their exclusion, I would argue, not principally from a global order of signs but from participation in the commercial Tanzanian music industry and from local opportunities for recognition. Underground rappers have created an alternative performance economy to contest their marginality. This alternative music economy is defined not principally by its distance from the global order of signs from which it appropriates but its relationship with local social relations of political-economic and cultural power. *Kampu* and *maskani* not only position rappers in relation to an order of already existing power relations but establish the significance of these relations. Through both their lyrics and performance, rappers are able to assert themselves as masculine subjects within a hierarchy of masculinities. They contest control over physical and social space. Underground rappers create, in the practice of underground rapping, their own registers of knowledge, skill, and creativity. This mode of being is characterized by the production of events, texts, and socialities.

An analytical frame that has been used to effectively engage with issues of marginality by, for example, MacGaffey and Bazenguissa-Ganga when exploring informal trade between Congo and Paris, is a form of resistance to exclusion. Drawing on the ideas of James Scott about resistance without protest and the "weapons of the weak," informal traders "have rejected the values of a system that has excluded and marginalised them" (MacGaffey and Bazenguissa-Ganga 2000, 157). While it may be tempting to view underground rapping as a form of resistance to exclusion from the commercial world of music production and dissemination, I think there is more at play here. Underground rappers in Dar es Salaam are not an oppositional culture as understood in cultural studies. They are frequently fans of commercial rappers and see them as role models. Underground rappers frame themselves as the equivalent of, rather than in opposition to, the successful commercial Tanzanian rappers. Their relationship with the commercial world of music production is filled with ambiguity. The networks and institutions from which underground rappers are excluded are also those which produce and broadcast the genre in which they see themselves as participating. Returning to Das and Poole's analysis of the margins of the state, their conception of the ways in which actors on the margins remake the conceptual boundaries of the state can be useful in thinking through the marginality or otherwise of underground rappers. Underground rappers, on the margins of the music industry in Tanzania, do not so much seek to reject that industry but to remake it. Excluded from the formal spaces for performance, recording and recognition these opportunities are recreated in *uswahilini* neighborhoods. Concepts of fame and celebrity are refashioned within the spaces of an alternative musical economy. Underground rappers, through performance, create their own networks of mobility for both themselves and their reputations. Observed from another angle, this alternative musical economy is an integral part of the wider Tanzanian music economy. While studios, radio DJs, and commercially successful rappers may not engage directly with underground rapping, it is part of a local economy of music and signs. While they may be excluded from the commercial spaces of music recording and performance, underground rappers still continue the practice of rapping in Dar es Salaam: as Das and Poole argue, that which is at the margin is a necessary entailment of the center. Despite clearly existing at the margins of the music industry in Tanzania, underground rappers use this position to contest their marginality and assert their presence sonically, socially, and creatively. In the process, they make and remake both themselves and an alternative music economy.

Bibliography

Abbink, J., and I. van Kessel. (2005). *Vanguard or Vandals: Youth, Politics and Conflict in Africa*. Leiden: Brill.
Agamben, G. (2005). *State of Exception*. Chicago: University of Chicago Press.
Appadurai, A. (1996). *Modernity at Large: Cultural Dimensions of Globalization*. Minneapolis: University of Minnesota Press.

Askew, K. M. (2009). "Musical Images and Imaginations: Tanzanian Music Videos." In K. Njogu and J. Middleton (eds.), *Africa*. Edinburgh: Edinburgh University Press.

Barber, K. (1997). "Preliminary Notes on Audiences in Africa," *Africa* 67, no. 3: 347–62.

Bennett, Andy. "Subcultures or Neo-Tribes? Rethinking the Relationship Between Youth, Style and Musical Tastes." *Sociology* 33, no. 3 (1999): 599–617.

Biaya, T. K. (2005). "Youth and Street Culture in Urban Africa: Addis Ababa, Dakar and Kinshasa." In A. Honwana and F. De Boeck (eds.), *Maker and Breakers: Children and Youth in Postcolonial Africa*. Oxford: James Currey.

Bradley, A. (2009). *Book of Rhymes: The Poetics of Hip Hop*. Philadelphia: Basic-Civitas.

Brennan, J. R., and A. Burton. (2007). "The Emerging Metropolis: A Short History of Dar es Salaam, circa 1862–2005." In J. Brennan, Y. Lawi, and A. Burton (eds.), *Dar es Salaam: Histories from an Emerging African Metropolis*. Oxford: Mkuki na Nyota.

Burton, A. (2003) "Townsmen in the Making: Social Engineering and Citizenship in Dar es Salaam, c.1945–1960." *International Journal of African Historical Studies* 36, no. 2: 331–65.

Butler, J. (1999). *Gender Trouble: Feminism and the Subversion of Identity*. New York: Routledge.

Charry, E. (2012). "A Capsule History of African Rap." In E. Charry (ed.), *Hip Hop Africa: New African Music in a Globalizing World*. Bloomington and Indianapolis: Indiana University Press.

Christiansen, C., M. Utas, and H. Vigh, eds. (2006). *Navigating Youth, Generating Adulthood: Social Becoming in an African Context*. Uppsala: Nordiska Afrikainstitutet.

Comaroff, J., and J. Comaroff (2000). *Millennial Capitalism: First Thoughts on a Second Coming*. Public Culture 12, no. 2: 291–343.

Das, V., and D. Poole. (2004). "State and Its Margins: Comparative Ethnographies," in V. Das and D. Poole (eds.), *Anthropology in the Margins of the State*. Oxford: James Currey.

De Certeau, M. (1988). *The Practice of Everyday Life*. Berkeley: University of California Press.

Dhillon, N., P. Dyer, and T. Yousef. (2009). "Generation in Waiting: An Overview of School to Work and Family Formation Transitions." In N. Dhillon and T. Yousef (eds.), *Generation in Waiting: The Unfulfilled Promise of Young People in the Middle East*. Washington, DC: Brookings Institution.

Di Nunzio, M. (2012) "We Are Good at Surviving": Street Hustling in Addis Ababa's Inner City, Urban Forum 23, no. 4:433–47.

Diouf, M. (2003). "Engaging Postcolonial Cultures: African Youth and Public Space." *African Studies Review* 46, no. 2: 1–12.

Englert, B. (2003). "Bongo Flava (Still) Hidden: 'Underground' Rap Music from Morogoro, Tanzania." *Wiener Zeitschrift fur Kritische Africastudien* 5: 73–93.

Englert, B. (2008) *Ambiguous Relationships: Youth, Popular Music and Politics in Contemporary Tanzania*. Wiener Zeitschrift für kritische Afrikastudien 14: 71–96.

Fikentscher, K. (2000). *'You Better Work!': Underground Dance Music in New York City*. Middletown, CT: Wesleyan University Press.

Geenen, K. (2009). "'Sleep Occupies No Space': The Use of Public Space by Street Gangs in Kinshasa." *Africa* 79(3): 347–68.

Graebner, W. (1997) "Whose Music?: The Songs of Remmy Ongala and the Orchestra Super Matimila." In K. Barberv(ed.), *Reading in African Popular Culture*. Oxford: International African Institute / James Currey.

Graeber, D. (2011) "Consumption." *Current Anthropology* 52(4): 489–511.

Haas, P. J., and T. Gesthuizen (2000). "Ndani ya Bongo: Kiswahili Rap Keeping it Real." In F. Gunderson and G. Barz, G. (eds.), Mashindano! *Competitive Music Performance in East Africa*. Dar es Salaam: Mkuki na Nyota.

Harrison, A. K. (2006). "'Cheaper than a CD, Plus We Really Mean It": Bay Area Underground Hip Hop Tapes as Subcultural Artefacts." *Popular Music* 25(2): 283–301.

Hebdige, D. (1979). *Subculture: The Meaning of Style*. London: Methuen.

Heinonen, P. (2013). *Youth Gangs and Street Children: Culture, Nurture and Masculinity in Ethiopia*, Oxford: Berghahn.

Honwana, A., and F. de Boeck. (2005). "Introduction: Children and Youth in Africa: Agency, Identity and Place." In A. Honwana and F. De Boeck (eds.), *Makers and Breakers: Children and Youth in Postcolonial Africa*. Oxford: James Currey.

Honwana, Alcinda. "Waithood: Youth Transitions and Social Change." In *Development and Equity*, 28–40. Leiden, The Netherlands: Brill, 2014.

Ivaska, A. (2011). *Cultured States: Youth, Gender, and Modern Style in 1960s Dar es Salaam*. Durham, NC: Duke University Press.

Jua, N. (2003). "Differential Responses to Disappearing Transitional Pathways: Redefining Possibility among Cameroonian Youths." *African Studies Review* 46(2): 13–36.

Kibona, Clark, M. (2013). "The Struggle for Hip Hop Authenticity and Against Commercialization in Tanzania." *Journal of Pan African Studies* 6(3): 5–21.

Lemelle, S. J. (2006). "Ni Wapi Tunakwenda': Hip Hop Culture and the Children of Arusha." In D. Basu and S. Lemelle (eds.), *The Vinyl Ain't Final: Hip Hop and the Globalization of Black Popular Culture*. London: Pluto.

MacGaffey, J., and R. Bazenguissa-Ganga (2000). *Congo-Paris: Transnational Traders on the Margins of the Law*. Oxford: James Currey.

Mains, D. (2007) "Neoliberal Times: Progress, Boredom, and Shame among Young Men in Urban Ethiopia." *American Ethnologist* 34(4): 659–73.

Masquelier, A. (2013). "Teatime: Boredom and the Temporalities of Young Men in Niger." *Africa* 83(3): 470–91.
Mose, C. (2013). "'Swag' and 'cred': Representing Hip-Hop in the African City." *Journal of Pan African Studies* 6(3): 5–21.
Moyer, E. (2006). "Not Quiet the Comforts of Home: Searching for Locality among Street Youth in Dar es Salaam." In P. Konings and D. Foeken (eds.), *Crisis and Creativity: Exploring the Wealth of the African Neighbourhood*. Leiden, The Netherlands: Brill.
Nguluma, H. M. (2003). "Housing Themselves: Transformations, Modernisation and Spatial Qualities in Informal Settlements in Dar es Salaam, Tanzania." PhD diss., Royal Institute of Technology, Stockholm.
Ngware, S. (2006). "Welfare through Civic Participation: Tabata Development Fund, Dar es Salaam." In D. F. Bryceson and D. Potts (eds.), *African Urban Economies: Viability, Vitality, or Vitiation?* London: Palgrave Macmillan.
Nyerere, J. K. (1966). *Freedom and Unity: Uhuru na Umoja*. Dar es Salaam: Oxford University Press.
Ogola, G. (2011). "The Political Economy of the Media in Kenya: From Kenyatta's Nation Building Press to Kibaki's Local-Language FM Radio." *Africa Today* 57, no. 3: 77–95.
Perullo, A. (2005) "Hooligans and Heroes: Youth Identity and Hip-Hop in Dar es Salaam, Tanzania." *Africa Today* 51, no. 4: 75–101.
———. (2007). "'Here's a Little Something Local': An Early History of Hip Hop in Dar es Salaam 1984–1997." In J. Brennan, Y. Lawi, and A. Burton (Eds.), *Dar es Salaam Histories from an Emerging African Metropolis*. Oxford: Mkuki na Nyota.
———. (2011). *Live from Dar es Salaam: Popular Music and Tanzania's Music Economy*. Bloomington: Indiana University Press.
Reuster-Jahn, U. (2008). "*Bongo Flava and the Electoral Campaign 2005 in Tanzania.*" *Wiener Zeitschrift für kritische Afrikastudien* 14: 41–69.
Reuster-Jahn, U., and R. Kiebling (2006). *Lugha Ya Mitaani In Tanzania: The Poetics and Sociology of Young Urban Style of Speaking*. Swahili Forum 13:1–196.
Reuster-Jahn, U., and G. Hacke (2011). "The Bongo Flava Industry in Tanzania and Artists' Strategies for Success Arbeitspapiere." Working Papers Nr. 127. Institut für Ethnologie und Afrikastudien: Johannes Gutenberg-Universität.
Sanders, T. (2008). "Buses in Bongoland: Seductive Analytics and the Occult." *Anthropological Theory* 8, no. 2: 107–32.
Smiley, S. L. (2009). *The City of Three Colors: Segregation in Colonial Dar es Salaam, 1891–1961*. Historical Geography, 37: 178–96.
Stroeken, K. (2006). "'Stalking the Stalker': A Chwezi Initiation into Spirit Possession and Experiential Structure." *Journal of the Royal Anthropological Institute* 12, no. 4: 785–802.

Suriano, M. (2007). "'Mimi Ni Msani, Kioo Cha Jamii': Urban Youth Culture in Tanzania as Seen through Bongo Fleva and Hip Hop." *Swahili Forum* 14: 207–23.

Szemere, A. (1996). "Subcultural Politics and Social Change: Alternative Music in Post- Communist Hungary." *Popular Music and Society* 20: 19–41.

Ugor, P. (2013). "Survival Strategies and Citizenship Claims: Youth and the Underground Oil Economy in Post-Amnesty Niger Delta." *Africa* 83(2): 270–92.

Weiss, B. (2005). "The Barber in Pain: Consciousness, Affliction and Alterity in Urban East Africa." In A. Honwana and F. De Boeck (eds.), *Maker and Breakers: Children and Youth in Postcolonial Africa*. Oxford: James Currey.

———. (2009). *Street Dreams and Hip-Hop Barbershops: Global Fantasy in Urban Tanzania*. Bloomington: Indiana University Press.

Chapter Three

Entertainers and Breadwinners

Music in the Lives of Street Children in Abidjan, Côte d'Ivoire

Ty-Juana Taylor

On a continent where nearly 40 percent of the population is under the age of fifteen, scholars, policymakers, politicians, and adults cannot afford to continue to ignore African youth—a substantial and ever-growing segment of the African population and, indeed, the global youth population, which currently stands at 1.2 billion people between the ages of fifteen and twenty-four.[1] As this bulging African youth population becomes more educated and media savvy, they are poised to become the next generation of leaders throughout Africa and the world. Understanding how populations of African youth see, observe, and engage with the world around them, especially through the production of culture, might offer scholars important insights not only into this generation's lives and experiences but also about the broader processes of social and cultural change taking place in Africa.

Many scholars engaging with youth in Africa have found the arts to be useful in understanding the unique experiences of youth cultures across the continent. Since the turn of the twenty-first century, scholars have found African youth utilizing the arts to articulate their conflicted postcolonial

---

1   United Nations Department of Economic and Social Affairs Population Division.

positionality and making sense of their global identity. Consistently, scholars of youth culture are seeing youth utilize music as a medium to contest social norms and/or express their individual and cultural identity in a globalized world. Often the message portrayed is politically driven, but in other cases it is simply a tool to amplify the voices, desires, and experiences of a generation.

But the voices, thoughts, and experiences of a specific population of youth have consistently been silenced or omitted from much literature on contemporary African youth culture—namely street children. In the context of Africa, where there are tens of millions of street children roaming its city streets, it is crucial that we gain a sense of how this population sees and engages with the world. Being an important segment of African youth culture that is little known, the broader topic of street children has gained uncharted momentum in academia.[2] However, limited scholarship has investigated how this population makes and utilizes the arts in everyday life, specifically popular music. Since street children draw upon the music and culture surrounding them, it is essential to consider the experiences of street children who often dwell in the same urban spaces as their colleagues with shelter and undergo similar struggles surrounding postcolonial positionality and individual identity.

Brief Discussion of Methodology

In a string of serendipitous acts while in the field (2010–14), I was introduced to a growing and significant population of Ivoirian youth: street children. I found that music was a huge part of daily lives of Abidjan street children, of whom there are estimated to be around a hundred thousand. Music functioned as a tool to aid them in forging an autonomous community of their own and creating their own space and subculture that draws from Abidjanese youth culture at large. The stories and experiences of these street youth informed the construction of this research work, as I spent a great deal of time observing the popular music culture in Abidjan through the city's *maquis* and party districts (*mille maquis*; *alloco drome*; and *la rue princess*) and observing how both youth who dwell in homes and those who reside on the streets of Abidjan use those spaces. Their narratives were woven

---

2   Heinonen, *Youth Gangs and Street Children*; Amantana, *A Sociological Study of Street Children in Ghana*.

around the streets of Abidjan, and the role and function of music and performance in the city.

Because my objective was to create an ethnography on the music culture of street children in Abidjan, the primary methods used in collecting data included interviews (semistructured individual interviews in groups and individual interviews), observation, audio and video recordings, and photography. Due to my population being highly mobile, and most being semiliterate, I opted for a purely qualitative study that focused on the words, thoughts, and actions of children in order to contribute to the limited ethnographic data available on African street children. My objective was to use the words of street children in Abidjan to comment on their culture, daily activities, ambitions, dreams, and philosophies. Over the span of five years, interviewing and collecting data,[3] from dozens of street children either living

---

3   To gain an understanding of the national imagination of street children in Côte d'Ivoire, I conducted archival research on the subject by studying material found at the Centre de Recherche et d'Action pour la Paix (Center of research and action for peace, CERAP). This research institute and school house a significant body of literature, including theses and dissertations on child labor, child abuse, street children, deviant/delinquent behavior, education, and health in Côte d'Ivoire and other parts of the world. While providing an arsenal of data, the works are written from the perspective of those with backgrounds in social work (the field that I have now transitioned into), health, or human rights law. And the information was generally collected by researchers interning at one of the major centers for street children in Abidjan or other parts of Côte d'Ivoire—Bureau International Catholique de l'Enfance (International Catholic office for children, BICE); Foyer Akwaba; Don Bosco; Marie Dominque; SOS Children's Village—not from interacting with children on the streets. However, the material from CERAP, coupled with my interviews with social workers, center employees, and interns, allowed me to gain substantial information about my research population from a national perspective.

Television also served as a research tool for me. My informants commonly shared how they spent many hours per day intensely watching music videos by peering over the fences of maquis (open-air restaurants) and discotheques (clubs), memorizing the contemporary dance moves that they will later practice and imitate to perfection with their peers in parking lots, grassy fields, and whatever other spaces or a paying audience allows. I also used the TV and its content as a source. By keeping abreast of audio recordings, music videos, TV programs, and material included in newspapers and magazines that focused on music and popular culture figures (primarily musicians) and current events in Abidjan, I became informed about the events and people that the children referenced in my interviews and the events that were impacting their lives and the arts.

in interim housing or those living on the streets, ages six to eighteen, several points were made evident while working with Abidjanese youth: 1) Urban Ivorian youth culture is heavily influenced by Ivorian popular music; and 2) musical performance (musicking)[4] is a common form of collateral by urban Ivorian youth, specifically homeless youth, to secure socioeconomic capital. This work thus discusses the complex nature of youth culture in Abidjan, especially its intersection with music, culture, identity, performance, and labor in the city.

The Intersection between Youth Culture and Popular Music

While evaluating street youth in Abidjan, Côte d'Ivoire, it became evident to me that not only were street youth immersed in the popular music scene, but the nation's prevailing urban youth culture is heavily influenced by that very same music scene, which was dominated by a single genre at the time: *coupé décalé*. Nearly all maquis continually played music videos and were full of youth on a nightly basis. Advertising trucks roamed the city amplifying Afropop and top-ten hits, and free concerts were frequently hosted by companies wanting to promote their product. Similarly, dancing competitions were encouraged in primary schools, church programs, and formalized components of children's television shows. In fact, as Stolozoff and Bradley have noted, the sound system culture dominates the urban scene in Abidjan.[5] Music is amplified and heard nearly everywhere—whether on the streets of Abidjan, dining, shopping, or watching television. In fact, it is rare to not encounter music in some shape or form in Abidjan's urban scene. With this as the context for youth culture in Abidjan, it is important to investigate

---

4   Musicking as a concept has a long history in Côte d'Ivoire and in the greater African context in general. Although ethnomusicologist Christopher Small coined the term "musicking" in the 1990s, it was J. H. Nketia who described the extramusical experience (i.e., musicking) in African music several decades prior, describing the "emotion stimulated by music. [Acknowledging that] dance can also be used as a social and artistic medium of communication, conveying thoughts or matters of personal or social importance through the choice of movement, postures, and facial expressions." More simply, Nketia speaks of the many extra components of musical performance (dancing, singing, observation, communication, affect, etc.) and how these elements all affect the participants and the musical experience, affecting more than auditory and visual stimuli.

5   Stolzoff, *Wake the Town and Tell the People*; and Bradley, *This is Reggae Music*.

how youth in the city engage with the pervasive presence of music (performing, listening, being in the space, and other extra-musical components), and musicking's impact on their culture and identity.

In the context of Abidjan, I evaluate how music is prevalent in Abidjanese youth culture, paying particular attention to the extra-musical components and their significance in Abidjan's everyday culture. I examine how Abidjanese youth *musick*, using music and its extramusical components to create and communicate their sense of identity, or their "ability to articulate differences between self and other."[6] This identity can be self-constructed or ascribed by others and is best defined as realizing the components that differentiate one person from another (e.g., race, religion, nationality, ethnicity, class, and age) along with the components that people have in common. This realization or ascription of identity is often played out in the streets of Abidjan. This link between music and identity formation is not only significant to youth in the country but also to the history of the nation at large, specifically Abidjan, as it served as the hub for African popular music for several decades. This long historical connection between musical expression and youth identity formation is best seen in the history of the Ivoirian popular music genre *coupé décalé*.

Coupé Décalé: A Musical Genre

Coupé décalé, the music-and-dance genre most popular among youth when in the field, was created by immigrants from Côte d'Ivoire in cosmopolitan Paris, France, in 2002 and gained its popularity in Côte d'Ivoire. The inventors of the genre are believed to be Douk Saga (Stephane Hamidou Doukouré), Molare, Solo Beton, Lino Versace, and Bobo Sango, all of whom were middle-class immigrants from Côte d'Ivoire who amassed substantial wealth while living in Paris. Coupé décalé, literally meaning, in French, "to cut and shift," has an alternate meaning among the genre's young urban Nouchi-speaking Ivoirian audience.[7] Within this linguistic context, coupé décalé connotes "cheating someone and running away," referring to the fraudulent, freewheeling nature by which its inventors acquired funds and wealth. And, consequently, the lyrical content focuses

---

6   Stokes, *Ethnicity, Identity and Music*, 8.
7   See Nouchi.com, accessed February 19, 2016, http://www.nouchi.com. Nouchi is an argot composed of Ivoirian French and several different indigenous languages.

on flaunting wealth, materialism, sexual desires, and/or introduces a new dance—a major component of the genre.

Coupé décalé was informed by a subculture marked by extravagance. The founding figures (jetsetters) of coupé décalé were imitators of the popularly known culture of sharp-dressed gentlemen who call themselves *les sapeurs*. Having origins among the Congolese in Brazzaville, les sapeurs forged a society, SAPE (Societe des Ambianceurs et des Personnes Elegantes [Society of tastemakers and elegant people]), which branches out to the Congolese and African diasporas. Les sapeurs are men from the working and middle classes who dress extravagantly in fine designer suits. The culture has significant roots in colonialism, as it was initially an attempt to imitate the colonizers. However, nearly half a century after independence, such trends continue: for some this style signifies Western acculturation, while other practitioners view the style as a sophisticated art where men cleverly use themselves as the canvas and their clothing as the paint. Aside from aesthetics, les sapeurs also have a political inclination. They are known for being pacifists, which is significant given the hostile conditions of much of Central Africa, where this culture started.

Douk Saga, though Ivoirian, embraced the sapeurs culture, adorning himself in extravagant clothing from France and Italy. To accompany his extraordinary attire, he lived a glamorous life, dancing, drinking, partying, and flaunting his wealth (the source of which was not ever publicly known) around those in the club. Douk Saga acquired a following with his high-society lifestyle, fancy clothing, grandiose behavior, and dancing at the nightclubs. With an audience before him, Douk Saga began to popularize a dance move that resembled the Congolese dance *ndombolo*—laying the foundations for the *coupé décalé* dance.

Initially only gaining popularity as a symbol of wealth and success, it was only after financing and management by David Monsoh (producer at OBOUO Music) that Douk Saga became a pop star. Monsoh financed his video and produced his first release, "Sagacité." Artists such as Douk Saga, Boro Sandji, Molare, Versace, and Solo Beton were a part of the first generation (beginning of the twenty-first century) or the jet setters of *coupé décalé*. The disc jockeys who were providing the music for these men's dances, and singing their praises as MCs in the clubs, decided to join the scene and contribute to the making of *coupé décalé*. The introduction of DJs, such as DJ Jacob, DJ Caloudje, and DJ Jonathan from 2004 to 2008 introduced the second generation of *coupé décalé*. Later, in the third generation—the most contemporary style of *coupé décalé* (beginning in 2008)—emphasis was placed primarily on dance. With artists such as DJ Arafat, Serge Beynaud, and Kiva Kedjevara breakdancing, crumping, street dancing, and acrobatics became crucial generic components.

Coupé décalé is sonically similar to its musical predecessor *zouglou*, both drawing significantly from the Congolese music genre *soukous*. However, while coupé décalé was birthed in Paris, zouglou was bred in the streets of Abidjan in the late 1980s and early 1990s by a generation of youth and young adults who wanted a platform to protest the unjust conditions faced by youth and students. Due to the use of the same distinctive popular dance rhythm, seen in example 3.1, the genres have a noticeably similar musical foundation. However, it is primarily coupé décalé's influx of layered electronic beats and lack of vocal harmonies that differentiates it musically from zouglou. Also, unlike zouglou, which has indigenous roots and initially utilized traditional membranophones (djembe) and idiophones (shakers, bottles), coupé décalé was bred in the electronic world-music scene, dependent upon the mixing, variation, and layering of synthesized sounds and beats by DJs.

The genre was first popularized with the 2004 release of the song "Sagacité" (also spelled *Saga Cité*, meaning "lively minded"), by genre founder Douk Saga. The song was originally performed in the Club Atlantis in Paris, France, in 2002 and thereafter spread to Abidjan. The genre was originally more focused on fashion, appearances, and its personification, more so than music. It is only through time that the style began to solidify as a genre and the music gained a specific form. The genre's initial single, "Sagacité" is "through-composed," meaning that it lacks any specific form (see table below). However, the song opens with the familiar dance rhythm heard in popular music genres throughout many other pop-music styles in West and Central Africa (see example 3.1):

Introductory lyrics to "Sagacité":[8]

Original Lyrics	**English Translation**
Hé hé	Hey Hey
Stéphane Doukouré	Stephane Dokouré
Douk Saga de la Sagacité	Douk Saga from "Sagacité" [Wisdom]
Le créateur du coupé décalé	The creator of coupé décalé
L'ennemie de l'homme c'est l'homme !	The enemy of man is man!

---

8   "Douk Saga Word Fest Douk Saga."

Les gens n'aiment pas les gens	Men don't like men
Affaire de prodada	Case of showing off
Seul le travail paie	Only work pays
Silence ici on travaille	Silence here, we're working
Le feu sans le feu	Fire without fires
Celui qui n'a pas peur n'a pas le courage	Whoever doesn't have fear doesn't have courage
David gai Fatigua de Milano	David gai Fatigua de Milano
Linon Versase	Linon Versase
Chacoulé	Chacoulé
Donc OFF! Le champion	So Off! The champion
Hé Hé	He He
Y'a une danse qui à été crée là: décalé	There's a dance that was created: décalé
coupé	coupé
Celui qui la crée s'appelle: sagacité	There was a creator whose name is: sagacité
Y'a une danse qui à crée la ho ho: décalé	There's dance that was created: décalé
coupé	coupé
Celui qui la crée s'appelle: sagacité	There was a creator whose name is: sagacité

The lyrics of "Sagacité" set the precedent for the genre, with its loose structure appearing to be an exchange of lyrical ideas from one singer to another. Therefore, although the music is quite repetitive, seemingly minimalistic in its construction, consisting of looped motifs, the lyrics seem extemporaneous. Perhaps this is why many scholars and nonfans of coupé décalé have critiqued the genre for being a musical form composed by nonmusicians. The vocal style is a mixture of speaking and singing that is slightly more melodic than rap. The music, however, is constructed with layering. These repetitive rhythmic motifs include the popular dance rhythm (see example 3.1), but after a few bars, a guitar motif enters, and more motifs played on digital instruments are added to the mix, each creating a multitude of layers to the polyrhythmic song. As obvious from the lyrical content, there is no narrative. In reality, it is the extra-musical elements (i.e., philosophy, ambiance, dance, and language) that became crucial elements of the genre's structure and its immediate popularity:

Example 3.1. Coupé décalé popular dance rhythm.

Philosophy

After the genre was transported to Côte d'Ivoire, coupé décalé (music and dance) became a way for Ivorians to escape the daunting realities at home, including war, lack of jobs, national instability, and economic decline. This was a drastic turn in Cote d'Ivoire's narrative. Historically, this nation, with over sixty ethnic groups residing within its borders, was seen as a beacon of peace and prosperity post-1960s, unlike many of its surrounding neighbors undergoing political and ethnic turmoil following independence.[9] President Felix Houphouët-Boigny's thirty-year presidency (1960–93) was thought to be a key component in the nation's stability, and the drastic decrease in cocoa prices (the nation's primary export) was thought to be the culprit for the country's economic decline.

In response to a collapsing economy and ever fewer job opportunities, the youth of Côte d'Ivoire, primarily students at the University of Cocody-Abidjan, began to vocalize their discontent about their nation's unacceptable economic, political, and educational conditions. Through revolts, music, dance, and student-led organizations, young Ivorians during the early 1990s introduced a major ideological change in the country that offered commentary on colonial allegiance and Ivorian identity. Prior to this period, the nation's identity was aligned with that of the French. But, after the drastic decline of cocoa prices in the 1980s due to a global recession, revolts, protests, and campaigns against the one-party system of Houphouët-Boigny, and the sudden devaluation of the country's CFA (Communauté Financière African [African financial community]) currency by half in 1994 (due to the International Monetary Fund), the sentiment toward the standing president and the metropole (France) changed. The presupposed inheritance of the so-called Ivorian miracle—an Ivorian notion of education, prosperity, and wealth that previous Ivorian generations had experienced—was deconstructed.[10] And, as a result, the disenchanted youth and young adults from this period challenged the country to move in a new direction.

---

9   Zolberg, *One-Party Government in the Ivory Coast*.
10 Blé, "Zouglou et Réalités Sociales des Jeunes en Côte d'Ivoire," 169.

In 1993, the nation's first and only president, Houphouët-Boigny, died. And his successor, Henrie Konan Bédié, took office (though unrightfully, since the person next in line for the presidency was the prime minister, Alassane Outtara). In a nationally reductive move, Bédié introduced a notion of national identity called Ivoirité. This move resulted in ethnic divisions within a nation that had, since French rule, welcomed immigrants from northern countries (Burkina Faso, Benin, and Mali) for agricultural labor. This biased legislation excluded many multigenerational immigrants from political positions, creating xenophobia along with ethnic and regional contention throughout the nation. In response to this assault on national unity, General Robert Guei, from Man in western Côte d'Ivoire, led a military coup in 1999 that sparked over a decade of sociopolitical unrest and eventually led to the physical division of the nation. Ivoirité's concept of nationalism intentionally excluded specific ethnic groups, and nearly half of the country's population (immigrants and those of Burkinabe, Malian, or non-Ivorian heritage) from the folds of Ivorian citizenship.[11]

At this point, ethnic, religious, and political divisions were brewing at home, and many were fleeing to France, where coupé décalé was formed. While zouglou was a tool to express the sentiment of dissatisfaction and protest by youth against injustice and mistreatment, coupé décalé instead aggrandizes a culture of materialism and wealth for the poor—"realizing" the Ivoirian miracle that the previous generation experienced was no longer within reach. And Douk Saga, the genre's founder, embodied the rags-to-riches persona, or a path to achieve the wealth and prestige one desired. Although some coupé décalé artists have used the genre as a platform to express their discontent with the government and comment on the general political and economic condition of the nation, the genre is primarily known as party and dance music. It encourages its audience to embrace the message of acquiring wealth and goods for nonutilitarian reasons, an essential tool for escapism during a period of great strife for many in Côte d'Ivoire during this period and a means by which Ivorian youth could situate themselves within a global world.

It is within this context that we can better understand the youth culture of Abidjan, both those who are homeless and those who are housed. Similar to other youth, those experiencing homelessness mimicked the actions and aspects of coupé décalé culture as another method to create a sense of self-esteem among their ranks—just as the other youth of Abidjan. One particular

---

11   McGovern, *Making War in Côte d'Ivoire*.

artist, DJ Arafat (who tragically and unexpectedly passed away on August 11, 2019), aided in setting new trends in coupe décalé and drawing street children to maquis to perform. Unlike previous artists, or the original jet setters, DJ Arafat did not follow the traditional aesthetics of the genre. Arafat instead mimicked many visual and aural aesthetic elements of American hip-hop culture with his wearing of caps, sunglasses, sagging pants, exposed boxers, tattoos, and unkempt facial hair, rapidly spoken lyrics (similar to the "mystical" genre), and the use of breakdancing. Later, following the growth and popularity of Afropop, his style evolved, eventually paying more homage to indigenous culture with his attire, song titles, and video themes, while still maintaining his own unique performance style. While several substyles within the genre exist, the earlier styles coexist alongside Arafat's version of the genre. Among the street children that I encountered and interviewed, Arafat was the most admired due to this shared narrative, conveyed in the lyrics of his song "Petit Nouchi," given below.[12] This song offers a narrative that many street children identified with.

Petit Nouchi

French Version

Commandant Zabra

Arafat Ayee ayee ehe enheuuu showtime

Tout le monde lève les mains si vous aimez le worobo

Avant j'étais un petit nouchi dans la rue oh oh (4x)

J'ai grandi dans un quartier que un appelle blockauss precisement a cocody a Abidjan

English Version

Arafat ayee ayee ehe enheuuuuu showtime

everybody hands up if you love the Yorobor

Before, I was a little man down in the street oh oh (4x)

I grew up in a neighborhood called Blockauss precisely at Cocody in Abidjan

---

12 Lyrics provided courtesy of Obouo Music.

C'est ainsi qu mon pere ma mis dehors et je me suis suis retrouvé dans la rue	Thus my father put me out and I found myself in the street
Arrivée dans la rue j'ai continue directement à youpougon cheze ma grande mere	Arriving in the street I continued directly to Yopougon to my grandmother.
C'est a dire la maman a ma maman. Ma grande mere meme qui a tout fait pour moi et	That is to say the mom of my mom. My grandmother who had faith in me is the reason that I became DJ eh
Qui a fait que je suis devenu DJ ehhh	
Avant j'étais un petit nouchi dans la rue oh ohh (4x)	Before, I was a little man down in the street oh oh (4x)
C'est moi seul qui les arrange	All the songs you hear are mine alone

"Petit Nouchi" was released in 2012 by DJ Arafat on his album entitled *Commandant Zabra*. The song is in both French and the Ivorian slang, Nouchi,[13] and offers a short narrative of the "little nouchi," a resilient or strong youth who was brought up in urban Ivorian street culture, where the argot Nouchi is prevalent. As evident in the lyrics, Arafat offers a personal narrative similar to that of many "street children," a life full of labor in the informal sector (i.e., thievery), mobility (physical migration around the city and social mobility), and resilience to the difficulties of life. The song states that growing up in Blockhauss (a region of Cocody), he settled into thievery at a young age. This lifestyle eventually led to his father kicking him out of the house.[14] With nowhere to go, he decided to live with his grandmother in Youpougon, a commune of Abidjan that formerly had a popular dance and party area known as Rue Princess). While there, he began his career as a DJ, working in maquis and

---

13   Nouchi.com, http://www.nouchi.com.
14   Since there was no mention of his mother, he may have been raised in a single-parent household.

clubs, eventually developing into the famous and successful musician known today throughout the country and much of the Francophone African diaspora.

While some of these elements of his misspent youth may be true, DJ Aarafat actually got his start as a DJ at Rue Princess in Youpougon at the rise of the coupé décalé scene in Abidjan in the early 2000s. His mother is the well-known risqué music artist Tina Glamour and his father, Pierre Houon, is an amateur musician. However, it is rumored that Arafat lived a tumultuous life plagued with abandonment and substance-abuse issues, so he might have lived in a single-family household and could have been raised by his grandmother.[15] Despite his past, Arafat has risen to fame, headlining for the nationally promoted six-stop tour, Caravane Pour La Paix et Reconciliation, which was sponsored by the current Ivorian administration in July 2010. Arafat is not only popular throughout the Ivorian diaspora but also in other Francophone African regions of the world. Whether the narrative of "Petit Nouchi" offers an autobiography of Arafat's life or not, the lyrics resonate with the stories of many street children, especially those in Abidjan. A life marked by parental abandonment, poverty, drugs, and final redemption in the form of celebrity status and wealth is a narrative of hope and possibility that resonates with the young urban poor. Because Arafat is a prolific and successful figure in contemporary Ivorian popular culture, many street children I interviewed look to Arafat and his honest method to wealth and success as the roadmap for their potential future.

> This pursuit of wealth and material goods within the context of Ivoirian youth culture is best described by anthropologist Sasha Newell as bluff or mimicry. By projecting the allusion of wealth (in this case, the images profiled in coupé décalé videos) youth in Abidjan create a source of social wealth for themselves. Newell notes that "it [is through] the ability to imitate with precision that many Ivorians locate their sense of prestige," noting that there is the façade of success and prestige being played out in the streets of Abidjan on a daily basis.[16]

This is seen in the founder of coupé décalé, Douk Saga, who imitated the fashion and style of les sapeurs, and the youth of Abidjan similarly mimicked the style, dance, and actions of Saga and other coupé décalé artists. While "mimicry" suggests that the youth of Côte d'Ivoire lack creativity, I would like to situate Newell's statement in the context of African music. In African music, an attentive level of repetition or mimicry is highly regarded and essential for mastery. John Miller Chernoff explains:

---

15   See http://www.mtv.com/artists/dj-arafat/biography/.
16   Newell, *The Modernity Bluff*, 1.

In African music, the chorus or response is a rhythmic phrase which recurs regularly. The repetition of a style is important as a way of maintaining the tension of an ensemble's beat, and the duration of the style is important in terms of the crucial decision of when to change to get the maximum effect. In the timing of the change, the drummer demonstrates his own awareness of the rhythmic potential of the music and his personal control of its inherent power, but most importantly, he demonstrates his involvement with the social situation in a dramatic gesture that will play upon the minds and bodies of his fellow performers and his audience.[17]

Chernoff notes the importance, beyond simple repetition, of a performer emulating or mimicking a performer's style, connection with the audience, intensity, and awareness. Therefore, mimicking, as an African sensibility, is linked to traditional forms of performance and held in high esteem. Similarly, within the context of Ivorian popular music, the ability to mimic well distinguishes one performer from another. This element is essential in informing the self-identity of youth performing on the streets of Abidjan, as they mimic the dance moves, gestures, and personality of artists, similar to how performers in traditional settings emulate the style and extra-musical aspects of master musicians.

The history of bluff as a concept can be traced to the beginnings of coupé décalé, when Ivorians embraced the music for its ability to trigger a memory into an imagined reality of success and wealth. Creators of coupé décalé were able to acquire (from unknown sources) funds to invest in the fashioning of their identities or bluffs of well-dressed wealthy, popular, and important figures. Ivorian youth—feeling hopeless due to national economic instability, war, and ethnic and religious divisions—envisioned themselves acquiring success similar to the jet setters (founders of coupé décalé). Therefore, they appropriated the style, language, music, and dance of the originators. This idea and feigned image of wealth, success, and fame stimulated hopes and dreams while the country went to war. The genre therefore fed into Ivorian youth's ideal of their future and their prospective memories. Anthropologist Sasha Newell's concept of *le bluff* can be enacted through buying (or appearing to have bought) substantial food and drink for your guests, wearing expensive clothing and accessories, or owning expensive material goods, such as technological gadgets (tablets, cell phones, smart watches) and cars that they cannot afford.

---

17   Chernoff, *African Rhythm and African Sensibility*, 113.

What makes this excessive expression of wealth unique and different from the "big man" syndrome that prevails in much of Africa is that the participants are aware of the conflation of wealth and social status. In fact, the client-patron system of the "big man" syndrome is nonexistent within this paradigm. Individuals are often borrowing from their peers to finance these bluffs (or shows of wealth), returning the favor when necessary. Newell explains that this investment in showy material goods is an expression of "modernity" by Ivorian youth. In a world where the western and northern hemispheres are thought of as being modern, and often depicted as having an excess of material products (cars, branded clothing, accessories, and food), marginalized youth in Africa aspire to these tangible symbols of modernity. Newell states that Ivorian youth are imitating such patterns to demonstrate their exchange or participation in a global "modernity." This engagement with "modernity" is not limited to Ivorian youth's purchasing habits. Homi Bhabha has discussed the constant cultural turmoil many postcolonial nations must endure in identifying their modern positionality within the Western narrative.[18] "Because the European colonial empire played a double game by encouraging 'natives' to abandon their cultural practices and recognize the superiority of European ones, but at the same time barricading access to European identity, the interpretation of mimesis reproduces colonial discourses. Both representations of native authenticity underlying mimetic enactments and those that describe successful 'acculturation' reinforce ideologies of modernity and the hierarchies they continue to legitimate."[19]

While the statements by both Newell and Bhaba seem to neglect the agency of the former colonies in realizing their own notion of modernity (or position within it), they do explain the arduous situation that formerly colonized nations and their youth find themselves in. To avoid the reification of African traditional culture as their own culture, African youth, especially Ivorian youth, have made "efforts at attaining 'modernity' through consumption as well as the relationship between fears of mimesis and the cultural construction of so-called modern identity in North Atlantic cultures."[20] However, within a post-colonial climate, youth are deliberately attempting to not replicate Western European and American culture which dominates much of global popular culture. This conflicted culture of consumption is most obvious in the history of the music genre and culture of coupé décalé,

---

18 Bhabha, *Location of Culture*, 171–79.
19 Newell, *Modernity Bluff*, 14.
20 Newell, 19.

where its foundation is based on aspects of African culture (African dance, les sapeurs, blend of African languages, repetition, and musicking).

Aesthetic Elements in Coupé Décalé: Ambiance, Dance, Fashion, and Language

The creator of the music and subculture of coupé décalé, Douk Saga, embraced Les Sapeurs culture, adorning himself in extravagant clothing from France and Italy. To accompany his extraordinary attire, he led a decadent lifestyle, dancing, drinking, partying, and flaunting his wealth. During his partying days, Douk Saga acquired admirers of his extravagant lifestyle, clothing, grandiose behavior, and dancing, creating a mood of delight or stylish ambiance. Douk Saga and his entourage were thought to be *ambianceurs*. Ambianceurs are those who create or are crucial for creating a euphoric atmosphere. This element feeds into the philosophy of the subculture and myth of socioeconomic movement surrounding the genre. Participants acquire social capital through being in the presence of an ambianceur, and as Newell shared, the facade is often financially supported by peers. So many contribute to the creation of the ambiance and the propping up of the ambianceur in Abidjanese youth culture.

Ambiance was an essential element of escapism that Abidjanese youth were experiencing in dealing with their nation's civil war (2002–7), xenophobia, and economic decline. Coupé décalé ironically helped youth deal with their present circumstances through longing for resources that many youth felt they deserved but could not afford. The ostentatious dress and flaunting of material items associated with coupé décalé amused listeners and established an ambiance that allowed youth to escape daunting realities at home, including war, lack of jobs, national instability, and economic decline. They could project their thoughts on their ambitions or prospective memories in lieu of focusing on the danger outside their door. Instead of advocating for rights and speaking up against injustice, as the previous generation had done with zouglou, youth instead used music "to share memories and thoughts . . . to strengthen their own identity [and to create a] link . . . with the client's cultural identity and personal history."[21] In the case of Abidjanese youth, coupé décalé was not intended to reify any tradition. Instead, the culture promoted or suggested a new positionality of youth in the world. It

---

21   Orth, "Music Therapy with Traumatized Refugees in a Clinical Setting," 2.

was a position not strictly tied to the metropole but one where youth blend African elements (dance, music, language) with their knowledge of the rest of the modern world (language, travel, clothing, material products).

Dance

Dance is a pivotal aspect of the genre, one that not only has direct ties to African music and dance traditions but simultaneously allows Ivorian youth to provide commentary on world events through movement rather than lyrical content. The standard movement—bowed legs, swaying arms, and rotating waist—differs slightly in choreography with each song. The songs directly correlate with a new dance. For example, *coupé décalé chinois* uses the same original forms: bent bowed legs, rotating waist, and rigid torso. However, the arm movements are meant to mimic martial arts motions with the occasional roundhouse or front kick interspersed. Similarly, *coupé décalé guantanamo* keeps intact the basic form, but arm movements are restricted as if the dancer is in handcuffs—wrists crossed—or in miming the holding of prison cell bars. These kinds of dance creations offer commentary on popular topics and issues (Guantanamo, bird flu, the growing presence of the Chinese in Africa, etc.) and influence virtually every new dance style created.

While the lyrical content may not be directly critical or engaged with these current political events, the dance movements clearly are. Coupé décalé chinois is an artistic expression of the growing and sometimes contested relation between the Ivory Coast and China. Since the beginning of the twenty-first century, China has had a significant presence in the Ivory Coast, facilitating several infrastructure contracts with the government. These government contracts have led to a larger Chinese presence in the country, as Chinese men often work on the construction projects. Similarly, *coupé décalé guantanamo* responds to the heavily criticized prison camp Guantanamo Bay, opened in 2002 by the George W. Bush administration. Other dance creations commented on the bird flu—or avian influenza—that primarily hit China and spread worldwide with pandemics cropping up across Asia and the rest of the world in the early 2000s. All of these world events were satirized and made into visual art through dance moves by coupé décalé artists, speaking to how Abidjanese youth are in dialogue with the rest of the world.

These dance moves were also seen as capital among homeless youth. In the vignette below, quoted from my previous work, a context is set where this population of youth are dependent upon their ability to follow, learn, and perform the most popular dance moves in order to survive on the streets.

> On the south side of Abidjan lives a group of about fifteen boys, ranging between seven to seventeen years of age, who sleep outside the club, Marcory Gaza. Adorned with bright neon lights, the club is located in the working class, residential neighborhood of Abidjan called Marcory. The children silently wait from late evening to nearly midnight for the weekend crowd that visits the club and maquis for entertainment. As midnight draws closer, the children awake from the cold pavement to entertain each other and coerce tips from the seated crowd of clubbers awaiting their food. The street was lined with open-air restaurants, each serving between 30–50 people. Each maquis had a seating area around 30 feet in length and 15 feet in width where customers sat at plastic outdoor tables waiting for their food, while listening to the blend of music from the surrounding amplified speakers. In this moment of idle time, while conversing with friends, the young boys entertain the club attendees and those dining at the maquis. Roaming from table to table to solicit funds, they perform complicated and contortionist-like dance movements (e.g., kpango, placali, and zouglou) to the music of DJ Arafat and Serge Beynaud amplified on loudspeakers outside the clubs.[22]

Not only were skills needed to draw tips and thus further their livelihood, but it was necessary to be in the space itself. Highly skilled dancers quickly dissuaded those who lack talent from such competitive urban spaces. Those who are successful and talented often dance at the entrances to discotheques and restaurants/maquis to amplified prerecorded music. Some may dance freestyle, while most follow the choreography they memorized from the tracks' corresponding music videos. Throughout the day, those same street children spend their time near maquis or restaurants where they study the most current music videos constantly streaming: usually those of coupé décalé artists. Because of the culture surrounding coupé décalé and its impact on the greater Ivoirian youth culture, dozens of street children I interviewed expressed aspirations of being a pop-music performer. The culture of coupé décalé was pervasive throughout the city and informed how many Ivoirian youth formulated their identity and considered their positionality in the discussion of modernity.

---

22 Taylor, "When the Streets Speak."

Language

In addition to introducing new dance and fashion and propagating a culture of ambiance among urban Ivoirian youth, coupé décalé aided in further popularizing Nouchi, a language which acted as a panethnic bond further uniting urban youth of Abidjan by melding Ivoirian French, several different indigenous languages, and American English. The word "Nouchi" is thought to mean literally "moustache," signifying a strong or powerful man; however, its exact definition has been contested.[23] No matter the language's exact definition and etymology, its role within coupé décalé is to further emphasize the genre's panethnic appeal, as the lyrics are primarily sung in French. The language also acts as a code between generations. Because of its chameleon-like ability to shift, the language is always changing, including new vocabulary and slang and redefining words. Youth often inject old words with new meanings and give meaning to vocables (nonsense syllables). Often coupé décalé artists utilize Nouchi in their lyrics, with many listeners not understanding them, not unlike contemporary rap in the United States. This language barrier signifies the barrier between participants and observers of the culture. Those who are familiar with the language and its frequent linguistic mutations are able to creatively use the language to articulate the sentiment of the everyday Ivorian and Ivoirian youth.[24]

Social and Economic Capital

Throughout its history, Cote d'Ivoire has acted as a major hub for music production, a vibrant cultural scene for creating and replicating styles and genres from surrounding nations and the metropole. It is currently a major center for music consumption, especially as a focal point in West Africa for concerts and music festivals. While I was in the field, the city hosted a plethora of concerts, offered a variety of music video stations (Trace Africa, RTI Music TV, Hit Africa), and aired several live music-centered television shows (Wozo Vacance). These entertainment activities, coupled with the sound system culture discussed earlier, demonstrate the country's strong affinity with music. Similarly, all of these events showcase popular and traditional dance styles as well, indicating the strong connection between popular music and dance. In

---

23   See http://www.nouchi.com.
24   Taylor, "Zouglou."

addition, for reasons needing further exploration, Ivoirian culture seems to strongly support and encourage dance and music performance among children, as seen in the national TV programming, classroom curriculum, and programming for youth at nonprofits.[25]

Because of the national popularity of dance and the potential profitability of dancing and rapping, as illustrated through the story of DJ Arafat, many youths are inspired. DJ Arafat's story inspired many children to revere his path to wealth and success. For instance, the following interviews offer the views of many participants on dance and labor:

Moise: ... I want all of you to know my true calling, which is to become a dancer so to financially help my family.

Junior: my name is Junior and ... I would like to become a dancer. [26]

The above and below are simply a few statements pulled from youths who saw music and dance as their path to fame and wealth, as well as an escape from the streets and a means of financially assisting their family. Even among nonstreet children, the youth I met in the city's maquis stated that they take to the streets to dance for money with their parents' consent after seeing the profits. Many children I interviewed and worked with looked to that profession as a source of labor or work. There are other examples of labor familiar among children beginning at a young age, such as working in the informal sector through selling various items, acting as parking boys, begging, washing windshields, assisting in the market, or other miscellaneous jobs. But dance had the potential for a way out, as DJ Arafat shared.

Interviewer: So, what did you do to feed yourself?

Child: I beg.

Interviewer: All right, but how do you manage to get food and clothes for wearing?

Child: I beg to obtain all these things.

---

25   *Human Rights Watch.*
26   From an interview by the author.

Interviewer: So, how did you manage to earn money and buy clothes?

Child: I beg and use it to buy foods and new dress and have bath.

Child: My name is [JM], when we get up we go and wash our faces and then go to beg and we come back around midday to play a bit.[27]

Children such as the ones quoted above, who depend on begging to obtain the necessaries of life, may envision success as a dancer as a feasible alternative.

Conclusion

Music is an important and critical tool in understanding Ivorian youth culture. Through music and dance, youth are able to demonstrate and articulate their positionality within the world. And, as seen through coupé décalé culture, youth have distanced themselves from the traditional reified concepts of African identity. Instead, they are melding traditional and global aspects of identity to formulate their own modern identity. Through musicking, youth are able to express their identity and comment on current events and engage with materialism, globalization, national identity, and socioeconomic capital. The youth culture informed by the genre of coupé décalé fed into Ivorian youth's ideal of their future. And the street children of Abidjan, as inhabitants of the streets, club areas, and maquis where the "bluff" (as discussed by Newell) is being manifested, accrued a similar sentiment and desire for themselves. Furthermore, prominent musician and dancer DJ Arafat has a myth shrouding him that he was himself a street child. Through dancing he gained publicity and fame, which eventually led to wealth. Therefore, the bluff (through dancing) allows street children to acquire social capital from peers and economic capital from observers similar to their icon, DJ Arafat.[28] Musicking, in the case of urban Ivorian youth, functions as a tool to energize their individual ambitions of success, prosperity and a dignified life in the midst of national crisis. Historian Osumare explains that

> the performativity of their movements—often unconscious but meaningful series of bodily postures, gestures, and movements . . . implicitly signify and mark a sense of social identity in everyday pedestrian activity. The performativity of

---

27 Interview by author.
28 Marie, "Breakdancing."

gestures and body language constitutes the manner in which we understand ourselves through our bodies, literally through the muscular and skeletal structure as well as semiotically and metaphorically.[29]

These movements, though imitative, explore and express how youth are deconstructing cultural societal norms and formulating their own position and identity in this globalized world.

Bibliography

Aliman, Usher. *Douk Saga: Ou l'Histoire Interdite du Coupé Décalé, un Destin Fracassé*. Abidjan: Les Classiques Ivoiriens, 2013.

Amantana, Vivian. *A Sociological Study of Street Children in Ghana: Victims of Kinship Breakdown and Rural-Urban Migration*. Lewiston, NY: Edwin Mellen, 2012.

Appert, Catherine. *Locating Hip Hop Origins: Popular Music and Tradition in Senegal*. Africa, 86, no. 2 (2016): 237–62.

Aptekar, Lewis. "Are Colombian Street Children Neglected? The Contribution of Ethnographic and Ethnohistorical Approaches to the Study of Children." *Anthropology and Education Quarterly* 22, no. 4 (1991): 326–49.

Beazley, Harriot. "The Construction and Protection of Individual and Collective Identities by Street Children and Youth in Indonesia." *Children, Youth and Environments* 13, no. 1 (2003):105–33.

Bhabha, Homi. *The Location of Culture*. New York: Routledge, 1994.

Blé, Raoul Germain."Zouglou et Réalités Sociales des Jeunes en Côte d'Ivoire." *Afrique et Développement* 31, no. 1 (2006).

Bradley, Lloyd. *This is Reggae Music. The Story of Jamaica's Music*. New York: Grove, 2001.

Chernoff, John. *African Rhythm and African Sensibility: Aesthetics and Social Action in African Musical Idioms*. Chicago: University of Chicago Press, 1979.

Cunningham, Hugh. "Children and Childhood in Western Society Since 1500." In *The Global History of Childhood Reader*, edited by Heidi Morrison, 368. 1st ed. New York: Routledge, 2010.

Da Silva, Rita de Cácia Oenning. "Reversing the Rite: Music, Dance, and Rites of Passage among Street Children and Youth in Recifie, Brazil." *World of Music* 48, no. 1 (2006): 83–97.

Dorf, Brandon. "Les Sapeurs Research Story: The Story about Les Sapeurs and their Lives." http://www. storify.com/dorffbr/les-sapeurs-research-story. Accessed May 17, 2016.

---

29 Osumare, *Hiplife in Ghana*, 86.

"Douk Saga Word Fest Douk Saga." http://www.greatsong.net. Accessed May 8, 2016.
Heinonen, Paula. *Youth Gangs and Street Children: Culture, Nurture and Masculinity in Ethiopia*. New York: Berghahn, 2011.
Human Rights Watch. https://www.hrw.org/topic/childrens-rights/child-labor. Accessed May 15, 2016.
Marie, Lucas. "Breakdancing: The Commodification and Globalisation of an Underground Subculture." In *Thinking Out Loud: A Collection of Articles on a Broad Range of Topics including Anthropology, Sociology, Philosophy, Politics, and Dance*. Edited by Lucas Marie. http://www.lucasMarie.wordpress.com. Accessed September 2, 2015.
McGovern, Mike. *Making War in Côte d'Ivoire*. Chicago: University of Chicago Press, 2011.
Mtv.com. http://www.mtv.com/artists/dj-arafat/biography/. Accessed February 20, 2016.
Newell, Sasha. *The Modernity Bluff: Crime, Consumption, and Citizenship in Côte d'Ivoire*. Chicago: University of Chicago Press, 2012.
Nketia, J. H. Kwabena. *The Music of Africa*. New York: W. W. Norton, 1974.
Nouchi.com. http://www.nouchi.com. Accessed February 19, 2016.
Orth, Jaap. *Music Therapy with Traumatized Refugees in a Clinical Setting. Voices: A World Forum for Music Therapy* 5, no. 2 (2005).
Osumare, Halifu. *The Hiplife in Ghana: West African Indigenization of Hip-Hop*. New York: Palgrave Macmillan, 2012.
Small, Chris. "Musicking: A Ritual in Social Space." Lecture at the University of Melbourne, June 6, 1995.
Stokes, Martin. *Ethnicity, Identity and Music: The Musical Construction of Place*. Oxford: Berg, 1994.
Stolzoff, Norman. *Wake the Town and Tell the People. Dancehall Culture in Jamaica*. Durham, NC: Duke University Press, 2000.
Tang, Patricia. *Masters of the Sabar: Wolof Griot Percussionists of Senegal*. Philadelphia: Temple University Press, 2007.
Taylor, Ty-Juana. *When the Streets Speak: Investigating Music, Memory, and Identity in the lives of Abidjanese Street Children*. PhD diss., University of California, Los Angeles, 2016.
———. "Zouglou." In *Continuum Encyclopedia of Popular Music of the World*. London: Bloomsbury, 2018.
United Nations Department of Economic and Social Affairs Population Division. http://www.unpopulations.org. Accessed May 2015.
Zolberg, Aristide R. *One-Party Government in the Ivory Coast*. Princeton, NJ: Princeton University Press, 1964.

Chapter Four

Young People, Music, and Sociopolitical Change in Postwar Sierra Leone

Ibrahim Bangura

Introduction

For eleven years (1991–2002), Sierra Leone was embroiled in a violent civil war that led to the death of approximately sixty thousand people, with more than a million leaving the country in search of peace and security in other parts of the world. Young people of all ages were caught up in the country's violent crisis as they became both victims and actors that played active or passive roles in the conflict. At the end of the conflict in 2002, several initiatives were undertaken by the government and its international development partners to stabilize the country and address the root causes of the conflict. However, a few years into the postwar reconstruction phase, young people in Sierra Leone, those who initially had high hopes at the end of the war, started to lose faith in government initiatives as the political elites failed to address the historical legacies of the conflict. Although the violence ended, there were no concrete policies and implementation strategies effected to address the root causes of the war. This inaction by the state was exacerbated by the popular perception of a return to the prewar status quo among young people. Now war-wearied and increasingly unwilling to use violence as a means of expressing their grievances, young people took to popular arts as the main tools of engagement with an indifferent state and its ruling class. Popular music in particular became a powerful form of sociopolitical expression, one that caught the interest and cultural imagination of both the younger and older generations. Young people started creating and producing songs on issues related to politics, the economy, corruption, and the marginalization of women and youth. The popular songs and comedy became instrumental in sensitizing the public to the concerns of young people while drawing the attention of the elites to the concerns and anxieties among the wider population.

The instrumentalization of popular arts by Sierra Leonean youth is not unique by any means. Popular arts and their everyday use by youth is common in other parts of Africa, and over the last three decades, this phenomenon has been the subject of extensive academic research in African studies.[1] Of particular interest to researchers has been the multiple ways in which young people interact with, shape, and use popular arts as a means of sociopolitical expression. To some extent, this focus on Africanist research could be attributed to young people's active politicization of cultural production in the context of violent conflicts and peacebuilding processes across the continent. Thus, popular arts culture in Africa has become central to the ways in which young people conceive, make, interpret, and use art as an instrument of social change. For most youth in Africa, popular arts play a vital role in forming identities, creating a sense of belonging and constituting citizenship politics that are linked with the current political atmosphere. As a number of scholars have argued, images and symbols from popular culture shape our identities, sexuality, political affiliations, social class, and notions of nationhood by producing and eliciting certain feelings and sentiments inside us.[2]

This chapter thus critically assesses the evolution of a popular youth-based music culture in postwar Sierra Leone and the ways in which it became a crucial cultural tool of a new consciousness among young people and the wider Sierra Leonean society. It examines, among other things, the types of songs produced by young artists and how they have been instrumental in providing a voice for young people; the influence of the songs on the public and their perceptions of the songs; and the contributions of popular music to the peacebuilding process in the country. The chapter examines the period between 2002 and 2007 in which the country experienced

---

1 See the works of authors such as Wale Adedeji on Nigeria, Brigit Englert on Tanzania, and Anne Schumann on Côte d'Ivoire.
2 Street, *Politics and Popular Culture,* 11; and Kaur, "Sister Fa and Nneka," 5.

a significant shift in popular music, the emergence of young musicians as a self-conscious political constituency, the decline in popular music between 2007 and 2015, and the reemergence of popular music between 2015 and 2019. In regard to methodology, the chapter adopts a phenomenological approach that draws on the experiences and voices of the young artists and their fans. Semistructured interviews and focus-group discussions (FDGs) were conducted with twenty-three popular arts artists and fifty-three youths in the neighborhoods of Sierra Leone's capital city, Freetown. Additionally, thirty-seven active participants in the Sierra Leonean culture industry in various ministries, departments and agencies (MDAs), civil society organizations (CSOs), academic institutions, and local community leaders were interviewed and engaged in FGDs.

Young People and Civil War in Sierra Leone 1991–2002

Several authors including Richards (1996, 2006), Keen (2011), Abdullah (1998), Brett and Specht (2004), Peters (2011), and Bangura (2016, 2017) have written extensively on young people and the civil war in Sierra Leone. These researchers have often attributed the involvement of youth in the conflict to poverty, high unemployment, widespread illiteracy, the endless marginalization of youth and women, and the perception of corruption and bad governance among ordinary people. Writing on young people and the conflict in Sierra Leone, Ibrahim Bangura stated:

> Two distinct strands of analyses have been used to explain both the causes and longevity of the conflict in Sierra Leone, both of which are of relevance to the country's young people. Poor governance and corruption have been widely argued to be the main factors responsible for the conflict, while the marginalization of youth and the influence of natural resources are thought to have fuelled the extent of the conflict and the severity of its impact.[3]

Political-economic and social factors such as poor governance, corruption, and the marginalization of young people significantly contributed to the eruption of violence in Sierra Leone. Historically, these underlying factors go back as far as the immediate postindependence period when the contestation for power and state resources between the country's two leading political parties, the Sierra Leone People Party (SLPP) and the All People's

---

3   Bangura, "We Can't Eat Peace," 39.

Congress (APC), divided the country along ethno-regional lines. The SLPP perceived the southeastern regions to be its stronghold while the APC perceived the northwestern regions to be its main political base. In a heavily contested election in 1967, the APC defeated the ruling SLPP, a defeat that the SLPP was unwilling to accept, thereby encouraging the military to step in. The elected Prime Minister Siaka Probyn Stevens was sent into exile in neighboring Guinea, where he stayed until 1968 when he was returned and reinstated as prime minister by junior officers (Stevens 1984). However, Stevens, a popular trade unionist who had built his political foundation on a democratic platform, returned home determined to consolidate power and protect his regime. To effectively do so, he downsized the military, adopted a one-party system of governance in 1978, and established a paramilitary unit, the Internal Security Unit (ISU), consisting mainly of his loyalists.[4] As such, opposition members were left with the unappealing options of joining the APC, leaving the country, or remaining silent in the face of a rising postcolonial dictatorship.

With the absence of an effective opposition to checkmate the excesses of the APC, young people took matters into their own hands, with students regularly facing off with the government on key issues relating to political corruption, a declining economy, and failed governance. Two historic student demonstrations in 1977 and 1984 and the heavy-handed response by the government exposed the government's unwillingness to use constructive, peaceful engagements when dealing with young people.[5] These violent reactions by the state culminated in the development of the foundations of a revolutionary movement that saw students and enlisted youth traveling to Libya for training in guerrilla warfare. It was during this contentious period that Foday Saybana Sankoh, who subsequently emerged as the leader of the Revolutionary United Front (RUF), was recruited by youths who were facilitating the mobilization of young people for training in guerrilla warfare in Libya (TRCSL 2004).

The civil war erupted on March 23, 1991, in Bomaru, a border town with Liberia, a part of the country that was considered seriously marginalized by the APC. The invading force of approximately 250 soldiers was soon joined by a readymade army of young, marginalized, and disillusioned youth. This also became the case for other factions that emerged such as the Civil Defence Force (CDF), the Armed Forces Revolutionary Council (AFRC),

---

4   Koroma, *Crisis and Intervention in Sierra Leone*.
5   Bangura, "Bridging the Gulf," 41–42.

and its splinter group, the West Side Boys. As indicated by Brett and Specht (2006), young people constituted a significant portion of all armed groups in Sierra Leone and performed several roles such as armed fighters, cooks, spies, sex slaves, and bush wives.

The nature of the violence demonstrated by young people who participated in the conflict provides an indication of the level of anger and resentment that they had often harbored for years against the state. Decades of ostracization culminated in the perception that violence was the most formidable means of engaging with a system that the youth believed had failed them. A former combatant interviewed by the author explained how young combatants perceived the state and political elites before and during the civil war:

> For many years the state failed us. We were nothing to politicians, we were young, poor, hungry and desperate, we tried to explain what we were going through to the elders in our communities, but they did not listen. To them, we were not capable of thinking, we were children and that hurt us deeply. Politicians did not educate us, but they used us as thugs. We were bitter, we were angry, and the gun became our voice. The war was the only period when we were respected, when we could teach those who treated us like animals, of what we are capable of doing. The table turned for 11 years, but they are still behaving as if nothing happened and it is all now like it used to be before the war. [6]

The statement above points to the fact that young people in Africa have been a misunderstood demographic and are often subjected to stereotypes, marginalization, and infantilization. The failure to constructively engage them by the state and its elites succeeded in denying them the identity, recognition and means of expressing legitimate grievances, which they harbored over time. Consequently, violence became the only effective tool they could use to challenge and deconstruct the dubious powers that held them hostage for decades and also to contest, unlock and unsettle such powers.

The APC was ultimately overthrown in 1992 by young soldiers from the war front led by Captain Valentine Esegrabo Melvin Strasser, who formed the National Provisional Ruling Council (NPRC). The inexperienced soldiers could not contain the RUF, and after four years of intense civil war, Brigadier General Julius Maada Bio, who had replaced Strasser through a palace coup in January 1996, initiated peace talks with the RUF in Abidjan, Côte d'Ivoire. The process was finalized by Ahmad Tejan Kabbah, a career diplomat who became the first democratically elected president after almost

---

6   Interview conducted in Makeni on July 14, 2019.

three decades of a one-party system of governance. Nonetheless, the agreement was short lived as the RUF violated it, and in the middle of the chaos, the military overthrew Kabbah on May 25, 1997, and established the AFRC.[7] After more than eight months of seeking to persuade the AFRC to peacefully hand over power, the Economic Community of West African States Monitoring Group (ECOMOG) forced the AFRC out of the capital, Freetown, and the conflict intensified until July 1999 when the Lomé Peace Agreement was signed between the government of Sierra Leone and the RUF in Togo. In spite of the agreement, the conflict was only officially declared over in 2002, as the RUF continued perpetrating atrocities against innocent civilians.[8] Respondents interviewed as part of this study indicated that the agreement mainly focused on appeasing the leadership of the RUF, failing to incorporate components that would have been geared to transforming the lives of young people in the postconflict context.[9]

The Evolution of Popular Music in Postwar Sierra Leone (2002–7)

From the history previously sketched out, postwar Sierra Leone was unsurprisingly characterized by a weak and declining economy, dilapidated sociopolitical systems and structures, deep-seated poverty, and limited socioeconomic opportunities and services (Koroma 2004). Consequently, there was a massive reliance on international support by the state to stabilize the economy and promote growth and development. However, a few years into the postwar reconstruction phase, the inability of the government to directly and adequately address the challenges that young people were contending with, led to a loss of confidence in the system. This was exacerbated

---

7   Kabbah, "Coming from the Brink."
8   The RUF continuously violated the Lomé Peace Agreement by attacking communities and killing innocent people. This led to civil society organizing a mass demonstration at the residence of Foday Saybana Sankoh, the leader of the RUF, on May 8, 2000. Twenty-one people including two soldiers were killed during the demonstration, but eventually Sankoh was arrested and jailed. This led to a change in the leadership of the RUF, with General Issa Sesay replacing Sankoh. Unlike Sankoh, Sesay was willing to comply with the agreement, and eventually peace was declared in 2002.
9   Based on interviews conducted for this chapter.

by perceptions of corruption, bad governance, and the general marginalization of youth by the prewar political elites who had reemerged and once again gained control of the socioeconomic and political space. As I have indicated elsewhere,

> Caught in the framework of a paternalistic society in which cultures, traditions, systems and structures had marginalized women and youth, young people had sought new modes of engagement with the emerging reality of a country in transition. With the war, they played prominent roles in the fighting forces, and in some cases, in their communities too. After the war, their leadership was again constrained by multiple factors, such that signs of youth marginalization started re-emerging in both urban and rural communities.... The re-emergence of the pre-war status quo led to a "withdrawal syndrome" as youth, tired of fighting the system, developed strategies for personal survival. At the same time, youth spaces for expression and engagement continued to shrink, being subject to interference.[10]

The relentless search for personal survival during the postwar years also led to the reengineering of the social space by youth. One set of youth focused directly on engaging the state and its elites through popular music, while the other focused on the establishment of other sociocultural platforms through which youth could constructively engage with one another on burning questions that concerned them and their society. The latter approach was organized around social clusters that met in local coffee booths called *ataya base*, which are referred to as the "youth parliament" by members. The *ataya base*, which initially consisted of young educated and frustrated youth, soon accommodated unemployed educated youth who were equally desperate and disappointed with the system. Drinking the strong Chinese green tea called *ataya* and sharing the little food they had, these youth cohorts intensely and critically examined the chaotic state of affairs in the country and what could be done to set things right. With no other social spaces available to them, young people spent most of the day, especially the evenings, socializing with their peers in the *ataya bases* and discussing their lived experiences, opinions, and perceptions of the state. *Ataya bases* became widespread in every district in the country, with structured leadership and bylaws in each of them to maintain discipline and order among its membership.

The *ataya bases* are in many ways emblematic of how vulnerable youth faced the endless hardships associated with an increasingly uncertain

---

10 Bangura, "We Can't Eat Peace," 45.

postcolonial world and created alternative spaces to help make sense of their lives and the world around them. Thus, the *ataya bases* are forms of "new social spaces"[11] that are not only a by-product of but also an active response by youth to historical processes surrounding and shaping their lives. Ironically, even though such platforms could have been used as a means of engaging, mobilizing, and enhancing young people's capacity to promote national development, they are usually dismissed as idle spaces for dropouts and hooligans.[12] This missed opportunity further widened the mistrust between the youth and political elites.

The emergence of these two social circles symbolized the unwillingness on the part of young people to demonstrate their frustrations using violence. As Foday Kallon, a rap artist interviewed for this chapter recounted:

> We knew we had to change as young people, we knew music was the way to go and we knew that the only way we could get the attention of our people and leaders was through singing songs that spoke to burning issues and questions. It was difficult as we had limited financial means to produce songs, but we were determined, and nothing could stop us. Soon after, artists such as Emerson, Dry Yai Crew, Jungle Leaders and Pupa Baja became household names. We sang on anything and everything that was going wrong in Sierra Leone and while politicians hated us for that, our people came to accept and love us.[13]

The songs produced by these young artists reenergized a country that was still trapped in the gripping aftermath of a violent civil war. A healthy nightlife resumed in a country in transition from violence to peace, with nightclubs and bars booming with business, playing popular Sierra Leonean songs to people of all ages.

Inasmuch as local music and arts were popular before the war, the difference was that the leading artists consisted of older musicians performing in bands or singing traditional songs. Musicians such as S. E. Rogie and his Palm Wine music (Maringa), Big Fayia of the Sierra Leone Military Band fame, Ebenezer Calender and his Goombay (Gumbe), which was later converted to Milo-jazz by Olofemi Israel Cole (a.k.a. Doctor Oloh) and Bunny Mack (Wai 2005) are still remembered for the songs they produced. Postwar Sierra Leone, however, experienced the emergence of a much more youthful collection of popular musicians. Young musicians such as Emmerson

---

11 Kennelly, Poyntz, and Ugor, "Special Issues Introduction," 259.
12 Based on interviews conducted in Freetown in July 2019.
13 Interview conducted in Freetown on July 23, 2019.

Amidu Bockarie, Pupa Baja, Innocent, Jungle Leaders, Baw-Waw Society and K-Man emerged during this period and immediately garnered widespread followership across the country. Additionally, the types of songs and the issues addressed in them started to speak directly to the everyday happenings in society, their effects on youth, and the kinds of change desired by Sierra Leoneans. Speaking on the reasons behind the emergence of young musicians and their interests in socioeconomic and political issues in postwar Sierra Leone, a political observer noted:

> The end of the civil war ushered in a lot of hope and desire for change. Several people had died, and millions have suffered unjustly over the years due to the failure of the state; the thought was that there would be no reverse to business as usual. Unfortunately, few years after the war, the political elites became comfortable again and nothing changed. The anger and frustration among young people led to some of them taking to music to express their concerns and be both the voice and conscience of the Sierra Leonean society. The young musicians took to doing what the academics and civil society could not do. They contested state failure and it caught the attention of a lot of people. [14]

In his 2005 article "Musical Artists and Social Change in Sierra Leone: A Reflection," Zubairu Wai wrote about his first experience with the new types of songs produced by young Sierra Leoneans and his impression of them:

> I stood there trying to absorb the shock and conceal my excitement at what I was hearing and seeing. It wasn't anything negative at all. It was just that I was stunned because it wasn't there when I left Sierra Leone in 1999 or not on this scale when I returned to visit in 2002. This time, in September 2005, something had changed. Music in Sierra Leone has come to not only be a means of artistic expression; it has become a very powerful tool in the campaign for socio-political transformation, the struggle for human dignity and morality in society. The popular artists in Sierra Leone are not only entertainers, but social commentators and educators as well. Their bravery is astounding especially at a time when the political dispensation seems to be sliding into a mild form of dictatorship and at a time when the government is frowning on dissent and suppressing free speech. The artists today are young women and men, mostly in their 20s. They represent a generation that has known nothing other than rottenness in Sierra Leone. Their consciousness is shaped by life's experiences and social realities and that is what is vividly portrayed in their songs. [15]

---

14   Interview conducted with Joseph Kamara in Freetown on July 19, 2019.
15   Wai, "Musical Artists and Social Change in Sierra Leone."

What Wai experienced in Sierra Leone then was a powerful cultural expression of the desires, hopes, and aspirations of the country's youth. It appears that in the immediate aftermath of the war, some youths were unprepared to remain reserved in the midst of the unwillingness on the part of the elites to address both the historical legacies of the conflict and the existing and emerging challenges that the youth were contending with. Thus, music became an effective means of expressing the concerns and suggestions of changes by a self-conscious political constituency: the youth. This is similar to how hip-hop music is used and perceived as a way of informing society of their challenges and at the same time a means of protesting and resisting the political elites. Writing on hip-hop music in Nigeria, Wale Adedeji states that

> no art exists only for its own sake but is often a medium to convey social messages and ideologies. The genre of hip hop goes beyond hedonism or the portrayal of affluence as widely perceived. In contemporary Africa, it has become a powerful force for education, information, and resistance.[16]

Like the case of Sierra Leone, hip-hop music in Nigeria became an essential component in the struggle for identity and recognition that succeeding governments have denied them. The everyday contestations and confrontations between youth and the political elites have degenerated into perennial crises such as the Niger Delta Crisis and the Boko Haram armed insurgency in the last decade and a half, leading to the deaths of hundreds of Nigerians. Hip-hop music thus became a more positive and constructive option of expressing grievances against the state by youth who did not want to resort to violence.[17]

In her article on young people and Bongo Flava music in Tanzania, Brigit Englert concluded that popular arts have succeeded in increasing what she described as the "visibility" and "voiceability" of Tanzania's youth:

> Bongo Flava music has helped to shape a generational identity of those Tanzanians who grew up in the era of liberalisation and multi-party politics. More importantly, this youthful musical genre has helped to increase the visibility and *voiceability* of youth in the Tanzanian public and thus at least indirectly encouraged the political participation of youth in political discourses. In this article I argue that it is not so much the critical lyrics of some of the songs which

---

16   Adedeji, "African Popular Culture," 15–16.
17   Based on interviews conducted with Paul Nyulaku, a peace and security expert in Nigeria.

have helped achieve this, than the fact that the successes of Bongo Flava musicians have conveyed self-consciousness to young people who experience that they can achieve more than hitherto thought.[18]

The ability of Bongo Flava music to provide the voice and visibility that youth have been denied for decades provides an indication of the effectiveness of music as an engine for social change. In Sierra Leone, the public voice that the songs provided a once-voiceless young generation triggered significant change in consciousness among the ordinary citizenry. The songs inspired those in the *ataya bases* who continuously played these songs as they engaged in discussions on the challenges that the country was contending with. Songs like "Borbor Pain," "Borbor Belleh," and "Two Fut Arata" by Emmerson Amidu Bockarie, "City Life" by Pupa Bajah and BawWaw Society, and "Doe don Clean" and "Pack for Go" by Jungle Leaders all provoked heated discussions and debates on corruption and bad governance among the populace and went a long way in energizing the vociferous call for change as the country moved toward presidential and parliamentary elections in 2007. Writing on youth, music, and politics in postwar Sierra Leone, Susan Shepler stated the following:

> The national elections of 2007 were notable for an explosion of popular music by young people directly addressing some of the central issues of the election: corruption of the ruling party and lack of opportunities for youth advancement. Though produced by youth and understood locally as youth music, the sounds were inescapable in public transport, markets, and parties. The musical style is a combination of local idioms and West African hip-hop. The lyrics present a young people's moral universe in stark contrast to that of their elders.[19]

The use of music as an aesthetic and authentic form of communicating their daily lived experiences created a space for young people to engage the state and present their perceptions of what a normal society for young people should be. Their ability to take the moral high ground when compared to the ruling elites pointed at the urgent desire for change in the country. Additionally, the songs by musicians opened discussions on the core issues undermining the human security of Sierra Leoneans. Thus, the elections were primarily issues based, unlike previous elections that were grounded in ethnic affiliations and tribal sentiments.

---

18   Englert, "Ambiguous Relationships," 71.
19   Shepler, "Youth Music and Politics in Postwar Sierra Leone," 1.

In his song "Borbor Pain," depicting the life of suffering young people in Sierra Leone, Emmerson[20] sang:

> Mi nah borbor pain ar no go runaway [I am a sufferer, I will never run away]
> e too bad e too bad so so struggle [Things are too bad, too bad, too much struggle]
> en di struggle everyday e de double [And the struggle is adding-up everyday]
> nah so wi go die pan de struggle [This is how we will die in the struggle]
> di system too hot na di jungle [The system is too difficult in the jungle]
> but idle wi life [And our lives are idle]
> noto so noto so e for be O
> noto so noto so e for be O noto so noto so . . . [not how it should be, not how it should be . . .]
> na di system na e mek ar dry so [It is the system that is making me lose weight]
> but mi nah borbor pain nosi ar no de go [But I am a sufferer, I will go nowhere]
> leh wi bear yeah? [Let us endure yeah?]
> wi nah borbor pain [We are sufferers.]

The song touches on the insufferable conditions that youth contend with, with the jungle motif suggesting that Sierra Leone is a lawless and wild postcolonial national entity where it is difficult for young people, who mostly suffer, to survive. The emphasis on the words "struggle" and "sufferers" connotes a sense of desperation and frustration amid a stifling environment that generally affects the fortunes of young people. The reference to the "system that is making me lose weight" speaks to the pervasive socioeconomic deprivation, mostly attributable to corruption and bad governance, which has led to the marginalization of youth but also to the immiseration of the entire populace.

Similarly, in the 2005 Jungle Leaders song "The System," they noted the plight of poor people in Sierra Leone and the effects of bad governance

---

20 Emmerson Amidu Bockarie is an Afropop singer who became prominent in the mid-2000s with his songs on corruption and social change. He has remained one of the most popular Sierra Leonean artists. Some of his songs on corruption and social change include "Borbor Bele," "2 Fut Aata," "Survivor," and "Yesterday Betteh Pass Tiday."

within a failed system that they perceive to be antipoor. Rather than working for the interest of the ordinary citizens, the ruling elites have turned against the very people they represent. Some of the lyrics of the song below speak specifically to economic hardship, corruption, unmet needs, and unfulfilled promises by the government:

> Papa nor dae wok [Father isn't working]
> Mama nor get mohni [Mother doesn't have money]
> Ar wan go skul, but the system make ar worri [I want to go to school, but the system worries me]
> D poh man sorri [The poor man is pathetic]
> as E sik so nar berrin [When he falls ill, he dies]
> How for liv dis life wae u nor get mohni [How do we live this life when you don't have money?]
>
> As u wake so nar mohnin [As you wake up in the morning]
> Nar d system yu dae see [The system is the first thing you see]
> Everyday dem promise [Every day they make promises]
> Never fulfill am for wi [Never to be fulfilled for us]
>
> School don open [Schools have re-opened]
> Tem for pay skul fee [It's time to pay school fees]
> Say di poh pipul dem still dae wondri [The poor are still worried]
> Korrupshion, bot dis tem E for don [Corruption, but this time it should end]
> Imagine Le 1.8 Billion wae jus los nar d bank [Imagine Le 1.8 billion disappeared in the bank]
> Wae d pipul ask dehm dis kweshion [When the people ask them this question]
> Den nor ansa [They did not answer]
> wetin we dae pa [What are we up to?]

Like "Borbor Pain," "The System" is an immensely popular hit and has remained one of the most popular songs in Sierra Leone for more than a decade. Not only did these popular songs convey a sense of despondency by a frustrated youth generation, but they also powerfully conveyed the wider anxiety and general sense of betrayal felt by ordinary people on the streets. The songs embodied the collective sentiments held by the people who lacked avenues of public expression. It is no wonder, then, that the songs succeeded in shifting public opinion against the government. With this shift, the ruling SLPP eventually lost to the opposition party, the APC, in the 2007 elections.

A youth activist had this to say on the influence of music on the outcome of the elections:

> Even though there were several factors responsible for the government losing the 2007 elections, one cannot deny the fact that the social consciousness promoted by local artists created the foundations for the willingness for change. The songs were used by opposition parties to their own advantage during campaign rallies and gradually the chances of the government retaining power dwindled and they lost the elections .[21]

Changes in the Music Industry 2008–16

The success of this youth-based activist movement in the music industry and its subsequent attraction of business-minded people inaugurated a shift from songs focused on social change to those with a Western orientation. As youths began to have access to transnational images/imageries and texts of popular artists and icons from the West, especially the United States and the United Kingdom, they began to imitate Western artists such as Eminem, Tupac, Jay-Z, and 50 Cent. They also began to aspire to the celebrity status of American rap artists and Hollywood stars and modeled themselves along the East-West divide that had started more than two decades earlier among rappers in the United States.[22]

Halifu Osumare (2008), Jesse Weaver Shipley (2012), and Brad Weiss (2009) have contributed to the rich literature on globalization and the transnational effects of Western music and artists on popular arts in Africa. The influence of Western music and artists on the evolution of popular arts culture in Africa in the last decades is an indication of the extent to which globalization has made it possible for African youths to access images/imageries and other cultural resources from the West. This has to some extent succeeded in shaping, for instance, the style and content of some

---

21   Interview conducted in Freetown on July 21, 2019.
22   It is worth mentioning that prior to the influence of Western artists, youths in armed groups such as the RUF and the West Side Boys were known for showing a Western influence with similar songs, graffiti art, and hip-hop clothes. In fact, the West Side Boys were named after the West Side Boys in the United States that Tupac and other famous artists had been part of. (See the work of Boima Tucker, "Musical Violence: Gangsta Rap and Politics in Politics.")

of the songs produced by local artists, as they are tweaked to have Western outlooks.

In the late 2000s in Sierra Leone, Amara Denis Turay (aka Kao Denero), a popular rapper, formed a record company called the Black Leo Entertainment, also known as Black Leo Family. Alhaji Bankaria Bah (aka LAJ), another rap artist who was regarded as Kao's rival formed the Red Flag Movement (RFM).[23] The colors of the Black Leo Entertainment are blue and black while that of RFM is red. The rivalry between the two groups intensified as they struggled to expand their fan base and claim supremacy over the other.[24]

This cultural war between opposing youth groups culminated in the evolution of gangs and clique-related violence in Sierra Leone. The social space was once again recalibrated, with the focus being on mobilizing young people to express themselves using violence. This change undermined the effectiveness with which young artists once contested social injustices and advocated for change in their society. As David Massaquoi, a lecturer at the Department of Peace and Conflict Studies, University of Sierra Leone, noted:

> The violence affected the agency that had been generated by young artists. The contribution to social issues became marginal and the focus was on attacking each other. The lack of an effective opposition and the failure on the part of academics to take on key issues had left artists as the voice of the people. That voice was lost for a while as desperate and marginalized youths adopted gangs and cliques as a social pathway to recognition and identity. Additionally, politicians focused on destroying the common voice that musicians had through politicizing them. Thus, there were those who were pro-government and those against government and that also led to tension and division among artists.[25]

The continued failure on the part of the state to address the challenges that young people were facing rendered them vulnerable and exposed to social acts of violence. Not only did young people become pawns in the perverse regime of the weaponization of violence and the instrumentalization of disorder by the ruling class, they were often hapless victims of a new regime of violence masterminded by their older compatriots. Thus, between 2012 and

---

23 Both Kao and LAJ had lived in the United States for several years, and it appears that they were inspired to play music while they were living there.
24 Office of National Security, "Youth and Emerging Crimes in Sierra Leone," 24.
25 Interview conducted in Freetown on July 25, 2019.

2017, Sierra Leone experienced a rash of violence because of the transformations in the music industry and the culture of violence it started promoting. An indigenous culture industry created by young people to narrativize the struggles of everyday life and to comment on the failure of the postwar ruling elite became an unwitting ally in the very system that it sought to challenge and change. A vulnerable youth generation, constantly preyed upon by postcolonial ruling elites primarily driven by greed and primitive accumulation, was simultaneously victimized and became unwitting tools of a failed state.

Another factor that came to negatively impact the industry was the perception of politicization of artists. A popular music producer then, Abdul Rahman Kamara, in an interview claimed:

> After the 2007 elections, everything changed. Political parties did their best to have the artists supporting them. If you sing a song that they believe is in their favour, they become happy with you, if they believe it goes against them, they get their supporters to go after you. Musicians openly took sides and that was not good for the country. Artists also took to making money from politicians and some sang songs for them that were critical of other parties and politicians. This did not help us, it made us look cheap and dishonest but that was what the politicians wanted, and they succeeded.[26]

It appears that sensing the impact that the artists had made on the 2007 elections, political parties either courted or discredited artists they believed were opposed to them. Respondents claimed that this became common during the drive to the 2012 elections. Popular musicians were either co-opted into powerful political blocks or were paid to be quiet. This culture of silence or co-optation into the reigning political culture of corruption undermined and weakened the initial activism and social movement ethos that animated and sustained politically conscious music by young artists in Sierra Leone.

"We Can't Let Them Ignore Us": Prospects and Challenges to Changes Desired by Youth in Sierra Leone

Even though a pervasive culture of violence and popular perception of the politicization of artists have permeated the music industry for almost a

---

26 Interview conducted in Freetown on July 26, 2019.

decade, this trend started changing after 2015. Musicians have once again started producing songs addressing critical socioeconomic and political issues. The 2016 hit song "Munku Boss Pan Matches" by Emmerson went a long way in characterizing as inept and corrupt then President Ernest Bai Koroma and the officials of his government. The song triggered another wave of heated public discussions on politics and the economy. It was produced at a time when Sierra Leone was going through difficult transitions due to the deadly Ebola virus disease (EVD)[27] and the economic meltdown from the fall in the price of iron ore in the world market. The twin challenges, coupled with the 2017 mudslide that killed over a thousand people in Sierra Leone, succeeded in further deepening economic hardship, poverty, and unemployment in the country (Bangura 2018). The revival of activist songs that once again inspired social consciousness had a direct impact on the conversations in the ataya bases. Ben Turay, the president of the Union of Ataya Bases in Sierra Leone had this to say:

> The songs that started coming such as "Munku Boss Pan Matches," "Good Do" by Emerson and "Big Trouble nar Small Salone" by LAJ and Rahim the Wizard were refreshing, and they re-energized the young population and Ataya Bases started discussing the songs in relation to the challenges that the country was contending with. The discussions were usually very heated as supporters of the ruling APC party and the opposition SLPP debated on politics and the economy. [28]

For almost fifteen years, Emmerson remained one of the leading artists, producing songs that inspired social and political debates and changes in the country. The popular perception of his neutrality in relation to national politics appears to have provided him with a credibility that gets people to listen to and respect the messages in his songs. Speaking on *Emmerson* and his constant contributions to popular music on socioeconomic and political issues, a social commentator named Alhassan Kamara[29] noted:

> Emmerson has contributed more than any artist to socio-political consciousness in Sierra Leone. He is fearless, brave and intelligent. His songs draw on issues that bother the common man and he produces songs on every government, which has earned him a high level of credibility that others do not have.

---

27 The EVD led to the loss of over 2536 lives with 17,318 cases reported in Sierra Leone from 23 May 2014 through January 31, 2015. See https://www.ncbi.nlm.nih.gov/pmc/articles/PMC5528867/, accessed July 26, 2019.
28 Interview conducted in Freetown on July 26, 2019.
29 Interview conducted in Freetown on July 24, 2019.

Similar to what happened during the 2012 elections, several artists took sides during the 2018 elections, which undermined their ability to provide the kind of neutral voice that appeared to exist during the 2007 elections. For instance, LAJ openly supported and campaigned for the APC and Kao Denero supported a new political party, the National Grand Coalition (NGC) led by Kandeh Kolleh Yumkella, a retired UN career diplomat. Kamara, who is quoted above, further indicated:

> The active involvement of musicians such as LAJ and Kao Denero in politics during the 2018 elections dented their credibility and the lens with which people look at them. They do produce incredibly good songs, but they are tagged as the voices of certain political parties rather than as artists that desire genuine changes in their society.[30]

Inasmuch as it is not wrong for musicians to be associated with and openly campaign for and defend political parties, based on the interviews conducted it appears that people want musicians to remain neutral, which gives them a semblance of objectivity and authenticity. This desire was expressed by a member of the Model Junction Ataya Base:

> Over the years, the academics, civil society and opposition parties have failed us. They kept quiet when everything that could go wrong, went wrong in Sierra Leone. They left us in the wilderness, and we could only count on our musicians to speak up for us. The prospect of losing them to politicians is not good for poor and voiceless Sierra Leoneans. They are what we have; we have lost everyone else.[31]

The hold on music and the psychological satisfaction derived from it as a source of voice and hope for the marginalized populace will only remain true if the songs are perceived to be authentic. While questions such as "Have the elites been listening?" and "Do they care?" were asked during interviews for this chapter, what people want to see is the persistence of artists in reminding the ruling elites of their duties and responsibilities to them.

Between 2017 and 2019, a new generation of youthful artists with little knowledge of the civil war emerged. They appear to be modernizing the music industry, which raises both hope and doubts as indicated by respondents. Ninety percent of the respondents indicated that they would like to see artists remaining vocal on sociopolitical issues and serving as the voice of Sierra

---

30 Interview conducted in Freetown on July 24, 2019.
31 Interview conducted in Freetown on July 12, 2019.

Leoneans. A young artist, Simche Lansana, popularly known as Protégé,[32] had a reassuring note in relation to the concerns of the respondents:

> As artists, we should serve a greater purpose other than ourselves. Music is the hope of the people and we will not deny them that. Young artists are equally affected daily by the poverty and economic hardship in the country. The music revolution will continue until the changes that people want to see are achieved.

Conclusion

For several decades, local music has been popular in Sierra Leone, with artists producing popular songs that are listened to across different generations. However, between 1991 and 2002, the country experienced a bloody civil war resulting from years of bad governance, corruption, and the marginalization of youth and women, among several other factors. With the inability of the government to address the historical legacies of the conflict and overcome the postwar challenges, young people started reengineering the social space, building a conscious political constituency, using popular arts, mostly in the form of popular hip-hop music to engage the state. Thus, between 2003 and 2007 a significant number of young artists started producing popular music that voiced the everyday socioeconomic and political challenges in their society. In the absence of official avenues to interact with the state and express legitimate grievances against the system, ordinary Sierra Leoneans came to accept these artists as their political voice and as wider representatives of the conscience of the country.

With the quality of the songs produced and the huge fan base they have amassed, young artists such as Emmerson, Jungle Leaders, Pupa Baja, and Baw-Waw Society succeeded in shaping the conversations and narratives around issues that young people and the general society contend with on a daily basis including corruption, bad governance, unemployment, and poverty. The songs analyzed in this chapter by Emmerson and Jungle Leaders provide particularly good insight into the style of lyrics that are produced mostly using a mix of Krio and English. However, these initial gains were gravely affected by changes in the music industry, as the rivalry between artists led to the evolution of cliques and gang-related violence at the end of the 2000s. Another factor that undermined the agency of artists was the popular

---

32   Interview conducted in Freetown on July 28, 2019.

perception that some of them were being corrupted by certain political interests, hence they lost the neutrality and authenticity that surrounded the industry in the immediate postwar period. In spite of the setbacks in the music industry, the outbreak of the deadly EVD, the collapse of the economy between 2015 and 2016, the mudslide in Freetown, and ordinary citizens' perceptions of corruption and bad governance, there was a resurgence in social consciousness and a renewed quest for identity among the new generation of musicians and some of the older artists. The people's lack of confidence in the political elites, public institutions, academics, and civil society, has left the artists as the perceived voice and conscience of the Sierra Leonean society, a role the young hip-hop artists themselves are keen to continue to play in the foreseeable future.

Bibliography

Adedeji, Wale. "African Popular Culture and the Path of Consciousness: Hip Hop and the Culture of Resistance in Nigeria," *Postcolonial Text* 8, no. 3–4, (2013): 1–18.

Abdullah, Ibrahim. "Bush Path to Destruction: The Origin and Character of the Revolutionary United Front/Sierra Leone." *Journal of Modern African Studies* 36, no. 2: (1998): 203–35.

Bangura, Ibrahim. "Bridging the Gulf: Civil Society and the Quest for Peace and Security in Sierra Leone." *Journal of African Peace and Security* 1 (2018): 36–50.

———. "Peacebuilding in Sierra Leone One and a Half Decades after the Civil War: At What Stage Does a War-Affected Country Cease to Be Post-conflict?" In K. Omeje (ed.), 91–110. *Peacebuilding in Contemporary Africa: In Search of Alternative Strategies.* New York: Routledge, 2018.

———. "We Can't Eat Peace: Youth, Sustainable Livelihood and the Peacebuilding Process in Sierra Leone." *Journal for Peacebuilding and Development* 11, no. 2: (2016): 37–50.

Brett, Rachel, and Irma Specht. *Young Soldiers: Why They Choose to Fight.* Boulder, CO: Lynne Rienner, 2004.

Englert, Brigit. "Ambiguous Relationships: Youth, Popular Music and Politics in Contemporary Tanzania." *Stichproben. Wiener Zeitschrift für kritische Afrikastudien* 14, no. 8 (2008): 71–96.

Kaur, Harpreet. "Sister Fa and Nneka—21st Century Global Diplomats: The Symbiosis between Music and Politics Explored through Female West African Artists." Master's Thesis, School of Sociology, Politics and International Studies, University of Bristol, UK, 2013.

Kennelly, Jacqueline, Stuart Poyntz, and Paul Ugor. "Special Issue Introduction:

Youth, Cultural Politics, and New Social Spaces in an Era of Globalization." *Review of Education, Pedagogy, and Cultural Studies* 31, no. 4 (2009): 255–69.

Koroma, Abdul Karim. *Crisis and Intervention in Sierra Leone* s.l.: Freetown, Sierra Leone: Andromeda, 2004.

Office of National Security. "An Assessment of the Youth Situation and Emerging Crimes in Sierra Leone." Freetown, Sierra Leone: Office of National Security, 2016.

Osumare, Halifu. "Global Hip-Hop and the African Diaspora." In *Black Cultural Traffic: Crossroads in Global Performance and Popular Culture*, edited by Harry J. Ellam Jr. and Kennell Jackson, 266–88. Ann Arbor: University of Michigan Press, 2008.

Peters, Krijn. "The Crisis of Youth in Post War Sierra Leone: Problem Solved?" in *Africa Today* 58, no. 2: (2011): 129–53.

Richards, Paul. *Fighting for the Rain Forest: War, Youth and Resources in Sierra Leone*. London: The International African Institute with James Currey, 1996.

———. "Young Men and Gender in War and Postwar Reconstruction: Some Comparative Findings from Liberia and Sierra Leone." In *The Other Half of Gender: Men's Issues in Development Washington*, edited by I. Bannon and M. C. Correia. Washington, DC: World Bank, 2006.

Schumann, Anne. "Music at War: Reggae Musicians as Political Actors in the Ivoirian Crisis." *Journal of African Cultural Studies* 27, no. 3, (2015): 1–14.

Shipley, Jesse Weaver. *Living the Hiplife: Celebrity and Entrepreneurship in Ghanaian Popular Music*, Durham: Duke University Press, 2012.

Shepler, Susan. "Youth Music and Politics in Post-war Sierra Leone." *Journal of Modern African Studies*, 48, no. 4 (2010): 627–42.

Stevens, Siaka Probyn. *What Life has Taught Me: The Stevens Family*. Freetown, Sierra Leone, printed by author, 1984.

Street, John. *Politics and Popular Culture*. Oxford: Polity, 1997.

TRCSL. *Truth and Reconciliation Commission's Reports*. 3 vols. Sierra Leone, 2004.

Wai, Zubairu. "Musical Artists and Social Change in Sierra Leone: A Reflection." *Patriotic Vanguard*, Freetown, Sierra Leone (2005). http://www.thepatrioticvanguard.com/musical-artists-and-social-change-in-sierra-leone- a-reflection. Accessed July 11, 2019.

Weis, Brad. *Street Dreams and Hip-Hop Barbershops: Global Fantasy in Urban Tanzania*. Bloomington: Indiana University Press, 2009.

Chapter Five

The Politics of Pleasure in Nigerian Afrobeats

Paul Ugor

The domains of leisure and consumption promote socialization of the self with the help of generation co-members aware of their shared history and destiny. When using new media (and engaging in leisure and consumption) young people are, virtual or real, regarded as fuller members of their community.
—Henk Vinken, "Changing Life Courses, New Media, and Citizenship."

Introduction

Although it has become common in African cultural studies to rate Nollywood as the most popular art form in Africa,[1] it is perhaps more accurate to argue that the booming and vivacious Afro hip-hop music is unquestionably the popular arts genre with the highest mass appeal in Africa today. The continental reach and global popularity of Afro hip-hop were brought home to me in the summer of 2015 when I embarked on a research trip to Ghana, Kenya, Nigeria, and Uganda. The music of Nigerian Afrobeat superstars such as Timaya, Flavour, Davido, Whizkid, Tiwa Savage, and other young musicians from Nigeria was being played enthusiastically in bars, nightclubs, hotel lobbies, public buses, street shops, radio and television

---

1   See Haynes, *Nollywood*; Haynes and Okome, "Evolving Popular Media"; and Krings and Okome, *Global Nollywood*.

stations, private homes, and on personal cell phones. Not only did people know the lyrics of these artists' songs, but they could dance to the music with the unique swag of the average Nigerian urban youth. This inescapable presence of contemporary Nigerian Afrobeats across Africa is not unique, for it emblematizes the wider popularity of the hip-hop genre beyond the continent's shores. As Khalil Saucier has observed, "Today, hip hop is arguably the fastest growing component of African youth culture. It can be heard in vibrant and chaotic urban areas and desolate and pastoral rural areas of Africa. It can be heard in both private and public spaces, while being piped through loudspeakers of one's personal music device."[2] With its current population of about 1.2 billion, out of which almost 77 percent are young people below the age of thirty-five, there is no doubt that the Afro hip-hop genre, created and patronized by African youth, is the most popular art form in the continent today. Thus, any meaningful conversation on popular arts culture in Africa must continue to address the place of this popular genre as it stands at the very center of the continent's cultural imagination.

Beyond the wild popularity of Nigerian Afrobeats music in many African countries, however, I was also particularly struck by the lyrical, sonic, visual, and thematic shifts in the songs and music videos of the artists. Born and raised in Nigeria, I was already a young adult by the early 1990s when popular Nigerian hip-hop music exploded onto the nation's entertainment scene. It had an unmistakable critical edge to it. Popular artists like Daddy Showkey, Baba Fryo, Sound Sultan, Eadris Abdulkarim, Duncan Mighty, T-Face Idibia, and other early hip-hop musicians who emerged from the local slums in Lagos and elsewhere railed against the hardships and vicissitudes of postcolonial urban life, the sickening indifference and unbridled greed of the political elite, the chronic lack of electricity and other social amenities, the precariousness of life in urban slums, and the general struggles of the working poor trapped in the underbellies of large cities in Nigeria. This musical style's particular mixed heritage is rooted in indigenous musical forms like Juju music, Afrobeat, highlife, and various traditional ethnic music forms, combined with elements of reggae, American rap, and R&B music. The criticality of this emerging urban youth culture was what made Nigerian hip-hop so popular among the youthful urban audience. Traced to the American hip-hop of black youth that emerged in the United States in the late 1970s, the leftist ideological commitment of early Nigerian hip-hop music is not surprising. As several studies on hip-hop have shown, the

---

2 Saucier, "Introduction: Hip-hop Culture in Red, Black, and Green," xiv.

genre emerged as a cultural tool and creative space for despondent African American and Latino youth in US inner cities to tell their own stories of everyday struggles and survival in the context of socioeconomic hardships and racial violence.[3]

Facing relentless racial discrimination, economic inequality, widespread political and socioeconomic disenfranchisement, and structural violence in the US justice system, black youth in the Bronx, Harlem and Washington Heights (New York), Compton and South Central (Los Angeles) and East Oakland and Marin County (northern California) turned to a popular genre created by young people themselves to convey their frustrations, express their anxieties and fears, and lament the deleterious impact of state violence and racial capitalism on black lives and other minorities in postsegregation America. Hip-hop in America thus began as a creative response by marginalized urban youth to "America's unfulfilled promise of economic inequality and inclusion."[4] David Toop eloquently captures the adverse socioeconomic conditions that gave rise to America's most vibrant urban youth culture when he notes how hip-hop arose out of a postsegregation era in which "ideals were shattered to be replaced by poverty and drugs, the despair that comes when high optimism goes unfulfilled."[5] So African American and Latino youth in America's inner cities, descendants of slaves and immigrants, "created an art form that responded to poverty and oppression, joblessness and police brutality, to drug wars and gang violence."[6] Although founded and popularized in the United States as the urban culture of marginalized youth, hip-hop soon struck a chord with many black, brown, red, and other disaffected youth globally because of what Halifu Osumare calls "hip hop's connective marginalities,"[7] referring here to the functional ways in which the genre's narratives of human suffering, dehumanization, and marginality—and the general existential anxiety these experiences create—resonated powerfully with disenfranchised youth globally. Hip-hop's gripping resonance with marginalized youth globally is thus an example of how black popular culture

---

3   See Basu, *The Vinyl Ain't Final*; Kitwana, *Hip Hop Generation*; and Toop, *Rap Attack 3*.
4   Kitwana, *Hip Hop Generation*, xx.
5   Toop, *Rap Attack 3*, xvi.
6   Jackson, "Introduction," xii.
7   Osumare, "Global Hip-Hop and the African Diaspora," 267.

travels internationally across nations and vast racial, ethnic, class, gender, and religious groups.[8]

It is no surprise, then, that the initial phase of Nigerian Afro hip-hop in the early 1990s and 2000s was as politically conscious as its source of inspiration in the United States. In his 2006 hit, "E Be Like Say," Tu-Face Idibia, for example, dedicates the song to "all the shady politicians" in Nigeria, reminding the ruling elite that power and wealth mean nothing if the people they represent do not have quality education, a functional health-care system, good road networks, and cannot live in peace and harmony among themselves. Creatively constituted as a forewarning to an inattentive and perhaps uncritical electorate, the song cautioned the masses to beware of the duplicity of Nigerian politicians who have mastered the lexicon of a global democratic culture and were now returning every four years to ask the people for support with bogus promises of improving social infrastructure and their everyday lives.[9] For TuFace and other pioneer Nigerian hip-hop artists, if their nation had become crisis ridden and unsafe, it wasn't because the ordinary wo/man on the street did not do his or her part; rather, it was because the politicians have failed in doing their jobs as public servants. The story of the rise and popularity of politically conscious hip-hop in Nigeria and other places in the continent is an interesting one: what it does illuminate is a global cultural traffic in which, as Kelly Jackson notes, "performances and representations derived from black cultural material have shown enormous mobility. They can end up in unlikely places, in contradictory alliances, can take on new and unintended forms, and can synthesize radically disparate materials."[10]

I have cited the above examples of politically conscious hip-hop in Nigeria only to foreground the shift in the lyrical focus of contemporary Nigerian hip-hop indicated at the beginning of this chapter. The version of Nigerian hip-hop I heard as I traveled across West and East Africa in the summer of 2015 was different. Both the lyrics and images seemed less political and more about material wealth and consumption; fame, glamor, style, and celebrity culture; love, sex, romance, and eroticism; image, performativity, and urban identity; transnational mobility and hybrid selves; high-class fashion, accoutrements of postmodern life such as glitzy cars, expensive media technology, lavish parties, mega-city landscapes, and beautiful young women, African

---

8   Elam and Jackson, *Black Cultural Traffic*.
9   Idibia, "E Be Like Say."
10   Jackson, "Introduction," 5.

and non-African alike. It is no surprise, then, that cultural critics are beginning to rail against this genre of popular music and asking crucial questions about the sociocultural expediency of this popular urban youth culture. In a highly controversial newspaper article, Rueben Abati, the famous Nigerian journalist, mounted a scathing critique of the supposedly depoliticized Nigerian hip-hop, arguing that it was a sign of a nation experiencing cultural crisis. Comparing the hip-hop artists to the earlier musicians of the 1970s and 1980s, Abati contended that Nigerian hip-hop has neither "meaning" nor "polish":

> Music is about sense, sound, shape and skills. But there is an on-going deficit in all other aspects except sound. So much sound is being produced in Nigeria, but there is very little sense, shape and skills. They call it hip-hop. They try to imitate Western hip pop stars. They even dress like them. The boys don't wear trousers on their waists: the new thing is called "sagging", somewhere below the waist it looks as if the trouser is about to fall off. The women are struggling to expose strategic flesh as Janet Jackson once did. The boys and the girls are cloaked in outlandish jewellery and their prime heroes are Ja-Rule, Lil'Wayne, Fat Joe, P. Diddy, 50 Cents, Ronz Brown, Chris Brown, Sean Kingston, Nas, Juelz Santana, Akon . . . Well, God Almighty, we are in your hands![11]

Although Abati conceded that this popular genre created by urban youth has brought Nigeria tremendous international recognition, he argued that Afro hip-hop is a cultural sign that "Nigeria is suffering from an identity crisis imposed on it in part by an emergent generation of irreverent and creative young Nigerians who are revising old norms and patterns."[12] Abati's acerbic reproach of Afrobeats is not new because American hip-hop itself has experienced such disparagement. Zoe Spencer's reading of American hip-hop concedes that "hip hop was the voice of the brothers and sisters who may have otherwise been written off—whose voices may have otherwise never been heard,"[13] but insists that the genre has been infiltrated and contaminated by American corporate interests. For Spencer, hip-hop as a collective entertainment culture among black urban youth has witnessed a weakening of its moral and cultural authority: "What they call "Hip-Hop" is a lie. It hates me, abuses me, hates and abuses itself and others. It abuses the concept of brother and sisterhood, Black identity, Black love, real relationships

---

11   Abati, "A Nation's Identity Crisis," 9.
12   Abati, 9.
13   Spencer, *Murda,' Misogyny, and Mayhem,* xi.

foundations, the black body, family, Black life and death, Black babies—and the Black community (the place where it was born)."[14] Like Abati, Spencer berates hip-hop for its "heavy beats that are accompanied by unintelligible verses, and clear and repetitive hooks that glorify money, women's behinds, guns, violence, sex, drugs, murder, and even one's own death or brush with death."[15]

Bakari Kitwana has also noted how the hip-hop genre, while making it possible for minority youth in the United States to make associations between blackness and poverty, it has ironically participated in promoting "anti-intellectualism, ignorance, irresponsible parenthood, and criminal lifestyles."[16] These harsh critiques of hip-hop are in fact not unique, as there is evidence that other popular music genres in Africa, in Nigeria at least, felt a pushback from the cultural elites. Wolfgang Bender, for example, has noted how the "stalky" jazz musicians in southern Nigeria and their fans were outraged when Bobby Benson introduced popular jazz music in 1947. To the educated African elite who were the jazz enthusiasts, "Jazz and social dancing was cultivated entertainment for respectable 'tamed negroes.'" But Bobby Benson later introduced popular jazz that was rather "savage . . . even vulgar."[17] Here, we see how popular music, whether created by youths or other artists both within and outside Africa, has often been scorned for its supposed lack of cultural refinement and political edge.

Although Abati was challenged by Afrobeats industry insiders, his harsh indictment of contemporary Nigerian hip-hop is significant in many ways. His critique functioned not only as a condemnation of the perceived vulgarization of a popular musical genre but also of its depoliticization. It was not just an expression of the cultural anxieties of the metropolitan elites about the prominence of youth in the public space but also served as a powerful criticism of Afrobeats' supposed political bankruptcy, especially its obsessive textualization of images of pleasure and enjoyment. I contend, however, that the problem is not so much with hip-hop as it is with African cultural elites who lack the critical skills and conceptual tools to make sense of emerging urban youth cultures and their unique aesthetics and unusual content, all of which fall outside of the normative patterns of meaning-making practices that Abati is so familiar with. As P. Khalil Saucier has argued, "Hip hop is

---

14 Spencer, xv.
15 Spencer, xvii.
16 Kitwana, *Hip Hop Generation,* xxi.
17 Bender, *Sweet Mother,* 88.

seen by many African youth not so much as a loss of culture and tradition [as Abati suggests] than as an addition. Like many things in Africa, things appropriated from outside are forever signified and reconfigured in locally meaningful ways."[18]

While the preponderance of imageries of material pleasure and consumption in Nigerian Afrobeats music has put the genre under intense scrutiny for its depoliticization, I'm interested in thinking about what "pleasure" might mean for young people in the context of postcolonial privation and existential crisis and how they integrate those meanings into popular art and culture such as Afro hip-hop. My aim is not to mount a moral critique that accounts for the appropriateness (or otherwise) of surplus images of pleasure in Afrobeats music but simply to explain why those images are there in the first place and how they function as aesthetic elements and new ways of being for young people in increasingly uncertain and perilous postcolonial conditions. I believe that the desire, intensity, kind, and the place where pleasure takes place all combine to tell us something not just about young people but also about the larger society itself. As Paul Zeleza has noted,

> It should not be so hard to understand the connections between leisure and transgressive behaviour, for after all, leisure involves a search for limit experience and moral transcendence; it constitutes a liminal time and space where the moral prohibitions of the conventional legal-rational order are commonly questioned, standardized and routine practices discarded, and repressed aggressive and sexual emotion vented.[19]

In her analysis of the dialectical relationship between pleasure and politics in African screen media, Lindiwe Dovey also calls attention to the manifold ways in which "many forms of local, domestic culture—including music, humour, 'heritage', comic books, writing, dance, African languages, and poetry" are all actively engaged in what she calls a "profound performance of the 'pleasure of politics' as well as the 'politics of pleasure.'"[20] Acutely aware of the contemporaneous conversations about how globalization has made possible the transnational circulation of global cultural resources for African youth, mostly in the form of images of consumption and other symbolic

---

18   Saucier, "Introduction," xx.
19   Zeleza, "Introduction," xvi.
20   Dovey, "African Film and Video," 3.

cultural goods,[21] I am particularly invested in building on these arguments to think more deeply and specifically about how pleasure functions both as a creative and discursive field for marginalized youth in Africa who have been systematically denied access to the consumer goods and other luxuries of life that their peers elsewhere take for granted. In doing so, I aim to elaborate on Deborah Posel's arguments against conservative understandings of consumption and pleasure and argue that historical contexts are significant factors in assessing when and how pleasure becomes a defining cultural force in postmodern life.[22]

I proceed from two premises. The first is Karin Barber's view that the "musical idiom can express not just cultural alignments and aspirations, but a new consciousness among its producers and consumers. It can be the locus where an emerging class consciousness is forged."[23] I'm interested in Nigerian Afrobeats not only as a musical idiom that documents social change but also as cultural repertoire defined by certain sociohistorical forces that then deploy a vast arsenal of aesthetic resources, including seemingly innocuous pastimes like pleasure in its articulation of a kind of political consciousness among young people and the wider society. I am inspired by Wolfgang Bender's position that "it is impossible to exclude history and politics from the study of musical developments."[24] So, while Abati and other conservative cultural elites may not see important meanings and sociopolitical, cultural, and moral values in contemporary Nigerian hip-hop, I aim to use the genre to demonstrate the ways in which pleasure in general operates as a useful aesthetic tool for young artists seeking to express covert moral and political messages to themselves and the world around them.

Second, I take as a point of entry the views of Stuart Hall and Johannes Fabian: that black popular culture has huge epistemological weight and discursive value not so much because it is consumed so widely, in this case by young people, but precisely because it is the site of contestations over the social meanings that ultimately shape how we see ourselves in relation to the larger world.[25] Popular culture offers us the dominant codes from where we

---

21 See Weaver, *Hiplife*; Osumare, "Global Hip-Hop and the African Diaspora"; and Weis, *Street Dreams and Hip-Hop Barbershops*.
22 See "Races to Consume."
23 Barber, "Popular Arts in Africa," 58.
24 Bender, *Sweet Mother*, 74.
25 Hall, "Notes on Deconstructing the Popular"; and Fabian, *Moments of Freedom*.

constitute the meanings that come to define how we operate socially. So, I'm interested in thinking about the ways in which pleasure functions as a cultural code for young people seeking to create meanings around their lives—their hopes, aspirations, and dreams—in an austere social environment habitually marked by the absence of pleasure. I engage with the discourse of pleasure and consumption in relation to Afro hip-hop as youth culture because I not only recognize its mass appeal, but as Khalil Saucier argues, I recognize how that popularity rests on the genre's ability to provide a sociocultural "space where African youth voice their opinions and participate in open, public discourse in ways that are often not possible through more traditional avenues of political and cultural participation."[26] It is the genre's unconventionality, both in terms of its content and form, that makes it culturally expedient as a discursive tool in the public domain. So to read it along the conventions of mainstream genres is counterproductive. Thus, the crucial question I address is this: what does it mean for young people to create and have access to pleasure when the overall effect of the existing postcolonial political-economic system is the denial of pleasure? I contend that much of the cultural anxiety expressed about nonmeaning, vulgarization, and the commercialization of Nigerian hip-hop are inattentive to the brutal history of relentless suffering and deprivation that contemporary Nigerian/African youth have faced since the early 1980s when neoliberal technocrats fobbed the structural adjustment program on African countries. I will attempt to map out that socioeconomic history as a way of illuminating how pleasure comes to function as a crucial tool of aesthetic formation in urban youth cultures.

Globalization, Precarity, and the Denial of Pleasure in Everyday Life in Nigeria

In her recent work tracing the expansive history of popular arts in Africa, Karin Barber notes how the forced introduction of neoliberal policies to Africa in the early 1980s, mostly in the form of privatization and deregulation, created two contradictory outcomes: "On the one hand, they made life worse for most ordinary people by increasing unemployment, removing social services and driving rural populations into hand-to-mouth existences in shanty-towns of bloated conurbations. On the other hand, they brought new goods, new connectedness, new access to international media

---

26   Saucier, "Introduction," xviii.

technology, which enabled the predominantly youthful urban population to occupy, if only provisionally and precariously, a kind of virtual global space."[27] The curious mix of extreme precarity and the superfluous circulation of new cultural resources and consumer goods in the form of media technologies has led to a flourishing regime of imaginative work in which young people are constantly creating varied cultural texts that not only help them cope with the insufferable conditions around them but also allow them the creative and critical voice to comment on the broader circumstances surrounding and shaping their lives. Thus, popular arts by African youth not only embody the social transcripts of the historical contradictions in which they are produced and consumed but also function as creative responses to those historical paradoxes. How might we then make sense of pleasure as a unique creative response to opposing historical conditions in Africa simultaneously marked by both chronic lack and excess cultural goods?

The introduction of structural adjustment policies to Africa in the mid-1980s occurred at a unique global moment in which neoliberal globalization went hand in hand with renewed processes of democratization.[28] Since so many Africans had long been ruled by brutal military dictatorships that had no oversight control from within or outside the country, democratization held a strong appeal to ordinary people because it embodied the promises and possibilities of freedom and the general restoration of human rights. Having lived under brutal military dictatorships for more than four decades, the idea of a democratic dispensation in which the rights of ordinary people were guaranteed by the constitution and other laws made by the representatives of the people had a strong fascination for nonelites. But the full social benefits of democratization, as the neoliberal argument logic went, was to open the markets, eliminate trade barriers, and allow for free transnational flow of goods and services. The argument was that a free market, combined with a free democratic society, will guarantee the democratization of wealth. The possibility of access to long-denied wealth and decent livelihoods in the era of democracy and neoliberal globalization held enormous purchase for the African populace.

But the reality on the ground was different. While military dictators were compelled by global political-economic forces to transition into what seemed

---

27   Saucier, 159.
28   Barber, *A History of African Popular Culture*; Jewsiewicki and Pype, "Popular Culture in Francophone Central Africa"; and Krings and Simmert, "African Popular Culture Enters the Global Mainstream."

like functional democracies, mostly as strategic political maneuvers to secure loans from global financial institutions like the International Monetary Fund and the World Bank, the political-economic policies these African leaders implemented on behalf of global financial organizations had devastating consequences for the people. Initially operating a national capitalism that emphasized welfarism for more than three decades, the new African democracies were forced to embrace privatization and deregulation. Aggressive privatization and deregulation meant that state-funded efforts in education, health care, housing, electricity and water, agriculture, and other crucial sectors were abandoned by the state and left solely in the hands of private investors whose primary interest lay in maximized profits. Huge cutbacks in funding for social services, mass retrenchments from the public sector, and the devaluation of national currencies all combined to trigger the collapse of indigenous industries, and with this decline came high unemployment rates, dire poverty and hunger, insecurity and crime, and a general state of unprecedented precarity experienced by people who had fought so hard for independence in hopes of a better life.

But the real social import of the neoliberal policies of the 1980s and 1990s is not to be grasped in terms of unemployment statistics and crime records. It is to be gleaned in the real impact it had on people's everyday lives. It had palpable material consequences. I remember the stories my mother told me of how she fed the entire family for a week with ₦ 5, which is perhaps less than ten cents today. Growing up in the 1980s in the era of food rations and other biting structural adjustment programs, my mother's stories of the good times of the pre-SAP (Structural Adjustment Program) era sounded like scenarios from a Nollywood movie. The direct effects of structural adjustment were the lack of income and food and, thus, hunger; needless deaths in ill-equipped hospitals with poorly trained doctors and nurses; the dearth of books, lab equipment, scholarships in schools, and thus poor-quality education; the absence of basic social services like electricity, water, and good roads—hence a poor standard of living. Privatization simply meant high prices for goods and services the people couldn't afford because of lack of jobs and wages. The lack of a steady family income also meant previous cultural pastimes such as family vacations and other forms of leisure activities that were possible because of the availability of disposable income in the pre-SAP years disappeared. The generation of Nigerian youth who grew up in the immediate post–civil war, pre-SAP era awash with petro-dollars experienced a different world from the uncertain and risky times that the contemporary Nigerian/African youth have experienced from the late 1980s onward. The youth of the post-SAP era have led brutal lives of absolute hopelessness, devoid of the necessities of life and any certainty about the future. While the younger pre-1980s generations took for granted socioeconomic services like scholarships and quality education, a reliable and functional health-care system, good electricity and water supply, good roads and a reliable public transport system, not to mention other social amenities, post-1980s youth could count on none of this. The pre-SAP youth generation, the ones ruling Nigeria today, experienced a life of plenitude, with pleasure, fun, and a general culture of leisure as their everyday reality.

Yet poor and marginalized youth and their families, in both rural and urban areas, are constantly bombarded by relentless images of excess wealth by their political leaders and their cohorts. As several studies have now shown, in the past five decades, Nigeria has earned billions of dollars in revenue from crude oil sales, but a significant chunk of that income has been stolen by the ruling elites in cahoots with their foreign allies.[29] While young people in Nigeria lead hopeless lives tormented by poverty, hunger, and a general lack of social opportunities, they see their political leaders living in palatial homes with their families, hosting lavish parties, sending their children to elite schools abroad, and flaunting their wealth in public spaces with luxurious cars and other postmodern gadgets: all part of a general culture of material extravagance displayed by the ruling elite. If politicians and other elites are not shamelessly displaying stupendous wealth, they are staging public spectacles of newfound wealth and power as Andrew Apter so astutely demonstrates in his work on the 1977 FESTAC in Lagos, Nigeria.[30] And as Michael Peel has noted in the case of the Niger Delta, as jobless and frustrated youth continue to see politicians and other local leaders "dressing well, living comfortably and driving fast cars, the understandable temptation" has been to try to imitate them or at least hang around waiting for crumbs from their tables.[31] With better communication technologies in the form of Android phones, laptop computers, and iPads, marginalized youth living in poverty can see the marked differences between their sordid lives and those of their privileged counterparts both within and outside Nigeria.

Not all African youth have reacted violently to the betrayal of their older compatriots, especially those running their crumbling postcolonial nations. While the proliferation of nonstate actors and the eruption of violence have

---

29 See Shaxson, *Poisoned Wells*; and Peel, *A Swamp Full of Dollars*.
30 See Apter, *Pan-African Nation*.
31 Peel, *A Swamp Full of Dollars*, 30.

Figure 5.1. A power generator and an improvised satellite dish designed by a young bar owner in Gbekobor Village in the Niger Delta region in Nigeria (courtesy of Paul Ugor). From this rural squalor and deprivation, the local youth who come to the bar see global images of wealth and glamour on the screen.

been the major outcomes of misgovernance and failed states in Africa, the majority of young people in Africa have turned to the informal sector to eke out a living and make sense of their lives. Despite a rigged system that is designed to prevent young people from thriving, the "flipside of a nation's abuses of power, everyday attrition and squalor [has] been a compelling story of ceaseless, inventive activity."[32] As I have argued elsewhere, "while difficult political, economic and social conditions persist across the entire African continent, Africa's youth, like their counterparts all over the world, are finding new and ingenious ways of making sense of not only their own lives, but also those of their families and communities at large."[33] This is what the Nigerian Afrobeats maestro Banky W meant in his measured response to Abati:

> Our country has not yet given us steady electricity, adequate education, safety from armed robbers or standard healthcare, yet artistes have risen like the Roses

---

32   Peel, *Swamp Full of Dollars*, xvii.
33   Ugor, "Extenuating Circumstances," 6.

that grow from Concrete . . . and these very artistes love and represent their country proudly on a global stage. This music industry has given hope, jobs and income to countless youth of today. We are Rappers, Singers, Producers, Sound Engineers, Managers, Promoters, Marketing Consultants, Record Label Owners and we will not apologize for making the best of our circumstances; and all this in spite of the fact that we have Marketers that exploit but refuse to pay for our Musical pieces, Royalties and Publishing income that hitherto has been non-existent, a Government that is just now very slowly starting to enforce anti-piracy laws, and Event Organizers that would rather pay 50 Cent One Million US Dollars than give D'banj or P-Square 5 Million Naira.[34]

At a broader social level, then, Abati's caustic critique of contemporary Nigerian Afrobeats represents an example of the many ways in which "work on 'African identities' often occludes one of the most important and fascinating aspects of the lives of youth in the postmodern Postcolony: an ability to live productively through the fractured, experimental, and decidedly unfixed nature of what it means to be African in the world today."[35] But more specifically, his analysis is indicative of how the cultural elites often misunderstand contemporary African youth cultures, especially how such readings often either ignore or misunderstand "the dialectical relationship between pleasure and politics, and the fact that—in much African screen media—this relationship is expressed in performative ways."[36]

Pleasure as Aesthetics and Protest in Contemporary Nigerian Afro Hip-Hop Music

I have sketched the fraught, contradictory existence led by contemporary Nigerian youth who, in the last three decades, have had to lead lives essentially marked by chronic deprivation on the one hand, and superfluous cultural resources made available by globalization on the other. While neoliberal globalization has brought African youth untold misery, hopelessness, and uncertainty, it has ironically also provided them new resources to craft individual and collective trajectories of survival and hope. The social import of structural adjustment for Nigerian youth, then, is that it led to the creation of serious constraints and contradictions but also new creative and social

---

34   Banky W, "Response to Mr. Reuben Abati's Article."
35   Hofmann, *War Machines*, xv.
36   Dovey, "African Film and Video," 1.

opportunities. But neoliberalism created a contradictory social environment not only for young people but for the postcolonial nation itself. In opting for an unregulated free market, privatization, and the unbridled prioritization of profits, the postcolonial nation-state has not only witnessed the weakening of its sovereign powers—with these powers now snapped up by unwieldy multinational economic empires[37]—but it also lost its moral authority to legislate on national culture, which is the main province of urban youth cultures.

In his analysis of the links between leisure culture and the political-economic forces in the era of Thatcherism and Reaganomics, Peter Bramham notes that whereas the political elites such as federal and state legislators, governors, neoliberal technocrats, policy planners, and other political tycoons could maintain cultural taste through their distribution of state resources in the form of welfare disbursement and collective consumption, neoliberal globalization and the concomitant shifts in the distributive power of cultural resources to market forces meant that the state had lost its singular authority and leverage to function as the regulator and arbiter of moral and cultural order. Having given up their place as the integument of national culture, ordinary people have been left to the mercy of global market forces. Bramham thus argues that "marketization of public services opened up a pandora's box of individualized desires that politics and society failed to regulate comfortably. Rather than an established missionary elite in control of national culture, there was the babble of diverse 'experts' providing very different discourses on lifestyles and leisure."[38] What the postmodernization of culture in the era of neoliberalism demonstrates is that consumption, pleasure, and other leisure activities are not mere innocuous pastimes, but crucial everyday cultural practices embedded with discourses heavily defined and impacted by politics and economics. What emerges is an active politics of the superficial, where visual imagery of pleasure and consumption in popular representations come to operate "as the primary form of public address not because commerce is powerful but because it addresses the public in a way that is beneficial to contemporary populations confronted at every turn by commercial interests."[39] This is what Bramham and Wagg mean when they assert that "people do make choices (and not only in leisure), but their choices are made within the structures of constraint which govern their

---

37 Hardt and Negri, *Empire*; Beck, *World Risk Society*; and Bauman, *Liquid Times*.
38 Bramham, "Choosing Leisure," 15.
39 Ommen, "Introduction," 9.

lives."[40] Pleasure is thus not that supposedly apolitical social activity as often perceived by the cultural elite but a powerful and meaningful cultural act defined by political, economic, and social contexts. Pleasure can thus function as another heuristic device through which we might make sense of social change, especially the larger social forces that shape young people's lives and the varied responses they formulate to those cultural forces.

Stuart Hall has argued that culture is not "a decorative addendum to the 'hard world' of production and things"[41] but a site of endless struggles over the meanings that come to shape the human experience. He insists that culture is now the arena of consensus and resistance where hegemonic forces arise, are secured, or forcefully contested. In the age of culturalism, therefore, culture can no longer be separated from articulations of power and globalization discourses. Culture, as David Held and Henrietta Moore argue, "is no longer something that exists outside the economy or outside of capital, but rather part of the self-definition of both capital and globalization, and a major driving force in corporate institutional innovation and in market strategization."[42] Recognizing leisure as part of culture, what I demonstrate is an example of how in a postmodern society where economic labor is no longer necessarily the center of individual lives and communities, "Leisure has become an ever-greater site of excess, escape, transgression, resistance and change."[43] As Henk Vinken argues in the chapter epigraph, pleasure can become an unconventional resource through which young people find community, socialize, and forge new ways of being and global citizenship. I will illustrate this claim by focusing on the songs and music videos of several Nigerian hip-hop musicians. I begin with the famous Nigerian Afro hip-hop artist Timaya.

Born Enitimi Alfred Odom on August 15, 1980, in Port Harcourt, River State, Timaya hails from Odi in Bayelsa State, Nigeria. A singer and songwriter, he is famous in the Nigerian and African music scene as a prodigious producer of popular Afro hip-hop genres such as Ragga, Dancehall, Afro hip-hop, Afrobeat, and Soca. Founder of the South-South hip-hop group Dem Mama Soldiers, his solo career began in 2005 when he released his single, "Dem Mama," which was later featured on his debut album, *True Story* (2007). This was followed two years later with his second album, *Gift and*

---

40 Bramham and Wagg, "Introduction," 5.
41 Hall, "Notes on Deconstructing the Popular," 79.
42 Held and Moore, "Introduction: Cultural Futures," 12.
43 Bramham and Wagg, "Introduction," 5.

Figure 5.2. Enitimi Alfred Odom, popularly known as Timaya.

Grace (2008). His national fame and global conspicuousness as an Afro hip-hop musician would come with his third studio album, *De Rebirth* (2009), featuring his lead single, "Plantain Boy."

Timaya's musical and creative output in the past decade and half shows a remarkable shift from an artist initially concerned with sociopolitical issues to one obsessed with pleasure, leisure, consumption, and other putative apolitical themes. His first major hit, "Dem-Mama," produced by K-Solo (a young producer he met in Mafoluku, Oshodi, a Lagos slum) was a bold critique of the militarization of democracy and governance in Nigeria. In an interview published in *The Punch magazine*, Timaya stated: "Dem-Mama was an account of the 1999 destruction of Odi, a river side community in Niger Delta. Soldiers were hunting down militants they alleged killed eight policemen. The village was burnt down, and numerous people killed. I bravely tackled the issue years later and won instant street credibility for my boldness." In a frantic bid to gain attention from the international community and an indifferent global corporate world, approximately fifty thousand young men and women in the oil-rich Niger Delta region in Nigeria took up arms against the Nigerian state and multinational oil corporations between 1999 and 2009. They violently agitated for self-determination and a fair treatment of the oil-producing communities by the Nigerian federal government. The angry youth blew up oil pipelines and sabotaged crude oil production in the region, kidnapped and took hostage foreign expatriates working for transnational oil companies, and bombed government offices and facilities. Unsettled by the violence, the major multinational oil companies operating in the Niger Delta feverishly withdrew staff from the oil fields and called off production, reducing national output by about 750,000 barrels per day, which at the time was roughly half the nation's daily output.[44] Desperate to restore oil production and the steady flow of oil revenues, the Nigerian federal government sent soldiers and other security forces into the Delta region to quell the violence. In Odi, Bayelsa State, seven policemen were said to have been killed by youths on November 4, 1999. The federal government responded with brutal force. A contingent of Nigerian soldiers invaded the town and mowed down everything on their path except for the community bank, the community center, and the Anglican church. Locals, mere defenseless civilians, were killed in their thousands.

Apart from the Odi, communities such as Kaiama, Yenogoa, Opia, Gbaramatu, and Okerinkoko, in Bayelsa State; Omuechem and Ogoni in Rivers; Ayakoromo and Okirika in Delta State; Egbema in Edo State; and Ilaje in Ondo State have all experienced scorched-earth operations by the Nigerian military and riot police, all supported with lethal munitions and huge financial and logistical backup by multinational oil companies.[45] And four years earlier, in November 1995, General Sani Abacha had ordered the judicial murder of internationally renowned writer and environmental activist Ken Saro Wiwa and eight other Ogoni environmental activists. By taking on the Odi Massacre in his hit single, Timaya had positioned himself in the national public sphere as a young artist who uses Afrobeats to do battle with the state and the global oil empire. Not only was the song a daring critique of the impunity of the Nigerian military, which had turned its lethal weapons on its own defenseless citizens, it was a denunciation of unhinged state violence carried out and aided by global corporate forces. Timaya's second, third, and fourth albums all showed strong signs of political commitment as a disenfranchised youth and popular artist.

In 2012, however, Timaya released his fifth album (*Upgrade*), which had hit tracks such as "Bum-Bum," "Sexy Ladies," and "Malonogede."[46] That

---

44   Douglas et al., "Oil and Militancy in the Niger Delta," 3.
45   See Amnesty International; Human Rights Watch; and Clarke.
46   Timaya, "Bum Bum," https://www.youtube.com/watch?v=V4tWUJKiT1M; "Sexy Ladies," https://www.youtube.com/watch?v=TA22O8N-Ybw; "Malo Nogede," https://www.youtube.com/watch?v=QixW_5QoU4Q

album, perhaps as the name suggests, was a significant marker of Timaya's makeover from a politically and socially conscious artist to the artist of pleasure, consumption, postmodern youth identity politics, and fun culture. His other tracks such as "Ukwu" (2013), "Sanko" (2014), "Bum-Bum" (2014), "I Concur" (2015), and "Rude Boy" (2017) all bear the marks of an artist who has transitioned from the precarious margins of society to a privileged urban youth floating in excess wealth and affluence. His music videos now display sensational images of sex, romance, and eroticism ("Ukwu" and "Bum Bum"); surplus wealth and a culture of consumption ("Rude Boy"); the stylization of African culture ("I Concur"); global fame and celebrity culture ("Bum Bum"); and the symbols of global wealth and networks ("Ukwu").

As these postmodern images proliferate in his musical texts, there is a seeming absence of political consciousness and criticality. Youth are leading their fun lives, indifferent to the dangers and precariousness of the world around them. This remarkable shift in textualization practices, Timaya asserts, was a response to a major critique from his Nigerian fans. When he released "Plantain Boy" as part of his album (*De Rebirth*, 2010), he was derided by young people for his obsession with depressing stories of urban struggles and adversity.[47] Although "Plantain Boy" was a celebration of the triumphs and accomplishments of a village boy who made it good in the city, bringing his mother joy and pride, the video's surplus images of extreme poverty, urban squalor, and postcolonial gloom did not resonate with the upwardly mobile and aspiring urban youth whose individual struggles and creativity have put them in a fairly privileged position of economic independence and social privilege.

Timaya's music videos since 2012, and indeed those of most Nigerian Afro hip-hop artists, are marked by a preponderance of sexual imagery and hypersexual exhibitionist displays. They feature beautiful, scantily clad young women in sensuous and skimpy lingerie, with voluptuous bodies, revealing cleavage and protruding breasts, immense bare bottoms, and bare-chested, handsome young men with flat six-packs wearing shorts, the ultimate global symbol of youth and sexual prowess. The songs are often about falling in love and the joys of sexual pleasure amid unrelenting social pressure. It is this crass display of sexual freedom and erotic pleasure that has triggered the moral panic about obscenity and moral corruption among youth by

---

47 "Plantain Boy," https://www.youtube.com/watch?v=15gzJf8_P3Y.

postcolonial legislators of national culture. This ubiquity of autoeroticism in Afrobeats hip-hop reveals two interesting aspects of the postmodern culture generally. First, it marks the widening of the sphere of sexual display, shrinking the traditional boundary between the private autoerotic realm and the public domain, and thus weakening the old dichotomies between private sex (considered good) and public sex (perceived as bad). The second is the rise of a new form of commodified eroticism in which cultural repackaging in the form of entertainment sex has been "sanitized from old ideas that freewheeling sex can 'deprave and corrupt' or, at least, offend."[48] It is in the latter regard that I believe erotic imagery in Afro hip-hop music videos functions to link sexual imagery to the wider processes of social order, thus making romance a political issue and a tool of liberationist politics for young people. Mamadou Diouf highlighted this unique cultural politics of urban youth in Africa when he observed that for alienated youth operating on the margins of society, whether as "migrant or clandestine workers, or sometimes as musicians, artists, and 'Golden Boys,' they become actors in the theatre of globalization, resolved to make their way into the world market's economy of desires and consumption."[49]

Other Afro hip-hop musicians across the continent are also embroiled in this popular purveyance of images and culture of excess consumption, materialism, and pleasure. David Kerr, for example, has documented how young artists of "Muziki," the popular Tanzanian hip-hop genre, engage in "performances of consumption, the shooting of videos abroad, most notably in South Africa and the United States" and how "cars, drinks, modern gleaming cityscapes and female bodies are essential elements of these video texts." According to Kerr, these "videos have become a space of competition between artists; a symbolic representation of their success."[50] James Yeku addresses a similar rhetorical performance of accumulation and success in Nigerian video films, showing how Nollywood movies are implicated in the desire for the public staging of identity and presence in Lagos. In the context of urban precarity, Owambe (Nigerian party culture of Yoruba origin) ostentation works as a compensatory aesthetic that creates a sense of self-possession, belonging, and dignity in the absence of social recognition. For Yeku, if the precarious urban space of Lagos is marked by a pathology of enduring lack as scholars of postcolonial urban space argue, Owambe aesthetics and

---

48   Hawkes, 10–11.
49   Diouf, "Engaging Postcolonial Cultures," 5.
50   Kerr, "Fantasy, Desire and Urban Space in Tanzanian Music Videos," 230.

"the diversion it makes possible functions as a modality of rehabilitating that pathology. The desire for happiness and to belong to the social spaces that party celebrations construct is always in deferral, therefore it [Owambe] signifies as a festive negation of postcolonial pessimism."[51]

What these accounts of the aesthetics of display and the politics of the superficial tell us is that Africans, especially urban youth, now take pleasure seriously even if academics and cultural critics like Abati do not. They do so because they understand that pleasure and other leisure activities, as Paul Zeleza argues, are "about the ordinariness and extraordinariness of daily life, poetry and prose to pleasures and pressures, pain and pathos, promises and possibilities of affective and effective living."[52] Leisure, pleasure, and other so-called nonwork, nonpolitical everyday activities, whether by youth or adults, "can tell us far more about the social content and contradictions of the broader structures and processes often analysed," Zeleza argues. [53] He insists that seemingly innocuous leisure cultures have "the potential of deepening our understanding of dynamics of African societies, of the complex constructions and contestations over resources, meanings, symbols, and time."[54] Let me now turn to the leitmotif of romance to show its politicization in popular Nigerian Afro hip-hop.

The Politicization of the Romantic in Afrobeats

There is a sense in which we can apprehend pleasure, especially in the form of romance, as a powerful discursive tool for urban youth. Rather than the current attitudes in which sex and romance are viewed as morally dangerous and socially disruptive, I argue it could productively be understood as a heuristic device for young people to make powerful commentaries and provide thoughtful insights on the broader social order and cultural values. As Gail Hawkes notes, the tendency in modern society has been to emphasize the experiential aspects of sex and romance over their structural dimensions. Scholars of sex and romance often indicate "less recognition of an ideological dimension of sexual desire and pleasure that operated at a less conscious level

---

51 Yeku, "Owambe," 5.
52 Zeleza, "Introduction," vii.
53 Zeleza, viii.
54 Zeleza, viii.

and that linked sensual experience to social order."[55] But the work of several African writers has shown how romance as private pleasure can be wielded as a political tool in the public domain. When Nadine Gordimer (*Occasion for Loving,* 1963/1994) and Athol Fugard (*Statements after an Arrest Under the Immorality Act,* 1974) narrativized the social tensions that erupted from the romantic adventures between interracial couples in apartheid South Africa, they were highlighting the concrete ways in which private matters—romantic pleasure—can be endowed with public associations. These activist writers showed how romance and sex can function as weapons of public revolt and resistance under oppression. Part of what I argue in this paper then is that popular Nigerian Afro hip-hop music offers important cultural insights into how romance functions as a powerful discursive device for youth to comment on and restructure the broader social order. I illustrate this politicization of romantic love with one Nigerian hip-hop artist—Teni. Below are the lyrics of her popular song, "Your Case":

[Intro]
Iye hey hey, huh oh oh, pem pem ijele bem
pem pem ijele bem, pem pem ijele bem
[Verse 1]
I slap police for your Case oo, I go to war for your Case oo
I go to court for your Case, I climb the bridge for your Case oo
Enter water for your Case oo, I punch the judge for your case oo
Anything you want baby, get for you baby
[Chorus]
For your case oooo elele le for your Case oo ho huh ho no,
For your case oooo elele le, for your Case oo ho huh ho no,
Cause my papa no be Dangote or Adeleke but we go dey ok yea yea
But my papa no be Dangote or Adeleke, but we go dey ok yea yea
I go go Oshodi for your Case; I go slap agbero for your Case
I go call M.C oluomo, I go report all of them
I go go Oshodi for your Case; I go slap agbero for your Case
I go call M.C oluomo, I go report all of them
[Verse 2]
So, tell me what the hell are you waiting for, if nah to chop indomie, you go chop
if nah to soak garri, you go soak, what the hell are you waiting for
If nah to fry akara you go fry, if nah to saok akamu you go soak
[Chorus]

---

55 Hawkes, *Sex and Pleasure in Western Culture,* 2.

For your case oooo elele le for your Case oo ho huh ho no,
For your case oooo elele le, for your Case oo ho huh ho no,
Cause my papa no be Dangote or Adeleke but we go dey ok yea yea
But my papa no be Dangote or Adeleke, but we go dey ok yea yea
I go go Oshodi for your Case; I go slap agbero for your Case
I go call M.C oluomo, I go report all of them
I go go Oshodi for your Case; I go slap agbero for your Case
I go call M.C oluomo, I go report all of them
For your case oooo elele le, for your Case oo ho huh ho no
For your case oooo elele le, for your Case oo ho huh ho no
pem pem ijele bem, pem pem ijele bem, pem pem ijele bem, pem pem ijele gbem.[56]

The lyrics feature a young lover who promises to go to any lengths for the sake ("your case") of love. Some of the promises s/he makes, such as to "slap [the] police"; "go to court"; "climb the bridge"; or "enter water [plunge into the sea"] are some of the most dangerous activities anyone can undertake in the precarious environment that is urban life in Nigeria. To slap a police officer in Nigeria is simply a one-way ticket to the grave. The courts are not public institutions of fairness, but a marketplace where the highest bidder buys justice. The places where the young lover promises to go for the sake of love are some of the most dangerous neighborhoods in Nigeria. Oshodi, for example, is a suburb of Lagos, with one of the largest markets in Nigeria and a busy railway terminal, but it is also notorious for criminal activities such as mugging, armed robbery, and drugs. To visit the Oshodi bus terminus in Lagos is to venture into a den of hardened criminals.

But the perilous actions the young wo/man promises to undertake as a sign of his/her love only serve as symbols of the extent of his/her emotional commitment to the partner. It is noteworthy that the young lover has a working-class background, not as rich as "Dangote," the famous Nigerian industrialist and wealthiest man in Africa or "Adeleke," a prominent politician in southwestern Nigeria. The subject promises to share whatever food s/he has with the lover: "indomie" noodles, "akara" (beans case), "garri" (cassava flour), and "akamu" (corn pap). These are the staple meals of the working poor and the intermediate class in Nigeria and other countries in West Africa. What the song does then is to mix the unique cultural symbols of working-class life in Nigeria with the metaphors of youthful romance in a seemingly depoliticized context. But collectively, the symbols of poverty, precarity, and urban danger

---

56   Teni, "Your Case": https://www.youtube.com/watch?v=hYx5ukr_YWw.

function to convey unflinching loyalty in a precarious social environment marked by moral bankruptcy. In the perilous environment of socioeconomic hardships so prevalent in urban Nigeria, love and sex are not by-products of affect but essentially emotional products for sale. It is a social landscape devoid of a culture of devotion where politicians are loyal only to their own pockets and not the people; where civil servants are devoted only to those that pay them under the table for public services; where everyone, including family members, is invested only in the self. In this treacherous cultural landscape of disloyalty and unreliability, the language of love and desire becomes an idiom of social reengineering where marginalized youth deploy love as a tool and symbol of moral critique of the dominant culture of corruption. Birgit Meyer addresses this form of politicization of pleasure in Ghanaian popular culture, noting how pleasure instantiates itself in popular video films as "the celebration of moral values and the defeat of evil."[57] While the cultural elites undermine or deride images of pleasure and enjoyment and frame them as the depoliticization of popular culture, they are inattentive to the unique ways in which young artists now use iconographies of romance and sex as cultural resources for critiquing the broader social order, especially its culture of corruption and the absence of loyalty and commitment to the nation and its people. In this political economy of romantic display, pleasure, enjoyment, and excessive consumption are no longer indexes of extravagant celebration and hypersexuality but crucial sites of popular contestation over limited access to social services and the consequent exclusions they engender across categories of gender, class, and generation. In this regard, romance and sex register as powerful public expressions of young people's creative freedom and social power.

Concluding Remarks

While leisure time continues to be socially framed as free time outside of productive work time (and hence meaningless), it is important terrain on which we might learn significant social truths about the existential politics of marginalized youth making sense of their lives in the face of unrelenting odds. While for some people "leisure is defined in relation to work or in terms of specific activities, there are those for whom leisure implies freedom, a state of being that is intrinsically rewarding, an end in itself that

---

57   Meyer, "Tradition and Colour at Its Best," 7–23.

requires no instrumental justification."[58] Because pleasure functions as an act of freedom, it is performative in the sense that it bypasses the idea of pleasure as nonwork and stages itself as a "status-placing activity, aimed at identity distinction, through which one displays to others one's habitus, capitals accumulated in various social fields such as education and economic wealth and income, and the symbolic power of tastes, preferences, perceptions, and dispositions learned and developed in one's upbringing within a particular family and class."[59] I find this idea of pleasure and leisure as freedom and play particularly useful for making sense of the surplus images of pleasure and material consumption in popular youth cultures such as contemporary Nigerian Afrobeats. When marginalized and voiceless youth manage to create beauty, wealth, and success from the modest cultural resources available to them in a social climate of continuing lack and privation, the public staging of extravagant consumption and romance functions to announce the social accomplishments of an alienated, underprivileged generation.

When Afrobeats fans criticized Timaya for his use of superfluous images of squalor and poverty to convey the struggles of contemporary Nigerian youth, they were expressing a preference for the dominant images that they want to shape their reality, knowing of course that precarity and uncertainty have been central aspects of their lives for more than four decades, and perhaps will always be in the foreseeable future. It is an expression of a desire for a different social reality when their current one is dominated by misery and the denial of the pleasures of modern life as experienced by their peers in more stable social climates. Like most of their counterparts across Africa, pleasure, fantasy, and excessive consumption are thus the new sites in which young people engage in the public display of power and where such displays "always involve the culturally, socially and politically saturated business of negotiation and value-judgment; and they always have cultural, social and political implications."[60] This is what Sharon Macdonald refers to as the "exhibitions of power and powers of exhibition" in her analysis of museums as public institutions of cultural power.

---

58 Zeleza, "Introduction," xiii.
59 Zeleza, xiv–xv.
60 See "Exhibitions of Power and Powers of Exhibition," 1.

Bibliography

Adejunmobi, Moradewun. "Charting Nollywood's Appeal Locally and Globally." *Film in African Literature Today* 28 (2010): 106–21.

Amnesty International. *Claiming Rights and Resources: Injustice, Oil and Violence in Nigeria.* London: Amnesty International, 2005a.

———. "Nigeria, Ten Years On: Injustice and Violence Haunts the Oil Delta." London: Amnesty International, 2005b.

Apter, Andrew. *The Pan-African Nation: Oil and Spectacle of Culture in Nigeria.* Chicago: University of Chicago Press, 2005.

Barber, Karin. *A History of African Popular Culture.* Cambridge: Cambridge University Press, 2018.

———. "Popular Arts in Africa." *African Studies Review* 30, no. 3 (September 1987): 1–78.

Basu, Dipannita, and Sidney Lemelle, eds., *The Vinyl Ain't Final: Hip-hop and the Globalization of Black Popular Culture.* London: Pluto, 2006.

Bauman, Zygmunt. *Liquid Times: Living in an Age of Uncertainty.* Cambridge, MA: Polity, 2007.

Beck, Ulrich. *World Risk Society.* Cambridge: Polity, 1999.

Bender, Wolfgang. *Sweet Mother: Modern African Music.* Chicago: University of Chicago Press, 1991.

Bramham, Peter. "Choosing Leisure: Social Theory, Class and Generation." In *New Politics of Leisure and Pleasure*, edited by Peter Bramham and Stephen Wagg. London: Palgrave Macmillan, 2011.

Clarke, Duncan. *Crude Continent: The Struggle for Africa's Oil Prize.* London: Profile, 2008.

De Waal, Alex. "Realizing Child Rights in Africa: Children, Young People and Leadership." *Young Africa: Realizing the Rights of Children and Youth.* Trenton, NJ: Africa World, 2002.

Diouf, Mamadou. "Engaging Postcolonial Cultures: African Youth and Public Space." *African Studies Review* 46, no. 2 (September 2003).

Douglas, Oronto, Von Kimedi, Ike Okonta, and Michael Watts. "Oil and Militancy in the Niger Delta: Terrorist Threat or Another Colombia?" *Niger Delta: Economies of Violence*, Working Paper No. 4. 2004. http://geography.berkeley.edu/ProjectsResources/ND%20Website/NigerDelta/WP/4.

Dovey, Lindiwe. "African Film and Video: Pleasure, Politics, Performance." *Journal of African Cultural Studies* 22, no. 1 (2010): 1–6.

Ellam, Harry Jr., and Kennell Jackson, eds. *Black Cultural Traffic: Crossroads in Global Performance and Popular Culture.* Ann Arbor: University of Michigan Press, 2008.

Fabian, Johannes. *Moments of Freedom: Anthropology and Popular Culture.* Charlottesville: University Virginia Press, 1998.

Hall, Stuart. "Notes on Deconstructing the Popular." In *Cultural Theory: An Anthology*. Edited by Imre Szeman and Timothy Kaposky. Oxford: Wiley-Blackwell, 2011.

———. *Representations: Cultural Representations and Signifying Practices*. London: SAGE, 1997.

Hardt, Michael, and Antonio Negri. *Empire*. Cambridge, MA: Harvard University Press, 2000.

Haynes, Jonathan. *Nollywood: The Creation of Nigerian Film Genres*. Chicago: University of Chicago Press, 2016.

Haynes, Jonathan, and Onookome Okome, "Evolving Popular Media: Nigerian Video Films." *Nigerian Video Films*. Edited by Jonathan Haynes. Athens: Ohio University Press, 2000.

Hawkes, Gail. *Sex and Pleasure in Western Culture*. Cambridge: Polity, 2004.

Held, David, and Henrietta Moore. "Introduction: Cultural Futures." In *Cultural Politics in a Global Age: Uncertainty, Solidarity and Innovation*. Oxford: Oneworld, 2008.

Hoffman, Danny. *The War Machines: Young Men and Violence in Sierra Leone and Liberia*. Durham, NC: Duke University Press, 2011.

Human Rights Watch. *Criminal Politics: Violence, Godfathers and Corruption in Nigeria*. 2007.

———. *Nigeria: Crackdown on the Niger Delta*. Vol. 11. No. 2(A), 1999.

———. *The Price of Oil: Corporate Responsibility and Human Violations in Nigeria's Oil Producing Community*. New York: Human Rights Watch, 1999.

Jewsiewicki, Bogumil, and Katrien Pype. "Popular Culture in Francophone Central Africa." In *Oxford Research Encyclopedia, African History*. Oxford: Oxford University Press, 2020.

Kelly, Robin. "Forward." *The Vinyl Ain't Final: Hip Hope and the Globalization of Black Popular Culture*. Eds Dipannnita Basu and Sidney J. Lemelle. London: Pluto, 2006.

Kerr, David. "'Maisha yetu ya kila siku kama vile movie': Fantasy, Desire and Urban Space in Tanzanian Music Videos." *Journal of African Cinemas* 11, no. 3 (2019): 225–40.

Kitwana, Bakari. *The Hip Hop Generation: Young Blacks and the Crisis in African American Culture*. New York: BasicCivitas, 2002.

Krings Mathias, and Tom Simmert. "African Popular Culture Enters the Global Mainstream." *Current History: Journal of Contemporary World Affairs* 119 (817) (May 2020): 182–87. https://doi.org/10.1525/curh.2020.119.817.182.

Krings, Mathias, and Onookome Okome, eds., *Global Nollywood: The Transnational Dimensions of an African Video Film Industry*. Indianapolis: Indiana University Press, 2013.

Jackson, Kelly. "Introduction: Traveling While Black." *Black Cultural Traffic: Crossroads in Global Performance and Popular Culture*. Edited by Harry J. Ellam, Jr. and Kennell Jackson. Ann Arbor: University of Michigan Press, 2008.

Macdonald, Sharon. "Exhibitions of Power and Powers of Exhibition: An Introduction to the Politics of Display." *Politics of Display: Museums, Science, Culture.* London: Routledge, 2010.

Meyer, Birgit. "Tradition and Colour at Its Best': 'Tradition' and 'Heritage' in Ghanaian Video- Movies." *Journal of African Cultural Studies* 22, no. 1 (2010): 7–23.

Osumare, Halifu. "Global Hip-Hop and the African Diaspora." Black Cultural Traffic: *Crossroads in Global Performance and Popular Culture.* Edited by Harry J. Ellam, Jr. and Kennell Jackson. Ann Arbor: University of Michigan Press, 2008.

Peel, Michael. *A Swamp Full of Dollars: Pipelines and Paramilitaries at Nigeria's Oil Frontier.* London: I. B. Tauris, 2011.

Posel, Deborah. "Races to Consume: Revisiting South Africa's History of Race, Consumption and the Struggle for Freedom." *Ethnic and Racial Studies* 33, no. 2 (2010): 157–75.

Saucier, P. Khalil. "Introduction: Hip Hop Culture in Red, Black, and Green." *Native Tongues: An African Hip Hop Reader.* Edited by P. Khalil Saucier. Trenton, NJ: Africa World, 2011.

Shaxon, Nicholas. *Poisoned Wells: The Dirt Politics of African Oil.* New York: Palgrave Macmillan, 2008.

Spencer, Zoe. *Murda', Misogyny, and Mayhem: Hip Hop and the Culture of Abnormality in Urban Community.* Lanham: University Press of America, 2011.

Toop, David. *Rap Attack 3: African Rap to Global Hip Hop.* London: Serpent's Tail, 2000.

Ugor, Paul. "Extenuating Circumstances, African Youth and Social Agency in a Late-modern World." *Postcolonial Text* 8, nos. 3 and 4 (2013).

Vinken, Henk. "Changing Life Courses, New Media, and Citizenship: The Impact of Reflexive Biographization on Young People's Democratic Engagement." *Young Citizens and New Media: Learning from Democratic Participation. Edited by Peter Dahlgren.* New York: Routledge, 2007.

Wagg, Stephen. "Introduction: Unforbidden Fruits: From Leisure to Pleasure." In *New Politics of Leisure and Pleasure*, edited by Peter Bramham and Stephen Wagg. London: Palgrave Macmillan, 2011.

Weaver, Shipley, Jesse. *Living the Hiplife: Celebrity and Entrepreneurship in Ghanaian Popular Music,* Durham, NC: Duke University Press, 2012.

Weis, Brad. *Street Dreams and Hip-Hop Barbershops: Global Fantasy in Urban Tanzania.* Indianapolis: Indiana University Press, 2009.

Yeku, James. "Class and the Aesthetics of Ostentation in Nollywood's 'Owambe' Genres." 2020, forthcoming.

Zeleza, Paul. "Introduction." *Leisure in Urban Africa.* Trenton, NJ: Africa World, 2003.

Part Two

Popular Online Media and Democratic Participation and Engagement

Chapter Six

The Regeneration of Play

Popular Culture as Infrapolitics on Instagram

James Yékú

Popular arts in Africa are steadily being produced on social media in recent years, signifying the discursive import of the internet, which Karin Barber argues is "the domain of the unregulatable" that has become "increasingly central to popular culture as more and more become connected."[1] Although what Jodi Dean calls communicative capitalism[2] suggests the internet is anything but unregulatable, there is the sense in which Barber's observation signals a necessary attention to the explosion of the popular narratives being produced by netizens using social media as a playground from which they contest and critique hegemonic structures. Understanding popular culture as an arena in which many nonelite cultural producers create aesthetic forms from the quotidian realities of their everyday urban lives, I examine the implications of Barber's claim in the context of the cultural symbols of youth production and popular laughter on Instagram. My analysis examines the Instagram postings of three young Nigerian comedians as playful texts of infrapolitics that expand our understanding of the intersections of popular play and youth involvement in a digitally enabled public sphere. While acknowledging that questions about internet access and class as well as the political and neoliberal underpinnings of the internet's infrastructure

---

1 Barber, *A History of African Popular Culture*, 142.
2 *Communicative Capitalism and Left Politics*, 1.

naturally figure into discussions of digital culture, I focus more on the cultural productions of the networked publics[3] that already exist among digital subjects who are generally uncritically impervious to how monetary value is being captured from their cultural and interactive encounters online.

The notion of "networked publics" refers to a "linked set of social, cultural, and technological developments,"[4] which Ito prefers to "audience" and "consumer" because of the ideas of passivity and consumption usually attributed to them. In any case, the existence of a digital divide is not sufficient reason to foreclose the media expressions or practices of those who already have access to the internet. My analysis constructs these new media users as creative subjects imbued with authorial power, making their capacity for self-representation a pertinent development in countries in which historically they have neither been visible nor heard. One of the inflections of this newfound creative voice among young people is the production of humorous narratives that amplify the interpretive gestures of youth culture in relation to the broader social and political contexts they inhabit. This chapter demonstrates that Nigerian popular culture has witnessed a widened, more vigorous influence of young people and forges new perspectives and deepens cultural and political discourses even as it inaugurates a new cultural order of youth agency on social media.

Although one of the popular digital platforms of narrativizing the self and performing visual identities on social media, Instagram is also deployed to articulate humor as a site of resistance to oppressive conditions. Hence, what we may call Instagram comedy to refer generally to comic narrations produced for digital platforms and circulated for the instant consumption and engagement of social media audiences, offers a sense of what Moradewun Adejunmobi presents as a tension between career option and social obligation in her discussion of the ethics of the performance of Nigerian stand-up comedy.[5] With a massive growth in Nigerian digital culture, we can read Instagram comedians as enabling not only a mediatization of the performance of the occupational self as guaranteed and widely accessible but also a performance model that fuses social and occupational identities. As more Instagram comedians generate financial value from their followers and online influence, it becomes clear that the performance of humor in the space is ultimately intended to be an occupational expression of a talent that shifts

---

3   Ito, "Introduction," 2–3.
4   Ito, 2–3.
5   Adejunmobi, "Standup Comedy and the Ethics of Popular Performance in Nigeria."

the fulfillment of social obligations to the margins. The monetary rewards of huge online followership trump the performance of social identities, although this is not totally ruled out.

Regardless of the tendency to function as occupational performances built on comic self-projections, Instagram comedy may be read as a domain of infrapolitics, with agents of state either sometimes unaware of the acerbic critiques of state failure that abound on the platform, or dismissive of the counterhegemonic discourses in an arena sometimes inaccurately designated solely as a space for the performance of innocuous or depoliticized celebrity culture. I will examine, therefore, the ways in which online popular culture foregrounds the performative representations of agency and voice on social media, paying particular attention to the production of playful agency, comic selves, and irreverence by young people on the platform. My analysis aims to uncover how social media in Nigeria is potentially a politically charged realm that stages constant performative tensions between popular culture and the representation of power in everyday life.

I use several examples to demonstrate the connections between playful and comic content like Instagram comedy and the critiques of the state by nonelite citizens whose major form of empowerment is the voice gained from access to the social web. For instance, my first example highlights the ill-preparedness of the Nigerian government to the Covid-19 pandemic of 2020. With the country on lockdown like the rest of the world, Nigerian citizens were basically suffering "lockdown in hunger" (see figure 6.1) as an already-bleak economic situation became exacerbated by the fiscal impact of both the pandemic and government's indifferent or selective response to the masses. As I will show shortly through my analyses of infrapolitics, this example not only addresses a recent global event but also uses the theme of romance to mask the critique of the Nigerian state. Three major Instagram accounts that reveal how young people are expanding the intersections between online visual rhetoric and the performative potentials of popular culture, therefore, offer a chance to provide some theoretical reflections on the nature of humor in Nigerian social media culture. Specifically, I examine the Instagram postings of three Nigerian youths who use their Instagram accounts to refigure power even as they speak back to it. Reading their comedy skits as texts of popular culture that overlap with dominant articulations of power, I will analyze other comic postings by @Samobaba_comedian[6] whose videos rework iconic scenes from Bollywood movies and repurpose them to comment on sociopolitical and cultural topics in Nigeria through

---

6   https://www.instagram.com/samobaba_comedian/.

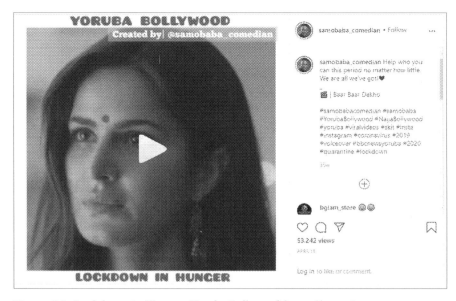

Figure 6.1. Lockdown in Hunger *Yoruba Bollywood.* https://www.instagram.com/p/B-_e5SMn9Jk/.

what I believe to be an infrapolitical interaction with power. Secondly, I examine @OfficerWoos[7] posted videos that narrate and caricature the activities of the Nigerian police, a state apparatus of coerced power and violence in Nigeria. Although not as fully explicated as the two previous examples, the last accounts I examine belong to two Instagram comedians whose postings offer a comic treatment of performative cross-dressing and its connection to the politics of gender inequality and identity performance in Nigerian social media. In a country that recently criminalized same-sex marriages, the playful organization of nonheteronormative identities and desires foregrounded in these videos are pertinent to understand the subversion of power on social media.

As a user-based digital platform, social media renders visible a media ecology in which consumers of the media are positioned as active producers of popular culture, with fascinating aesthetic dimensions to their cultural productions. In an earlier work in which I addressed the ways online Nigerian political narratives render visible an infrapolitical reconstruction of humor through the trickstoid character of Akpos,[8] I stated that digital technolo-

7   https://www.instagram.com/officerwoos/.
8   Yékú, "Akpos 'Don Come Again.'"

gies reinvigorate humor and enable ordinary citizens to produce counterdiscourses that may serve as "hidden transcripts of resistance."[9] As postcolonial humor continues to mock the volatile travesty of the state's actions and its apparatuses of systemic oppression through social media, I am particularly interested here in how several young people in Nigeria now use Instagram to perform new political identities that mock power. While focused on a new genre of Nigerian humor, I show that social media remains embedded in broader social and cultural discourses,[10] and young people are at the very center of a new cultural activism that disciplines power through performative play and ridicule. The core of my analyses thus focuses on the ways in which Instagram, especially as an expressive and performative space for humorous sensibilities, may constitute an infrapolitics of youth agency in Nigeria.

Performative Agency and the Regeneration of Play

Agency may be encountered as the capacity for self-representation and public communication through which young Nigerian netizens independently express perspectives that may otherwise be unheard without the authorizing affordances of social media. Social media affordances are the utilitarian possibilities enabled by the material designs of digital environments. As actions guided by the materiality of web environments and design,[11] they are the spatial conditions of virtual design and interface that enable the expression of action, as perceived by users of digital media. Through these new humor-enabling media spaces, we may appreciate the means by which young people "encounter the state, and how they engage, deconstruct and wrestle with it"[12] as a practice of everyday life. Although their agency is structured by the fact of social media as American media ecologies owned by corporations with interests in profit, we can still appreciate performative presentations organized around humor on social media as facilitating important encounters between popular culture and the state. As George Ogola has noted, the realm of popular culture provides us a lens through which to witness change differently, learn about alternative narrations and histories, and revise some of the problematic generic frames that characterize the reading of the African state. This realm is much more inclusive and less linear, undisciplined, and

---

9   Scott, *Weapons of the Weak*, 29.
10 Yékú, "Akpos 'Don Come Again,'" 246.
11 Bucher and Helmond, "Affordances of Social Media Platforms."
12 Obadare and Willems, *Civic Agency in Africa*, ixxx.

quite difficult to frame.[13] Through a playful reconstruction of cultural and sociopolitical issues, young people perform comic selves that render visible their participation in the public sphere. A carnival of subversive humor is, therefore, the basis for the recent scrutiny of political excess by ordinary nonstate actors, most of whom are young. I am employing the term "performative agency" to gesture toward the performance of identities organized around the capacity of individuals to produce and circulate certain cultural meanings as subjectively defined practices of transforming and reproducing social structures. Performative agency is produced in the space between aesthetic self-presentations on social media, on the one hand, and the resistance to hegemonic culture, on the other. The Instagram postings I analyze, like many other cultural sites of performative agency and speech on Nigerian social media, affirm in radical ways the connections between the rhetorical strategies of popular culture and civic expressions of identities such as citizenship.

Nadine Dolby asserts that citizenship is "an active process that involves the core of people's daily existence, including the ways in which they interact with and use popular culture."[14] This reading, which marks the centrality of popular culture to how people express citizenship is an idea I emphasize throughout, and enables me to imagine an intersection between popular culture as a domain for identity performance and social media as an avenue that fosters new forms of political subjectivities for young people. Although Dolby's cultural analysis was in relation to popular television and youth identity politics in Africa, the exegeses I offer here reveal how expressions of citizenship and identity in contemporary Africa can also be fully appreciated through the economies of symbolic meanings netizens produce and circulate on social media. Performative citizenship in online media is the product of the spectacular reconstruction of speech through user-based media, and manifests in how netizens can now use popular culture to represent the self, subvert the mechanisms of domination, and play humorously but with criticality at existing political-economic and cultural power structures. This last point—playing with power—impels us to clearly articulate the way in which the idea of play is mobilized in this chapter. The democratizing effect of the social web not only collapses boundaries but also requires us to "rethink our mediascapes not in accordance with old 'closed' dichotomies of user and producer, gamer and creator, but in terms of a flexible, paratextual, open—and

---

13 Ogola, "Popular Media in Kenyan History," vii.
14 Dolby, "Popular Culture and Public Space in Africa," 31–47.

often irreverent and playful—dynamic.[15] While aware that in the context of digital research, play has specific semantic resonances that evoke its application to contexts such as game theory and multiplayer online gaming, my approach to social media as a performative ecology understands play from a cultural perspective that frames and deploys it as central methodology of analyses. Rather than a fringe activity that is marginal and unserious, play is beginning to pervade every aspect of social and cultural life, especially as the core of human activity.[16] Pearce stresses how social media are more recent digital domains for play, aside from gaming environment:

> If we telescope out to the larger picture, we find that networked play is not simply confined to the game worlds. . . . In fact, network play has insinuated itself into many other aspects of life. It could be argued that YouTube is a networked playground of sorts, . . . We see games and play increasingly embedded in social networks, in mobile phones, on web sites, and in domains as diverse as education, military and corporate training, activism, even politics.[17]

In addition to its unique deployment in digital culture, the sense of play in this work is its incorporation into other aspects of life such as activism and politics facilitated through the agency of play and the play of agency expressed through popular culture. While there are several anthropological and sociological perspectives on the concept of play that might be productive for my reflections here, I find Karin Barber's notion of generative materialism beneficial for my analysis.[18] This is a method of reading she deploys in her critiques of the production of plays by the Oyin Adejobi Theater Company. In her exploration of the popular Yoruba theatre company in *The Generation of Play*, we see a similarity between performance improvisations and how young netizens playfully use humor to respond to the rapid changes of urban postcolonial malaises through new genres of digital self-making, the agency of play, as well as the self-fashioning strategies of user-generated cultural contents. Barber's methodology is informed by Henri Lefebvre's generative approach, which takes real life as the point of departure in an investigation of how the ideas that express it and the forms of consciousness that reflect it emerge.[19] This is the basis for Berber's treatment of popular theater

---

15 Richardson and Hjorth, "Mobile Games," 264.
16 Pearce, *Emergent Cultures in Multiplayer Games and Virtual Worlds*, 278.
17 Pearce, 278.
18 Barber, *A Generation of Play*, 7.
19 Barber, 8.

as constitutive of the production of ideas as a never-ending process, one of continual experimentation and innovations and something that is evident among young social media users with the right technical skills to repurpose previous narratives and produce humorous "plays." On this premise, Barber's generative methodology emphasizes how plays are generated from the provisional domains of everyday life:

> Plays were generated out of the people and ideas available. Narratives were drawn from a wide range of written and oral sources and freely adapted. . . . Characters were excavated from the experience of the actors. In the generation of a play, the theatre company "made do" as well as "make up", improvising not only the dialogue . . . but also the larger structure of the drama.[20]

Barber's explanation of the emergence of play makes it important for my analyses. It is a question of method that in the context of social media articulation of popular culture may be seen in the unique ways some young Nigerian makers of comic content perform humor in spaces like Instagram, YouTube, and, recently, TikTok. If the generative approach focuses on the processes of producing popular cultural genres that are in flux and emergent, the regenerative approach to the free play of performative identities equally underscores the digital affordances that enable online performers to deploy innovative self-fashioning as the basis for their playful expression of authorial agency and creative talent. Like their theater forebears studied by Barber, the everyday life experiences, commonplace narrative texts, and ongoing events and histories all serve as grist for young people's creativity online. And these cultural repertoires function as new sites of symbolic contestations over power. This is how ordinary people potentially succeed in using digital platforms, which in the real sense of things serve the ideological goals of neoliberal capitalism, to push back against their own immediate oppressive ideological conditions and remains the core logic of regenerated play on social media. That resistance arguably emerges from the structural fluidity of these digital genres is perhaps another reason to read these Instagram postings in relation to infrapolitics.

Free adaptation and the reworking of the contents of plays indicate connections between the popular theater and some of the processes of generating Instagram comedy skits, which also include freely adapting and readapting existing narratives, real or fictional, as well as reworking materials from older media in a process known as remix culture,[21] which resembles the citational

---

20   Barber, 131.
21   Lessig, *Remix*.

gestures of oral traditions. Barber's analysis is strictly limited to a theatrical conceptualization of play; the same generative approach that informs play as a performance practice may be found in the playfulness that netizens mobilize in their expression of voice online. As I have noted, this dimension of play is similarly constructed on a model in which a pastiche of prior ideas and performance practices become the springboard for the creative reinterpretation of everyday life. Without any attempt to exoticize forms of indigenous popular genres, I am suggesting that there is a modular affinity between some of the processes of producing performance forms such as Yoruba popular theater, and the many expressive sites of humorous performances on social media. In this digital realm, innovative self-presentations by creative producers of content shape the reworking and remixing of existing material and serves as the mode of cultural production, with content being as unpredictable as the forms in indigenous performances. A similar "creative potentiality"[22] that hovers around every moment of the production of Yoruba popular theater/play may be potentially located in Instagram comedy and other forms of humorous performances on social media where one can also find a repertoire of self-making improvisations and creative playfulness. This expression of the playful is partly enabled by the material affordances of social media and is one of the major means by which young people interpret their sociopolitical realities and challenge systems of rule and domination. We may speculate that play is the primary mode of the performative challenge to postcolonial agonies on social media, and it is why the counterhegemonic contents produced appear to be hidden as texts of resistance.

Infrapolitics, Youth Culture, and Instagram Humor

Arguably, the default cultural logic in Nigerian social media is humor, which expresses the playful construction of power online. Humor is a creative means of transcending the oppressive conditions of postcolonial states; it is a coping mechanism as Achille Mbembe and other scholars have shown,[23] and figures as an aesthetic response to the material and functional urgings and designs of digital affordances. Social media platforms center users and their creative expressions online, making them visible through interactive design, interface, and other connective functions. These inspire performative play and self-presentations, which in the Nigerian context are articulated through humor that seeks to deconstruct the normativity of oppressive

---

22 Barber, *A Generation of Plays*, 9.
23 See Mbembe's *On the Postcolony*, for instance.

power. In other words, the medium enables a propensity for play, delivered through the mechanism of humor. This perspective is my sense of play as a regenerative practice, a noncentralized and potentially carnivalesque space that offers some creative individuals the opportunity to interrupt the spread of hegemonic culture. In humorous online forms of play, therefore, are performative displays of hidden politics of dissent that invite us to rethink how social media marks a critical segment of the urban, digitally connected, and contemporary African youth population as a generation of playful subjects performing resistance to state domination.

James Scott's sense of infrapolitics conveys the sense that it is "an unobtrusive realm of political struggle" in which can be discerned "the circumspect struggle waged daily by subordinate groups."[24] In other words, rather than the open politics associated with liberal democracies, infrapolitics signifies "much of the cultural and structural underpinning of the more visible political action"[25] that animates the public sphere. Infrapolitics describes the ways in which the encounters and tensions between the powerless and the powerful are defined by deceptive and invisible tactics, with the dominated class feigning deference, while the powerful subtly assert and instrumentalize their mastery. Since the powerless, whom James Scott imagines as peasants, serfs, untouchables, slaves, laborers, and prisoners, are unable to express themselves freely in the presence of power, they look for hidden practices and cultural forms of resistance to resist disempowering conditions. In another cultural context, Asef Bayat's discussion of the nonmovements of the Middle East locates infrapolitics as "the quiet encroachment of the ordinary"[26] that encapsulates "the discreet and prolonged ways in which the poor struggle to survive and to better their lives by quietly impinging on the propertied and powerful, and on society at large."[27] For the marginalized young netizens in the Nigerian media environment, online lives and presence similarly figure as a site of politics discreetly negotiated through the symbols of culture.

Although the context of Scott's argument is apparently different, I would argue, following Ebenezer Obadare's deployment of the term in the framework of civic society: that humor is an important infrapolitical practice that has taken on new configurations in online environments. Netizens in Nigeria create an array of discourses hidden in visual and humorous forms in online

---

24 Scott, *Weapons of the Weak*, 183.
25 Scott, 184.
26 Bayat, *Politics as Life*, 14.
27 Bayat, 14–15.

locations, and these serve as a critique of power delivered behind the backs of the dominant classes. While there is sufficient evidence to show the presence of the Nigerian political class on social media spaces such as Twitter and Facebook, a platform such as Instagram—which is mostly populated by Nigerian entertainment celebrities, is hardly a place where the political elite may interact with or co-opt politics—as evident in their use of Twitter. The implication of this fact is that the powerless can use humor on Instagram in an infrapolitical manner that critiques and disavows practices of rule and domination. Humor's capacity to "ruffle the social matter and rupture hegemonic narratives,"[28] in line with Ebenezer Obadare's assertion, compels us to focus on its poetics, practices, and possibilities that connect "civil society to [infrapolitcal] zones of existence that are frequently unorganized."[29] This present inquiry is intended to show how Instagram similarly functions as one of these invisible zones of hidden political engagements, one in which young people generate humorous videos that implicitly structure and shape dominant articulations of hegemonic culture. New articulations of humor on social media, we should note, offer us opportunities to imagine culture as a regenerative practice, while presenting a comic archive of the ways in which information technology links people around the country into new chains of filiations and affiliation, sociality, and solidarity, as well as play and performance. Much of this is driven by the creative interventions of young Nigerians, both in the country and in its diaspora, and it is their playful reconstructions of the present political moment in Nigeria that we find the most enduring argument of digital media's animation of popular laughter.

My sense of the online cultural productions of Nigerian youths is their manifestations as the creative labors of ordinariness. By that I mean how regular, everyday young people creatively interpret reality and produce new meanings. Rather than mark ironic evasions as well as the subversions of official institutions as the major strategies of popular culture, Karin Barber imagines the popular as an eruption of ordinary aesthetics unbounded by structural limits. In other words, we must address ourselves to "how ordinary people succeed in establishing and institutionalizing their own unofficial modes of operation and making them work despite the absence of a consistently functioning centralized structure"[30] in order to understand the contingent, emergent improvisations of cultural performances. How this

---

28 Obadare, *Uses of Ridicule*, 245.
29 Obadare, 254.
30 Barber, *Generation of Plays*, 10.

generative moment of the popular manifests in the "shifting, apparently formless, apparently chaotic scene of postcolonial Nigeria [in which] clear and complex world do crystalize"[31] offers a reengagement with youth culture that yields insights on popular culture as a mode of a playful engagement with politics. Playing, as an ordinary, nonserious online activity makes Instagram an appropriate space for youthful investments in infrapolitics and its dynamics of popular, covert resistance.

There are several studies that analyze the relationship between youths and technology, especially the impact of new media on youths. One of such studies that foreground this engagement of youths with the digital world is Danah Boyd's *It's Complicated*, a work that offers one of the earliest accounts of the ways in which digital-networked publics impact the lived realities of teenagers. Boyd argues that through social media, "teens reveal their hopes and dreams, struggles and challenges" online and that digital platforms make "the struggles youth face visible," even as this sort of online environment "mirrors and magnifies many aspects of everyday life, good and bad."[32] Unlike Boyd's work that pinpoints the anxieties often propagated concerning the impact of social media on youths, my analysis uncovers the playful forms of authorial agency that young people in places like Nigeria mobilize to mimic and represent hegemonic culture. In the context of African cultural and media scholarship, there are some analyses that focus on youths and social media, although Nigerian netizens who produce cultural forms are not youth by default. Krystal Strong and Shaun Ossei-Owusu, for instance, examine how African diaspora youths employ social media to connect with home and negotiate the isolating conditions of exilic locations.[33] Mamadou Diouf's idea of youth culture in Africa frames this interaction between local and global forces, as "the condition of young people in Africa, as well as their future, is heavily influenced by the interaction between local and global pressures: the fragmentation or dissolution of local culture and memory, on the one hand, and the influence of global culture, on the other.[34]" On social media, many young people are engaged in a translocal space from which they use cultural forms to assert voice and perform resistance to hegemonic power.

---

31   Barber, 10.
32   Boyd, *It's Complicated*, 212.
33   Strong and Ossei-Owusu, "Afroexploitation and the New Media Creative Economies of Cosmopolitan African Youth."
34   Diouf, "Engaging Postcolonial Cultures: African Youth and Public Space," 2.

Also, Paul Ugor's work on youth culture offers a fascinating argument on areas as diverse as the underground activities of young Nigerian youths in the informal oil economies of the Niger Delta, as well as Nollywood's amplification of youth culture and agency. In his writings, Ugor argues that young people in general are at the very center of the ordinary struggles against economic and political domination in Africa and acknowledges the role of technology in the creation of a new cultural space and community that is both imagined and virtual. It is from this space, Ugor writes, that "the views of young people about their immediate world are being expressed. In this sense, Nollywood now dramatizes postcolonial anxieties especially about what it means to be a young man or woman in both urban and rural Africa."[35] Although Nollywood's representation of the melodramas of youth culture is well documented and solidly important, social media offers an equally productive avenue for the articulation of youth culture and agency, considering the visibility and immediacy of voice it affords postcolonial African subjects to narrate their own stories. Although how the term "youth," which is central to much of Ugor's recent scholarship, is directly applicable to the filmmakers who tell the African story is not always clear, important in his analyses are what he refers to as the "production possibilities occasioned by small media technology for youth."[36] These possibilities, he argues, allow them to "playfully engage with discourses of nation, citizenship, democracy, culture, religion/faith, and postcolonial experience[37]. Again, play as a *creative* and generative practice that allows authorial and narrative power is best located on social media in contemporary culture, with digital networks of sociality and performance serving as the ultimate locations of self-authorial possibilities.

The concluding section of this chapter now turns to three examples from Instagram to support the assertion that young people creatively use technology to negotiate their personal, social, and cultural experiences in postcolonial Nigeria. Unlike the ephemeral aesthetics of Snapchat, Instagram aims to be a social media environment in which the idea of permanence is invoked to attract users to capture and share "a moment and record it forever in time."[38] As Nigerian users post images and share life worlds from the country online, they are recording and sharing important moments of the

---

35 Ugor, "Small Media, Popular Culture, and New Youth Spaces in Nigeria," 398.
36 Ugor, 388.
37 Ugor, 388.
38 Systrom, cofounder of Instagram.

country's postcolonial crises. These captured moments eventually constitute an online archive of memories of contemporary politics in the country. The fans and followers who like and comment on these videos are implicated in the various threads of textual constitution at work in every shared and interactive moment on the platform. We should note, as Richardson and Hjorth suggest, that in user-based environments such as that of Instagram, the popular forms produced are "inherently playful, collaborative, shared, frequently comprises the recontextualization, repurposing, remixing, and recirculation of existing media content."[39] These popular texts render visible the ways in which young netizens are at the forefront of some of the creative expressions of popular culture currently being produced place in the Nigerian cultural terrain, even as they mark social media as the space in which youths now lay claim to a rational understanding of citizenship and performative agency. In addition to a political self-fashioning that overlaps with infrapolitics, the forms of popular culture in these platforms are visual signifiers of the politics of popular culture as well as their performative visualization of state domination. This online effort to map and visualize power is in many instances more important than whether power is materially displaced.

@Samobaba_comedian

My first example is @Samobaba_comedian's Instagram account, which exemplifies the localization of global media culture in Nigeria, especially through creative digital appropriations of Bollywood film. The Instagram account presents a growing repository of audience (re)interpretations of Bollywood narratives by this young netizen who overlays the original film texts with Yoruba-language conversations that radically depart from the prior cultural contexts and social meanings of the Bollywood films. @Samobaba_comedian is replaying a popular cultural form in a local context in which it is made to resignify new layers of authorial intentions. The result of this creative redesign is a new "text" appropriated after contact with a foreign media narrative to tell new stories in local contexts and distributed through social media (see figure 6.2).

These examples are important symbolic forms that are not only remediations of Bollywood narratives by a young netizen but also an apt reiteration of the propensity of social media to imbue popular audiences around the world

---

39   Richardson and Hjorth, "Mobile Games," 264.

Figure 6.2. Yoruba Bollywood. https://www.instagram.com/samobaba_comedian/.

with creative authority. The examples are virtual and visual echoes of the theoretical explications of Matthias Krings's work on African appropriations. Krings reveals that "people in Africa appropriate and make meaning out of foreign life-worlds[40] through creative adaptations of such foreign media content. In this framework, Krings imagines appropriations to be "the material result of local interpretations—namely, by those producing these copies and who in so doing articulate their "readings" of the foreign "originals.""[41] Based on this, it is not far-fetched to imagine texts such as these creative reinterpretations of Bollywood content on Instagram as digital appropriations that demonstrate how the creative economies of social media bring into being a culture of film viewership rendered as a productive location of laughter and new cultural meanings. This is the sense that we also get in Brian Larkin's analyses of a similar dynamic. Larkin's work on the Nigerian lovers of Indian films stresses how the consumptive site of Bollywood by audiences in northern Nigeria involves the creation of parallel modernities.[42] What is presented through Instagram is a vision of digital culture in which appropriation serves as a major idiom of interaction among creative networked publics.

While there is a humorous appropriation at play in these Instagram videos, they also present the account as one invested in the performance of popular

---

40 Krings, *African Appropriations*, 7.
41 Krings, 7.
42 Larkin, "Indian Films and Nigerian Lovers," 407.

culture, especially as the new texts are deployed as creative avenues by a non-elite subject to critique political and hegemonic cultures in Nigeria. In one of these videos, for instance, the subject of the narrative is the 2019 presidential elections in Nigeria and the various contestations around its postponements. With the election postponed hours before it was set to begin, many social media users in Nigeria criticized the electoral body (INEC) for rescheduling the elections on logistical grounds. The "Election Postponement" video on the Instagram account is a cultural text that stages the voice of its creator in a performative mode that highlights how social media gives voice and visibility to ordinary citizens as new cultural actors who produce online narratives that interpret reality and the forces surrounding and shaping it. I am using the idea of "voice" in the manner explained by Nick Couldry[43] as the act of giving accounts of ourselves and the worlds we inhabit despite the neoliberal politics that structure and even hinder public voices. Because voice matters as a mode of public agency, the question of whether monetary value is captured by the corporate owners of these platforms or if online humor can upstage power is of less interest to me for now. The capacity for speech and performative self-representations is equally important.

In another video, entitled "Sex for Marks," the Instagram comedian engages with the exploitative practice of academic marks for sexual favors among faculty in Nigerian universities (see figure 6.3). While underscoring the inequalities of power in such sexual transactions, the video succinctly addresses how female students are often exploited by male lecturers who often subject their victims to more agony by not giving the student the mark promised. Dr Ashaffa's seating position in this video indicates he is pleased with himself as a man validated through the subjugation of a woman, while the girl who has come to complain about her poor mark is staged as a victim of that phallic domination. In addition to the sexual conquest at play in this text is a double enactment of oppression, which enables an appreciation of the power imbalance that the creator of the video alerts viewers to through the rhetoric of his onscreen imagery. To emphasize the thematic focus of this narrative, the comedian intensifies the chains of intertextualities in his skit by incorporating Eedris Abdulkareem's "Mr Lecturer." The track is a 1990s classic of Nigerian hip-hop and examines the same vexing theme of sexual exploitation as a form of hegemonic masculinity in Nigerian higher education. The deployment of Abdulkareem's "Mr Lecturer," itself a song that is actually a pastiche of other songs, serves to indicate @Samobaba's deliberate

---

43   Couldry, *Why Voice Matters*.

Figure 6.3. "Sex for Marks," *Instagram*, https://www.instagram.com/p/Bqy6fNnh4qB/.

investment in social media as an ecology in which his visual symbols of cultural activism on Instagram are also reiterations of earlier cultural forms. While his use of indigenous language in these videos presents a creative adaptation of Hindi texts in which Yoruba emerges as the linguistic modality of mediating the playful encounters of the two different cultures, Yoruba also expands the multilingual archive of cultural forms on the Internet.

These two videos employ strategies of humor in a manner that can only be understood by Yoruba speakers and also prove to be digital appropriations of a foreign media culture that embodies some of the new ways through which popular audiences creatively respond on social media to more established media forms. Other approaches include the increased use of Nollywood clips as Internet memes, for instance. Without the creative reformulations of these Instagram videos, the original Bollywood films may never be "seen" by audiences in Nigeria. Although the original narratives of the Indian originals are absent, the traces of their presence in a Nigerian context further cement the globalism of Bollywood and its local regeneration online. To return to the engagements with official power by ordinary people, I now turn to an example by another young netizen whose stylistic approach concerns the mockery of police officers.

@Officerwoos

Although the depiction of Nigerian police officers by @Officerwoos in his Instagram postings may be contingent on the use of caricature and exaggerated melodramas, they accurately represent the police culture in the country in a way that recalls Achille Mbembe's claim in his discussion of the aesthetics of vulgarity in postcolonial states. He writes that "ordinary people have a certain conception of the aesthetics and stylistics of power and the way it operates and expands."[44] This understanding of official power is expressed, in the case of Instagram postings by @Officerwoos, through humorous skits in which one or more police officers interact with the public to confirm the perceived notion that policing in Nigeria, as the public face of political domination, is an abject site of impunity and corruption. This Instagram account, therefore, produces satirical videos intended to make visible the contradictions of Nigerian police behavior, while inviting followers and fans to participate in the discourse of police violence as the ultimate metaphor of the failures of the state. The representation of the police in Nollywood and other cultural forms such as stand-up comedy and newspaper cartoons in Nigeria is not new; what may be unprecedented is how several young Nigerian netizens, who are ordinary members of the public, can actively preoccupy themselves humorously and "safely" with a police culture notorious for its wanton human rights abuses.

In one video posted by @Officerwoos, a group of police officers stops a car, and the senior officer orders the driver to produce various documents, as is a customary procedure of the Nigerian police. When they observe that the driver has every official paper required, one of the police officer proceeds to ask ridiculous and unnecessary questions about both the car and the owner's destination. Seeing that its driver appears to be well prepared, the capricious police officer asks for money, but all the driver has is a twenty naira note (less than twenty cents), which is in a manner of speaking paradigmatic of

---

44   Mbembe, *On the Postcolony*, 109.

the various narratives of corruption by the police in the Nigerian cultural imagination. The currency is torn, but the police officers do not mind, as they gladly accept it. The acceptance of the torn currency itself is a satirical statement that the police exist not to enforce order at the so-called roadblocks but to impose arbitrary caprices and illegalities on the people. While the mockery of a culture of bribery in the police service is conspicuous in an Instagram video that recirculates a well-known narrative, what is significant is the fact that this mockery opens up a space from which ordinary people seek to sanitize state power by ridiculing it. As Achille Mbembe notes of this strategy, it is with the conscious aim of avoiding police trouble that

> ordinary people locate the fetish of state power in the realm of ridicule; there they can tame it or shut it up and render it powerless. This done, the fetish takes on the status of an artifact, an artifact that is a familiar friend, a member of the family, for the rulers as for the ruled. This double act of distancing and domesticating is not necessarily the expression of a fundamental conflict between worlds of meaning that are in principle antagonistic.[45]

Rather, it is an expression of the fraught relationship between state power (represented in the form of tainted officialdom) and ordinary citizens who, sometimes covertly, work in ways to undermine the state's dubious operations. To underscore their commitment to infrapolitics, comedians such as @Officerwoos (see figure 6.4) produce hidden texts on Instagram to satirize and lampoon the state, uncovering the excesses and abuses of state power in the process. Only a few institutions in Nigeria symbolize tyrannical power the way police culture does in its underhanded, sleazy practices that squeeze and oppress everyone in its path. This culture of police brutality eventually led to the famous 2020 #EndSARS hashtag movement that is also the routine subject matter of many a social media text of comedy in recent months.

A point that needs to be reemphasized in relation to @Officerwoos is how his account paradoxically makes clear Mbembe's assertion that "ordinary people locate the fetish of state power in the realm of ridicule" as a way of undermining oppressive power. The idea in his profile that he "NO BE ORDINARY PERSON" ("I am not an ordinary person" in Nigerian pidgin English) is particularly relevant. Oladaposi Gbadamosi, the owner of the account, is indeed an ordinary citizen who is rejecting the tag of ordinariness in his bid to reveal and mock the performative inadequacies of a state agency, thereby constituting a public identity as a man of power acting with force

---

45 Mbembe, 108.

Figure 6.4: @Officerwoos. *Instagram.* https://www.instagram.com/officerwoos/

and violence against the state. By rejecting the label of "an ordinary person," he is in fact enunciating the "uncommonness" of his daring encounter with a powerful postcolonial state, an encounter that reveals corrupt policing as a larger failure of government.

His Instagram account, therefore, serves as a performative and aesthetic mediation of ordinariness that allows us to encounter everydayness of life as a quotidian space saturated by predictable details of existence rife with a history of corruption and violence—as in the case of the Nigerian police @Officerwoos represents in his videos. His videos clearly show that the most emblematic representation of the abuse of power by the Nigerian state is the police. And to have the policing culture routinely scrutinized and caricatured as @Officerwoos does, in a digital space with less governmental presence than Twitter and Facebook, is to be invested in a covert form of resistance to state power and officialdom. There are several other videos from this Instagram account that show the chaotic underbelly of Nigerian police culture, and they all demonstrate that social media generates creative spaces from which young people can toy with power in order to make its strategies of abuses visible. Through countless videos on various social media platforms, these young netizens insert their creative agency into the discourses on the workings of oppressive power, deconstructing through performative self-presentations that may intentionally or inadvertently constitute infrapolitics.

I take my final examples of young netizens' humorous engagement with the dominant culture from the Instagram accounts of two young Nigerians, @mamafelician.Africa and @mamatobi. There are two male comedians that belong in a separate subgenre of Instagram comedy because of their

Figure 6.5: Instagram comedians as cross-dressers, https://www.instagram.com/p/CKmknOinq5X/.

employment of cross-dressing as a performative tactic (see figure 6.5). Their many videos present a masculinist vision of African women in a different and often transgressive sense that shows how male comedians reconfigure the performance of masculinities through corporeal strategies that upset fixed notions of gender and African maleness. Their performances in these humorous online texts show masculinist narratives about women operate through a playful ambivalence. In the context of popular culture in Nigeria, these social media accounts indicate some of the ways in which humor and masculinity studies can intersect, especially given the mostly patriarchal nature of many

African societies. In the framework of Ghanaian youth culture and the discourse of festive transvestism or cross-dressing, as Karin Geoffrion shows, is "understood as a contemporary ritual that mainly serves the purpose of reinforcing and reproducing gender binaries as well as heteronormativity."[46] These two examples present an optic by which we can appreciate how the performance of subversive masculinity through humorous cross-dressing unsettles such binaries. The Instagram accounts not only show that masculinity can be creatively reconstructed to express alternative identities and interpretations of gender but also represent and construct masculinity in a manner that imagines a subversion of its hegemony. Aside from male-to-female cross-dressing, however, there is one other Instagram account that reverses this form through the performance of hegemonic masculinity by a female who plays multiple comedic roles to comment on sociocultural issues in Nigeria. Unlike the male comedians that cross-dress in a way that denigrates women through performances of gender that are sometimes exaggerated notions of femininity, @Maaraji's performances of masculinity question the very notion of masculinity as a troubling expression of the oppressive forces of patriarchal culture. Her videos may not exclusively incorporate cross-dressing as a performative form, yet when she plays the roles of men in her comic narratives, she also equally forces her fans to rethink the ways in which masculinity is a social construct that may support or unsettle gender inequalities, depending on its deployment.

The cross-dressing event, as evidenced by these Instagram humor accounts, is a mediated spectacle in which the very condition for the existence of an alternative gender identity that violates heteronormative ideals of society is informed by play generated as a practice of offending hegemonic power structures. Although I do not intend to conflate homosexuality and cross-dressing, there are reasons to read these Instagram humor accounts in relation to the legislative regulation of sexual bodies and pleasures in the country's cultural imagination. Although the Nigerian government may have recently enacted a bill to criminalize gay organizing and postings, Instagram comedies are saturated with explicit thematic content that promote gay culture. The employment of cross-dressing is symbolic in that framework because it inserts itself into a potentially volatile space of oppression that is well positioned to extend punishment to digital actors whom some Nigerian state agents are increasingly seeking to censor. For a country in which to live openly as a gay person is often a silent and secret struggle against cultural

---

46   Geoffrion, "Ghanaian Youth and Festive Transvestism," 49.

and juridical prohibitions, to be able to cross-dress openly and give playful hints of a public transgression of a state-backed enforcement of prohibited sexuality is itself an act of boldness. Through this approach, the relationship between these Instagram accounts that use cross-dressing and infrapolitics may become clear. The male-bodied representations of gender fluidities in these online performances make visible an open challenge to state power that is concurrently veiled because of the absence of any active attention to the platform. With such inattention, these digital actors can push back against the Nigerian government's recent criminalization of nonheteronormative identities. As enactments of queer gender identities and subjectivities that refuse and destabilize the fixed and singular conceptions of gender signified by the Nigerian legislative apparatus of disempowerment, these videos are infrapolitics texts that resist the juridical discursive proscription of nonnormative sexual identities.

Conclusion

Instagram comedy, used here to refer to the thousands of social media comic skits that are currently reconfiguring the landscape of comedy in Nigeria, reveals a performance of humor organized around playful self-presentations that serve as potential iterations of infrapolitics. The Instagram comedy skits analyzed in this chapter have offered an opportunity to connect contemporary youth culture in Nigeria to a performative expression of citizenship and agency in which civic engagement with the state is asserted through infrapolitical relations with the state on Instagram. The comic contexts of some of the videos may not be immediately evident to a non-Yoruba audience, but the point is to show how the performance of humor generates and regenerates conditions of play among young people with access to the internet. Overall, there has to be a consideration of the fact that social media in various ways has expanded popular culture and aesthetics as we examine the creative expression and practices of young people and other nonelite youths with access to the internet. My goal in this paper has been to use the Instagram accounts of Nigerian Instagram comedians to think about the cultural productions of African youths and the significations of new discourses in the context of user-generated media. I have examined examples of Instagram comic videos as texts of popular culture produced by young people in response to digital affordances and for expressing their comic personas on social media. The texts and performative practices of the comedians I examine are important because they function as social transcripts of popular resistance, as the mechanisms of infrapolitics by which young people regenerate and re-create play as a modality of performing identities that represent the excesses and abuses of power.

Bibliography

Adejunmobi, Moradewun. "Standup Comedy and the Ethics of Popular Performance in Nigeria." In Popular *Culture in Africa: The Episteme of the Everyday*, edited by Stephanie Newell and Onookome Okome, 175–94. London: Routledge, 2014.

Barber, Karin. *The Generation of Plays: Yoruba Popular Life in Theater*. Bloomington: Indiana University Press, 2003.

Bayat, Asef. *Life as Politics: How Ordinary People Change the Middle East*. Amsterdam: Amsterdam University Press, 2010.

Bucher, Taina, and Anne Helmond. "The Affordances of Social Media Platforms. In *The Sage Handbook of Social Media,* edited by Jean Burgess, Thomas Poell, and Alice Marwick, 223–53. London: SAGE, 2016.

Couldry, Nick. *Why Voice Matters: Culture and Politics After Neoliberalism*. Los Angeles: SAGE, 2010.

Diouf, Mamadou. "Engaging Postcolonial Cultures: African Youth and Public Space." *African Studies Review.* 46, no. 2 (2003): 1–12.

Dean, Jodi. *Democracy and Other Neoliberal Fantasies: Communicative Capitalism and Left Politics*. Durham, NC: Duke University Press, 2009.

Geoffrion, Karine. "Ghanaian Youth and Festive Transvestism." *Culture, Health & Sexuality* 15 (2013).

Hjorth, Larissa and Richardson, Ingrid. "Mobile Games: From Tetris to Foursquare." In *The Routledge Companion to Mobile Media,* edited by Gerard Goggin and Larissa Hjorth, 256–66. New York: Routledge, 2017.

Ito, Mizuko. "Introduction." In *Networked Publics*, edited by Kazys Varnelis, 1–14. Cambridge, MA: MIT Press, 2008.

Larkin, Brian. "Indian Films and Nigerian Lovers: Media and the Creation of Parallel Modernities." *Africa: Journal of the International African Institute* 67, no. 3 (2007): 406–40.

Lessig, Lawrence. *Remix: Making Art and Commerce Thrive in the Hybrid Economy*. London: Bloomsbury, 2008.

Mbembé, Achille. *On the Postcolony*. Berkeley: University of California Press, 2001.

Obadare, Ebenezer, and Wendy Willems. *Civic Agency in Africa: Arts of Resistance in the 21st Century*. Woodbridge, UK: James Currey, 2014.

Ogola, George. *Popular Media in Kenyan History: Fiction and Newspapers as Political Actors*. New York: Palgrave Macmillan, 2017.

Pearce, Celia. *Communities of Play: Emergent Cultures in Multiplayer Games and Virtual Worlds.* Cambridge, MA: MIT Press, 2011.
Scott, James C. *Weapons of the Weak: Everyday Forms of Peasant Resistance.* New Haven, CT: Yale University Press, 1985.
Strong, Krystal, and Shaun Ossei-Owusu. "Naija Boy Remix: Afroexploitation and the New Media Creative Economies of Cosmopolitan African Youth." *Journal of African Cultural Studies* 26, no. 2 (2014): 189–205.
Ugor, Paul. "Small Media, Popular Culture, and New Youth Spaces in Nigeria." *Review of Education, Pedagogy, and Cultural Studies* 31, no. 4 (2009): 387–408.
Yékú, James. "Akpos Don Come Again: Nigerian Cyberpop Hero As Trickster." *Journal of African Cultural Studies* 28, no. 3 (2016): 245–61.

Chapter Seven

"This Is Very Embarrassing and Insulting"

Flash Fiction Ghana and Transgressive Writing

Kwabena Opoku-Agyemang

Introduction: Flash Fiction and New Media Spaces

Consistent with statistics in what is conventionally tagged "Sub-Saharan" Africa, the expansion of internet access in Ghana has been dramatic since the turn of the millennium.[1] This remarkable increase in access has consequently revolutionized modes of African cultural production, particularly in urban Ghana. The prevalent nature of digital technology has in turn allowed both professional and amateur creative writers to harness new forms of imaginative

---

I would like to thank Adwoa Opoku-Agyemang of the University of Michigan, Kwame Otu of the University of Virginia, and Paul Ugor of Illinois State University for their valuable feedback.

1. According to *Internet World Stats*, countries like Ghana, Kenya, and Nigeria experienced an explosion of internet users by 37,902 percent, 21,564 percent, and 59,653 percent respectively.

expression via online media platforms.[2] One burgeoning avenue for such endeavors is flash fiction in online spaces where these writers tend to explore issues related to themes that challenge orthodox cultural norms.[3] They treat such themes in order to provide alternative perspectives to established sociocultural values fostered by older forms of technology related to orality and print in Ghana.[4] The internet allows this new breed of young writers to use these digitally based genres to extend the literary engagement with contemporaneous sociocultural issues. The creative efforts of these writers thus open up research possibilities to ascertain how this emerging genre of writing differs from and complements existing imaginative works. But, perhaps more critically, there are also attempts to understand the ways in which this type of writing stands out as a unique field of creativity.

While Ghanaian popular culture has been a subject of study for the past two decades, thanks to the excellent work of researchers such as Joseph Oduro-Frimpong, Stephanie Newell, and Esther de Bruijn,[5] Africanist scholarship has yet to examine the exciting work being done by the mainly young, amateur writers using digital technology in Ghana, even though these writers are prolific. Flash fiction is a particularly accessible genre for these writers because of its fluid form, which on the surface appears restrictive due to its brevity but actually allows for an exploration of a variety of themes through its unique deployment of literary elements such as plot, theme, and characterization.[6] Despite its supposed stylistic constraints, the iconoclasm of flash fiction allows for a distinctive way of addressing a wide spectrum of unexplored and contentious meanings and ideas. In "The Remarkable

---

2 This trend is similar to what Shola Adenekan notes in "Transnationalism and the Agenda of African Literature in the Digital Age" with regard to Nigeria and Kenya.

3 Flash fiction is a creative prose genre with stories that usually number between three hundred and a thousand words. Ashley Chantler compares complementary and sometimes competing definitions in "Notes Towards the Definition of the Short-Short Story."

4 See respective examples for orality and print in Dinslage, "A Comparative Study of the Transmission of Moral Codes of Sexual Behaviour in Folktales"; Opoku-Agyemang's "Rituals of Distrust: Illicit Affairs and Metaphors of Transport in Ama Ata Aidoo's "Two Sisters"; and Adichie's 'Birdsong."

5 See "Sakawa Rituals and Cyberfraud in Ghanaian Popular Video Movies"; and "Sensationally Reading Ghana's Joy-Ride Magazine," respectively.

6 Interviews with the writers for this chapter revealed that they experimented with flash fiction because of the potential associated with the brevity of the form.

Reinvention of Very Short Fiction," Robert Shapard defines the form as "very short fiction" that is "ten times shorter than a traditional story," even though he admits that "numbers don't tell us everything." In other words, it is difficult to use figures or length to delineate what stories fall into this category. In an attempt to speak to this conundrum, Frederick Luis Aldama calls flash fiction "stories that one can apprehend in one visual gulp" in "A Scientific Approach to the Teaching of a Flash Fiction." Despite mixed metaphors of vision and taste, it is clear that the defining feature of flash fiction is the reader's ability to read the full text without breaks due to its compact nature. The submission guidelines page on *Flash Fiction Ghana* recommends work that falls between five hundred and a thousand words, while an early post on the website defines flash fiction as "very tight and concise . . . [pulling] the reader into the story with the barest minimum of exposition and [getting] into the . . . conflict quickly." The post points out that structural elements of a plot occur "in as few words as possible." This strategy in turn provides a platform for an explosion of meaning and, by extension, multiplicity of interpretations. Accordingly, what may be initially perceived as a constraint is indeed the catalyst through which the story extends itself. As Chantler notes, short-short stories aim at unease, which should "disturb us with its not quite homely or acceptable truths" (2008, 45). I connect this unease to the speculation that ensues from what is left out of the text.

One of the most popular venues for Ghanaian flash fiction is the website *Flash Fiction Ghana*, which as its name suggests, hosts flash fiction from Ghanaian writers. The website was created by Daniel Dzah, a young Ghanaian interested in curating brief creative pieces by young Ghanaians to form a community of readers and writers.[7] He launched *Flash Fiction Ghana* in June 2012 and started with three successful submissions in the following month. The website has been on a break since 2018, when it launched an anthology of selected works. During its active period, it hosted more than a hundred works of short prose fiction and other subgenres that include romance, science fiction, horror, comedy, and mystery. In terms of themes, some of these submissions tend to tackle transgressive relationships such as nonnormative sexualities, extramarital affairs, multiple romantic relationships, among others. Through their exploration of themes that violate and

---

[7] The first post on the website starts by greeting "bloggers, writers and everyone else who stumbled across this blog." The website also recommends that stories do not exceed a thousand words.

critique entrenched social norms, young amateur writers reimagine and reinterrogate the mainstream Ghanaian sociocultural landscape.

In this chapter, I examine how short online fiction from *Flash Fiction Ghana* addresses transgressive or illicit relationships. Because illicit relationships are typically frowned upon and thus perceived as not meant for open discussion, flash fiction becomes a productive vehicle for treating transgressive themes in the popular public space or cultural imaginary. By performing a close reading of two pieces of flash fiction by two young women writers who treat themes related to sexual transgression, I suggest that the interplay between notions of what is done in private and what is accepted in public becomes a vehicle through which the writers implicitly critique a society uncomfortable with confronting a thriving culture of illicit relationships, especially when exposed. This discomfort is thrown into sharp relief by juxtaposing the transgressive relationships with orthodox concepts of the family. The stylistically restrictive nature of flash fiction thus allows these young amateur writers to reappraise and challenge the normative Ghanaian family model. This process of creative reinterpretation by popular online flash fiction is not necessarily intended as negative criticism of the mainstream culture but functions to eventually make space for speculating about possible resolutions to the social problems that the writers grapple with.

By illicit relationships I mean socially transgressive associations that contravene conventionally accepted expectations with regard to how people relate to each other. For the purposes of this chapter, transgressive relationships focus on societally unaccepted behavior such as fornication, adultery, and incest. While the first two may be rampant and sometimes even acknowledged publicly, incest is regarded as taboo in many Ghanaian societies.[8] The actions and characters associated with these societal vices are treated in Akua Serwaa Amankwah's "May I Borrow Your Husband?" (2013) and "Red Means Stop" (2014) by Adelaide Asiedu, both of which appear on *Flash Fiction Ghana*.[9] In both stories, transgressive relationships are counterbal-

---

[8] See Ampofo's "'When Men Speak Women Listen': Gender Socialisation and Young Adolescents' Attitudes to Sexual and Reproductive Issues"; Kofi Awusabo-Asare and John K. Anarfi, "Rethinking the Circumstances Surrounding the First Sexual Experience in the Era of AIDS in Ghana"; and Quarshie et al., "Some Epidemiological Characteristics of Perpetrators and Victims of Incest in Contemporary Ghana: Analysis of Media Reports."

[9] In an interview with Amankwah, she revealed that she had to ask the web administrator to eventually take down the story after offline complaints about the lascivious nature of the piece mainly from professional acquaintances.

anced by a conventional notion of the nuclear family. Because in Ghana the family is typically understood to be the foundation of society (and the nation for that matter), transgressive relationships in the texts challenge sanitized conceptions of Ghana. Anne McClintock and Susan Strehle, for example, have presented convincing arguments that situate the family and the nation within complex relationships in postcolonial contexts.[10] I argue that this challenge to normative values in popular online flash fiction helps to create a less limiting notion of Ghana and thus functions to enable a more inclusive and diverse Ghanaian society that embraces and decriminalizes those with nonnormative cultural propensities.

Honest Immorality versus Deceptive Morality in "May I Borrow Your Husband?"

Set in contemporary Ghana, "May I Borrow Your Husband?" is the story of Roxanne Asante, a second-year student in a Catholic school who daydreams in her religious studies class, which is taught by a nun, Sister Theresa. Asante writes in her diary during class. In her entry, she attacks various groups of people, after which she writes a poem. The poem constitutes the majority of the story and proposes "borrowing" the husband of her neighbor. She then pivots to fantasize about attacking her teacher before returning to expand on her plan to steal her neighbor's husband. At the end of the story, the nun has caught the young girl in the act of writing in her diary and has sent the diary (which contains both the diary entry and poem) to the dean of the school as evidence of her "embarrassing and insulting" deeds. In an accompanying memo, the nun informs the dean that she has dismissed Asante from her class indefinitely and recommends that the dean mete out the appropriate punishment to the young lady. The story itself is, therefore, the nun's report to the dean containing the diary entry, which contains the poem.

Amankwah starts the story with Asante's greeting, "Good *moaning* diary" (the emphasis is mine). She immediately informs her readers that the use of "moaning" is not a mistake, instantly foreshadowing a salacious tone and theme. She is stylistically reinforcing the tendency of flash fiction to explode meaning from the outset but, perhaps most crucially, signaling a deliberate traversal of established literary conventions with the aim of improving her

---

10 See "'No Longer in a Future Heaven': Gender, Race, and Nationalism" and *Transnational Women's Fiction: Unsettling Home and Homeland*, respectively.

sense of self-awareness. After all, by using two similar-sounding words that have very different meanings, she lets her diary know that rather than engage in plain phatic communication, she would rather pun on a word that simultaneously connotes complaint and sexual pleasure. Phatic communication is usually processed as a filler that performs a social rather than informative function; it therefore carries no semantic weight.[11] In this light, utilizing "moaning" in place of "morning" underlines her interest in performing actions that have relevant meaning and tangible effect on her life. Playing on "morning" again suggests that she is beginning to explore her sexuality and understand her social environment. This does not necessarily imply naïveté on her part, even if the morning can be a stylistic emphasis of her youth.

She uses another pun, "horngry," which is an amalgamation of "horny" and "hungry." "Horngry" is a bolder and more adventurous example than "moaning" and reveals her quest to not only play with words but also to control language by creating words that fulfill her intentions and desires. She fills gaps that for her, conventional language fails to address, thus underlining the importance of transgression in catering for the spaces that convention is unable to speak to. Her blending of the two words is, moreover, a clever play on Ghanaian pidgin that allows her to critique convention in her own way. Pidgin, which is an alternative form of English, is mainly used among young people in Ghana.[12] In Pidgin, the transitive verb "to eat" ("chop") has different interpretations that include reference to having sex; thus, her play on the two words makes it clear that while she might be hungry in the conventional sense, she wants to not only have sex but also initiate it.

She is obviously not interested in the class proceedings, and her poem characterizes her as a curious young lady who is comfortable with embracing her sexual side and contemptuous of people who are not genuine. Her poem includes lines that reveal her love for "a lot of things" including "lap dances and reading the *Kama Sutra*/ I like chocolate sauce and whipped cream . . . / for all the naughty reasons you can think of." Highly self-aware, she embraces these examples of kinky behavior because being in control of herself appears to make her comfortable with who she really is. Her disdain for a range of people follows: "people who clown themselves with too much

---

11 See Žegarac and Clark, "Phatic Interpretations and Phatic Communication."
12 Dako and Huber explain the nature of Ghanaian pidgin in "Pidgin in Ghana: A Theoretical Consideration of its Origin Development," "Student Pidgin (SP): The Language of the Educated Male Elite," and *Ghanaian Pidgin English in Its West African Context: a Sociohistorical and Structural Analysis*, respectively.

makeup," "couples who own a dog and call themselves mommy and daddy," and "trashy little tarts who call themselves models" are among various groups that consistently suggest a disconnect between their appearance and reality—or their public and private selves. This disjunction in turn points to the absence of honesty. The people who use excessive makeup are actually fooling themselves, she asserts. She opines that ownership of pets does not make one a parent, while models typically use makeup and are also, by extension, clowning. The overt social constructed-ness of these people irritates her. As such, these groups represent the public acts of cultural refinement, beauty, and moral rectitude that she detests. They are the precursors that trigger the attack on Sister Theresa, whom Asante claims to hate as well. The emergence of her rhetorical aggression, consistent with these other attacks, appears to stem from the dissonance between appearance and reality in her lecturer.

This figure of authority and knowledge in the classroom space is akin to a "block of steel in a habit." Asante fantasizes about throwing away her "wimple, her veil, and her whole effing habit" and then, giving her "real clothes" and a man who would "teach her the art of loving." Sister Theresa's religious raiment is an outward marker of her purity and moral rectitude in society, but Asante views these clothes as inauthentic modes of maintaining power, respect, and order, all grounded in both self- and public deception. In stripping her of these garments, Asante therefore flirts with chaos. This collapsing of the dichotomy between private and public allows Asante to envisage a relationship in which chaos and order interlock; when these binaries meet, they morph into disorder. By stripping the nun of her sartorial symbols, Asante essentially abrogates the constitutive signs of Sister Theresa's moral power, thereby challenging and undermining her cultural capital in the public domain. But by doing so, Asante symbolizes a young woman who is unsatisfied and impatient with cultural pretenses of Ghanaian society and therefore challenges its collective bigotry. Asante imagines her teacher in "real clothes," which would signify her "real" self. This self would have a man to "teach her the art of loving." An allusion to Christian Grey of the bestselling novel *Fifty Shades of Grey* indicates sexual domination, while suggesting that Sister Theresa would reject her calling by breaking her vow of chastity, a fundamental portion of her divine mandate. If nuns are figuratively married to God, then by letting a man replace God and by allowing chaos to subsume order, Asante replaces one order with another. That new order is grounded in honesty and candor. If chastity is interpreted to mean that the religious are not matrimonially attached to any person or being, then Asante radically underlines the potential of her brand of honesty to revolutionize Ghana's social landscape. Asante thus sees the chaos in revolutionary and ironic terms: revolutionary in the sense that it suggests the religious order should be replaced or toppled, while the irony presents itself in the fact that these revolutionary fantasies occur in a religious and educational institution that ought to function as a tool of acculturation and socialization into the existing moral and cultural order.

After reproaching her teacher, Asante proceeds to attack her neighbor, Emelia Dawson. In the poem, Mrs. Dawson is a "mousy little woman, a prosaic package, she wears glasses, walks like a tortoise." Consistent with the earlier mockery of people who "adopt" animals, the animal imagery strengthens her disdain for this plain woman who could not possibly satisfy her husband due to her ordinariness. The choice of the mouse and the tortoise further highlights the meekness and sluggishness of Mrs. Dawson. For Asante, a woman has to be aggressive by physically and sexually satisfying her male partner in order to "keep" him. This belief fuels her accusation: "You don't treat him right, Dammit!" According to her, "A woman has got to treat her man right!" Her charge consequently addresses and then overturns conventional wisdom in Ghana that states that women are to be pursued, while men are the pursuers.[13] Most crucially, it undermines a Ghanaian cultural code demanding that women be sexually passive while men, energized by toxic masculinity, are active/aggressive.

In a reversal of gendered objectification, Asante positions Mrs. Dawson's husband Brian as a prize to be coveted and won. He is "ruggedly delicious," a "chocolate Adonis of goodness," and "a Greek god." Recalling her use of "horngry," she aims to devour him in bed. In addition, her employment of classical Greek imagery is not used to promote the man's power; it is used to position him as a prize, a sensual object to be competed for and won.[14] Again, convention is overturned as Asante aims to push an agenda that gives her agency. In order to compete, the young lady realizes she has to prepare accordingly. Asante contends in the poem that dressing "like you're going

---

13 This conservative type of thinking is broadcast in Ghanaian popular culture including songs. Akosua Adomako Ampofo and Awo Mana Asiedu survey trends related to this issue in "Changing Representations of Women in Ghanaian Popular Music: Marrying Research and Advocacy," 265–68.

14 Nick Galli and Justine J. Reel examine the ways in which the mythical figure of Adonis influences "the ultimate form of masculinity" among a type of male athlete in "Adonis or Hephaestus? Exploring Body Image in Male Athletes."

to throw the trash away" and by wearing "voluminous skirts and shapeless getups/ like something out of Noah's ark," Mrs. Dawson lacks the tools to consume her husband; she is an archaic woman who is no match for Asante's "gorgeous" self. She therefore aims to use her beauty and youth to snatch the man from his wife. Accordingly, she ends the poem with "And when I say borrow . . . I kind of mean forever." On the one hand, using "kind of" signifies an empty semantic gesture because from the poem it is clear that she is determined to "confiscate" her neighbor's husband. On the other hand, however, "kind of" can be interpreted literally as a coy way of affecting uncertainty and giving Mrs. Dawson the impression that she is not interested in keeping the man forever. The suggestion that she could easily consume and discard him can be seen in her maverick stance that stems from the different genres of communication she uses.

From the diary entry to the poem, the girl's inner thoughts consistently converse with the outer social context of a culture of chastity and temperance and suggest the failure of the teacher to have a positive, practical impact on the students. The teacher might satisfy the demands of the lesson plan, syllabus, lesson outcomes and objectives, and even the course structure in lecturing about the importance of moral values. Moreover, considering the title and context of the class, the teacher expects to impart values such as sexual abstinence, faithfulness in marriage, self-control, and other such "decent" and conventionally accepted moral values to her students, who are supposed to internalize these positive values.[15] However, if the student does not reflect these values in her thoughts, then there is a detachment that undercuts the intended impact of those in authority. This disconnect is even more ironic if these students excel in their exams because in reality their high level of academic competence is not commensurate with their ability to obey the moral code. Ultimately, Amankwah uses the story to critique societal constructions of excellence and morality, which she presents as propped up by shaky foundations. The work suggests that these foundations are unstable because they are diametrically opposed to the practical realities of young people's everyday lives that they precariously support. This is seen even in the form and style of the teacher's writing.

---

15 Thompson Mumuni, for instance, found that a majority of Ghanaian secondary school students and teachers in the Upper East Region of Ghana had a favorable perception of and attitude to subjects related to religious and moral education.

The tone of the brief memo reflects societal convention and authority, acting as a counterbalance to the content of the girl's diary. Sister Theresa complains that as she was "busily lecturing Chastity and Temperance, this girl was writing this poem." By focusing on her role, the teacher attempts to deflect from potential blame in the problem that her student presents. She again inadvertently portrays herself as being occupied by the teaching material rather than being concerned about having a relevant impact on her student, whom she further alienates by referring to as "this girl." It is also important to note that the nun deems indefinite dismissal from her class as the appropriate initial punitive action and leaves the rest of the direct action on the student to the dean. This decision to remain punitive rather than rehabilitative reflects the irrelevant structure of the system, which emphasizes and prioritizes convention, instead of relevancy.

In line with Sister Theresa's role, it is again possible to argue that her disgust at the actions of her student stems from an implicit rejection of her, not only as an authority figure but even as a potential lover.[16] In attacking the nun and Mrs. Dawson, Asante leaves no room for redemption for her teacher. She not only strips away her authority; she destroys any chance at positioning her as having a sexual or even romantic interest in her teacher. It must also be noted that Asante was also engrossed in her poem while the nun was engrossed in her teaching. Their lack of communication and social engagement highlights the contrast and disconnect between them, thus not only granting veracity to Asante's dismissal, but also reinforcing the antagonism between the two characters and possibly informing the nun's punitive decisions.

Sister Theresa goes on to ask the dean to liaise with the girl's parents in order to warn Mrs. Dawson about the intentions of the young girl toward her husband; and as it turns out, Mrs. Dawson happens to be the nun's younger sister. The story does not inform the reader as to whether this "sister" is the generic "oh, she's my sister" that Ghanaians know so well, or is a blood relative.[17] The nun may be following standard procedure, but her decision to pass along the "problem," as it were, frees her from dealing with

---

16   Homosexuality is still illegal in Ghana, falling under the category of "unnatural carnal knowledge." The constitutional unacceptability is complemented by a conflation of traditional and contemporary social stigma, according to Owusu et al., in "Attitudes and Views on Same-Sex Sexual Behavior in Ghana."

17   Many Ghanaians use the terms "brother" and "sister" to refer to close acquaintances not related to them.

rehabilitating the girl. It must be emphasized that rehabilitation itself does not come into play, as she advises: "Please feel free to give her any punishment you deem appropriate." By being interested in punitive rather than remedial measures, Amankwah invites criticism of the ways in which authority figures in Ghana fail to improve their society through humane, productive, and sustainable means.

In terms of style and structure, Amankwah incorporates three different genres: a diary entry, a poem, and a memo. Each mode of communication has a unique tone: the diary entry and poem are similar to each other in this regard, since they have the same narrator; Sister Theresa uses the latter genre to stand in for the general sanitized and "official" societal reaction to adultery, subversion, and immorality. The diary entry and poem are more personal and appear to be an honest portrayal of an adolescent girl's method of dealing with psychological and physiological development, as well as her social environment. Using poetry in a fictive piece moreover underlines poetic license and could probably explain away some of the spelling mistakes—and by extension, even justify some of the strong language and countercultural stance of the text. The anger and shock in the official memo are, however, clear. The rhetorical choices and genres therefore function to highlight the sharp contrast between the two major characters in the narrative. Even though Asante imagines that the nun will be subsumed by chaos were she to shed her façade, the reality is that Sister Theresa wields the cultural and social power. This reality explains the actual action in the story where the nun seizes the creative material and hands it over to the dean. So, Asante's voice is taken away, and she is promptly written out of the story (and thus out of the social established order).

Amankwah uses stylistic structures to mirror the societal structures at play by making the nun's memo to the dean the larger story. This is because the poem is contained in the diary entry, which is contained in the memo. In terms of authority, the three genres accordingly form concentric circles that move outward from the weakest to the strongest component and highlight an interplay between power structures and convention to prevent the poem and diary from breaking out of the memo. In setting up this structure, Amankwah uses content to illustrate the tension that occurs between two extreme positions in terms of moral perspective. The transgressive story, both in form and content, thus creates possibilities of theorizing the dangers that young people face when they attempt to challenge authority, especially when the attack on the social order emanates from a young lady coming to terms with her identity.

Meaning Stop, but Suggesting Go: Colors and Motive in "Red Means Stop"

"Red Means Stop" is divided into three parts, with each segment told from the perspective of a different member of a family that comprises an unnamed young woman and her parents whose names are also not mentioned. The narrative starts with the daughter dressing seductively and leaving the house to go work in a brothel. She thinks her parents are either asleep or working and is therefore emboldened to go out unmonitored. The second part is told by the mother, who is having an online affair with a man far away from where she lives in Accra. She also thinks that her husband and daughter are working and sleeping, respectively, and she recounts how she and her online lover progressed in their affair from emails to Skype conversations. The final part revolves around the father, who pretends to be at work to avoid his daughter and wife and heads to his regular brothel. Like the other two, he believes that everyone else is fast asleep. The story comes to its proverbial full circle when he opens the brothel door, and the new girl who has been offered to him turns out to be his daughter. His wife, on the other hand, is not caught and neither does she catch either family member. Each portion of the story is united by a red motif: tight red dress for the daughter, blinking red light on the mother's laptop computer, and red ink on the brothel signboard for the father.

Unlike the first story where the family is indirectly threatened through a diary entry and poem, in "Red Means Stop," there is a more direct attack on the nuclear family with adulterous and incestuous actions that have occurred or are about to happen. These actions are stylistically reinforced by symbols and objects that undermine the strength and "sanctity" of the nuclear family as the foundation of the broader sociocultural order. One major mode of reinforcing illicit relationships in this story is through the color red. The title of the story comes from a popular public education saying in Ghana on the functions of a traffic light. A Ghanaian children's song contains the line "Red means stop, yellow means get ready, green means go."[18] While the title of the story implies that illicit relationships are wrong, the warning that accompanies the color plays an ironic role: the actions that are publicly admonished by the color take place under the guise of privacy. The author thus uses this

---

18   Eric Baah Mensah studies this song in "Songs that Aid Reading in Kindergarten Schools: A Case Study of Three Selected Kindergarten Schools in Agona Kwanyarko, Ghana" to underline its utility in improving reading practices among children.

disjunction to underline the disconnect between public perception and private reality. The daughter, for instance, wears a red dress that is described as:

> Tight. Actually, it's more than tight, its seams cling[sic] to my body. Its red and my brown could easily be the same fabric, but my brown is skin and the red is my dress. Somewhere in between my thigh and my knee, the red gives way once more to my brown. In truth, the mirror reflects more brown than red; perfect.

This description is reminiscent of a scene in Ama Ata Aidoo's short story, "In the Cutting of a Drink" in the 1969 *No Sweetness Here* collection where the village-based narrator who has gone to Accra for the first time describes the dressing of a young lady, saying, "There was no space between her skin and her dress" (36). This young lady is most likely a prostitute, as the narrator says that she and her colleagues "were all bad women of the city" (36).[19] Brenda F. Berrian also argues that "bad" city women such as the young lady in Aidoo's story are symbols of uprootedness who are perceived as not living within the cultural parameters of familial context.[20] And yet, the young lady in "Red Means Stop" has a home that she returns to after she engages in prostitution. It might therefore be hasty and reductive to assume that women who engage in these behaviors do so because they do not enjoy the protection of a family. After all, "Two Sisters," another of Aidoo's short stories in the same collection, features a character involved in an illicit relationship with a rich married politician for his money, despite having a close relationship with family.[21]

In the extract, the red represents the dress while the skin represents the young lady's flesh, which is what is exposed to attract her clientele, enabling her to engage in transgressive behavior. If the color red is supposed to signify a stop to illicit behavior, then in symbolic terms the dress serves the opposite purpose by supplementing the sexual function of the girl's skin. The young lady is at pains to remind her audience that the brown is skin while the red is cloth but that due to how the seams cling to her body, they play the same role of encouraging illicit behavior. This is especially true if the red and

---

19   Lloyd W. Brown explains the interplay between rural conservative perspectives and the sexualized urban space in "Ama Ata Aidoo: The Art of the Short Story and Sexual Roles in Africa," 172–76.
20   See Berrian's "African Women as Seen in the Works of Flora Nwapa and Ama Ata Aidoo," 338.
21   See Humann's "The Question of Mercy: Gender and Commodification in Ama Ata Aidoo's 'Two Sisters.'"

brown could "easily be the same fabric." Similar to the collapsing of binaries in "May I Borrow Your Husband?," the public face becomes subsumed in the private reality. The private reality is reflected in the mirror; and in saying, "In truth, the mirror reflects more brown than red," the daughter gravitates toward honesty. This scene is therefore a figurative way of revealing her reality, which is that illicit or transgressive behavior is more pervasive than society would want to admit.

In a symbolic sense, the house embodies the failure of society to protect young people like the daughter from illicit behavior. Similar to her dress, the house and its accessories become enabling stakeholders. The clock tells her "it's time to go," and as she narrates her way out of her house, moving methodically to the brothel, the reader gets the sense that she has escaped its confines many times. Many homes in Ghanaian cities have walls that primarily prevent unwanted intruders.[22] In her case, however, "The wall is a walkover, literally." Thus, she steps out of her home confident that she will not be caught. She is explicit in connecting her confidence to being unmonitored. "Nobody sees me, except the night. I have no fears. The night may be your foe, but it is my ally, my element." She again underlines the importance of privacy to her being herself.

Confidence stemming from the same logic permeates the second section. In this case, the red color comes from the laptop that the mother uses to conduct her online affair. The red light indicates that her battery is dying, so she plugs in the charger, promptly changing the color to green. Using the traffic light analogy, she manipulates the blockade in order to continue with the transgressive relationship. Like her daughter, she utilizes the structures around her to maintain her own illicit relationship. The green light, to further the analogy, reveals the honesty that drives the mother's actions. In the previous scene, her daughter turns on the light when she is alone and then operates in the darkness when she leaves the house. In a similar sense, the light does not reveal the mother's actions to the public; it rather facilitates her conversation with her lover. As she chats with him, she acknowledges that what she is doing is immoral. She admits that she should feel indignant and even insulted but justifies her behavior. Nevertheless, by claiming that her husband is a "broken record" and that she is "tired of trying to fix things," she is similar to Sister Theresa in that she deflects blame from herself to the other party in her socially sanctioned relationship.

---

22 See Asiedu and Arku, "The Rise of Gated Housing Estates in Ghana," and Pellow's "Cultural Differences and Urban Spatial Forms."

The mother also uses space as a way of justifying the illicit relationship. When she states that "Accra is a dot on the map compared to where he is," she uses anonymity to show the way in which these relationships operate as a counterbalance to publicly acclaimed relationships. Like her daughter, she gains confidence in the assumption that her family members are either asleep or working. Accordingly, her tone changes from diffidence through defensive justification to bold resolve to continue in the relationship with this man. Her cable is "firmly plugged in. But it's alright." Again, she states that while she should want to see the light go red, she would rather not. The symbol that would have stopped the illicit action is thus elided in the text, allowing her to do "some work of [her] own."

In the final section, the red color is the ink on the signboard to "Verna's Place," which is the brothel that the father frequents. The underlying irony is perhaps strongest in this symbol, where the red designates a place for illicit acts. There is also the obvious but unstated reference to the red-light district, and the red ink on the signboard proclaims, "Verna's Place." The father is not only familiar with the place; he is "even more familiar with Verna and her girls." In other words, he is an active stakeholder in the business. And yet, the problem with legally defining prostitution in Ghana as "women's business" means that women, and not men, are punished by law.[23] Multiple media reports in Ghana that talk about the crime of prostitution thus tend to dwell on punitive measures taken on women and not the largely male clientele.[24] The irony of ignoring the gendered angle of the supply-demand nature of prostitution deepens with the fact that this man has become a "premium member" of Verna's place. Like his wife, he acknowledges the immorality of his actions by admitting that her establishment is "less than respectable." This ability to transition between public and private personae to condemn the very act they engage in implies that hypocrisy and the absence of honesty combine to serve as a critique of the sociocultural construction of respectability.

Again, like his wife, he justifies his actions by calling his use of the brothel his only "respite" from the "constant yapping" from his wife and daughter about material possessions and the fact that he is an "absent husband/father."

---

23   See Ansah's "Structural Relations of the Sex Trade and its Link to Trafficking."
24   See "23 Prostitutes Busted at Osu" and "17 Nkrumah Circle Prostitutes Nabbed" as examples, where both the headlines and the content do not mention the predominantly male clients. Accompanying pictures also do not usually include male clients.

Nevertheless, in calling his actions a "business of sorts," he hints at the importance of using illicit behavior as a means of coping with the pressures of publicly sanctioned relationships. His lack of interest in his nuclear family belies his heightened excitement at finally becoming a premium customer. Verna places sexy pictures of her employees on the doors to the rooms where they engage in prostitution, and as the father enters the door, he finds that the "picture looks vaguely familiar, but only vaguely." While he fails to heed to the warning of potential incest, his shock mirrors his daughter's when the final recognition takes place.

Ending the story with the rhetorical question "Daddy?!" is an effective way of highlighting the brevity with which flash fiction teases out these illicit themes. It is also a nod to the societal response to illicit relationships: there is no identified effective or sustainable way of responding to them. Essentially language fails when it encounters transgressive relationships. Combining the question mark with the exclamation mark again suggests multiplicity in the confusion that occurs in dealing with these aspects of societal relations. In "Red Means Stop," the reader has no idea what happens after the initial recognition. The lack of resolution appears deliberate because it inaugurates a multiplicity of questions and responses that have huge implications for the larger society and its cultural and moral codes.

Conclusion: Expansiveness in Brevity

In a newspaper article commemorating the first celebration of micro-fiction, David Gaffney recommends that flash fiction writers "make sure that the ending isn't at the end." He advises to "place the denouement in the middle of the story, allowing us time, as the rest of the text spins out, to consider the situation along with the narrator, and ruminate on the decisions his characters have taken." Amankwah and Asiedu take the opposite route, as they seem interested in letting the resolution be driven by their characters and the audience. By using the limited space afforded them to tease out the nuances and complexities of troubling social issues, they ignore the societally accepted codes and rather seem to place their readers in awkward positions (like the dean in the first story) with the pressure to do what is "deem[ed] appropriate." Their relatively radical break from such cultural conventions as proposed by Gaffney is mirrored in both their choices of genres and the treatment of countercultural themes.

In "Migrant Forms: *African Parade*'s New Literary Geographies," Stephanie Bosch Santana historicizes the challenges that African writers have had to contend with in terms of finding outlets to publish their work. These obstacles, while limited to African-language fiction in Santana's article, can be extended to other genres of creative expression written in English but that do not enjoy the levels of audience reception that established forms such as the novel, play, or poem do. In Ghana, flash fiction has not received much attention historically, but digital technology now has expanded access and allows for greater participation in creative writing. As this chapter has revealed, young women are able to use the opportunity created by *Flash Fiction Ghana* to not only reach a wide audience but also to interrogate and critique the wider culture.[25] *Flash Fiction Ghana* thus joins other established platforms such as the Kenya-based *Jalada* and the Nigeria-based *Saraba* in the subregion in forming a vibrant online community of young creative African voices that imagine the world around them in diverse ways. These new voices respond to the larger society by engaging with the political-economic, moral, and cultural issues that affect them.

This chapter has attempted, through meticulous close reading of flash fiction, to demonstrate the utility of considering transgressive or illicit relationships as crucial parts of Ghanaian society in an online space. The fact that these relationships thrive, especially among young people, is a testament to the need to further investigate the ways in which they work with societally acceptable relationships to construct an idea of the nation. As has been mentioned previously, both stories stop short of proposing answers to the dilemmas they raise. This strategy could be deliberate. Or it could be a symptom of operating within highly restricted writing spaces. Regardless of the reason, both Amankwah and Asiedu succeed in forcing their readers to confront the reality of transgressive behavior in Ghanaian society. The question of what to do next recalls Achebe's famous quote in his last novel, *Anthills of the Savannah*: "Writers don't give prescriptions. They give headaches!" Perhaps like Achebe, these young writers are beginning to "give headaches" to normative social values, assumptions, and cultural codes by questioning their cultural relevance to people's everyday lives.

---

25 The nature of *Flash Fiction Ghana* posts allows audience members to respond to the stories, and the stories have been shared on other websites such as *Pulse Nigeria*.

Bibliography

"23 Prostitutes Busted at Osu." https://www.ghanaweb.com/GhanaHomePage/NewsArchive/23-prostitutes-busted-at-Osu-604745. Accessed August 7, 2018.

Adenekan, Shola. "Transnationalism and the Agenda of African Literature in a Digital Age." *Matatu - Journal for African Culture and Society* 45, no. 1 (2014).

Adenekan, Shola, and Helen Cousins. "African Short Stories and the Online Writing Space." In *The Postcolonial Short Story: Contemporary Essays*, edited by Maggie Awadalla and Paul March-Russell, 199–213. London: Palgrave Macmillan, 2013. https://doi.org/10.1057/9781137292087_13.

Adjei, Jonathan. "17 Nkrumah Circle Prostitutes Nabbed | Kasapa102.5FM." https://kasapafmonline.com/2017/07/17-nkrumah-circle-prostitutes-nabbed/. Accessed August 8, 2018.

"Africa Internet Users, 2019 Population and Facebook Statistics." Internet World Stats: Usage and Population Statistics. https://www.internetworldstats.com/stats1.htm.

Aidoo, Ama Ata. *No Sweetness Here*. London: Longman, 1970.

Aldama, Frederick Luis. "A Scientific Approach to the Teaching of a Flash Fiction." *Interdisciplinary Literary Studies* 16, no. 1 (2014): 127–44. https://doi.org/10.5325/intelitestud.16.1.0127.

Amankwah, Akua Serwaa. "May I Borrow Your Husband?" https://flashfictionghana.com/2013/07/05/may-i-borrow-your-husband-by-akua-serwaa-amankwah/. Accessed June 2, 2015.

Ampofo, Akosua Adomako. "'When Men Speak Women Listen': Gender Socialisation and Young Adolescents' Attitudes to Sexual and Reproductive Issues." *African Journal of Reproductive Health* 5, no. 3 (2001): 196–212.

Ampofo, Akosua Adomako, and Awo Mana Asiedu. "Changing Representations of Women in Ghanaian Popular Music: Marrying Research and Advocacy." *Current Sociology* 60, no. 2 (2012): 258–79. https://doi.org/10.1177/0011392111429229.

Ansah, Nancy. "Structural Relations of the Sex Trade and Its Link to Trafficking: The Case of Ghana." *Agenda* 20, no. 70 (2006): 100–106. https://doi.org/10.1080/10130950.2006.9674782.

Asiedu, Adelaide. "'Red Means Stop.'" *Flash Fiction from Ghana*, June 3, 2015. https://flashfictionghana.com/2014/08/08/red-means-stop-by-adelaide-asiedu/.

Asiedu, Alex Boakye, and Godwin Arku. "The Rise of Gated Housing Estates in Ghana: Empirical Insights from Three Communities in Metropolitan Accra." *Journal of Housing and the Built Environment* 24, no. 3 (2009): 227–47.

Awusabo-Asare, Kofi, and John Kwasi Anarfi. "Rethinking the Circumstances Surrounding the First Sexual Experience in the Era of AIDS in Ghana." In *The Continuing HIV/AIDS Epidemic in Africa*, edited by I. O. Orubuloye, J. C. Caldwell and J. Ntozi, 9–18. Canberra: Australian National University, 1999.

Berrian, Brenda F. "African Women as Seen in the Works of Flora Nwapa and Ama Ata Aidoo." *CLA Journal* 25, no. 3 (1982): 331–39.

Brown, Lloyd W. "Ama Ata Aidoo: The Art of the Short Story and Sexual Roles in Africa." *World Literature Written in English* 13, no. 2 (1974): 172–83. https://doi.org/10.1080/17449857408588301.

Chantler, Ashley. "Notes Towards the Definition of the Short-Short Story." In *The Short Story*, edited by Ailsa Cox, 38–52. Newcastle, UK: Cambridge Scholars, 2008.

Dako, Kari. "Student Pidgin (SP) : The Language of the Educated Male Elite." *Institute of African Studies Research Review* 18, no. 2 (2002): 53–62.

Dinslage, Sabine. "A Comparative Study of the Transmission of Moral Codes of Sexual Behaviour in Folktales." In *African Oral Literature: Functions in Contemporary Contexts*, edited by Russell H. Kaschula, 46–53. Claremont: NAE, 2002.

Flash Fiction from Ghana. https://flashfictionghana.com/. Accessed September 5, 2014.

Gaffney, David. "Stories in Your Pocket: How to Write Flash Fiction." *Guardian*, May 14, 2012. https://www.theguardian.com/books/2012/may/14/how-to-write-flash-fiction.

Galli, Nick, and Justine J. Reel. "Adonis or Hephaestus? Exploring Body Image in Male Athletes." *Psychology of Men & Masculinity* 10, no. 2 (2009): 95–108. https://doi.org/10.1037/a0014005.

Huber, Magnus. *Ghanaian Pidgin English in Its West African Context*. John Benjamins. https://benjamins.com/catalog/veaw.g24. Accessed January 26, 2017.

Humann, Heather Duerre. "The Question of Mercy: Gender and Commodification in Ama Ata Aidoo's 'Two Sisters.'" *Obsidian III* 5, no. 2 (2004): 125–36.

"June | 2012 | Flash Fiction From GHANA." Accessed February 21, 2015. https://flashfictionghana.com/2012/06/.

McClintock, Anne. "'No Longer in a Future Heaven': Gender, Race, and Nationalism." In *Dangerous Liaisons: Gender, Nation, and Postcolonial Perspectives* edited by Anne McClintock, Aamir Mufti, and Ella Shohat, 89–112. Minneapolis: University of Minnesota Press, 1997.

Mensah, Eric Baah. "Songs That Aid Reading in Kindergarten Schools: A Case Study of Three Selected Kindergarten Schools in Agona Kwanyarko, Ghana." Master's thesis, University of Education, Winneba, 2016.

Newell, Stephanie. *Ghanaian Popular Fiction: "Thrilling Discoveries in Conjugal Life" & Other Tales*. Oxford: J. Currey, 2000.

Oduro-Frimpong, Joseph. "Sakawa Rituals and Cyberfraud in Ghanaian Popular Video Movies." *African Studies Review* 57, no. 2 (September 2014): 131–47. https://doi.org/10.1017/asr.2014.51.

Opoku-Agyemang, Kwabena. "'Rituals of Distrust': Illicit Affairs and Metaphors of Transport in Ama Ata Aidoo's 'Two Sisters' and Chimamanda Ngozi Adichie's 'Birdsong.'" *Research in African Literatures* 44, no. 4 (2013): 69–81. https://doi.org/10.2979/reseafrilite.44.4.69.

Owusu, A. Y., J. K. Anarfi, and E. Y. Tenkorang. "Attitudes and Views on Same-Sex Sexual Behavior in Ghana." *Global Advanced Research Journal of Social Science (GARJSS)* 2, no. 8 (2013): 176–86.

Pellow, Deborah. "Cultural Differences and Urban Spatial Forms: Elements of Boundedness in an Accra Community." *American Anthropologist* 103, no. 1 (2001): 59–75.

Quarshie, Emmanuel N.-B., Joseph Osafo, Charity S. Akotia, Jennifer Peprah, and Johnny Andoh-Arthur. "Some Epidemiological Characteristics of Perpetrators and Victims of Incest in Contemporary Ghana: Analysis of Media Reports." *Journal of Child Sexual Abuse* 26, no. 2 (2017): 121–39. https://doi.org/10.1080/10538712.2016.1277573.

Santana, Stephanie Bosch. "Migrant Forms: African Parade's New Literary Geographies." *Research in African Literatures* 45, no. 3 (2014): 167–87. https://doi.org/10.2979/reseafrilite.45.3.167.

Shapard, Robert. "The Remarkable Reinvention of Very Short Fiction." *World Literature Today* 86, no. 5 (2012): 46–49. https://doi.org/10.7588/worllitetoda.86.5.0046.

Strehle, Susan. *Transnational Women's Fiction: Unsettling Home and Homeland.* New York: Palgrave Macmillan, 2008.

Thompson, Mumuni. *Teachers' and Students' Perception of and Attitude Towards RME.* Riga: LAP LAMBERT Academic Publishing, 2013.

Žegarac, Vlad, and Billy Clark. "Phatic Interpretations and Phatic Communication." *Journal of Linguistics* 35, no. 2 (1999): 321–46.

Chapter Eight

Capitalizing on Transgression

Popular Homophobia and Popular Culture in Uganda

Austin Bryan

In 2009 Uganda became associated with deep-seated homophobia in the popular imagination of the Global North. This fraught relationship grew in part from the international mainstream media's coverage of Uganda's 2009 and 2014 Anti-Homosexuality bills, evidenced by Rachel Maddow's 2010 interview with David Bahati,[1] the bill's author, and the 2011 BBC documentary "The World's Worst Place to Be Gay,"[2] which Kwame Otu theorized as a neoliberal "homophobic safari."[3] Videos of Ugandan parliamentarians slapping their hands on their chamber seats chanting "Our Bill! Our Bill"[4] (Martin Ssempa explicitly shouting "eat da poo poo" to his congregation)[5] and the nondescript images of Kampala urban youth

---

1 See "Rachel Maddow/David Bahati Full Interview." 2010. MSNBC. December 9, 2010. http://www.msnbc.com/rachel-maddow-show/rachel-maddowdavidbahati-full-interview.
2 See Scott Mills, "The World's Worst Place to Be Gay: https://www.bbc.co.uk/programmes/b00yrt1c.
3 Otu, "LGBT Human Rights Expeditions in Homophobic Safaris," 126.
4 See "Parliament Passes Anti-Homosexuality Bill into Law." 2013. NTV Uganda. https://www.youtube.com/watch?v=ZYeIiB3ua8g.
5 The video has been viewed over ten million times in one YouTube version. The clips in this particular video are taken from the film *Missionaries of Hate* (2010).

in graphically homophobic soundbites, all circulated to the metropoles.[6] Scholars have simultaneously refuted the depiction of Africa as inherently homophobic, while criticizing the depiction of the Global North as a space of "safe," "liberal," so-called democracies for sexual and gender minorities, pointing out that this notion is particularly untrue for black sexual and gender minorities.[7] Nonetheless, these popular depictions in global mainstream media, framed as evidence of Africa's deep-seated homophobia, helped craft the most important aspect of the Global North's image of a homophobic Uganda, hence inaugurating the social figure of the destitute queer Ugandan in need of saving.

In February 2014, the Anti-Homosexuality Bill was signed into law by Ugandan President Yoweri Museveni, a man who, at the time, had been in power for twenty-eight years. Despite many prominent Ugandan LGBTI activists' disapproval, in March 2014 the United States imposed $118 million sanctions in addition to several other international organizations who cut aid to Uganda, hitting HIV/AIDS services particularly hard.[8] Not long after, in May 2014, I found myself in Kampala responding to an acutely pointed question from an intern at an HIV clinic where I was doing fieldwork: "Why does Obama support the gays?" The question was not invoked because of my positionality as a gay man doing fieldwork in a country where it was criminalized to "aid and abet homosexuality" but in my status as a US citizen.[9] Throughout my three months of fieldwork at the HIV clinic

---

6   See Sam Lazaro, Fred de. 2012. "In Uganda, Gays Face Growing Social, Legal Hostility."PBS NewsHour. https://www.youtube.com/watch?v=dKHApaNDEaQ.

7   See Awondo, Geschiere, and Reid 2013; Nyanzi 2013; Cheney 2012; Epprecht 2008; Boyd 2013; Lusimbo and Bryan 2018; Jjuuko and Mutesi 2018; Kinsman 2018.

8   The United States, along with Denmark, the Netherlands, and Norway threatened to cut aid. This negatively affected the work of HIV clinics and in recent years had led to the national movement to develop an HIV Trust, which would decrease Uganda's dependency on foreign aid for HIV/AIDS response (*Reuters* 2014).

9   The Anti-Homosexuality Act (2014), which prohibited homosexuality, included related offenses such as "aiding and abetting homosexuality," "conspiracy to engage in homosexuality," "procuring homosexuality by threats," "detention with intent to commit homosexuality," the prohibition of "same sex marriage," and the "promotion of homosexuality."

Figure 8.1. A copy of the tabloid newspaper, *hello!*, from August 11, 2015, with the cover headline "New Celebs, Corporates Gay Fans Busted." Ugandan artists Maryn, Eddie Kenzo, Weasel, and Sheebah Karungi, all suspected to be "gay fans," are on the cover.

I found that for many of my fellow twenty-something interns, my status as a US citizen meant I had explaining to do on behalf of my "neo-colonial government," as one young-person put it. The puzzle was that although I was warned by many in the United States not to discuss homosexuality in Uganda, to my own surprise, in this HIV clinic I could not escape the topic.

Given this charged context, I begin by unpacking, first, the Global North's imagination of a homophobic Uganda and second, the popular homophobia of Uganda. I believe both the North's and Uganda's cultural sensibilities with regard to homosexuality work together to reregister, renegotiate, and redefine what constitutes a queer transgression in contemporary Ugandan popular culture. To the Global North, the popular homophobia of Uganda is transgressive. This transgression has resulted in varied discourses, debates, and even interventions around social and cultural belonging, citizenship, and transnational movement. Vice versa, for a majority of Ugandans homosexuality is imagined as "Western" and perfectly acceptable to be *protected* in the Global North. Not only is advocacy for the "human rights" of sexual and gender minorities perceived as transgressive by Ugandans, these actions are also framed as "promoting homosexuality." I do not want to reduce popular homophobia to merely a critique of the Global North, recognizing that this would advance a lived reality of human rights abuses for sexual and gender minorities (Bryan 2016). And, perhaps most importantly, such popular homophobia constitutes a productive site of scholarly inquiry for understanding "resistance" where there is "power" (Foucault 1978).

By transgressions, I am referring to the cultural sites at which the norm cracks, fissures, and faults. While popular culture has always had a yearning for the transgressive, taboo, and nonnormative, Uganda's popular homophobia and the Global North's popular imagination have distinctly provided new possibilities for sexual and gender minorities to transgress the very transgressive nature of popular culture. This chapter will attempt to understand the life of queer individuals and their cultural production within the "political economies of anti-queer animus" (Thoreson 2014). From international Ugandan pop songs by lesbian artists such as Keko or her alleged lover Queen Sheebah Karungi, homophobic memes of transgender socialites such as Bad Black, to tabloid frenzy over "leaked nude photos" of artist Shivan Pavin, I demonstrate the ways in which Uganda's popular culture is queer and has "always been queer" (Hendriks 2017). While these women themselves may not be popular with *all* Ugandans, their cultural or creative output reveals how they have generated popular discourse around homosexuality that affects all Ugandans and that this discourse is now a site of participation for them. But for those transgressing normative culture, this transgressive discourse is generating new possibilities for economic, political, and sociocultural life making. Thus, the imagery from both the Global North and Uganda become contestatory sites for sexual and gender minorities to sell themselves to a global market. This global market in the political economy of homophobia is not typically a market of cash but one of "reputation." With each homophobic tabloid article published, or follower gained on social media, social opportunities such as earning enough Ugandan shillings to eat, gaining employment, elevating oneself to the "elite" of Uganda, or securing the chance to move to the Global North emerges for these "minoritized" sexualities and genders. The transgressions (such as being openly transgender, unapologetically lesbian, or visibly gender nonconforming in Uganda) are used and flipped by sexual and gender minorities in creative ways, especially in the realm of popular culture. The real cultural power or capital of these minorities is the affective *power* in being "disgusting." Consequently, sexual and gender minorities like Keko, Bad Black, and Shivan Pavin, flip, damage, exploit, and capitalize on the one thing that they can control regarding others: their "disgust" (Ashworth 2017).

Situating Queer Transgressions in Popular Culture

My approach lies at the intersection of anthropological studies of popular culture, youth culture, and postcolonial queer theory. I begin by situating my framework at this intersection and then turn to sociohistorical, ethnographic, and linguistic analysis to theorize how Ugandans are capitalizing on transgression. Starting from Karin Barber's (1987) theorization of popular arts as the "active exploitation of their unofficial status," Thomas Hendriks (2017) poses a provocative question at the close of his article on queer(ing) popular culture in Kinshasa: "If popular culture itself is always already queer, what new possibilities and futures are generated through this (over)production of transgressive capital?" Hendriks defines "transgressive capital" by the opportunity it provides for the *fioto* (effeminate male) interlocutors he works with in urban DRC to build reputations within the "culturally salient field of ambiance" (2017). To investigate the new possibilities and futures generated from overproduction of transgressive capital in Kampala, I turn to the social lives and cultural production of three young, queer, Ugandan women to push for an understanding of an emerging gender ideology (Oyewumi 1997) and to examine what possibilities and futures are generated from their successes (and failures) in their own reputation building in the realm of African popular culture.

Because the meaning of what it is to "be popular" is elusive, it is important to begin by clarifying what "popular culture" is and what constitutes "the popular" in African cultural production. Karin Barber found the elusive nature of the popular to be precisely its strength. Building on her work, I understand popular culture as a type of "popular consciousness" (Barber 1987), which despite its fleeting nature may give clues about cultural practices and the people who make use of them. Pinpointing what constitutes the popular was historically understood through the "distinctions" of taste, art, social class, mass culture, and high culture (Bourdieu 1986). And as Barber recently noted, these distinctions, while easy to identify are even easier to problematize (Barber 2018). I consider mass circulation less important than discourse and more acutely what "moments of freedom" (Fabian 1998) such discourse creates. Studies of African popular culture through analysis of political songs (Nyairo and Ogude 2005), slogans (Lawuyi 1988; Guseh 2008), and even "youth language" (Mous and Roland 2004; Beck 2011) have helped scholars refine their understandings of African society. Additionally, there has been a resurgence of interest in anthropological studies of popular culture in

Africa investigating questions of difference, belonging, identity, and citizenship (Becker 2012; Newell 2012; Pier 2015; Kerr 2014). Increasingly, popular culture in Africa has been understood as a site for analyzing citizenship practices, political engagement, economic activity, and activist ideologies within the context of global capitalism (Becker 2012). For example, Clark notes that African feminisms in hip-hop present challenges to patriarchy, gender norms, and the politics of respectability in and out of alignment with African feminist ideologies (Clark 2018). Similarly, in analyzing the reality television show *Big Brother Africa*, Dolby found everyday engagements with popular culture are central to understanding "cultural citizenship" in the emergent public spaces, such as reality television, apart of African futures (Dolby 2006).

A resituating of popular culture also requires a rethinking of "youth culture" (Bucholtz 2002; Schwartz and Merten 1967). In my analysis, I understand youth to be a category framed less through the fixation of age but instead through "relations to markers of adulthood" such as (un)employment, marriage, and social status (Kerr 2014). Because ending the liminality between youth and adulthood is contingent on marriage and raising children, the stage of "youth" often feels perpetual for queer Ugandans I spoke with. Uganda is a youthful country. Over 70 percent of the country's population is under thirty years of age, and (although the state of Uganda puts the numbers closer to 13 percent), the youth unemployment rate is at 83 percent for people aged fifteen to twenty-four years old. Finally, recognizing that there are multiple exclusions that poor, queer, young women experience because they are marginalized in multiple ways, it is almost impossible to untangle neatly the intersections between these different systemic hindrances and limitations. Nonetheless, the formal and informal creative economies, especially popular culture, have become vibrant cultural spaces for young people to build a "reputation" and generate an income, however small.

The internet, a significant mediator for production and consumption of popular culture in Kampala, is important to consider particularly when taking a closer look at youth culture. Much of the ethnographic evidence I draw from in this chapter moves between physical and virtual space. Because of the importance of the internet and the resurgence of interest in the study of popular culture, a rethinking of publics and the complex ways in which folks share information online will benefit studies of the popular in Africa (Srinivasan, Diepeveen, and Karekwaivanane 2019). The internet as a vibrant site for popular culture is now an alternative route for the expression of popular sentiments and sensibilities. However, as scholars such as Ligaga argue from their work on online space in Kenya, "The internet is not a simple alternative space, but one that fosters an oppositional culture...whereby online popular cultures often reproduce hegemonic tendencies and is 'rife with contradictions, indicative of the same kinds of relationships of which it is reflective."[10] It is this 'oppositional culture' in Ugandan popular culture and how it generates a sphere of imagination and a market for transgressions within it that I explore in this chapter. I argue that the virtual transgressions by sexual and gender minorities provide new "safer spaces" (Bryan 2018b) to attract their audience, thus inaugurating a new cultural economy or market for them.

Queering Ugandan popular culture does not need *doing* but rather *revealing*. I take note of Barber's warning that "we should not decide too hastily that works which appear conservative are completely and impenetrably so."[11] The conservativism of Ugandan popular homophobia reveals criticisms, reservations, doubts, anxieties, and possibilities of alternatives in textual loopholes, cracks, and silences. For as Hendricks (2017) notes, "The failures of heteronormativity open up possibilities for the expression of queer desire."[12] I similarly recognize the failures of popular homophobia in Uganda as openings for queer visibilities as these sites hold the potential for the accumulation of "transgressive capital" (Hendriks). Queer folks have used this capital for their own pursuits such as entertainment, activism, or building "reputation." Looking at ways in which queer folks resist oppression outside of formalized activist or advocacy spaces (which are increasingly NGOized in Uganda) reveals the heterogeneity of African queer liberation movements often overlooked in Africanist literature.

The chapter is based on twenty-four months of ethnographic fieldwork in Uganda between 2014 and 2019, as part of a larger project on the daily lives of sexual and gender minorities living in Kampala. I draw directly and indirectly on interviews conducted with artists, activists, journalists, internet users, members of civil society, and state officials. Since 2013, I have been regularly following Uganda's queer activist community in the capital, Kampala, and since 2014 have met hundreds of community members. I draw on participant observations on community events such as small private gatherings to public film screenings and larger festivals such as Pride Uganda. I also

---

10   Ligaga, "Virtual Expressions," 13–14.
11   Barber, "Popular Arts in Africa," 8.
12   Hendriks, "Queer(ing) Popular Culture," 13.

draw heavily from my participant observation in 2014 at an HIV clinic and support organization in Kampala. Further, I draw on online conversations and observations I have had through Facebook, YouTube, and WhatsApp, popular social networking and media sites in Uganda. Researching popular culture, sexuality, and youth under the criminalization of homosexuality is a major concern of this research, which is why I have anonymized informants who are not publicly "out" and focused on queer public visibilities. Discussing these topics with informants was built upon many months of establishing rapport and informed consent. Treating the digital as another field site came with its own limitations. Although Uganda has experienced an increase in internet usage, many people remain offline. Recent legislation such as the OTT tax, popularized as the "social media tax," has been seen by the international community as a way of suppressing online engagement and critiques of the government. Despite this, queer Ugandans have been producing transgressions between the physical and the virtual to build reputations. I now turn to the ethnographic evidence to illustrate how "capitalizing on transgression" operates in Ugandan queer popular culture.

Finding an "International" Artist in an HIV Clinic

The homophobia at the HIV clinic introduced in the beginning of this chapter *produced* queer visibilities. Working with the communications director for the clinic, together we designed campaigns to combat stigma against people living with HIV, while simultaneously debating whether or not Ugandans were "recruited into homosexuality" at boarding schools or if US citizens could "now marry dogs."[13] This popular homophobia was not without risk for the lives of queer Ugandans visiting the clinic. When two young Ugandan men came to the clinic for "couples testing," whispers circulated among the interns about the suspected "gay couple." Some interns even went into the private room when the two men were being counseled, pretending to pick up a file, just to get a closer look at the spectacle. This type of discrimination at clinics is well documented in Uganda, and unfortunately this

---

13   The immediate historical context here was 2014 when same-sex marriage was being legalized in more US states.

is a common experience for sexual and gender minorities who seek services at many health-care facilities in the country.[14]

Viral videos that circulated about homosexuality in Uganda were vastly different from the depictions of popular homophobia I had seen in the United States. For example, a ten-minute-long YouTube video of a white evangelical Christian woman meticulously explaining how Michelle Obama was a transgender woman was one of the most popular at the clinic. I wondered how these conspiracy videos—likely produced by US conservatives—were ending up on the mobile phones of young Ugandans at an HIV clinic in the country's capital. More theoretically, I wondered whether these health workers *believed* what they were seeing as the truth or merely entertainment. One of the more senior staffers at the clinic, a pharmacist, clearly found the homophobia entertaining when watching the video. The comedy of everyone huddled around a phone in the busy clinic hall, escaping for a fleeting moment, built camaraderie among the otherwise overworked staff. Among those watching the Michelle Obama transgender conspiracy video, the pharmacist seemed skeptical yet highly entertained.

I was also entertained by such transgressions. On another occasion, in 2014, I was in a tiny shared office at the same HIV clinic reading the online version of the local tabloid newspaper, *Red Pepper*, attempting to find an article about "Keko," a popular Ugandan musician that Fiona, a twenty-eight-year-old intern, had mentioned. According to Fiona, Keko was an alleged "homosexual." Finally, we found the incriminating quote from Keko, which read: "If Sevo [Ugandan President Museveni] signs the anti-homosexuality bill, we are always going to be third world. Development is tolerance." The *Red Pepper* gave its own analysis, which Fiona followed without contention:

> For over the years it has been rumored that female rapper Keko is a lesbian. It has been claimed that the singer is in a gay relationship with fellow singer Sheeba Karungi, and actually stay together in a rented apartment in Kiwatule. Neither of the two has ever denied the allegations. And now Keko has almost confirmed these allegations by blasting the president over the antigay bill.[15]

---

14 Peters, "'They Wrote "Gay" on Her File'"; Bryan, "Even If They Spit At You, Don't Be Surprised"; King et al., "HIV and Transgender Women in Kampala, Uganda—Double Jeopardy."

15 *Red Pepper*, "Keko Blasts M7 over Anti Homosexuality Bill."

Figure 8.2. Keko photographed in the tabloid newspaper *Red Pepper* in 2014.

When I asked Fiona if Keko was truly a lesbian she said, "that's what they are saying," adding "but they want to catch her in the act!" When I asked "why?" she responded by saying, "Because they want to imprison her." She paused briefly and then continued, "But they don't have enough evidence yet." I was curious as to how Keko could still be such a popular celebrity in Uganda despite the rumors. These allegations circulated at a time when "aiding and abetting homosexuality" could mean jail time. Keko has since reflected on that time and has told journalists about the fear she felt. If it was so widely believed that she was a lesbian, why was Keko not the first to be arrested? Why did her legal, sexual, and gender transgressions not destroy her reputation and any market for her music? Fiona, in an attempt to address my concerns, emphasized how "people don't mind whether she *is* or *not* [referring to homosexuality]—yes, she dresses like a boy, but Keko has become *international*."

Growing up in a strict conservative Christian family, Keko built fame in 2010 when she was twenty-four, with the release of the song, "Fallen Heroes."

In the song she appeared alongside other established Ugandan artists, a move that earned her notoriety. The following year, in 2011, she released the popular single "How We Do It," which made both the Ugandan charts and the MTV Africa charts. Many tabloids attributed this feat to Keko becoming a "household name" in East Africa and obtaining major marketing contracts. For example, an endorsement deal with Pepsi and an East Africa advertising campaign with Mountain Dew generated relatively large capital for her and solidified her reputation in the East African music industry. Later, in her follow-up track to "How We Do It" entitled *"Alwoo"* (cry for help), she triggered controversy because the lyrics were about domestic violence. My own introduction to Ugandan queer popular culture was Keko. Although she became popular in many respects from her music alone, Keko's queer transgressions in the wake of the Anti-Homosexuality Act increasingly became a part of her reputation whether she approved of this or not. Prior to this moment, her gender transgressions as a more "masculine presenting" woman were contextualized within East African hip-hop, but now her gender transgressions were increasingly used as evidence of her homosexuality. For example, Fiona equated Keko's fashion (dressing "like a boy") with homosexuality. Similarly, when Keko critiqued the government passage of the Anti-Homosexuality Act, the *Red Pepper* reported that she "confirmed these allegations [of homosexuality] by blasting the president over the antigay bill."

However, the violence of state sponsored homophobia has many cracks in which popular homophobia *produces* queer popular culture. The homophobia that was being sponsored by the state at the time was a part of why queer visibilities were being revealed and queer transgressions became normalized. A thriving market for popular media on homosexuality, however homo/transphobic, emerged. Although Keko was not yet openly queer (she later came out as lesbian in an interview in 2017), she was *suspected* to be, and this transgression alone created the discourse that elevated her reputation. Accusations (a "speech act") were directed at many figures in Ugandan popular culture (including fellow rappers); but when these were directed at Keko they stuck because of her queer "embodiment." The most "authentic" transgressions are embodied. By merely existing, and adorning the cultural accoutrements of toxic masculinity, Keko transgressed the normalized sexuality and gender projects at work in Uganda. Keko faced backlash for her gender transgressions, which she acknowledged in 2017. While Keko's sexual orientation was concealed throughout her career, her gender was visible. She was accused of homosexuality repeatedly and photographed with her suspected girlfriend Karungi (see figure 8.2). Her gender transgressions, coupled with sexual transgressions, established Keko as an outspoken artist for Ugandans to watch and for capitalists in the Global North to market.

Keko suggests Uganda is "Third World" in her reported slam of the Anti-Homosexuality Act in the *Red Pepper*. This is a trope that global northerners use to cast the continent as "backwards" and in need of "postures of empowerment" (Moore 2016), intervention, and development. As for several commenters on the article, it came as no surprise because Keko had been aligned with the Global North from the perspective of the Ugandan audience. This was the case for Fiona, who carefully described Keko as having "become international." "Becoming international" is a pursuit that reaches beyond the borders of queer popular culture; it is an aspiration for many Ugandans, most of whom would leave the country if they could. Even the pharmacist, a woman who I came to know, had a US-born daughter and a Ugandan-born son both living in the United States attending community college. The Global North was an aspiration at a time when countries like Uganda were (and still are) increasingly being globally incarcerated or enclaved off. "Becoming international" is an aspiration because it presents the possibility for a better future. "International" for Fiona did not mean that Keko's songs were played in neighboring Kenya or Rwanda (although this, too, could constitute "the international"); it meant Keko's songs were played in North American and European countries (however rarely they were actually on the radio). Keko's relevance in the United States was solidified by her frequent trips abroad. "Becoming international" made Keko closer to global northern "modernity." She could be a gay woman, outspoken against policy and the Museveni regime because she was not just any Ugandan woman: she was Keko, whose reputation was built on the transgressive political economy.

As she spoke out, thus transgressing Ugandan norms, she normalized herself to the Global North and capitalized on their newfound interest in her reputation. Featured in a CNN short documentary, which follows Keko to her recording studio in 2014 and to an event for her NGO called "Sober Up" (against drug abuse), a clear narrative emerges. A covert queer voice (framed as "outspoken" even though soft-spoken throughout the interview), Keko used her managed transgressive capital to become a story of empowerment. In 2017 Keko tweeted, "My gay ass is free yes free and there will be a wedding you best believe" and later "Thank you Canada for giving me a new home. . . . I feel free like a new person. It was a burden to live in a box and walk on eggshells." Although it is not public whether Keko went to Canada as a refugee based on sexual orientation or gender identity, she was in a country she believed made her "free." She had capitalized on her differences in

Uganda, first as a woman rapper (transgressing the hegemonic masculinity of the industry), later as an alleged lesbian, and finally as an "out" lesbian in Canada. Keko's story illustrates the power transgressive lifestyles have to build new futures for African youth.

Meet "The Caitlyn Jenner of Uganda"

After the rehearsals for Mr. and Ms. Pride Uganda, a beauty pageant that was part of the Pride Uganda 2015 festivities, I was chatting with Bad Black about an interview she was about to give. Bad Black, a transgender woman living in Kampala, is well known in the community. Since being outed routinely in local newspapers, online blogs, and on viral social media posts, Bad Black is increasingly breaking into the mainstream Ugandan media. In a loud whisper so others around the compound could hear, Bad Black told me that she would make a national TV appearance the following day because "they want to meet the Caitlyn Jenner of Uganda." I did not know what station it would be on, but in the following days an eleven-minute video clip of the interview circulated around WhatsApp groups entitled "Meet Uganda's Transgender (Bad Black)." The talk show, on *Morning Flavor Entertainment with Luzze Andrew Anderson*, begins with Anderson prefacing the interview with how "excited" he is to have Bad Black as a guest on the show. Quickly, he turns to sensational, religious-based, trans/homophobic invasive questioning. Referring to Bad Black, who is sitting in front of him crossing her legs with a ruffled pink blouse, a black skirt, and heels, he speaks directly into the camera to the imagined audience:

Andrew Anderson: But now, because if 'he' says 'transgender' that is the same thing that Caitlyn was saying. Caitlyn, that is—
Mama wa ba—
Tata wa ba Kardashian.
Yye agamba—
[English translation: Mother of—,
Father of the Kardashians.
They say—]
Because at the end of the day, do you, do you get attracted to women or male guys?
That is—
Is the biggest question
Because everyone *bwogamba* (when you say) a person who is gay *ekitegeeza abeera ayagala basajja banne* (which means a man likes fellow men).

CAPITALIZING ON TRANSGRESSION   221

Figure 8.3. Screen grab of Bad Black interviewed by Luzze Andrew Anderson on Morning Flavor Entertainment, a popular Ugandan morning talk show based in Kampala.

| | You get the point?
| | That is someone who is you know, gay.
| | So, with you, if you say 'I'm a transgender' because it's 'transgender person' is the person—
| | *Yye nga bamukyuusizza*
| | [English translation: When they are changed—]
| | Officially this is P.G.—
| | Forgive me, P.G.—
| | Parental Guidance is advised.
| | So, if young kids are watching you can just keep away from this one here.
| | (Turning back to Bad Black)
| | So, with you, which people do you get attracted to?

Bad Black: Okay, first of all, I'll explain the word 'transgender.'
| | Transgender means someone identifies as transgender woman—
| | Because I'm born in a male body—
| | But it's not a body I'd like to be in.
| | Yes, because I feel so much of a woman.
| | So, that's why I'm called a transgender because that doesn't mean you have to be transitioned already.
| | No. It's what you feel.
| | It's how you identify yourself.

You can just wake up one day and you're like—
I'm a transgender person who, you understand?
That's what you feel.
But me.
This is what I really feel.
I get attracted to men because I'm a transgender person.
I'm a transgender woman—

Andrew Anderson: That means you have your private parts are for a male person?—

Bad Black: It does not matter, yes, it is—
But deep inside me I feel I am a woman.
Most of the things in me are for women despite the biological part.
I feel I'm a woman and that's why I'm a transgender person.[16]

Throughout the interview, Bad Black, who now goes by Keem Love Black, remains remarkably composed in the face of such aggressive questioning. Months later, after the video had gone viral and mostly lost its immediate audience, I was chatting with Bad Black about the impact the visibility had on her daily life at a popular restaurant in Kampala. Curious about how she could continue to sit there, on national television, with such a homophobic interviewer, she responded with sass, "And he [the interviewer] is even gay—I had sex with him before!" I was surprised, considering the interviewer, Luzze Andrew Anderson, often posted on social media sexist homo/transphobic context, such as on January 20, 2017, when he posted a photo of a young woman with the caption: "She fucked around. . . . who wants to see her nudes doing another gal . . . we want 5009 likes then I post the. [*sic*]." While grossly disrespectful, alongside the on-air interview he did with Bad Black, such a post illustrates the way homo/transphobia and heterosexism are being capitalized on in targeting sexual and gender minorities in Uganda. Directly soliciting his followers to "like" the photo to release "nudes" of an unnamed woman who he alleges had sex with "another gal" represents the appeal that transgressive sexualities and genders have for the heterosexual audience. Entertainers and media producers in need of popular content to build their own reputations and stay relevant often rely on the transgressions of sexual and gender minorities. These transgressions become content, build followings, and in turn help media companies sell advertisements. However,

---

16   I would like to thank Grace for helping me translate the Luganda to English in this video clip.

perpetually confused by Bad Black's witty, sexual, and sensational humor, I often had a difficult time deciphering what was authentic and what was fake in her assertions. With time, I found this distinction did not matter as much as my reaction. It was what she was saying—the unexpected, sexual, twisted, transgressive—that *mattered* because it was a form of cultural capital.

While it is certainly debatable if Bad Black is indeed the "Caitlyn Jenner of Uganda" (there are strong competitors such as the brilliant community organizer Cleopatra Kambugu Kentaro who has her own documentary on Netflix), the idea is representative of how transnational frames are used for local transgressions. For example, in the *Morning Flavor* interview the interviewer, when attempting to introduce Bad Black, says she is "like Caitlyn, that is—*Mama wa ba*—*tata wa ba Kardashian* [Mother of, father of, the Kardashians]," at first confusing Caitlyn Jenner for "the father" of the Kardashians before respecting this framework as incorrect and shifting to use the classificatory "mother." While this level of respect is extended to Caitlyn Jenner, a white American Republican transgender woman with an estimated net worth of $100 million, the same privilege is not extended to Bad Black, a poor, openly HIV+, transgender Ugandan woman who is repeatedly referred to with the wrong pronouns throughout the interview. More broadly, using Caitlyn Jenner as the point of entry to discuss a local transgender life reregisters "transgender" as not only "Western" and "un-African" but also as a homogenized experience. Even though Bad Black was sitting in front of the interviewer as a Ugandan transgender woman, she was still labeled as "gay," "Western," "foreign," and "un-African." To Bad Black's own face, Ugandan transgender visibility was not only being questioned but also being erased.

While this was not the first time that Bad Black appeared on popular media in Uganda, since this interview was aired (and perhaps more importantly, since it was circulated on the internet), her reputation has grown tremendously. Now she has over fifty-two thousand followers on Facebook (her primary site for content dissemination), where she actively posts and engages her audience with provocative content. From documenting her "pregnancy" and "birth" in 2017 and advocating for the release of the jailed medical anthropologist and critic of the Museveni regime Stella Nyanzi to rubbing shoulders with Ugandan socialites at appearances in Kampala's nightlife, Bad Black's content uses the (long-standing) popular fascination with queer transgression to build an audience. Reclaiming and reinventing the homo/transphobic in Uganda and the political economy for transgressive content, Bad Black has, despite the risks, generated hundreds of transgressive posts covering sexuality and gender advocacy but also Ugandan politics. This

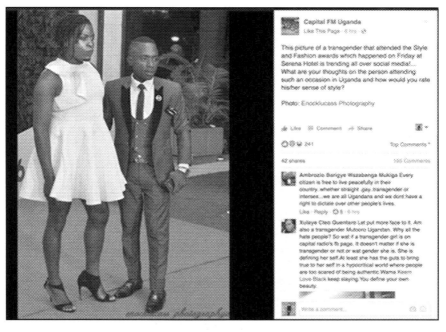

Figure 8.4. Screenshot of Capital FM Uganda's Facebook post of Bad Black at the red carpet event for the 2017 Style and Fashion Awards in Kampala.

transgression—the transgression of an individual expressing fluid gender expression, sexual identities, and queering the compulsory heterosexuality of Uganda became a stereotype to capitalize on for Bad Black because it was the life she *wanted* to live.

Bad Black flips the script on the expected shame that comes along with being an openly transgender woman in Ugandan society. Instead of viewing this as a detriment in the existing Ugandan political economy, she produces media content that is inherently transgressive from essentially accepted norms. While Bad Black engages in queer activism (with LGBT organizations in Uganda), she also uses popular media coverage, such as outings and negative (sometimes *violent*) coverage in tabloids, newspapers, blogs, and social media memes from attending events organized by the elites to build her reputation. For example, in 2016, Bad Black was photographed and made into a meme on Facebook by Capital FM Radio, Kampala's major radio station, after she wore a dress to the Style and Fashion Awards at the Serena Hotel in Kampala (see figure 8.4). The caption, which acknowledged that the image was "trending all over social media!" invited users to comment on what their "thoughts on the person attending such an occasion in Uganda" were and asked users "how would you rate his/her sense of style?" Such a post could have dire consequences for the average Ugandan being accused and outed, particularly in terms of social exclusion. For Bad Black, these things had already happened: loss of family, home, and employment. Her marginalization was so severe that her nonconformity simply became a channel of cultivating a popular reputation. In response to the backlash on Ugandan social media to her look at the Fashion Awards, Bad Black (taking after her mentor Stella Nyanzi) continued to generate transgressive content for her Facebook followers, such as the meme of herself as a 2021 Uganda Woman MP Candidate with the platform "Rich People United" to further circulate on social media (see figure 8.5). Similarly, when Bad Black posted a meme of herself next to a Ugandan socialite known for her own transgressions such as scamming a *mzungu* (white person or foreigner) for 11 billion Ugandan shillings (over $3 million USD), bleaching her skin to appear whiter, and her time spent in prison, social media followers actively engaged (see figure 8.6). This flipping is often outside of the notions of respectability that activists subscribe to, which may have them questioning whether such visibility (and its backlash) does more harm than good.

Bad Black uses a transgressive approach to build reputation and although at times this reputation is not respectable, she uses this transgression even within the growingly essentialized LGBT activist community as an opportunity to cultivate discourse, followers, and an audience. While elite activists do not necessarily belittle Bad Black and her activism, they certainly do not circulate her memes with the actual members of parliament or foreign dignitaries that they meet with on a regular basis when advocating for policy change. Nonetheless, the content Bad Black creates from her images of a transgender future help make such elite activists even more respectable. Bad Black is the actively, visibly gender nonconforming "nonnormative body" that makes NGOized LGBT advocacy look normalized in the Ugandan context. Because Bad Black is making a liveable queer life for herself outside of professional activism and cultivating a mainstream audience to accept her queer transgressions (at least as a form of entertainment), she is certainly a key player in making sense of contemporary popular culture in Uganda.

Figure 8.5. A meme posted by Bad Black on July 10, 2019, which illustrates a fictional political poster for her candidacy for a 2021 Woman Member of Parliament seat for Kampala.

Figure 8.6. A meme posted by Bad Black on her account inviting users to choose who "rocked the ASFA Awards" between "a transgender queen" (herself) and "an ex-convict, broke sex worker" (a photo of the Ugandan socialite "Bad Black" who shares her name).

Her cultural production, however transgressive to both Ugandan and Global North sentiments, builds her reputation and increases her capital.

Fleeting Transgression

I first met Shivan Pavin in 2016 with Keith King, a Ugandan transqueer artist who profiled her for a project documenting members of the Ugandan queer community. Shivan Pavin, an up-and-coming artist in Uganda's music industry, had popular tracks out on the NTV-Uganda charts and was also openly lesbian. Her face was adorned with six different piercings, from her eyebrows to her lips, which made it easy for Keith King to fashion an "edgy look" throughout the makeshift photoshoot in the back of the popular queer club, Ram, and on the street outside. We reviewed the photos from the shoot and learned more about her life over drinks at the bar in downtown Kampala. Shivan, then twenty-eight, told Keith and me about the difficulties she experienced on account of her sexuality—her struggles getting her first track out in the industry, her challenges raising her child from a rape, and her then complicated love with a Ugandan transgender man. She talked to us for about an hour, and throughout the conversation, it was clear to me Shivan was a fighter who cared little about other people's judgments. After discussing her new song, the theme song of Pride Uganda 2015, "This Is Me I'm Kuchu" (about being a queer person in Uganda), she told us about the discrimination she faced in Uganda for her queer transgressions:

> When I came out I lost contacts, I lost friends, I lost jobs. I asked people 'can you help me with this show?' And they said, 'no we cannot work with someone like you.' But no matter what happens I am never going back into the closet. You either accept me or leave it.[17]

Formal LGBTI activism became a major motif of her recent work, which gained a new and perhaps more consistent audience for her music. Previously she was producing music videos in Luganda, the local language, that mostly followed Luganda love song tropes such as the "village girl" finding love with a (rich) "big man." After her turn toward LGBTI activism, she was regularly considered a guaranteed invite to any LGBTI organizational event that needed a musical performance (which was at least once a month from 2015 to 2016). Shivan found a steady stream of gigs that also held a mission for her worth fighting for. Other *kuchu* musical groups in Uganda have similar goals as Shivan, including the group known as Talented Ugandan Kuchus (TUK). In 2016 Shivan was profiled by *Kuchu Times*, a LGBT media house created by Ugandan activist Kasha Nabagasera. Shivan was quoted saying, "If we don't have a right to be who we are why did God create us? Why are we surrounded with hate?" Shivan explained that the reason she started writing and producing songs on LGBTI activism was in response to the police brutality experienced by sexual and gender minorities, particularly in reference to September 2016 when the Uganda Police Force stormed the venue for Pride Uganda, arrested activists, seized cameras from journalists, and cut off the hair of some pageant performers, many of whom were transgender women.

Shivan's first tracks were about popular love in Luganda, a language of central Uganda. These songs reveal how Shivan first capitalized on transgression

---

17   Pavin, interview, October 20, 2015.

Figure 8.7. Screenshot from Shivan Pavin's music video "Back Off" illustrating her turf war.

with female (hetero)sexuality. Although in the love stories she is in pursuit of a male lover, the songs do have feminist undertones, particularly in the way she writes the story: making the decisions and fulfilling her own goals. However, the music video usually juxtaposes visual sexuality with the more sexually modest lyrics. This constituted transgression, which would turn into discourse, circulation, and finally "reputation" building for Shivan. Heterosexual transgressions operate in a parallel way to queer transgressions. Since her rise in popularity in 2016, Shivan has not produced any tracks or albums and has largely disappeared on social media, with only a few scattered (unpopular) posts since 2017. Shivan's story illustrates the fleeting nature of transgression. Producing transgressive capital, first and foremost, requires a public. For Shivan, an artist who has (up to this point) failed to enter the *mainstream* like Keko, and failed to go viral like Bad Black, the transgressions she was making, for whatever reason, lost value. Her content, while radical in its own right, was perhaps overshadowed by the many other artists that were competing for transgressive capital. Shivan's controversies, which consisted at certain points in time with leaked nude photos, her consistent acquisition of piercings, or feminist messages such as in her popular track "Back Off," gave her a reputation but one that did not transgress enough to sustain or translate into a secure material future.

A fleeting reputation is something most cultural producers experience. In the case of the queer transgressive in Uganda, a lost reputation is the loss

Figure 8.8. Screenshot from "Back Off" illustrating Pavin's Luganda love narrative.

of capital. This reputation is what allowed artists like Keko and activists like Bad Black to become celebrities. Keko, who came from a modest background in Uganda, traveled regularly internationally, hosting concerts and releasing albums before a permanent move to Canada, where she now lives with her partner. Her reputation in Uganda has been established, and her desired standard of living has been sustained. For Bad Black, a transgender woman who, at one time, was kicked out of her family home, lived in a slum in Kampala, sold sex to survive, and is HIV+, the life as a meme queen elevated her in part out of poverty.

Popular Homophobias and Capitalizing on Transgression

This chapter has prioritized a reconsideration of sexual and gender minority agency in theorizing how popular homophobia is flipped, and sexual and gender transgression is capitalized on in building and sustaining formidable cultural capital. In doing so, individuals such as Keko, Bad Black, and Shivan Pavin have, successfully and unsuccessfully, directly and indirectly, pursued a better future for themselves and their identities. By not allowing themselves to be shamed by oppressive patriarchal and masculinist forces, they have used this novel resistance to build reputations and brands that include relatively vast potential economic, political, and cultural value. The pursuits of capitalizing on transgression have played out in interestingly different directions for Keko, Shivan, and Bad Black in their shared interest for cultural capital.

The ethnography and biographies I present above demonstrate how African popular culture is now a rich site for understanding contested power relations. The chapter has taken a closer look at this cultural dynamic in regard to Ugandan youth with contested or nonnormative sexualities and gender who are otherwise disenfranchised. These youth use popular culture to their advantage by engaging the dominant discourse around it to conceptualize and enact their social and cultural roles as citizens that "belong." The youth producing and engaging in the Ugandan popular imaginary provide evidence that because the popular always leans toward the queer, transgressions have always been a part of popular culture and will continue to transform it as a site of constituting power and resistance (Hall 2002). These fights create anxiety for the state, which increasingly intervenes in popular culture, and particularly cultural and creative expressions mediated through the digital sphere, by arresting, prosecuting, and jailing those who insult the state. In Tanzania, ten of the most popular songs in the country were censored and banned under accusations of "sexual" transgression. In Uganda, five people have been jailed—including artists attempting to break into the industry—for "insulting" or "threatening" the president. In a context where building a reputation is as important a skill as any other, such transgressions encapsulate the potential for a type of reputation building.

There are shared connections to reaching the Global North in the most elite circles of Ugandan popular culture because the elite are the most connected to the extractive capital of the Global North. This is a popular mindset as illustrated by the tolerance of Keko. Further, parties at embassies and meetings with Ugandan MPs for LGBT activists connect them with the Uganda elite. The divisions of elite and nonelite are influenced almost entirely by social categories of the Global North. Yet again, preference for power is in the hands of Global North interests. When Bad Black, Shivan Pavin, and Keko engage in transgressions that resemble those of Global North modernity, they will always gain reputation and higher status in Uganda. However, if their transgressions are only localized, only pertinent to the Uganda elite, they will lose their cultural capital as artists in tune only with the modernity of the Global North. This partly fuels the gay "myth of affluence." Finally, the heterogeneity of the transgressions is important to consider. While the popular figures I have referenced in the chapter are all engaged in some of culturally transgressive work, the pursuits for making life liveable are inherently different and the outcomes are often not similar. While it is important to address the (anti-homosexuality) law, I contend that the law itself does not define the transgressive behavior. Rather, law gets used repeatedly as a cultural framework, reference point, or point of entry to any discussion on queer life in Uganda because it is one of the only frames that scholars and citizens alike have for conceptualizing transgressive queer lives. Moreover, the law is merely a tool of justification. This language becomes a way to justify the popular actors themselves treating others as transgressive. The stronger the popular justification for the law, the greater "value" the transgression has for that individual.

I have thus demonstrated the unique and complex ways in which transgressions are what create the space to enter the local and global market. The market I refer to is a unique space or cultural economy that is yearning for the transgressive because the cultural order has been standardized. The normative genders and sexualities are not headlined because they do not differ from the normative regimes of dominant culture. When Keko, Bad Black, or Shivan engage in transgressive acts, they crack the normativity and with it make headlines, find a public, and build a reputation. This reconceptualized brand can be managed and sustained, like that of Keko, in which she stayed silent on her sexuality, minimized her "politics," and continued producing tracks. This reputation can also be manipulated, distorted, and damaged as Bad Black has illustrated. She took her transgressions and established a consistently transgressive "Bad Black" that never stayed out of the headlines. Her audience is still growing: for her, this is just the beginning. Yet this reputation can be lost, as it was for Shivan Pavin. The fleeting nature of transgressive work and competition in the local and global market for reputation was eventually Shivan's downfall. What all three experiences demonstrate is how transgressive capital generated new possibilities for the future for marginalized African youth, while creating new inequalities and failures for others in the realm of popular culture.

Bibliography

Ashworth, Michael. 2017. "Affective Governmentality: Governing through Disgust in Uganda." *Social & Legal Studies* 26, no. 2: 188–207. https://doi.org/10.1177/0964663916666630.

Awondo, Patrick, Peter Geschiere, and Graeme Reid. 2013. "Homophobic Africa?: Toward a More Nuanced View." *African Studies Review* 55 (3): 145–68.

Barber, Karin. 1987. "Popular Arts in Africa." *African Studies Review* 30, no. 3: 1. https://doi.org/10.2307/524538.

———. 2018. *A History of African Popular Culture*. Cambridge: Cambridge University Press.
Beck, Rose Marie. 2011. "Urban Languages in Africa." *Africa Spectrum* 45, no. 3: 11–41.
Becker, Heike. 2012. "Anthropology and the Study of Popular Culture: A Perspective from the Southern Tip of Africa." *Research in African Literatures* 43, no. 4: 17. https://doi.org/10.2979/reseafrilite.43.4.17.
Bourdieu, Pierre. 1986. *Distinction*. 1st ed. London: Routledge.
Bryan, Austin. 2016. "And That's How I Survived Being Killed: Testimonies of Human Rights Abuses from Uganda's Sexual and Gender Minorities." Sexual Minorities Uganda.
———. 2018a. "'Even If They Spit at You, Don't Be Surprised': Health Care Discrimination Against Uganda's Sexual and Gender Minorities." Sexual Minorities Uganda.
———. 2018b. "Kuchu Activism, Queer Sex-Work and 'Lavender Marriages,' in Uganda's Virtual LGBT Safe(r) Spaces." *Journal of Eastern African Studies* 13, no. 1: 1–16. https://doi.org/10.1080/17531055.2018.1547258.
Bucholtz, Mary. 2002. "Youth and Cultural Practice." *Annual Review of Anthropology* 31, no. 1: 525–52. https://doi.org/10.1146/annurev.anthro.31.040402.085443.
Clark, Msia Kibona. 2018. "Feminisms in African Hip Hop." *Meridians* 17, no. 2: 383–400. https://doi.org/10.1215/15366936-7176538.
Dolby, Nadine. 2006. "Popular Culture and Public Space in Africa: The Possibilities of Cultural Citizenship." *African Studies Review* 49 no. 3: 31–47. https://doi.org/10.1353/arw.2007.0024.
Fabian, Johannes. 1998. *Moments of Freedom: Anthropology and Popular Culture*. Charlottesville: University of Virginia Press.
Foucault, Michel. 1978. *The History of Sexuality: An Introduction*. Translated by Robert Hurley. Reissue ed. New York: Vintage.
Guseh, James S. 2008. "Slogans and Mottos on Commercial Vehicles: A Reflection of Liberian Philosophy and Culture." *Journal of African Cultural Studies* 20, no. 2: 159–71. https://doi.org/10.1080/13696810802522288.
Hall, Stuart. 2002. "Notes on Deconstructing the Popular." In *Cultural Resistance Reader*, edited by Stephen Duncombe, 185–92. Brooklyn, NY: Verso.
Hendriks, Thomas. 2017. "Queer(Ing) Popular Culture: Homo-Erotic Provocations from Kinshasa." *Journal of African Cultural Studies* 31, no.1 (July): 1–18. https://doi.org/10.1080/13696815.2017.1341833.
Jjuuko, Adrian, and Fridah Mutesi. 2018. "The Multifaceted Struggle against the Anti-Homosexuality Act in Uganda." In *Envisioning Global LGBT Human Rights*, edited by Adrian Jjuuko, Nancy Nicol, Richard Lusimbo, Nick J. Mulé, Susan Ursel, Amar Wahab, and Phyllis Waugh, 269–306. (Neo)Colonialism, Neoliberalism, Resistance and Hope. School of Advanced Study, University of London.

Kerr, David. 2014. "Performing the Self: Rappers, Urban Space and Identity in Dar Es Salaam." University of Birmingham.
King, Rachel, Justine Nanteza, Zubayiri Sebyala, Joy Bbaale, Enos Sande, Tonia Poteat, Herbert Kiyingi, and Wolfgang Hladik. 2018. "HIV and Transgender Women in Kampala, Uganda – Double Jeopardy." *Culture, Health & Sexuality* 21, no. 3: 1–14. https://doi.org/10.1080/13691058.2018.1506155.
Kinsman, Gary. 2018. "Policing Borders and Sexual/Gender Identities: Queer Refugees in the Years of Canadian1 Neoliberalism and Homonationalism." In *Envisioning Global LGBT Human Rights*, edited by Nancy Nicol, Adrian Jjuuko, Richard Lusimbo, Nick J. Mulé, Susan Ursel, Amar Wahab, and Phyllis Waugh, 97–130. (Neo)Colonialism, Neoliberalism, Resistance and Hope. University of London Press.
Kwame, Edwin Otu. 2017. "LGBT Human Rights Expeditions in Homophobic Safaris: Racialized Neoliberalism and Post-Traumatic White Disorder in the BBC's The World's Worst Place to Be Gay." *Critical Ethnic Studies* 3 no. 2: 126. https://doi.org/10.5749/jcritethnstud.3.2.0126.
Lawuyi, Olatunde Bayo. 1988. "The World of the Yoruba Taxi Driver: An Interpretive Approach to Vehicle Slogans." *Africa* 58, no. 1: 1–13. https://doi.org/10.2307/1159867.
Lusimbo, Richard, and Austin Bryan. 2018. "Kuchu Resilience and Resistance in Uganda: A History." In *Envisioning Global LGBT Human Rights*, 323–46. (Neo)Colonialism, Neoliberalism, Resistance and Hope. School of Advanced Study, University of London.
Missionaries of Hate. 2010. Vanguard. Current TV. http://www.imdb.com/title/tt2158249/plotsummary.
Moore, Erin V. 2016. "Postures of Empowerment: Cultivating Aspirant Feminism in a Ugandan NGO: Postures of Empowerment." Ethos 44, no. 3: 375–96. https://doi.org/10.1111/etho.12124.
Mous, Maarten, and Kiessling Roland. 2004. "Urban Youth Languages in Africa." *Anthropological Linguistics* 46, no. 3: 303–41.
Newell, Sasha. 2012. The Modernity Bluff: Crime, Consumption, and Citizenship in Côte d'Ivoire. Chicago: University of Chicago Press.
Nyairo, Joyce, and James Ogude. 2005. "Popular Music, Popular Politics: Unbwogable and the Idioms of Freedom in Kenyan Popular Music." *African Affairs* 104 (415): 225–49.
Nyanzi, Stella. 2013. "Dismantling Reified African Culture through Localised Homosexualities in Uganda." *Culture, Health & Sexuality* 15 (8): 952–67. https://doi.org/10.1080/13691058.2013.798684.
Oyewumi, Oyeronke. 1997. *The Invention of Women: Making an African Sense of Western Gender Discourses*. 1st ed. Minneapolis: University of Minnesota Press.
Peters, Melissa Minor. 2016. "'They Wrote "Gay" on Her File': Transgender Ugandans in HIV Prevention and Treatment." *Culture, Health & Sexuality* 18 (1): 84–98. https://doi.org/10.1080/13691058.2015.1060359.

Pier, David G. 2015. *Ugandan Music in the Marketing Era: The Branded Arena.* https://doi.org/10.1057/9781137546975.
Reuters. 2014. "U.S. Cuts Aid to Uganda, Cancels Military Exercise over Anti-Gay Law," June 19, 2014.
Schwartz, Gary, and Don Merten. 1967. "The Language of Adolescence: An Anthropological Approach to the Youth Culture." *American Journal of Sociology* 72, no. 5: 453–68.
Srinivasan, Sharath, Stephanie Diepeveen, and George Karekwaivanane. 2019. "Rethinking Publics in Africa in a Digital Age." *Journal of Eastern African Studies* 13 no. 1: 2–17. https://doi.org/10.1080/17531055.2018.1547259.
Thoreson, Ryan Richard. 2014. "Troubling the Waters of a 'Wave of Homophobia': Political Economies of Anti-Queer Animus in Sub-Saharan Africa." *Sexualities* 17, no. 1–2: 23–42. https://doi.org/10.1177/1363460713511098.
"Uganda Court Rules against Homophobia." 2010. Al Jazeera English.

Chapter Nine

Twitter, Youth Agency, and New Narratives of Power in #RhodesMustFall

Jendele Hungbo

Introduction

The agency of youth in the numerous narratives surrounding the South African liberation struggles as well as the postapartheid attempts to keep racism and other forms of discrimination at bay has received considerable scholarly attention.[1] In much of those critiques, the critical approach has often been to emphasize the multiple issues of history and memory and how they relate to questions of race among the different categories of people who make up the national entity now famously styled "the rainbow nation." This thriving debate provides an opportunity for critical reflections on how much unity can be ascribed to the rainbow nation, which, on the surface, appears beautiful and exhibits peaceful coexistence. Such bourgeoning narratives of the awesomeness of the 'peaceful' transition from a segregated apartheid state to a supposedly democratic and inclusive 'new' South Africa are often not only popularized by the state, but by the global media, which often peddles the prevalent myth of a national euphoria surrounding the supposed

---

1 Pillay, "Silence is Violence"; Nel, "Social Media & New Struggles" and "Twitter Activism."

reconciliation of the different races in the new South Africa. What these narratives of national cohesion mask, however, are the uncomfortable compromises and concessions made by both sides of the racial divide to arrive at the much-celebrated peaceful transition. Though much of the bitterness of the past became known through the innovative Truth and Reconciliation Commission hearings, it was this same body that provided the public with a moral gauge with which to measure the readiness for compromise and forgiveness going forward.[2]

While history and memory cannot be disregarded in any discussion of the trajectory of the South African nation, a look at more recent examples of deep-seated disparities, especially at social and economic levels, suggests that there needs to be a bit more nuance in order to capture the lingering uneven positionality of the numerous layers of identity in the country. South African youth readily come to mind as one major disenfranchised group we need to further understand, as their experience of apartheid and the postliberation struggles related to it is quite different from that of the older generation of South Africans.[3] While the older generation encountered apartheid firsthand and lived through its excruciating realities, the younger generation's understanding of it has been mainly through narratives of angst and the current dispossessions steeped in the systemic structures of inequality sustained by the racially contrived system of segregation. Kristi Kenyon and Juliana Coughlin highlight this generational difference in chapter 14 of this edited volume. It is also important to acknowledge the peculiarity of the various struggles related to relations of power in South Africa. There is the need to look beyond race, as there are complex ways in which race and class structures are closely intertwined, thus making the country different from others in the region in fundamental ways.[4] As Abebe Zegeye argues, "The manner in which race and class simultaneously affect citizenship and democratization, and thereby also identity formation among South Africans needs to be considered"[5] seriously when dealing with issues around the experiences of different sections of the population. Such considerations, I argue, need to also cut across the different epochs in recent South African history. In other words, the telling footprints of race on class structures, material living conditions, and everyday life realities in South Africa provide an interesting

---

2 See Bairstow, "Amnesty, Reintegration and Reconciliation"; Bar-Tal, "From Intractable Conflict"; Graybill, *Truth and Reconciliation in South Africa.*
3 See Theron and Malindi, "Resilient Street Youth"; Evans, "Unsettled Matters."
4 See Friedman, *Race, Class and Power.*
5 Zegeye, "Media, Youth and Identity," 22.

backdrop for making sense of the conduct of different sections of the population, including young people.

South African youth in particular continue to grapple not only with the brutal legacies of apartheid but, like most of their counterparts on the continent, they constantly battle with the endless disempowering consequences of neoliberal globalization and the political-economic power imbalances that this globalization fosters in the developing world. The inequities fostered by neoliberalism have in turn been exacerbated by the actions and inactions of the ANC ruling elite, whose abysmal record of governance has created very few opportunities for young people. One of the immediate outcomes of this relentless history of disenfranchisement has been a festering angst among young people who feel betrayed by their local leaders and the world. Such resentments have found powerful expression in recent mass movements led by young people in universities across South Africa. And online media have provided the key political weapons in these mass movements. It is the mobilizing power of social media in these youth-led movements that I examine in this chapter. I focus particularly on the discursive behavior of the young undergraduates who were mainly involved in the #RhodesMustFall campaign at the University of Cape Town (UCT) between March and April 2015, demonstrating how they instrumentalized social media in clearing and reorganizing public space to promote freedom and inclusivity, thus renegotiating power relations with postapartheid hegemonic forces.

#RhodesMustFall and Transformation Consciousness

The mass youth movement generally known as "Rhodes-Must-Fall" began with a student's protest at the University of Cape Town in March 2015. There had been various open and underground mobilizations among students on university campuses across South Africa around the larger discourse of the need for transformation in education, especially at the tertiary level. But the effort of a particular UCT student, Chumani Maxwele, who specifically targeted the statue on the university campus of former British colonialist and former prime minister of the Cape Colony (1890–96), Sir Cecil Rhodes, triggered and symbolized the bigger campaign to decolonize education and rescue both curriculum and the superstructure of the academy from the shackles of racial discrimination.[6] It also raised questions about the pervasive inequality that had continued to generate a lot of tension in South

---

6   See Coetzee, *Writing Under the Skin*; and Roelofs, *Flying in the Univer-topia*.

African society, especially when viewed from the perspective of the advantages and disadvantages arising from racial belonging.

The protest that sought the removal of the statue of the colonial businessman and mining magnate from the campus began on March 9, 2015, when Maxwele defaced the statue of Cecil Rhodes on the main campus of the university in Cape Town, leading to other similar defacements on subsequent days.[7] For the students, both black and white, the presence of the statue and several others of its kind (as well as certain artworks on campus) promoted institutional racism and an assault on the sensibilities of black South Africans, who were the main victims of colonial raids and apartheid for centuries. The protest quickly assumed the dimension of a mass movement that provided an opportunity for mainly black students and faculty in the higher education sector to articulate grievances bordering on discrimination perceived to be based on racial considerations and the request for redress. It also lent credence to the argument that South Africa is still a work in progress, despite the general tendency to hold it up as a miraculous triumph in the blending of racial groups and identities to produce an enviable coexistence of different racial and sociopolitical interests. Indeed, the series of service delivery protests, xenophobic violence, and fatal criminal activities in the country, which are often linked to pervasive inequality after the demise of apartheid, further reinforce the fault lines of the "new" South Africa. It is therefore no wonder that the restiveness that reared its head in the higher education sector was also being attributed to social inequality, which perpetually relegates black students (and in some cases black faculty) to a position of marginality, while their white counterparts continue to enjoy privileges arising from a structurally skewed postracial neoliberal system.

Social media particularly provided a great impetus for mobilization and sustenance of the protest. Twitter was perhaps the most vibrant social media platform in this regard as the campaign styled #RhodesMustFall became popular with regular tweets, retweets, and updates keeping young participants abreast of events around the protest. The significance of Twitter as an online media platform in the campaign went beyond that of a social space that enabled a group of young people to connect virtually and socially across space and time. It also provided a forum for robust civic engagement and conscientization toward the critical issues of social transformation so central to the campaign, especially in historically white institutions in South Africa. Twitter provided an opportunity through this civic engagement codified as

---

7   See Kros, "Rhodes Must Fall"; and Nyamnjoh, *#RhodesMustFall*.

#RhodesMustFall for young people in South Africa to, in the words of Carli Coetzee, "draw attention to historic dirt"[8] and cause action to be taken.

The effectiveness of this youth-led campaign was evidenced by the response of the UCT authorities as the statue of Cecil Rhodes was indeed pulled down by the university a month after the beginning of the sustained protest. In this regard, #RhodesMustFall can be regarded as the deconstruction of a fraught history championed by young people in South Africa and beyond, mainly through social media activism. Such deconstructions become significant in the constant probing of the dynamics of social engagement, especially in instances of marginality where history and memorialization are heavily influenced by hegemonic sentiments. For the youth, the violent history handed down to them and the agency of the political establishment represented by the ruling African National Congress (ANC) have become inadequate in dealing with the harsh realities of the moment. The new social spaces created by innovations in science and technology thus became the alternative avenues from where young people could effectively renegotiate power relations with a new political establishment that operates with old repertoires of repression. As Henry Jenkins argues, "Whatever inequalities remain in terms of access to technologies, skills, and other social resources, we have found many instances where new media has provided tools and infrastructures by which marginal groups engage and participate in the public sphere."[9] New media have come to significantly alter the skewed architecture of the public sphere as "subordinate groups can use networked media to expand the civic domain, even as elite groups seek to constrain the definition of what is 'legitimate' in the public arena."[10] New online media now function both as existential tools and as alternative spaces for young people to challenge old forms of power that have been reinvented and reintegrated into a postapartheid democratic state. This mode of challenge, however, continues to be a heavily contested discourse, especially regarding the deployment of violence in the pursuit of resistance politics and the quest for a new social order.[11]

The emergence of new media technologies and the social contestations they have fostered have gained enormous critical purchase in cultural studies scholarship because they offer important avenues for drawing links between contemporary technological innovations and ongoing processes of social

---

8   Coetzee, *Writing under the Skin*, 105.
9   Jenkins, "Youth Voice, Media and Political Engagement," 24.
10 Jenkins, 24.
11 See Nuttall, "The Shock of the New-Old."

transformation. As Alun Munslow argues, since modern society "has experienced social, political and ecological revolutions, and new technology, the growing need has been to make the past intelligible to the present."[12] For young people in South Africa, the vaunted histories of social and political revolutions passed on to them by the older generation seem to have fallen short of expectations. While they are acutely aware of the barbarity of the apartheid regime and the phenomenal struggles and sacrifices of the older generation to secure freedom for them, the insufferable conditions of their lives continue to undermine that heroic past. The contradiction of the moment, of a black majority rule that has brought very few changes to their lives and those of their parents, has led to young people's search for new cultural spaces of expression and identity formation. They now find empowerment and solace in a technological revolution marked by the advent of new social media resources with the attendant opportunities for self-expression and the recalibration of their identity. In South Africa, race has been seriously implicated in discourses on access to the media. Mainstream media in South Africa have been dominated by the white minority population, which continues to deploy its powers toward the reinforcement of the hegemony of the few. The rise of big media conglomerates has meant the deployment of huge capital in the media business, making it difficult for the previously disadvantaged black population to participate or be adequately represented in the highly competitive postapartheid media environment. As Mvuzo Ponono notes, "In a society with a commercial media system that reinforces an elite national discourse, certain sections of the South African population are often omitted as participants from the media sphere due to any combination of education, income, language and place of residence."[13] What Ponono's argument affirms is that the democratic order that was birthed in South Africa in 1994 did not translate into much balance in terms of access to media and by extension the projection of the narratives of all the different identities making up the polity. While South Africa continues to be celebrated by the ruling elite and the global media as a miraculous exercise in multiethnic/cultural coexistence, narratives of marginality by disenfranchised groups are often eclipsed from the mainstream media.

---

12   Munslow, *Deconstructing History*, 8.
13   Ponono, "Centring the Subaltern," 141.

Theory and Method

This chapter proceeds from the perspective of critical internet studies that, in the words of Daniel Trottier and Christian Fuchs, allows us to analyze "larger contexts such as power structures, the state, capitalism, gender relations, social struggles, and ideologies which shape and are shaped by the digital media landscape in dialectical processes."[14] Such a perspective provides the opportunity to transcend the limitations of the Laswell model of communication inquiry. The linearity and unidirectional character of the Laswell model, which limits itself to the five elements of who said what, to whom, via which channel, and to what effect are then surpassed to look at broader sociohistorical dimensions and undertones of discursive engagements in the media. This approach emphasizes the idea of sociality, participation, and engagement in a community of discussants, which social media like Twitter offer in situations where mainstream media may not be available to the general populace.[15]

Critical internet studies build on the idea of signification so central to cultural analysis. Drawing heavily on semiotics and linguistics, Stuart Hall and his British cultural studies cohort relied on the new science of signs in formulating new insights into the process of meaning making in the media. This structuralist approach emphasized the ways in which language is not an objective conveyor of reality, but only a medium through which meaning is produced. So, meaning no longer depends on "how things were" but on how they are signified.[16] Language in communication, then, is a function of culture, not nature: there is not a direct correlation between language and its material referents. And because meaning is socially produced through language, some meanings are made to gain credibility and legitimacy over others. Signification, then, becomes a site of social struggle over meaning, and by extension, consent and power.[17] The critical paradigm that informs internet studies is thus a move away from the surface analysis of media message content and their effect on the generative aspects of language. The emphasis is on language as a process of coding, not a set of coded messages.[18] The instability of meaning associated with language means that media

---

14 Trottier and Fuchs, "Theorizing Social Media," 3.
15 See Carpentier, *Media and Participation*.
16 Hall, "Rediscovery of Ideology," 77.
17 Hall, 70.
18 Hall, 71.

messages are reconceived not in terms of how they convey reality but how they normalize ideology, "producing [inventing] nature as a sort of guarantee of truth."[19] This new insight into signification as a central tenet of media work raised crucial questions around representation. If situations could be defined, shaped, and organized to look a certain way, then reality was no longer a given set of facts: it was the outcome of a construction.

In the case of South Africa, the various sites of social contestation, which include power, land, politics, history, and memory, make a critical studies approach almost imperative. And, what's more, glaring inequality has stratified the two major races in the country, creating deep-seated animosities that make a forgetting of the historical realities of the country almost impossible. In this specter of inequality, the majority black South African population continues to see the experience of the past mirrored in the present with the possibility for redemption waning considerably. It is in this regard that this chapter draws on postcolonial theory in several ways for a nuanced understanding of the discursive practices that can be gleaned from the #RhodesMustFall movement on Twitter. Though a "diffuse and nebulous term" in itself, postcolonial cultural studies offers many possibilities in reading and understanding power relations in previously dominated societies.[20] While the kind of settler colonialism witnessed by South Africa during the apartheid era differs greatly from much of the experience in the rest of the African continent, the idea of subjugation that both apartheid and colonialism represent tends to put them in a common basket to a certain degree. In postcolonial thinking, we find different dichotomies and binaries brought about largely by essentialized notions of race, class and, more recently, gender. In a deeper sense, a combination of anti-imperialist tradition and the attempt to give the subaltern voice in the quest for the affirmation of humanity further defines the postcolonial project. In doing this, the consideration of historical realities may extend far back beyond the advent of official subjugation. As Yasmeen Daifallah argues, "Decolonial thinkers often invoke pre-colonial traditions in their efforts to fashion 'national cultures'—modes of being, understanding, and self-expression specific to a decolonizing collective experience."[21] This argument speaks to Munslow's idea of "deconstructive consciousness,"[22] which challenges master narratives of

---

19 Hall, 75.
20 Ghandi, *Postcolonial Theory*, viii.
21 Daifallah, "Politics of Decolonial Interpretation," 810.
22 Munslow, *Deconstructing History*, 67.

the colonial project by digging deeper into the preexisting realities of colonial subjects. For Daifallah:

> Since colonization is defined as a process of cultural (psychic, epistemic, ideological) as well as political and economic domination, its undoing has to entail a process of cultural de-colonization, including a thoroughgoing critique of the effects of colonialism, an unearthing of the modes of life it eradicates or distorts, and a provision of alternative visions for social and political life.[23]

Daifallah further contends that "one of the distinguishing marks of modern European colonialism was its effect on colonized subjects' worldviews and self-perceptions, and not only their modes of social, economic, and political organization."[24] One of the primary achievements of postcolonial thought then is its exploration of culture as a site of resistance to domination during and beyond the colonial age.[25] It is this mode of critical analysis that recognizes culture as the primary terrain of struggles against postcolonial domination that I bring to bear on my analysis of the #RhodesMustFall movement led by students.

For an effective analysis of the discursive characteristics of the engagement on Twitter during this campaign, it is important to define a manageable scope that offers primary data for that purpose. Content in the form of posts with the hashtag Rhodes Must Fall (#RhodesMustFall) on different Twitter handles was therefore tracked for one month beginning on March 12, 2015, when the campaign gained visibility on social media trending with the hashtag. The selected tweets excluded pictures and videos, as the focus of this study is limited to written texts only. A qualitative close reading of the posts is undertaken in the mode of critical discourse analysis for a nuanced understanding of how they functioned in relation to the sociopolitical circumstances under which they were produced. Critical discourse analysis has been identified by several scholars as a useful theoretical and methodological analytical tool for both media and cultural studies, especially where the purpose of engagement is to gain a deeper understanding of communication in context.[26] In other words, there is a kind of social and linguistic pragmatism

---

23   Daifallah, "Politics of Decolonial Interpretation," 810.
24   Daifallah, 810.
25   Daifallah, 811.
26   See Ainsworth and Hardy, "Critical Discourse Analysis" ; Blommeart, *Discourse*; Scollo, "Cultural Approaches to Discourse Analysis"; Wodak, "Critical Discourse Analysis."

that needs to be applied to discourses in order to draw out critical perspectives that might become useful in their interpretation. All the major proponents of critical discourse analysis as indicated above therefore subscribe to an interplay of text and context in the reading of discourse and discursive practices in order to arrive at meanings that mirror the significant dynamics of conversation. For Blommaert, discourse is "a general mode of semiosis, i.e. meaningful symbolic behaviour."[27] In essence discourse "comprises all forms of meaningful human activity seen in connection with social, cultural, and historical patterns and developments of use."[28] The way people communicate, therefore, has a lot to do with the crucial cultural and historical circumstances surrounding them.

Twitter and New Modes of Participation

As a social network tool, Twitter has become one of the most successful platforms, gaining significant advantage and preference over similar ones that have emerged in recent times.[29] Though based mainly on the creation of personal profiles similar to other social media platforms like Facebook, LinkedIn, Instagram, and the like, Twitter offers a significant opportunity for engagement in a unique online community. One key characteristic of the platform is the brevity of posts, which are generally known as "tweets." In the beginning, the platform allowed only 140 characters per tweet. Though the limit was doubled to 280 characters per tweet in 2018, Twitter users seem to have absorbed the habit of brevity as most tweets remain within or even far below the number of characters allowed on the platform. While tweets can be replied to, commented on, liked, or retweeted, they can also be posted as a thread where they are longer than the number of characters allowed for single tweets.

The first "hashtagged" tweet about the #RhodesMustFall movement was by Jerome September, who posted through the handle @JeromeSeppie on March 12, 2015: "UCT students demanding the removal of the Rhodes statue #UCT #RhodesMustFall." His tweet was directed at ENCA, SABC News, and UCT SRC. This tweet signaled the beginning of the struggle.

---

27 Blommaert, *Discourse*, 2.
28 Blommaert, 3.
29 See Grant, Moon, and Grant, "Digital Dialogue?"; Evans "Twitter as PR"; and Trottier and Fuchs, "Theorising Social Media."

It was an unequivocal reporting of the main objective of #RhodesMustFall and the beginning of a clustering of participation and further mobilization of a virtual community for the actualization of the objective. The clusters at which the initial tweet and most of the subsequent ones were directed are quite significant for the purpose of mobilization and mileage. In other words, different communities of discourse began to coalesce around individuals and organizations who became instant opinion leaders with attendant online popularity. Some popular news agencies, including @SABCNewsOnline, @etvnews, @eNCANews, @News24, and celebrities played significant roles in the discourses and counterdiscourses that characterized #RhodesMustFall. In one of his subsequent tweets the same day, Jerome refers to Xolela Mangcu, a black South African academic who taught at the University of Cape Town at the time and who had become famous on mainstream and social media for his views on the need for transformation in the country. The tweet that read "Prof Mancgu speaking in support of the students' demand for #RhodesMustFall at #UCT today" had a photograph of the teacher holding a microphone to his mouth and surrounded by students (see Figure 9.1).

Though Jerome might not be identified as a celebrity, his tenacity at tweeting on the events of the campaign created a buzz of activities and some attention around his Twitter handle with spiraling likes and retweets of his posts, thus keeping the movement alive in the public imagination.

The engagements on Twitter were not just one-sided. While many participants posted in favor of the fall of Rhodes, there were also several participants who did not see any propriety in hounding down historical statues and other similar public art. For those in disagreement with the organizers of the movement, the removal of colonial monuments might be too cosmetic and might even have unintended negative consequences for the kind of South Africa envisaged by the "rainbow" metaphor. A popular television comedian in South Africa, Gareth Cliff, @GarethCliff, seemed to disagree with the fallists[30]: "when I die rich, I won't leave a cent to educational institutions or scholarships. I'll just end up with turds on my statue" (March 18, 2015). Tweets such as this provided an indication that different people have different perspectives on the issue of the removal of colonial statues from South African public places. What his tweet suggested was that prominent figures

---

30 During the protests, "fallists" became a popular term used in public discourse to describe the young activists and their supporters who favored the removal of the statue of Cecil Rhodes from the University of Cape Town.

Figure 9.1. Prof. Mangcu addressing students during the #RhodesMustFall protest.

who bequeathed their wealth to public institutions were being attacked by beneficiaries of the same institutions that benefited from their magnanimity and philanthropy. What is interesting, though, is that the positions that people held during the time of the campaign had little or nothing to do with their skin color. While there were some white participants who tweeted in support of #RhodesMustFall, there were black tweeters whose posts did not support the struggle of the students, thus complicating simplistic notions of race and protest culture in South Africa.

But there is a clear consciousness of identity formation woven into some of the tweets that appeared during the protest. A participant, @Noloyiso, who is identified online as Noloyiso Lange, said, "As a result of this #RhodesMustFall business I think I'm gonna stick to my natural hair." There is an incredible way in which the politics of the body is implicated in this preference in identification, which seeks to define the participant as black and against white colonial culture. Wearing black hair is one of the ways in which people in racialized environments attempt to retain their identity as against the attempt by some black people to wear long, blondish artificial hairpieces. It is pertinent to note, however, that this is not limited to South Africa alone. The various instances of teenagers and children who have been discriminated against by school officials in the United States provide palpable evidence of the ways in which black hair might function both as a source of distress and revolt in the popular culture. So much so that the famous Nigerian writer, Chimamanda Adichie, acknowledges the politics of black hair, especially among black women.[31]

Many of the tweets also referred to events of South Africa's recent history. In a tweet, Dela Gwala, @indie1activist wrote: "Rhodes was a racist mass murderer & UCT needs to transform- race, gender, sexuality and class. What's up for debate?" (March 21). One other tweet that seems to capture the essence of history and memory associated with the anti-Rhodes struggle on Twitter came from Transkei Moon with the handle @feminist_morake: "There's a pain that comes with seeing a man known to have massacred your people every day as part of your learning experience." In a challenge to the master narratives of history, Yammie Hearts and Curves with the handle @OyamaBotha tweets, "'Slavery is not African history. Slavery interrupted African history—Mutabaruka." This tweet is a quote taken from another individual named Mutabaruka. It is most likely from a public address at one

---

[31] See Weatherford, "Chimamanda Adichie on Black Hair and the Narrow Definition of Beauty."

of the numerous rallies held during the campaign. The quote tweeted here foregrounds the question of the veracity of historical accounts and the question of which version of history is indeed to be taken seriously. As Jacques Depelchin argues, the history of the wielders of power often remains preeminent until "more and more of the vanquished who survive the ordeal gather enough courage to tell parts of the story."[32]

The survivors in this case are the young black South Africans who became courageous enough to raise questions about the political-economic and social landscape and the issues around transformation that gained traction during the campaign. The competing histories and narratives that have coalesced around the new rainbow nation, bifurcated around the interests of racial capitalism on the one hand and decolonial struggles on the other, thus exemplifying the broader argument that has been made in postcolonial studies about the project of nationhood as the outcome of cultural production (i.e., as the work of mythification and employment). This is what Homi Bhabha meant when he insisted that "as a form of cultural elaboration," a nation is "an agency of ambivalent narration that holds culture at its most productive position, as a force for 'subordination, fracturing, diffusing, reproducing, as much as producing, creating, forcing, guiding'."[33] It is this politicization of culture, especially by young people contesting existing narratives of nationhood and belonging in the new South Africa, that I bring to bear on my analysis of Twitter activism in the #RhodesMustFall campaign.

Youth, Agency, and Responsive Citizenship in #RhodesMustFall

The #RhodesMustFall movement, at some point, became a struggle that drew sympathy from different racial groups across the country as skin color was no longer the only determinant of participation. It created a new civic culture that changed the face of social and political engagement through the media in South Africa. More than anything else, the #RhodesMustFall campaign redefined the question of agency in the media, especially among the disenfranchised youth in South Africa. Civic agency can be said to be an offshoot of active citizenship. It is a conscious action by citizens aimed at effecting a change in the character of their environment by means other

---

32   Depelchin, *Silences in African History*, 9.
33   Bhabha, *Narrating the Nation*, 3–4.

than elections.[34] Through civic agency, people do not simply become change agents, they also see themselves as such, thereby creating an identity that associates them with new beginnings or a new social order. For most young people in Africa, like we have seen in the student leaders of #RhodesMustFall, a form of excitement surrounded the process of seeking radical change in the polity. There is also the willingness of the marginalized but politically conscious youth to take risks and rupture the old ways of thinking and acting as James Yeku, Godfrey Maringira, Austin Bryan, and Kwabena Opoku-Agyemang have shown in their chapters in this volume. As Chris Wells contends, "How young people engage must be considered in light of the socio-political context in which their civic identities develop."[35] This can explain the vehemence of the online civic agency of the young South Africans behind #RhodesMustFall.

On a broader level, the #RhodesMustFall movement provides crucial cultural insights into the new forms of political activism engaged in by young people in Africa. It has become common, for example, for politicians, political commentators, and the media to bemoan the apolitical character of the younger generation, especially their supposed lack of interest in formal democratic processes such as political campaigns and elections. This political apathy is not unique to young people. For most people, politics has become a ruthless game of chicken managed by powerful people—one that holds few solutions to the daily concerns and struggles of most people's lives. The uninspiring nature of contemporary politics in Africa has triggered nothing but cynicism and frustration among ordinary citizens, especially young people. The overbearing influence of "big money," the unconscionable indifference to the struggles of ordinary citizens it promotes, and the pervasive culture of unaccountability and impunity neoliberal globalization has fostered in the global political culture have all led to a massive disengagement of ordinary people from formal democratic systems. But the mass movements galvanized by young people in Africa in recent years suggest that they have found new ways of engaging in political activism outside of the formal democratic structures and processes created by the state, that is, if we understand political and civic engagement as a process of social transformation.

Excluded from the highest echelons of political parties run by the older political elites, ignored in the formal decision-making processes of the

---

34 See Dahlgren, "Doing Citizenship"; "Young Citizens"; Bakardjieva, "Reconfiguring the Mediapolis."
35 Wells, "Two Eras of Civic Information," 617.

nation-state, and ignored in the general considerations that inform national policy decisions, young people have found creative ways of bypassing the formal political institutions hijacked by the older generation to insert and assert themselves in the political landscapes of their nations in powerful ways. African youth, like most of their counterparts worldwide, now spend much of their time online, communicating and interacting with their peers through new media technologies. As Dahlgren rightly observes, many young people using new online media to communicate are also becoming "what is called 'producers,' that is, they are users who in a variety of ways are generating their own media content. For young people in Europe and elsewhere, the net, and social media in particular, are not just something they "visit" on occasion in order to seek something special; the net and social media are increasingly part of the terrain of their daily lives."[36] The #RhodesMustFall campaign is thus a powerful example of the multiple ways in which media-savvy African youth are deploying new media, mostly online, in bringing about radical social change to societies and political-economic systems that have failed them and brought endless suffering and indignities to their lives and societies.

What this new media ecology dominated by young people tells us about African youth is profound. While a number of Africanists have for decades framed African youth as powerless

people devoid of agency and thus prone to the immiserating forces of neoliberal globalization— a state of precarity often compounded by the devious in/actions of the local ruling elite—mass youth-led actions such as the #RhodesMustFall campaign point to the extraordinary ways in which disenfranchised African youth have found ingenious ways to express their views and empower themselves. In this way they can bring about fundamental social change that has a direct bearing on their lives. Although their backs are still against the wall, with greater odds stacked against them than most of their peers around the globe, African youth have found the new political tools to shake up old institutions sustained by colonial ideologies and new ways to deconstruct the disempowering workings of neoliberal hegemonies, thus unsettling entrenched postcolonial forces and helping to animate radical change in policies that help reinvent their lives. With the new resources of online media and their mobilizing power, young people in Africa are no longer a derided and ignored demographic, for new media have become the new political and cultural weapons with which the younger African generations

---

36   Wells, 14.

renegotiate power relations between old and new political-economic systems that continue to make their lives miserable, marked by the chronic lack of social opportunities.

Conclusion

This chapter has attempted to examine the agency of South African youth in their attempts to socially transform the higher education landscape through the instrumentality of social media, with specific focus on the deployment of Twitter during the #RhodesMustFall campaign. The analysis centered on the discursive practices of the young participants in the campaign and how they have deployed the inherent powers of Twitter to effect change in the narratives of power that define the South African nation. Access to new online media has brought about a powerful shift in the power base, at least at the political level, which has begun to significantly alter the dynamics of social experience for young people through a more broad-based participation in public discourse. The poorest and the most marginalized are beginning to find some opportunities for public expression in new platforms provided by information and communication technologies. Social media platforms like Twitter constitute one of the most vibrant of such platforms where young people reclaim and assert their agency.[37] Though Tim Unwin acknowledges the ways information and communication technologies reinforce inequalities globally, he nonetheless stresses their ability to create new, alternative avenues for seeking redress and setting different courses of action that may bring to public consciousness the predicaments of the less privileged. This creation of a new public consciousness is central to the cultural functions that Terence Ranger, Johannes Fabian, David Coplan, and Karin Barber ascribed to African popular culture.[38]

This critical approach and consciousness on the part of the youth based mainly on a Habermasian theoretical perspective serves the purpose of teasing out the redemptive capabilities of social media platforms, especially in diverse communities where some dominant groups may claim privilege over others. This kind of perspective, Unwin argues, offers "valuable insights

---

37 See Unwin, *Reclaiming Information and Communication Technologies*.
38 See Ranger, *Dance and Society in Eastern Africa*; Fabian, "Popular Culture in Africa: Finding and Conjectures"; Coplan, *In Township Tonight*; and Barber, "African Popular Arts," 13.

into ways through which poor people might be able to benefit from such technologies."[39] Such insights usually begin with a kind of self-evaluation which involves a critical assessment of conditions around livelihood and the available opportunities with which a change can be brought about. In putting the necessity for this kind of evaluation in proper perspective, Unwin contends that "self-reflection was the means through which emancipation could be achieved."[40] When pushed further, especially through different forms of education that assist in building consciousness, self-reflection has the capacity to result in what Richard Heeks describes as "enlightened self-interest."[41] Such self-interest often propels the individual mind into becoming more active in the service of deprived communities. It is this delicate link between new technologies, processes of self-reflection, and possibilities of radical agency and social change that the #RhodesMuastFall movement represents.

Bibliography

Ainsworth, Susan, and Cynthia Hardy. "Critical Discourse Analysis: Why Bother?" *Critical Discourse Studies* 1: 2 (2014): 225–59.

Bairstow, Timothy. "Amnesty, Reintegration, and Reconciliation: South Africa." *Military Review* 89: 2 (2009): 89–98.

Bakardjieva, Maria. "Reconfiguring the Mediapolis: New Media and Civic Agency." *New Media & Society* 14, no. 1 (2012): 63–79.

Barber, Karin. "African Popular Arts." *African Studies Review* 30, no. 3 (September 1987): 1–78.

Bar-Tal, Daniel. "From Intractable Conflict through Conflict Resolution to Reconciliation: Psychological Analysis." *Political Psychology* 21, no. 2 (2000): 351–65.

Bhabha, Homi. "Introduction: Narrating the Nation" in *Nation and Narration*, edited by Homi Bhabha, 1–7. London: Routledge, 1990.

Blommaert, Jan. *Discourse: A Critical Introduction.* Cambridge: Cambridge University Press, 2005.

Bosch, Tanja. "Twitter Activism and Youth in South Africa: The case of #RhodesMustFall." *Information, Communication and Society* 20: 2 (2017): 221–32.

Carpentier, Nico. *Media and Participation: A Site of Ideological-democratic Struggle.* Bristol: Intellect, 2011.

---

39 Barber, 6.
40 Barber, 12.
41 Heeks, *Information and Communication Technology*, 8.

Coetzee, Carli. *Writing under the Skin: Blood and Intergenerational Memory in South Africa*. Woodbridge, UK: James Currey, 2019.

Coplan, David. *In Township Tonight: South Africa's Black City Music and Theatre*. 2nd ed. Chicago: University of Chicago Press, 2008.

Dahlgren, Peter. "Doing Citizenship: The Cultural Origins of Civic Agency in the Public Sphere." *European Journal of Cultural Studies* 9, no. 3 (2006): 267–86.

———. "Young Citizens and Political Participation: Online Media and Civic Cultures." *Taiwan Journal of Democracy* 7, no. 2 (2011): 11–25.

Daifallah, Yasmeen. "The Politics of Decolonial Interpretation: Tradition and Method in Contemporary Arab Thought." *American Political Science Review* 113, no. 3 (2019): 810–23.

Daniels, Glenda. *Fight for Democracy: The ANC and the Media in South Africa*. Johannesburg: Wits University Press, 2012.

Depelchin, Jacques. *Silences in African History: Between the Syndromes of Discovery and Abolition*. Dar es Salaam: Mkuki Na Ntoya, 2005.

Evans, Angelica. "Twitter as a Public Relations Tool." *Public Relations Journal* 5, no. 1 (2011): 1–20.

Evans, Joanna. "Unsettled Matters, Falling Flight: Decolonial Protest and the Becoming-Material of an Imperial Statue." *The Drama Review* 62, no. 3 (2018): 130–44.

Fabian, Johannes. "Popular Culture in Africa: Finding and Conjectures." *Africa: Journal of the International African Institute* 8, no. 4 (1978): 315–34.

Friedman, Steven. *Race, Class and Power: Harold Wolpe and the Radical Critique of Apartheid*. Pietermaritzburg: UKZN, 2015.

Ghandi, Leela. *Postcolonial Theory: A Critical Introduction*. St. Leonards: Allen & Unwin, 1998.

Grant, Will, Brenda Moon, and Janie Grant. "Digital Dialogue? Australian Politicians' use of the Social Network Tool Twitter." *Australian Journal of Political Science* 45, no. 4, (2010): 579–604.

Graybill, Lyn. *Truth and Reconciliation in South Africa: Miracle or Model?* Boulder, CO: Lynne Rienner, 2002.

Hall, Stuart. "The Rediscovery of Ideology: The Return of the Repressed in Media Studies." In *Culture, Society and the Media*, eds. Michael Gurevitch, Tony Bennett, James Curran and Janet Woollacott. London: Methuen, 1982.

Heeks, Richard. *Information and Communication Technology for Development*. New York: Routledge, 2018.

Jenkins, Henry. "Youth Voice, Media, and Political Engagement." In *By Any Media Necessary: The New Youth Activism*, edited by Henry Jenkins, Sangita Shresthova, Liana Gamber-Thompson, Neta Kligler-Vilenchik, and Arely M. Zimmerman, 1–60. New York: New York University Press, 2016.

Kros, Cynthia. "Rhodes Must Fall: Archives and Counter Archives." *Critical Arts* 29, no. 1 (2015): 150–65.

Munslow, Alun. *Deconstructing History.* London: Routledge, 1997.

Nel, Reggie. "Social Media and the New Struggles of Young People against Marginalization: A Challenge to Missional Ecclesiology in Southern Africa." *Stellenbosch Theological Journal* 1, no. 2 (2015): 511–30.

Nuttall, Sarah. "Afterword: The Shock of the New-Old." *Social Dynamics* 45, no. 2 (2019): 280–85.

Nyamnjoh, Francis. *#RhodesMustFall: Nibbling at Resilient Colonialism in South Africa.* Bamenda: Langaa, 2016.

Pillay, Suntosh. "Silence is Violence: (critical) Psychology in an Era of Rhodes Must Fall and Fees Must Fall." *South African Journal of Psychology* 46, no. 2 (2016): 155–59.

Ponono, Mvuzo. "Centring the Subaltern: Interpreting Mainstream Media Messages in a Fractured Country." *Communitas* 23, no. 2 (2018): 139–54.

Ranger, Terence O. *Dance and Society in Eastern Africa, 1890–1970: The Beni Ngoma.* Berkeley and Los Angeles: University of California Press, 1975.

Roelofs, Portia. "Flying in the Univer-topia: White People on Planes, #RhodesMustFall and Climate Emergency." *Journal of African Cultural Studies* 31, no. 3 (2019): 267–70.

Scollo, Michelle. "Cultural Approaches to Discourse Analysis: A Theoretical and Methodological Conversation with a Special Focus on Donal Carbaugh's Cultural Discourse Theory." *Journal of Multicultural Discourses* 6: 1 (2011): 1–32.

Theron, Linda and Macalene Malindi. "Resilient Street Youth: A Qualitative South African Study" Journal of Youth Studies 13: 6 (2010): 717–36.

Trottier, Daniel and Christian Fuchs. "Theorising Social Media, Politics and the State: An Introduction." in *Social Media, Politics and the State: Protests, Revolutions, Riots, Crime and Policing in the Age of Facebook, Twitter and You Tube,* edited by Daniel Troitter and Christian Fuchs, 3–38. New York: Routledge, 2015.

Unwin, Tim. *Reclaiming Information and Communication Technologies for Development.* Oxford: Oxford University Press, 2017.

Wells, Chris. "Two Eras of Civic Information and the Evolving Relationship between Civil Society Organizations and Young Citizens." *New Media & Society* 16, no. 4 (2014): 615–36.

Wodak, Ruth. "Critical Discourse Analysis" in *The International Encyclopaedia of Language and Social Interaction,* edited by Karen Tracey, Cornelia Ilie, and Todd Sandel, 278–89. Chichester: John Wiley & Sons, 2015.

Zegeye, Abebe. "Media, Youth, Violence and Identity in South Africa: A Theoretical Approach" in *Power, Politics and Identity in South African Media,* edited by Adrian Hadland, Eric Louw, Simphiwe Sesanti, and Herman Wasserman, 17–51. Cape Town: HSRC, 2008.

Chapter Ten

Resisting Political Oppression

Youth and Social Media in Zimbabwe

Godfrey Maringira and Simbarashe Gukurume

Introduction

In a national context embroiled in political-economic crisis, Zimbabwean youth have configured social spaces on social media platforms to resist political oppression. This chapter focuses on the ways in which youth respond to political oppression in Zimbabwe through the creative utilization of cyberspace and popular entertainment, more particularly, social media such as Facebook, Twitter, popular humor, and music. The chapter asserts that social media platforms now function as new forms of popular culture, which youth produce in textual, photographic, and video forms in responding to and challenging oppressive politics and regimes in Africa. While the posts can be viewed as "movements" and "emerging forums,"[1] we assert that they are embedded in and with political tones that mediate political engagement with adamant political elites. While this is not a new phenomenon, we explore how these online spaces have been appropriated by youth as "new" and viable political instruments in responding to a government heavily backed by

---

1   Barber, "Popular Arts in Africa," 1.

the military. The extent to which youth have mobilized themselves against the government on social media have of late driven the government to block the use of internet during mass demonstrations in Zimbabwe.

For instance, in the January 2019 mass protests mobilized by young people through social media platforms, the state responded by ordering a complete internet and social media shutdown for almost a week. This desperate attempt by the state to censure youth activism on social media demonstrates that the youth are not only politically innovative on social media but also that their active engagement with the oppressive state is real and consequential. Youth engagement on social media platforms in Zimbabwe spurns the idea of new media as sources of mere entertainment, as it is politically charged with varied meanings that speak to the current and ongoing political mischief in the Zimbabwean context. While the memes, video clips, political poems, and songs created by youth are somehow entertaining, the motive is mostly political (i.e., it aims to engage with a devious state that is apparently driven by the desire to subjugate its citizens through military authority and power. Even as people laugh at the memes, the Facebook wall postings, and the hilarious comments on Twitter handles, their understanding of these messages are rooted in political undertones and meanings.

We therefore argue that while the social media space/platform is a source of popular entertainment for young people, it also functions as a formidable site of political contestation. While social media platforms serve as the new sites of generational connection and comradeship for young people through pleasure and other forms of entertainment, these platforms also serve as new battlegrounds of social engagement with powerful forces that shape young people's lives. It has become imperative, therefore, to analyze and understand how the oppressive state has become so interested in what young people post on social media and the ways in which the public responds to such postings. We argue that social media spaces are not entirely social or apolitical but also double as active political spaces in which the dictatorial regimes in power in Africa are increasingly being challenged, weakened, and undermined. Politicians have not been indifferent to young people's emerging media literacy and savviness. Instead, they have created their own social media accounts as a way of responding to a huge and growing youth population that has converged on social media for both popular entertainment and political activism. As several chapters in this collection show, cyberspace is now an unavoidable cultural space, a politically charged battleground of ideas for both young people and the ruling elite in Africa.

National Context: The Zimbabwean Crisis

It is important to note that since its independence in 1980, Zimbabwe has been in multiple crises. The military has often been deployed by the state to do the work of political violence.[2] In addition, the military has been largely involved in politics, which scholars have referred to as the militarization of politics and politicization of the military.[3] However, it is not the purpose of this chapter to dwell on how violence has been perpetrated over time by the military and the ruling elite. This information has been presented elsewhere.[4] While the Zimbabwean state has a long history of perpetrating violence against its own citizens, we focus on the most recent crisis, which happened during the post-2000 era when social media became so popular in Zimbabwe.

In the last decade or so there has been a growing number of youth visibility on social media.[5] While the initial motive was to connect with distant friends and relatives, of late, social media has been instrumentalized by Zimbabwean youth to respond to oppressive politics. In the Zimbabwean situation, the state has been an epicenter of violence, in particular through the deployment of soldiers, the central intelligence organization, the police, and the military intelligence .[6] The violent actions of the state security apparatuses were driven by the political zeal to keep former president Robert

---

2 Alexander, "Dissident Perspectives on Zimbabwe's Post-Independence War, Africa"; Alexander, "Militarisation and State Institutions"; Maringira, "Political Violence within Army Barracks"; Maringira, "Soldiering the Terrain of War"; Maringira, 'On Entering the Military Organisation"; Maringira, "When the Military became Militarised."

3 Maringira, "Soldiers and the State in Zimbabwe"; Maringira, "Militarised Minds: The Lives of Ex-combatants in South Africa"; Maringira, "When the War De-Professionalises Soldiers: Wartime Stories in Exile"; and Masunungure, "Zimbabwe's Militarized, Electoral Authoritarianism."

4 Ranger, "Nationalist Historiography, Patriotic History and the History of the Nation"; Raftopoulos, "The Crisis in Zimbabwe, 1998–2008"; Muzondidya, "From Buoyancy to Crisis, 1980–1997"; Maringira, "Politicization and Resistance in the Zimbabwean National Army"; Maringira, "Soldiers as Victims"; Maringira, "Householding by Rank and File."

5 Mare, "Tracing and Archiving 'Constructed' Data on Facebook Pages and Groups"; Mare, "A Complicated but Symbiotic Affair."

6 Maringira and Carrasco, "'Once a Soldier, a Soldier Forever': Exiled Zimbabwean Soldiers in South Africa"; Maringira; Richters and Gibson,

Mugabe in power.[7] The violence has been mainly physical, brutalizing opposition political party members and perceived supporters and sympathizers of the Movement for Democratic Change led by Morgan Tsvangirai, currently led by Nelson Chamisa.[8] But political violence remains evident in the post-Mugabe era, with the military being deployed to carry out gun violence on civilians. For instance, after the disputed 2018 elections and the recent protests over fuel prices, soldiers were deployed and killed several protestors in the streets of Harare. However, the response to state brutality by the people was limited, as the state controlled all forms of information-sharing mechanisms and the media. For a long time, and even up until now, the Zimbabwean state has had only one television station and control over all the ideological state apparatuses. This is done through a very tight rein on the process of issuing media licences to newspapers and television and radio broadcasting stations. All the radio stations in the country are monitored and controlled the oppressive state.[9] The government therefore has been overseeing the type of information the citizens get. Given this situation, there has been very limited information on political violence shared through the state-controlled media institutions. The only alternatives to state-sponsored information are often through rumor and gossip. As Nduka Otiono has noted, rumor is a subversive weapon of resistance in urban space in Africa.[10] However, in politically volatile situations, rumor and gossip function as tools to govern the marginalized people. ZANU-PF's control of the mass media in Zimbabwe should be understood within the context of mounting local and international criticism on its policies, governance and abysmal human rights record.[11]

However, with the emergence of social media such as Facebook, Twitter, and WhatsApp to mention just a few, the youth have been at the center of bustling media activities in Zimbabwe, resharing and reposting messages aimed at resisting political hegemony of the politicians in control of state power. Technologically savvy youth have taken advantage of the liberalized

---

"Zimbabwean Army Deserters in South Africa"; Gukurume, "Surveillance, Spying and Disciplining the University."

7 Maringira, Gibson, and Richters, 'It's in My Blood."
8 Alexander, "Squatters"; and Raftopoulos, "State in Crisis."
9 Willems, "Selection and Silence"; Chuma, "Mediating the 2000 Elections in Zimbabwe"; and Chari, "Media Framing of Land Reform in Zimbabwe."
10 Otiono, "Street Stories."
11 Ranger, "Nationalist Historiography."

nature of online social media to produce and circulate critical popular cultural texts that contest state propaganda and hegemony. In fact, with increasing ownership of smartphones and internet connectivity, young people have become citizen journalists in ways that trumps state-controlled media. Unsettled by young people's role in generating and circulating media content on social media, the state is working quite hard to suppress social media. For instance, in January 2019, there were widespread protests over the deteriorating economic situation in the country. The government of Zimbabwe deployed the military to deal with protestors. In order to commit violent acts away from public scrutiny, the government shut down the internet. There was an internet blackout in Zimbabwe for almost a week. It was hard for citizens, especially the victims of state violence, to share the information of what was happening at that time.

The closure of internet by the government of Zimbabwe was clear testimony of how the government fears youth creativity and agency, especially its newfound abilities to generate and share information about government brutality on its own citizens. While most of the people in and outside Zimbabwe thought that the postcoup/post-Mugabe era in Zimbabwe would bring about much-awaited political freedom and prosperity, it never happened and remained a pipe dream in the lives of many, especially the youth. Apart from shutting down the internet and social media, the state also responded by ordering telecommunications companies to stop social media promotions and hike the prices of data, thereby making access to online platforms a prohibitive pastime for young people. The government also hastily introduced a cybercrime bill,[12] which sought to criminalize online activism. In fact, young comedians like Comic Pastor[13] and *Gonyeti*[14] have been arrested for producing and circulating politically charged skits on social media, hence in our presentation of different posts on Twitter and Facebook, we use pseudonyms to protect these youths from state reprisal.

Postcoup Narratives on the Wall

Writing on his Twitter handle, Tom talked about how in postcoup politics, President Emmerson Mnangagwa had failed to change the country,

---

12   Gukurume, "#ThisFlag and #ThisGown Cyber Protests in Zimbabwe."
13   https://www.youtube.com/watch?v=OihhocC7Kl8.
14   https://www.youtube.com/watch?v=OihhocC7Kl8.

especially its economy and politics. In a highly critical piece posted on his Twitter handle he states that "ZANU-PF is more dangerous to Zimbabweans than Corona virus. The world should be worried of COVID-19, but we are more afraid of the regime and its gun-toting enablers who violently took over power through a military coup in Nov 2017. They have killed more than COVID-19" (May 16, 2020). The comparison of the postcoup regime to a killer reveals how President Mnangagwa has failed to fulfill the expectations of many people. A dream for a "new Zimbabwe" has been thwarted. Another young Facebook activist, James, talks about Zimbabwe as a "fascist state," which has destroyed people's dreams. In James's writing, the national dream is depicted as the only social and political resource that young people can hang-on to, yet it has been hijacked by political elites. For James, there was a strong emphasis on the idea of the "dream," which is the province of young people and their usual concern with futurity. In the post, Zimbabwe is humanized as a subject that can dream, a subject with aspirations but that is held down by what he called a "fascist" state. For this young Facebook user, the national dream had been crushed by a predatory class of vicious men, essentially political "gangsters" enriching themselves to the detriment of everyone else. He condemned the Zimbabwe military generals as a group of elites engaged in massive business deals in the extractive economy named in various UN reports, especially in connection with the looting of diamonds in the 1998–2002 Democratic Republic of Congo War. He also talked about the military involvement in mineral deals in Zimbabwe in diamond mining, especially the shady partnership with a Chinese arms conglomerate, Norinco, in a joint venture known as Anjin, as well as the army's involvement in the dubious distribution of platinum mining rights. He presented the military generals as uninterested in genuine political change. For him, all that the military did through its coup-installed president was to present a facade of national change under the mantra of "Zimbabwe is open for business." This was nothing but an empty political mantra, which many of the youth criticized. He clearly states that the "open for business" political mantra was nothing other than a political ploy to hoodwink the majority of citizens and businesspeople in and outside Zimbabwe. For the young Zimbabwean activist, the new mantra was just a "dog's breakfast" that many dogs would never touch.

On his Facebook wall, James juxtaposed the former president Robert Mugabe and the postcoup president, Emmerson Mnangagwa. He presented Robert Mugabe as a leader who had some modicum of restraint, while the word "restraint" does not exist in Emmerson Mnangagwa's political dictionary. He noted how the Emmerson Mnangagwa regime spends lavishly on consumer goods and lifestyles, with the president traveling around the world in an ultra-luxury hired Swiss jet. He emphasized how corruption and patronage have been taken to another level. The new regime continues to milk a hemorrhaging nation and its economy. He zeroed in on the culture of corruption, referring to it as "massive" in the different sectors of the economy. In his castigation of the regime, he noted how state officials have engaged in primitive accumulation and likened the current Zimbabwean regime to the corrupt and brutal regimes that were presided over by Mobutu Seseko (Congo), Sani Abacha (Nigeria) and Idi Amin (Uganda), respectively. There are few, if any political changes, that are likely to be seen, noting that there can never be reforms without reformers. In this regard, he foresees the current regime as a regime of politicians driven by an ideology of looting, while much of the general population sinks deeper into poverty. What James's commentaries suggest, we argue, is that the Facebook wall is no longer just an apolitical social space for innocuous interaction between young people and their peers, but now doubles as a discursive political space where frustrated youth articulate their grievances with the status quo.

In his summation of the wall post, he questions whether Zimbabwe was going to explode. James asserts that Zimbabwe is likely going to implode again. Although unclear about how this implosion will happen, he notes that another coup must be avoided, and the most likely alternative to rescue the country from implosion was to engage in a national dialogue that would then pave the way for a national transitional authority to deal with the twin evils of the "militarization of the state" and the "politicization of the military" in Zimbabwe. In concurring with these sentiments, another youth participant, Amos, posted on his Facebook wall noting that

> simple wisdom says problems are never solved at the same level they were created. Expecting president Emmerson Mnangagwa to be a reformer is wishful *mukoma* (my brother). Thank me later. (Amos, Facebook, May 2, 2019)

The assertion reveals that President Emmerson Mnangagwa is viewed as a problem himself as well as the creator of certain national problems. However, on his Twitter handle, the current president's sympathizer and advisor argues that the president will leave a positive legacy. There were various responses to this, with some respondents asking if the presidential advisor smokes marijuana. This was contested by one of the youth activists who vociferously noted that that will be a "positive legacy in your pocket." On the same platform, another responded in Shona local language saying, "*Musadero mudhara. Ko kungodya makanyarara*" (Please don't say that, just enjoy your life and don't mess with us). The engagement went on with others responding, stating that the only legacy that the president will leave is that of poverty, mass murder by the military in the streets, and a crippled health-care system.

Engaging the Postcolonial State through Tweeting

The state continues to do violence on unarmed civilians, with no intervention from either within or outside the country. There has been military deployment to deal with civilian protests, and in the process, ordinary defenseless civilians have been killed. One of the youth activists (Tatenda) took to his Twitter handle and noted the following:

> Case number OTP-CR-174/19 has been opened at the International Criminal Court implicating MR E. Mnangagwa in the murder of innocent civilians by the military on 01 August 2018. (posted June 7, 2019)

Interventions to stop indiscriminate military deployment have never happened, hence youth inform their fellow citizens on the urgency and possibility of holding the current regime to account. As the Zimbabwean state continues to use the military to arrest and detain its citizens, the youth have found alternative ways of tweeting to document these human rights violations and voice out their concerns. Farai for example noted that

> the continued assault on civil society leaders and indeed the continued closure of political space is unacceptable. The harassment of . . . is gross human rights abuse. The incarceration of seven activists is paranoia at its worst. This is a #fascistState. (@Farai, June 5, 2019)

The post above was regarding the civil society members who were arrested on arrival at the Robert Mugabe International Airport in Harare between May 20, 2019, and May 27, 2019. Civil society leaders have been criticized by the government for plotting against the state and mobilizing protests. As such, the state largely portrays civil society as an enemy of the state. This framing of civil society as a threat to state security, especially as agents of regime change, points to the continuities from the Mugabe regime. Young people now contest this dominant narrative on Twitter and Facebook as well as through comedy skits. This reveals the ways in which the all-powerful state is being challenged, especially how the youth contest the political detentions of civil society leaders. Karin Barber[15] saw this form of resistance to oppressive regimes in popular culture as a powerful social movement where popular arts take the form of an emerging political forum for marginalized voices. Our view is that in the age of media globalization, such forums have emerged in the form of online social media.

This reality has energized the political elites themselves to turn to online social media to assert themselves. In the face of a dwindling economy, the new president of Zimbabwe took on the issue on Twitter, stating the following:

> With unjustified price increases affecting all, we are demanding a stronger and more responsive social dialogue, protecting both our workers and our reforming economy. Zimbabwe will only be truly open for business when collaboration is put ahead of confrontation. (@President of Zimbabwe, June 5, 2019)

The response to this post was swift and terse. Many youths were clearly agitated, and some replied to his post on Twitter stating, "President Mnangangwa, You have failed.' Another one said, "If only these cosmetic words can be translated into action on the ground." Others questioned "to whom are you demanding this dialogue?" Another one questioned the president's post on Twitter and notes that "it's difficult to reconcile this message with the August 1 and January shootings and the constant presence of soldiers among civilians . . . but you are here preaching non-militancy. Only confrontation can save us now!" Thus, while the president encouraged citizens to engage in a "social dialogue," the young citizens are skeptical of such familiar political rhetoric that seeks to quieten the people. For most of the young people in Zimbabwe, especially from the fiery rhetoric of those active on social media, the emphasis is on confrontation rather than dialogue. They also questioned who the president wants a dialogue with as mentioned in his post. With people losing trust with the regime, most of the youth agitate for a confrontational approach to resolving the current Zimbabwean crisis. One youth activist responded, "The critical line will be crossed soon and a violent confrontation will be inevitable. You are pushing people towards war" (Nhamo, Twitter, April 18, 2019). While it is not clear as to what the youth mean by "the critical line," it is important at least to note the rise of a direct engagement with the president (in this case, on Twitter) and the inevitable

---

15   Barber, "Popular Arts in Africa."

violent confrontation that the encounter between the state and its young citizens suggests.

The Twitter posts reiterate that the president did not comprehend the reality on the ground, especially the everyday life struggles young people face. As Vimbai noted:

> On the ground are queues, shortages and hyper-inflation. So when any one speaks of reforms and progress its utter rubbish. . . . Its voodoo economics. (@Vimbai, May 13, 2019)

The post was in response to the government assertion that the Zimbabwean currency was gaining value on the international market. For him, when the economy is not performing well but the president believes it is, that is "voodoo economics." However, as noted above, the reality is that people are suffering. One of the youth activists' posts emphasized that

> once again, the solution is simple. The political crisis needs urgent resolution. Dialogue between Emmerson and our President @nelsonchamisa is the only thing that can create a soft landing for Zimbabwe. Without it the country is headed for an implosion. Another 17 Nov. (@Tambaoga, June 21, 2019).

There has been a call for a national dialogue between the opposition political party, the MDC (led by Nelson Chamisa), and the ruling ZANU-PF government (led by the current president, Emmerson Mnangagwa). The call for national dialogue is continuously being made because the 2018 national elections were contested by the opposition political party, which believes that elections were rigged in favor of the current president. The election results were challenged in the Constitutional Court in 2018 after the elections, but the court declared the current president the winner. One of the youths raised his concerns on Twitter handle: "It has never happened in the history of democracy that the majority becomes the loser and the minority becomes the ruler. Nelson Chamisa and the people of Zimbabwe are right to demand what is rightful [*sic*] theirs' (Garikai, Twitter: April 13, 2019). The call for dialogue, which includes the main opposition political party, the MDC, has not materialized because the opposition party had a set of conditions to be met before being involved in the national dialogue. As noted by one of the youth activists,

> The whole bunch are cruel clueless quislings. When a goat is found on the 20th floor of a building, the question is not how to get it down but how it got there? (@Ruramai, May 17, 2019)

This was a question about how the current president was elected to the position. It was a contested decision held by the Constitutional Court, and not through the electoral votes of the people of Zimbabwe. The opposition political party (the MDC) and many youths shared their sentiments and asserted that the current president was an illegitimate leader. They contend that if the current president, through the help of the military, had managed to rig an election, they would not be able to rig the economy. The youth shared these concerns and reiterated that the spiraling economy was a result of political illegitimacy and that it had to be resolved. On Twitter, one of the youths posted the following:

> The wheels have come off. Massive prices [sic] hikes mean that inflation will jump to 500% this month (May 2019). The parallel exchange rate will hit 1:9 in the next few days. There is a shortage of everything particularly fuel, drugs and electricity. Emmerson has taken us back to the Stone Age (@Kuda, June 3, 2019).

Regarding this issue, the government had estimated that the inflation rate would go down and that people should not panic. The reality was that inflation was soaring.

> The worst government and the worst "leader" since the creation of modern Zimbabwe in [1980] (@Farai, April 14, 2019).

In this regard, the current administration was ranked as the worst government presided over by the worst "leader" (@Tonderai, April 14, 2019). The people quoted here do not even want to call the president a real leader; his leadership is questionable not only because of how he came into power through a contested election but also because of the corrupt manner in which he runs the state. This sentiment is particularly strong among the youth, who in turn utilize social media to articulate their frustrations. These frustrations are understandable given the youths' protracted systematic exclusion from the economic and political corridors of power. In some of the messages posted on Twitter, young people complained about the president's failure to deliver jobs he promised when he came into power and failure to address the deepening economic crisis. So here we see how young people successfully producing and circulating counterhegemonic discourses about the state and ZANU-PF through the new discursive resources available in cyberspace. For instance, since taking over from Mugabe in November 2017, the current president utilized state-controlled media to propagate the mantra that "Zimbabwe is open for business" and claims that the current regime is transforming the fortunes of the country for the better. In response, many young people have resorted to social media to contest such claims and show how the living conditions of ordinary Zimbabweans continue to deteriorate under Mnangagwa's leadership. It is for this reason that George Karekwaivanane argues that through Facebook, ordinary citizens like these young people produce and reproduce "counter publics" that contest ideologies and discourses propagated in state-controlled public spheres.[16]

Revolts and Protests: Organization on Social Media

In a fraught postcolonial state like Zimbabwe where social and political spaces are understood to be closed to the popular public, the youth have neither been silenced nor have they rested. The youth devise innovative ways in which to mobilize protests and resistance on social media by posting videos and making commentaries that invoke anger among citizens, highlighting the multiple ways in which the current regime's politicians continue to lead lavish lifestyles while the majority of the citizens sink into dire poverty. For instance, in 2016 many young people organized nationwide protests through social movements such as #ThisFlag and #Tajamuka, which mobilized extensively through social media platforms.[17] The relative success of these social movements that mobilized protests through social media reveals the potential of youth to convoke "unruly publics" online through social media.[18] In fact, Gukurume argues that social media have enabled youth not only to resuscitate critical and rational political debates but to also reclaim their political space and voice.[19] Interestingly, young people are now able to achieve this critical engagement with the all-powerful state through humor and rumor. Young people in Zimbabwe circulate jokes, songs, stories, and other creative texts that mock corrupt politicians who engage in extravagant lifestyles while the majority wallow in abject poverty.

---

16   Karekwaivanane, "Tapanduka Zvamuchese."
17   Karekwaivanane.
18   Karekwaivanane.
19   Gukurume, "ThisFlag."

For instance, one of the current regime's politicians imported a Lamborghini worth US$400,000.[20] Currently Zimbabwe is experiencing a huge shortage in foreign currency, but when reckless politicians evidently spend the little money the country has on exotic cars, it is a cause for concern, especially for the majority of the marginalized youth in the country, the majority of which remain unemployed and impoverished. Because the minister belongs to the current regime in power, he was exempted from paying import duty for the expensive car he brought to the country. In response, many concerned youth activists took to Twitter and articulated their reservations about this flamboyant lifestyle led by the ruling elite. For instance, one stated on Twitter that "I think this car MUST spark a revolution. This is UNACCEPTABLE MADNESS" (Tarisai, Twitter). While the Lamborghini is a symbol of wealth, it also represents the arrogance and insensitivity of politicians in Zimbabwe. In a bleeding postcolonial economy marked by declining fortunes for the ordinary citizens, the least state officials can do is maintain a modest lifestyle. As stated by another youth activist:

> Lavish arrogance in the midst of a dysfunctional economy where millions can't afford basic livelihood is a slap in the face of those lowly paid soldiers whose monthly salaries are equivalent to USD$20 yet are abused to shoot and crush those who denounce poor governance (@Fadzai, April 7, 2019).

While the call for a revolution is not possible in a highly militarized public space, youth took it to social media platforms to call for dissent. The military is ever present in the streets in Zimbabwe, including the central intelligence operatives. In order to respond to and engage with the government misuse of funds, corruption, and rising youth unemployment, young people have found effective alternative spaces of engagement with the corrupt state on Twitter and Facebook. On Twitter, youth rally not only ordinary citizens but also the junior soldiers and other security officials deemed to be suffering just like their civilian counterparts. The galvanization of the junior soldiers is real, as the youth activists invite them to understand the harsh realities of the economic crisis facing the country, which includes the military personnel. It is therefore important to note that social media outlets such as Twitter have made it possible for young activists to invite and dialogue with the marginalized lot within the military hierarchy, especially the junior state security

---

20 https://www.zimlive.com/2019/06/12/my-lambo-is-us420k-not-us210k-boasts-zanu-pf-mp-wadyajena/.

personnel thought to be the arm behind the political henchmen unleashing violence on the people.

When the current president went on a local radio station and talked about the introduction of a new currency to solve the economic crisis facing the nation, several people responded to the president with cynicism. The president emphasized that the Zimbabwean currency is the strongest currency in the region. But such unfounded claims were received with widespread mockery and jokes by many young people. Young people and ordinary citizens asserted that Mnangagwa was out of touch with reality. One of the youths said, "We will no longer be governed by criminals. We need a new government not a new currency" (@Fungai, May 23, 2019. Twitter). Another youth posted the following on Twitter:

> A currency that is not recognised as legitimate and is not tradable in the region ever be the strongest in the region. You cannot have a running race against yourself in your house and declare yourself the winner. It can't. (@Garikai, May 23, 2019)

The ways in which the president is engaged on Twitter allow us to understand how the youth have shaped the rules of engagement for themselves by creating a safe and viable online space of sociopolitical activism. While their existence and contestations are real and powerful, they remain invisible and unreachable to the devious agents of state terror. James Yeku makes a similar argument in this collection about the power of humor and how online spaces have become safe havens for young comedians who are critical of the state and its policies.

Like the president, many other government officials are also active on Facebook and Twitter. For instance, on the fuel shortage, the deputy minister of energy posted on Twitter that one way to resolve the fuel crisis was for people to buy bicycles. This was met with an uproar. One youth activist on Twitter stated that

> we are not refusing to buy bicycles, but let our leaders lead by example, let them purchase ZIM 1 (presidential motorcade) bicycles first and then we will follow suit. The day we will hear ZIM 1 (presidential motorcade) bicycle bell by the roadside then *munhu wese mubhasikoro*! (everyone will be on the bicycle). (@Gumede, May 19, 2019)

The ZIM 1 is the popular nickname for the presidential motorcade in Zimbabwe, hence the youth demand that the president himself first buy and use the bicycle as his motorcade. If it is difficult for the president to travel by bicycle, it will be the same for the citizens. This form of popular resistance is entirely political: and this response to the government call for citizens to buy bicycles suggests that the policy is impractical and insensitive.

Resistance or Engagement? Theorizing Popular Online Media Activism

In understanding resistance and creative ways of engaging an authoritarian state, we draw inspiration from W. Willems, who asserts that in a Zimbabwean context, we should privilege everyday forms of resistance embedded in humor and rumor over a dominant scholarly obsession with dramatic revolutions and grand rebellions.[21] While popular mass violence instills fear as A. Kleinman suggests,[22] it is important to understand the ways in which young people's posts on Facebook, Twitter, and other social media platforms function as nonviolent and nonsensationalist repertoires of sociopolitical resistance and engagement with an insensitive state. Drawing from Karin Barber's[23] idea of the intersections between popular arts and politics, we argue that young people's postings on Facebook and Twitter, especially as part of everyday popular culture, "penetrate politics" but are also themselves penetrated by the same politics. African youth in general are a category of the continent's population understood to be in what Diana Singerman calls the limbo of '"waithood," an extended period of stagnation between youth and adulthood marked by unemployment and precarity due to the vagaries of the neoliberal order.[24] While this waithood limbo creates entrapment, social anxiety, and angst, social media spaces provide a vantage point and alternative political space that allows youth to realize the sociopolitical power they have as an important force within a politically charged polity.

We assert that youth response on Facebook and Twitter to political crises indicates how young people have bypassed the domination of news, which was previously controlled by a few political elites. As Paul Ugor has argued elsewhere, sociocultural and political spaces are not entirely dominated by

---

21   Willems, "Beyond Dramatic Revolutions and Grand Rebellions."
22   Kleinman, 'The Violences of Everyday Life."
23   Barber, "Popular Arts in Africa."
24   Singerman, "Youth, Gender, and Dignity in the Egyptian Uprising."

political elites but negotiated by and with youth.[25] Interestingly, the social media wall ceases to be just an ordinary wall for generational communication and interaction among young people. It becomes a discursive space and a political tool for young people to resist state control and hegemony. Using Bourdieu's concept of the "field of cultural production" as a site of power and contestations, the wall becomes a "field," a battleground of ideas where the struggle for ideological hegemony is fought between the state and the youth.[26] Indeed, for Bourdieu, the "cultural field" is an arena of contestation between various social agents and actors (in this case, the state and young people) who occupy different positions of power. This is evidenced by the very fact that it is not just Zimbabwean youth who post on social media walls: the government responds to these youth postings. Thus, even though African youth have often been viewed as languishing in the limbo of "waithood," judging them as hapless victims of the sociopolitical hegemony perpetuated by authoritarian regimes in power, their social media activism resists the idea of "waiting" and the absence of agency associated with this limbo state. This resistance in the so-called waithood is mediated through cyberspace, particularly on social media. Of import here is that the online texts are unmediated popular texts that are in conversation with political elites. The online activism of disgruntled Zimbabwean youth is a poignant example of the many ways young people have become producers of their own media content, which is often charged with political motivations and interests. As Peter Dahlgren notes, the online media provides a political platform that allows young people civic engagement with the state to ensure democratic ideas are achieved.[27] By mobilizing protest against the state through online new media, engaging and subverting state propaganda and authority, young people in Zimbabwe are actively fashioning their imagined futures through active attempts at refashioning the failed postcolonial state.

For Alcinda Honwana, the so-called waithood generation in Africa desires radical social, economic, and political shifts.[28] By employing their "active agency" on Facebook and Twitter, African youth can never be said to be entirely in a "limbo of waithood." They are never in a prolonged "suspension"

---

25 Ugor, "Niger Delta Wetland, Illegal Oil Bunkering and Youth Identity Politics in Nigeria," 7–8.
26 Bourdieu, *The Logic of Practice*.
27 Dahlgren, "Young Citizens and Political Participation: Online Media and Civic Cultures."
28 Honwana, "Youth, Waithood, and Protest Movements in Africa."

nor have their present and futures been impaired as Africanist scholars have often postulated.[29] By actively responding to bad political practices, African youth attain social and political recognition in popular spaces such as the social media and beyond. This emerging dynamic of media and social activism by young people challenges what Diane Singerman posits as African youth's permanent state of "wait employment":[30] our research reveals that they go beyond the endless wait for work to sociopolitical engagement with constituted authority. African youth are a resilient group and a politically productive constituency. Their networking on social media and ability to connect and reconnect make youth a generation capable of resisting political threats. Thus, Vigh deployed the concept of "social navigation" to depict the different ways in which African youth move in between spaces in politically volatile situations.[31]

In this regard, youth have the capacity to journey between different social media platforms, posting and engaging politicians in varied ways. Reminiscent of Pierre Bourdieu's concept of social capital,[32] youth have managed to utilize the sociopolitical resources among them as a form of social capital. This social capital is often produced and mobilized online through various popular "cyber-publics" such as Facebook forums and hashtag movements created by politically conscious youth to articulate their grievances and frustrations. Social movements like #ThisFlag and #ThisGown established by unemployed graduates are powerful illustrative examples.[33] This social movement mobilized support through its Twitter handle and Facebook page and has managed to submit petitions to the government and organized street protests and other symbolic ways of resistance and dissent. Through social media, seemingly simple hashtags created by young people morph into powerful discursive spaces capable of initiating critical and subversive conversations and debates between the authoritarian state and marginalized youth. Thus, social media has become an important resource and repertoire of political action and resistance for young people in Africa. Such activist work is rooted in the media literacy of African youth who are able to utilize their knowledge to innovate and initiate political debates or discussions on social media platforms.

29 Singerman, "Economic Imperatives of Marriage," 5–7.
30 Singerman, 5–7.
31 Vigh, "Motion Squared: A Second Look at the Concept of Social Navigation."
32 Bourdieu, *On Social Capital.*
33 Gukurume, "ThisFlag."

Indeed, in a highly charged postcolonial context characterized by a shrinking public sphere and a state-controlled media, we argue that social media has now provided an alternative space and counterpublic where young people engage, debate, and subvert state control and authority. We submit that young people's creative use of social media and cyberspace should be understood as cultural evidence of a new form of quiet resistance to the state. This emerging dynamic of youth consciousness in popular culture in Africa is a powerful example of the argument by some scholars that the often-neglected everyday forms of practices such as popular humor and rumor should be understood as subaltern resistance.[34] Social media spaces have afforded the subaltern youth a platform for speaking truth to power in a variety of ways. In this chapter we have demonstrated how social media can be imagined as a form of subaltern public sphere that now enables young people's resistance and dissent to the discursive hegemony of the state. Through a meticulous reading of young people's debates and narratives in cyberspace, we assert that social media and popular culture have enabled young people to creatively resist political control and to engage in antihegemonic struggles against the excesses of the state.

Conclusion

This chapter has argued that while political oppression is characterized by state violence against many of the youth, social media has provided a social and political space in which young people continue to resist and engage with the tyrannical state. In a context where political violence saturates the sociopolitical lives of the people in Zimbabwe, social media not only function as popular entertainment spaces for young people but also doubles as a sociopolitical space in which youth agency is deployed to actively engage with the oppressive postcolonial state. We have argued that youth knowledge of social media use is now a viable political resource that allows them to form both apolitical social networks and active sociopolitical communities of resistance on and beyond online spaces. Zimbabwean youth are not only able to connect and reconnect with their counterparts locally and globally but are also able to mobilize and remobilize ordinary citizens to protest against authoritarian regimes in power. Youth now employ their innovative new media skills to counter the hegemonic politics of the postcolonial state and its various

---

34 Willems, "Beyond Dramatic Revolutions."

apparatuses. We have also argued that insofar n as the state depends on the heavy handedness of the military on the streets, through social media mobilization and remobilization, Zimbabwean youth have to some extent weakened the dictatorial practices of the modern state.

Bibliography

Alexander, Jocelyn. "Dissident Perspectives on Zimbabwe's Post-independence War, Africa." *Journal of the International Africa Institute* 68, no. 2 (1998): 151–82.

———. "Squatters, Veterans and the State in Zimbabwe." In *Zimbabwe's Unfinished Business: Rethinking Land, State and Nation in the Context of Crisis,* edited by Amanda Hammar, Brian Raftopoulos, and S. Jensen, 83–117. Harare: Avondale, Weaver, 2003.

———. "Militarisation and State Institutions: 'Professionals' and 'Soldiers' Inside the Zimbabwe Prison Service." *Journal of Southern African Studies* 39, no. 4 (2013): 807–28.

Barber, Karin. "Popular Arts in Africa," *African Studies Review* 30, no. 3 (1987): 1–78.

Bourdieu, Pierre. *The Forms of Capital.* Cambridge: Polity, 1986.

———. *The Logic of Practice.* Stanford, CA: Stanford University Press, 1990.

Chari, Tendai. "Media Framing of Land Reform in Zimbabwe." In *Land and Agrarian Reform in Zimbabwe: Beyond White-Settler Capitalism*, edited by Sam Moyo and W. Chambati, 291–330. Dakar: CODESRIA, 2013.

Chuma, Wallace. "Mediating the 2000 Elections in Zimbabwe: Competing Journalisms in a Society at the Crossroads." *Ecquid Novi: African Journalism Studies* 29, no. 1 (2008): 21–41.

Dahlgren, Peter. "Young Citizens and Political Participation: Online Media and Civic Cultures." *Taiwan Journal of Democracy* 7, no. 2 (2011): 11–25.

Gukurume, Simbarashe. "#ThisFlag and #ThisGown Cyber Protests in Zimbabwe: Reclaiming Political Space." *African Journalism Studies* 38, no. 2(2017): 49–70.

———. "Surveillance, Spying and Disciplining the University: Deployment of State Security Agents on Campus in Zimbabwe." *Journal of Asian and African Studies* 54, no. 5 (2019): 763–79.

Honwana, Alcinda. *The Time of Youth: Work, Social Change, and Politics in Africa.* Sterling, VA: Kumarian, 2012.

———. *Youth, Waithood, and Protest Movements in Africa.* London: International African Institute, 2013.

Karekwaivanane, George. "'Tapanduka Zvamuchese': Facebook, 'Unruly Publics', and Zimbabwean Politics." *Journal of Eastern African Studies* 13, no. 1 (2019): 54–71.

Kleinman, Arthur. "The Violences of Everyday Life: The Multiple Forms and Dynamics of Social Violence." In *Violence and Subjectivity*, edited by V. Das, A. Kleinman, M. Ramphele, and P. Reynolds, 226–41. Berkeley: University of California Press, 2000.

Mare, Admire. "A Complicated but Symbiotic Affair: The Relationship between Mainstream Media and Social Media in the Coverage of Social Protests in Southern Africa." *Ecquid Novi: African Journalism Studies 34*, no. 1 (2013): 83–98.

———. "Tracing and Archiving 'Constructed' Data on Facebook Pages and Groups: Reflections on Fieldwork among Young Activists in Zimbabwe and South Africa." *Qualitative Research* 17, no. 6 (2017): 645–63.

Maringira, Godfrey. "Householding by Rank and File: The Married Quarters of the Zimbabwean National Army." *Comparative Studies of South Asia, Africa and the Middle East* 37, no. 3 (2017): 456–62.

———. "Militarised Minds: The Lives of Ex-combatants in South Africa." *Sociology* 49, no. 1 (2015): 72–87.

———. "On Entering the Military Organisation: Decivilianization, Depersonalisation, Order and Command in the Zimbabwe National Army." *Political and Military Sociology: An Annual Review* 44 (2016): 103–24.

———. "Politicization and Resistance in the Zimbabwean National Army." *African Affairs* 116, no. 462 (2017): 18–38.

———. "Political Violence within Army Barracks: Desertion and Loss among Exiled Zimbabwean Soldiers in South Africa." *Social Dynamics* 42, no. 3 (2016): 429–42.

———. *Soldiers and the State in Zimbabwe*. London: Routledge, 2019.

———. "Soldiers as Victims: Behind Military Barracks in the Post-colonial African Army." *African Security Review* 26, no. 1 (2017): 77–86.

———. "Soldiering the Terrain of War: Zimbabwean Soldiers in the Democratic Republic of the Congo (1998–2002)." *Defence Studies* 16, no. 3 (2016): 299–311.

———. "When the Military became Militarised: Accounts of Zimbabwean National Army Deserters in Exile in South Africa." *African Security Review* 25, no. 1 (2016): 21–30.

———. "When the War De-Professionalises Soldiers: Wartime Stories in Exile." *Journal of Southern African Studies* 41, no. 6 (2016): 1315–29.

Maringira, Godfrey, and Carrasco Lorena. "Once a Soldier, a Soldier Forever": Exiled Zimbabwean Soldiers in South Africa." *Medical Anthropology* 34, no. 4 (2015): 319–35.

Maringira, Godfrey, Annemiek Richters, and Diana Gibson. "Zimbabwean Army Deserters in South Africa: Military Bonding and Survival." *Africa Peace & Conflict Journal* 6, no. 2 (2013): 32–43.

Maringira, Godfrey, Diana Gibson, and Annemiek Richters. "'It's in My Blood' The Military Habitus of Former Zimbabwean Soldiers in Exile in South Africa." *Armed Forces & Society* 41, no. 1 (2015): 23–42.

Masunungure, Eldred. "Zimbabwe's Militarized, Electoral Authoritarianism." *Journal of International Affairs* 65, no. 1 (2011): 47–64.

Muzondidya, James. "From Buoyancy to Crisis, 1980–1997." In *Becoming Zimbabwe, A History from the Pre-colonial Period to 2008*, edited by Brian Raftopoulos and Alois Mlambo, 167–200. Harare: Weaver, 2009.

Otiono, Nduka. *Street Stories: Orality, Media, Popular Culture and the Postcolonial Condition in Nigeria*. PhD diss., University of Alberta, 2011.

Raftopoulos, Brian. "The Crisis in Zimbabwe." 1998–2008. In *Becoming Zimbabwe, A History from the Pre-colonial Period to 2008*, edited by Brian Raftopoulos and Alois Mlambo, 201–32. Harare: Weaver, 2009.

———. "The State in Crisis: Authoritarian Nationalism, Selective Citizenship and Distortions of Democracy in Zimbabwe." In *Zimbabwe's Unfinished Business: Rethinking Land, State and Nation in the Context of Crisis*, edited by Amanda Hammar, Brian Raftopoulos, and S. Jensen, 217–41. Harare: Weaver, 2003.

Ranger, Terence. "Nationalist Historiography, Patriotic History and the History of the Nation: The Struggle over the Past in Zimbabwe." *Journal of Southern African Studies* 30, no. 2 (2004): 215–34.

Singerman, Diane. "The Economic Imperatives of Marriage: Emerging Practices and Identities among Youth in the Middle East." *Middle East Youth Initiative Working Paper* no. 6. Wolfensohn Center for Development and Dubai School of Government, 2007.

———. "Youth, Gender, and Dignity in the Egyptian Uprising." *Journal of Middle East Women's Studies* 9, no. 3 (2013): 1–27.

Ugor, Paul Ushang. "The Niger Delta Wetland, Illegal Oil Bunkering and Youth Identity Politics in Nigeria." *Postcolonial text* 8, no. 3–4 (2014): 1–18.

Vigh, Henrik. "Motion Squared: A Second Look at the Concept of Social Navigation." *Anthropological Theory* 9, no. 4 (2009): 419–38.

Willems, W. "Beyond Dramatic Revolutions and Grand Rebellions: Everyday Forms of Resistance in the Zimbabwe Crisis." *Communicare: Journal for Communication Sciences in Southern Africa* 29, no. 1 (2010): 1–17.

———. "Selection and Silence: Contesting Meanings of Land in Zimbabwean Media." *Ecquid novi* 25, no. 1 (2004): 4–24.

Part Three
Popular Arts, Everyday Life, and the Politicization of Culture

Chapter Eleven

Dressing *en Style*

Fashion and Fandom in Niger

Adeline Masquelier

In the eyes of countless Nigerien male youth, no one currently epitomizes style as successfully as Wizkid, the young Nigerian pop sensation who was catapulted to global stardom in 2016 after the chart success of "One Dance," the song he produced with Canadian rap artist Drake. That same year, Wizkid, whose real name is Ayodeji Ibrahim Balogun, was named Nigeria's best-dressed pop star by *Vogue* magazine (Frank 2016). On the African continent, where he has practically become a household name, he is extolled as much for his trendsetting looks as for his crowd-pleasing sound. He is undoubtedly the most famous ambassador of the Nigerian musical movement known as Afrobeats. Afrobeats (to be distinguished from the jazzy Afrobeat sound pioneered by Nigerian artist Fela Kuti in the 1970s) combines Congolese soukous, Ghanaian highlife, Ivoirian dance music, and Jamaican dancehall. In Niger, Wizkid's adoring fans scrutinize his fashion choices but also emulate them—no matter the cost. Many of them have incorporated in their wardrobe the skinny jeans, colorful T-shirts, bomber jackets, and trucker hats favored by their idol; they also copy his hairdos and his way of talking; some of them go as far as taking the alias, Wizkid. In recent years the Afropop wunderkind has expanded his sartorial repertoire to include styles ranging from high-end fashion brands to athleisure to traditional Nigerian clothes. Whether he appears in casual streetwear or formal made-to-order clothes, he ends up setting new trends—the red beret "look," the colorful high tops paired with an all-black outfit, and so on—which his devotees quickly embrace. In sum, the Lagos-born artist always seems to be on the cusp of reinvention. One might even argue that his reputation as a fashion guru rests largely on his ability to smoothly navigate a wide, ever-evolving range of sartorial styles so as to keep his followers engaged and wondering about his next move.

Though Wizkid is not associated with a distinctive look or style, many of the clothes he wears are rapidly adopted by fans aiming to develop a sartorial personality that identifies them as followers of the star. In 2016 a style known as Wizkid became popular among adolescent boys after images of the Nigerian star, wearing cut-and-paste logo tees from the luxury streetwear brand Hood By Air (or HBA),[1] circulated online. The style consisted of black-and-white T-shirts adorned with bold graphics and logos and hemmed with patterned fabric of the same color. Assorted shorts or jeans complemented the look. Whereas the original T-shirt (with the iconic HBA logo) available in New York shops cost as much as six hundred dollars, fake versions of the same T-shirt sold at a fraction of the original price. By dressing like their idol, WizKid followers demonstrate simultaneously obsessive regard for the singer and cultural capital.

A number of urban youths I met in Niamey, Niger's capital, took inspiration from Wizkid's adoption of HBA's gilded streetwear to fashion the uniforms they wore on special occasions at their *fadas*, social gatherings over heavily sweetened tea and card games.[2] At the *fada*, young men (*samari* in Hausa) whose futures are overshadowed by economic uncertainty unburden themselves from social pressures while pursuing a quest for recognition through forms of experimentation that frequently rely on the performative power of dress. As platforms where young men develop consumerist desires, share ideas about style, and engage in practices of sartorial ostentation, *fadas* function as social laboratories.

A generation or so ago, the large majority of *fadas* brought together *samari* who had just discovered hip-hop and dressed in baggy pants and extra-large shirts known as *deux-places* (two seats). Other *fadas* coalesced around male

---

1 First appearing in 2006, the label Hood By Air (HBA to fans) soon garnered a cultlike following among affluent teenagers, avant-garde adults, and pop stars in the United States and beyond, thanks largely to its potent version of "ghetto gothic," a unique blend of streetwear and high fashion that subverted standard images of gender, race, and class.

2 *Fada* originally refers to the chief's or the emir's council in Hausa, the lingua franca of Niger. The plural form is *fadodi*, but it is often Frenchified in the media as *fadas*. To highlight the cosmopolitanism of these forms of sociality, I use the French plural form.

youth's shared affinity for reggae and Rasta wear. Yet others united young men who called themselves *sapeurs* (urban dandies) and paraded in expensive designer clothes.³ In the past decade many *fadantchés* (*fada* members in Hausa) have professed their devotion to *coupé-décalé*, a bass-heavy style of Ivoirian dance music with hip-hop-style vocals that draws heavily from Congolese rhythms; many of them dress like their musical idols in low-riding skinny jeans and skin-tight shirts.⁴ Initially associated with the flashy performances of Ivoirian migrants in Paris, *coupé-décalé* was later adopted in Abidjan—where it brightened the mood at the height of the 2002–4 civil war—before spreading to the rest of West Africa. Conspicuous consumption is the guiding principle of *coupé-décalé*. Devotees strive to wear brands (Gucci, Adidas, and so on) even if that almost always means acquiring counterfeits. More recently, Afrobeats, which borrows from a number of musical traditions, including *coupé-décalé*, has begun to inspire the iconography and style of new *fadas*.

Professing fondness for reggae, *coupé-décalé*, or hip-hop has typically meant embracing a musical culture rather than following a specific musician. Increasingly, however, *samari* seek inspiration from single artists whom they fully emulate: the dress, the hairdo, the talk, the body language. In this regard, Wizkid has become an important point of reference for young men seeking to fashion distinct personas by drawing on the sartorial power and charisma of the celebrity of the moment. The jersey the Afrobeats star designed in 2018 in collaboration with the US athletic wear manufacturer Nike (and which featured the logo of the star's own label, Starboy) reportedly sold out in minutes worldwide.⁵ Wizkid is not just a brand ambassador. He has become a prominent social influencer with millions of followers on Twitter. His seemingly effortless ability to initiate sartorial crazes by transforming ordinary items into stylish stuff has made him an inescapable fashion icon in the eyes of many young Nigerien men. Not to be outdone, many young women also confess a passion for the young musician; they avidly

---

3   *Se saper* means to dress elegantly in colloquial French. A cult of elegance known as *la SAPE* (Société des Ambianceurs et Personnes Élégantes) emerged among Congolese urban youth in the 1970s, inspired by an older tradition of colonized Africans emulating European fashions. Centered on the conspicuous consumption of Parisian finery, it operated as a counterculture under Congo-Brazzaville's Marxist regime (Gondola 1999).
4   In Nouchi, an Ivoirian argot, *coupé-décalé* means "scam and cram."
5   On the garment, the Nike swoosh was plastered right below the Starboy logo.

consume his celebrity through its immaterial (videos, images, and so on) and material (concerts) manifestations.[6]

In this chapter I explore how *samari* emulate the *style* of pop music celebrities like Wizkid in an age when economic conditions have simultaneously excluded them from the labor market and targeted them as consumers. "*Style*" (*samari* typically use the French term, which sounds global and fancy, though they also speak of *estila*, giving the term a Hausa inflection) here refers not only to the dress practices of a celebrity but also to his walk, talk, swagger—the acts of stylish individuation his fans associate with him. In sum, it consists of the myriad performances of identity made available for mass consumption through the large-scale reproduction and circulation of the celebrity's image, words, and voice. *Samari* speak of dressing *en style* ("in style"), by which they mean that they imitate the dress practices and body language of their favorite star, signaling their membership in a technologically mediated community of fans. Dressing *en style* attracts attention. We might describe it as a mode of "reflexive conspicuity" (Nakassis 2016, 58) for it not only calls attention to the wearer but also demands that he be recognized by highlighting his desire to be seen. While the practice draws on the virtual cosmopolitan persona fashioned by musical stars, it finds validation within the universe of *fada*, where young men's looks are forged and their reputations crafted. *Style* is essentially performative, reflexively mediating and materializing a tangle of relationships between media representations, marketed goods, and modes of subjectivity. As spaces of experimentation attuned to the world out there, *fadas* are where these stylish performances are most visibly instantiated.

Based on ethnographic research conducted in Niamey, a multiethnic metropolis, and in Dogondoutchi, a provincial town of some forty thousand heterogeneous Hausa speakers, I examine the role of ostentatious consumption in the constitution of male fandom in urban Niger. Aside from casting themselves as die-hard fans of famous musicians, cash-strapped *samari* who dress *en style* demonstrate an ability to navigate a constantly evolving stylistic landscape. Through a consideration of their transient, fashionable practices, I want to make a simple point, namely that "imitation" here cannot be reduced to a lack of creativity. Ever since Thorstein Veblen (1899) argued that the lower and middle classes in nineteenth-century America sought to distinguish themselves from their peers by emulating the consumptive practices of higher-ranking individuals, imitation has been dismissed as a superficial

---

6 Young women claim to be particularly fond of Wizkid's love songs.

endeavor, lacking value and authenticity. From this perspective, dressing above one's station by wearing cheap copies of expensive brands amounts to fakery. The stylistic pursuits I consider here through the lens of fandom and fashion suggest that emulation turns out to be a far more complex practice, forged at the intersection of distinctly gendered experiences of juniority, sociality, and consumption.

Veblen rightly pointed to the aspirational nature of conspicuous consumption in his discussion of how the working class, rather than wanting to bring down the bourgeoisie (as Karl Marx would have it), wished to look like them. Nevertheless, emulation should not be confused with conformity. By dressing like their musical idols, *samari* are flouting—rather than conforming to—adult norms and Muslim prescriptions. Their pursuit of fashion instantiates a mode of playful engagement through which to temporarily break free from normative obligations and organized power. As a form of aspirational practice, it serves as a kind of gatekeeping device for urban youth "in the know," signaling their engagement in proximate circuits of exchange and prestige. Far then from being considered the province of the deficient and the uninspired, the ability to imitate, I argue in what follows, is imbued with social capital.

Dress and Consumption

It is by now well established that dress and fashion were critical to the making of a distinct African modernity (Allman 2004b). In their studies of how colonized Africans engaged with a cosmopolitan world, Rhodes-Livingston anthropologists took people's adoption of colonial dress styles as an index of urbanization. Godfrey Wilson (1941) thus wrote that the sartorial cults and stylistic codes embraced by migrants to Copperbelt cities were symbolic means of earning respect and perhaps even power. These optimistic narratives were countered by the work of Frantz Fanon (2008) and other scholars who claimed that colonized subjects' desire for "Western" fashion was a symptom of their suffering and self-hatred. Seeking to distance themselves from analyses that equate colonized and other marginalized populations' acts of consumption with victimization, scholars have more recently emphasized the agency, creativity, and improvisational strategies of consumers. Thanks to the contributions of the Birmingham school, the role consumption practices have played in the formation of rebellious youth cultures in the United Kingdom is by now well-known (Hall and Jefferson 1976). Drawing on the notion of style as signifying practice, Dick Hebdige (1976) argued that British Teddy Boys in their Edwardian jackets, rockers in their pompadour hairstyles, and punks flaunting ripped clothing held together by safety pins resisted dominant ideologies by subverting the meaning of ordinary objects. Meanwhile Michel de Certeau (1984), focusing on quotidian practice, submitted that consumption was a form of production: consumers use commodities to suit their own agendas and aspirations, and in the process, they transform them. From this perspective, the hegemony of "Western" fashion has been continually challenged through innumerable acts of consumption and repurposing, including the production of visibly oppositional styles (Allman 2004a; Schneider 2006).

The "consumption as production" paradigm has inspired a new generation of scholars to examine how marginalized young people forge new, self-directed modes of achieving adulthood, measured more in terms of access to commodities than to productive labor (Liechty 2003; Weiss 2009). In contexts of precarity and material scarcity, excessive spending often emerges as a performance that, while "made up," has real consequences for the definition of social success and the making of habitable futures. *La Sape*, a cult of elegance originally centered on the conspicuous consumption of Parisian finery, is a well-documented instance of the productivity of "waste." By engaging in sartorial competitions such as *la dance des griffes* (the dance of designer labels), young Africans at home and abroad could momentarily contest their disenfranchisement (Gandoulou 1984; Gondola 1999). Whether they are analyzed as bluff (Newell 2012), antilanguage (Heath 1992) or politically charged spectacles (Bastian 2013), dress practices in the Global South must be understood as pragmatic performances through which individuals position themselves on a competitive social landscape, enabling them to project an image of success against all odds.

In colonial Niger, urban elites used dress to distinguish themselves from their rustic counterparts, contributing to emerging hierarchies of taste and style. At the center of the colonial public sphere was the civil service, a resolutely male world. In the early decades of postindependence, the civil service afforded opportunities of advancement to educated young men who dressed the part, demonstrating how clothing was a "readily available practice for popular expressions of African aspirations" (Hansen 2000, 52). This era was short-lived, however. To recite what is by now a familiar narrative, when debt-ridden Niger sought assistance from international lenders to confront a plummeting uranium market (one of Niger's main exports), it found relief albeit with heavy strings attached: that is, policy prescriptions to deregulate prices and markets, scaling back public services, and privatizing public institutions. Aimed at creating a suitable climate for economic growth, the structural adjustment programs were implemented in spurts from the late 1980s onward. They were supposed to be temporary corrective measures, a bitter "policy medicine" (Clark 2005, 6) with short-term side effects. Unfortunately, the side effects, which included widespread unemployment, turned into a permanent condition. Not only did they widen social inequalities, but they also encouraged the corruption they were supposed to eliminate. They also profoundly affected Nigerien participation in consumerism.

Whereas elites ultimately benefited from the privatization of public enterprises and the deregulation of markets and labor regimes, much of the population has faced considerable financial insecurity. Young people, in particular, have borne the brunt of these punishing economic policies. The formal labor market cannot absorb large cohorts of job seekers.[7] Formal education, once the ticket to a prosperous future, no longer guarantees stable employment in the civil service. Positions are restricted to well-connected candidates. Some educated *samari* take poorly paid, flexible jobs as schoolteachers but others prefer to wait for better opportunities. Meanwhile, their unschooled counterparts navigate the informal economy, realizing marginal gains. Forced to rely on parental support, many *samari* worry about the future. In particular, they worry about marriage.

For Nigerien males, one transitions to adulthood by marrying.[8] *Samari* with limited prospects cannot hope to attract a wife. If they earn an income, it is often not enough to provide adequately for dependents. Unable to follow their plotted life trajectory, they linger in a state of "waithood" (Singerman 2007). To experience waithood is to be caught in a temporal limbo between childhood and adulthood or, as Marc Sommers (2012) put it in his ethnography of jobless Rwandan youth, to be "stuck." It is a predicament many young people all over the planet are currently confronting.

Young Nigerien men who must postpone their plans of marrying and achieving social maturity experience their enforced immobility as a burden. Many of them have created *fadas* (or joined existing ones) to confront

---

7   Niger is the world's youngest country, with a population growing at 3.9 percent per year. Today roughly 75 percent of Nigeriens are under twenty-five years of age. Such demographics put great pressure on the state to invest resources it does not have in education and health care.

8   Women cross the threshold of adulthood by becoming mothers, that is, by acquiring a dependent.

unemployment, boredom, and alienation—or simply to hang out with peers. At the *fada,* they forge new modes of sociability and new expressions of self-esteem in the absence of direct avenues to sustainable livelihoods (Masquelier 2019a). They dream big dreams away from social dictates and parental pressures. Retired or stably employed members of the older generation routinely complain about the tea-drinking and card games that take place at the *fada,* hinting that they perceive these practices as symptoms of self-indulgence and dissipation rather than products of widespread structural inequalities.[9] "At the *fada,* they do not work, they just waste their time," is how a retired policeman described the shared youth culture "based around hanging out" (Jeffrey 2010, 35) that has developed in urban neighborhoods throughout Niger.

Significantly, the very conditions that impede these male youth from reaching adulthood make it possible for them to experiment with a range of identities before settling into mature social roles. These processes of experimentation are particularly visible in the domain of dress and fashion. Young men's fashions often mix playfulness with provocation. Rather than wear the locally tailored, long-sleeved tunic and drawstring pants that signify piety and respectability, many *samari* opt for low-riding jeans of foreign provenance, a controversial dress style known as *checkdown* that exposes the wearer's undergarments. Young men often invoke their juniority to justify their transgression of adult norms through lavish expenditures and sartorial pursuits. "I am a *petit* [junior]. I get to spend money on myself. That's what youth do," is how Ibrahim, a young man who earned an income unloading produce at the market, put it, implying that when he "grew up," much of that income would be directed toward the care of dependents. Ibrahim, who lived in a crowded, multigenerational compound, spent much of his time at the *fada* when he wasn't working. He enjoyed the freedom that came with being a youngster. Yet he often complained he was treated as an errand boy by his uncles and aunts. While they defer adult futures through their immersion in fashion, *samari* also long for those futures. In the face of an ever more receding horizon, many of them nevertheless believe that capitalizing on the potentialities of youth is a more effective strategy than rushing into marriage and acquiring dependents.

In Muslim-majority Niger, *samari* who "dress like Ivoirians" are frequently accused of contravening the modesty, self-restraint, and frugality they

---

9   Card games are perceived by many Nigeriens to be un-Islamic on the assumption that they generally involve playing for money.

should ideally embody as members of the Ummah, the global community of Muslims (Masquelier 2019b). Aside from denouncing young men's lack of religious commitment, some Muslim preachers decry their insobriety and disrespect for social conventions. At the turn of the millennium, young men who adopted the dress of hip-hop performers were severely admonished by Muslim religious elites for wearing baggy pants that dragged on the ground, gathering dirt and thus invalidating their daily prayers.[10] Today it is *checkdown* that inspires virulent criticisms on the part of pious Muslims.

Meanwhile those who join *fadas* are excoriated as worthless young men who spend their waking hours drinking tea while others toil. Their "unbridled" consumerism is the object of frequent criticism on the part of the older generation. If many parents worry about the improvidence of youngsters, others are more sanguine, asserting that *samari* must experience youth before they can embrace the responsible mantle of adulthood (Masquelier 2007).

On the face of it, the denunciations of youthful hedonism resonate with Veblen's indictment of the conspicuous pursuits through which elites and would-be elites built themselves up in American society at a time of severe social inequality. According to Veblen (1994), the display of accumulated wealth was critical to the upper class's ability to earn social recognition. By pointing to the way that members of the middle and lower classes felt compelled to emulate the spending habits of the rich to create an appearance of prosperity, Veblen's model of conspicuous consumption highlights how "the struggle for pecuniary reputability" (1994, 16) shapes the lives of those who, far from enjoying the wealth of the "leisure class," often spend above their means. In Niger young men themselves often admit to spending money they do not have in order to create the respectable appearance that signals access to resources. As a place of competitive sociality, the *fada* provides a Veblenian platform for consumerism in some of its most vivid, performative manifestations. Yet, all the same, we cannot reduce the lavish spending of impoverished *samari* to wasteful expenditure, as Veblen argued was the case among lower- and middle-class Americans seeking to emulate their wealthier peers. Nor can we assume that the young men are somehow mistaken about their priorities, as their critics often claim.

---

10   Before worship, Muslims perform ablutions so they can reach the ritual state of purity, free from any physical impurities or uncleanliness. To avoid the possibility of having to pray in soiled clothing, reformist Muslims told men to wear ankle-length pants.

Emulation and the "Look" of Success

Samari are well aware of the importance of dress in social life. They share an intense preoccupation with fashion and invest heavily in the acquisition of trendy outfits, borrowing money to purchase new attire when necessary (although parents often pay for their adolescent children's clothes to the extent that they can afford to, most of them balk at the notion of purchasing costly brands). Drawing on the spectacular power of clothes, they fashion distinct personas and routinely take pictures of themselves, which they post on social media (or they engage in mock sartorial battles). Like the carefully rehearsed dance competitions they stage between *fadas*, these informal performances often become critical sites for the making of "vernacular cosmopolitanisms" (Bhabha 1994).[11] The clothes, the dress performances they enable, and the images that are produced can thus be said to constitute a "prestige economy" (Fuh 2012, 501) that is as vibrant as it is competitive. The circulation of these images on social media broadens the performers' reputation among peers, contributing to their "fame" (Munn 1986) and making it easier to attract women and sustain their attention—a key concern for *samari*, whether or not marriage is on their mind. As projects of self-enhancement, *samari* dress performances thus operate along both competitive and seductive registers.

It is worth noting that sumptuous sartorial displays have a long history in this region of West Africa. In precolonial times, cloth was used as a measure of value and a unit of exchange throughout West Africa. Imported textiles—acquired from long-distance traders in exchange for slaves, leather, or ivory—were a luxury. They served to distinguish ruling elites from commoners (Nicolas 1986). Through the conspicuous consumption of finery, high-ranking individuals made sartorial statements that spoke of prestige stretching across tributary and kinship networks—what Jane Guyer (1995) called "wealth in people." By wrapping themselves in layers of expensive cloth, they literally insulated themselves from the masses (Worden 2010).

---

11 Inter-*fada* dance competitions are important events requiring much training and preparation. "The winners win prize money. And they receive the applause of spectators. It's such an honor. Coeur de Lion [a *fada*] won many times. They gave glory to the neighborhood," is how a young man described the centrality of these "tournaments of value" (Appadurai 1986, 21) for everyday life.

Codes of dress and regalia thus reinforced social hierarchies, simultaneously enhancing the visibility of ruling elites and asserting their superior status.

As the price of imported textiles dropped, commoners adopted elites' practices of adornment, seeking to elicit *daraja riga*, the respect well-dressed individuals enjoy. The spread of Islam, which associated Muslim identity with the voluminous and pricy open-sleeved gowns worn by male members of the traditional elite, facilitated this process. Given how wealth is a sign of God's blessing, Muslim pilgrims who financed their own trips to Mecca demonstrated both religious commitment and material success. As such, they became models to be emulated. Meanwhile, new sensibilities brought on by education, urbanization, and waged labor reshaped consumerist desires and dress practices. Upwardly mobile Nigeriens drew on the language of clothes to distance themselves from their less-educated counterparts.

Today many Nigeriens agree that these inflationary consumer competitions are unsustainable. When in the 1990s, unemployment rose, prices soared, and precarity spread following the abject failure of austerity measures, large numbers of young men heard reformist Muslim leaders' denunciation of conspicuous consumption and embraced their call to frugality (Masquelier 2009). Cloth nevertheless remains one of the primary "bodily signifiers of wealth" in Niger (Barber 1995, 214). Even as Nigeriens lament the cost of conspicuous expenditure, they are often caught in the aspirational logic that dictates the rules of spending in contexts where wealth, recognition, and virtue are entangled. Hence young men struggling to secure decent livelihoods may splurge on clothes. Those who remain dependent on kin for subsistence but have no dependents of their own channel their resources toward projects of self-fashioning. "I spend all my money on clothes," said a recent high school graduate, who labored in rice paddies and vegetable gardens to earn some cash.

For young men unable to achieve social mobility, dressing well is "both an end and a means" (Hansen 2010, 48). More than simply a matter of looking good, it is about creating an appearance of prosperity and sartorial savoir faire such that they can feel confident under the discriminating gaze of others. *Samari* know that dressing well opens doors. Whether they vie for the attention of young women (who often measure a suitor's wealth and his potential as a provider based on the clothes he wears, the motorcycle he drives, and so on), participate in neighborhood dance competitions (dressed in the *fada*'s uniform), or simply eye one another's outfits at a local bar, *samari* routinely engage in sartorial performances through which they redefine the meaning of success.

Figure 11.1. A young sapeur strolling in a Dogondoutchi street on a Saturday night.

In documenting how dress and fashion have been centrally implicated in the forging of a distinct African modernity, anthropologists have put the accent on processes of "bricolage, hybridity, and creolization" (Hansen 2004, 4–5). Along this register, dress practices are described as matters of individuation rather than emulation. Yet as Sasha Newell demonstrates in his ethnography of consumption and citizenship in Abidjan, we should not dismiss imitation on the assumption that it signals a lack of originality—a failure of creativity. For the *bluffeurs* (young men who project the appearance of success beyond their financial means) Newell (2012, 1) writes about, "There is no shame . . . in being derivative." Not only does the imitation of European styles and designs critically participate in the production of value in Côte d'Ivoire, but it is also a matter of national pride.[12] Nigerien devotees of Wizkid who display their passion for the Afropop star by faithfully imitating his fashion choices would probably see eye to eye with the *bluffeurs*. Just as Ivoirian young men draw prestige from their sartorial performances by imitating Europeans with great precision, so *samari* find fulfillment in dressing and behaving as much like their favorite pop star as possible. "The fans of Wizkid will search until they find the right T-shirt, the right hat so they look *just* like him. They are obsessed with his appearance. It's like a madness," a young man explained.

In his analysis of men's fashion shows in Trinidad, Daniel Miller (2019) highlights the distinction people make between fashion and style. "Fashion," he explains, leads to the dissolution of individual identity; it entails following sartorial conventions and blending in. To be in fashion is to be dressed like everyone else. "Style," on the other hand, is a highly personalized, self-controlled mode of forging identity through dress. With style, Miller (2019, 72) notes that "there is the search for the particular combination of otherwise unassociated parts which can be combined to create the maximum effect." Along the semantic continuum associated with dress practices, *samari*'s conception of *style* falls somewhere between the definitions of "fashion" and "style" offered by Miller. To dress *en style* is at once a personally cultivated performance and an expression of group identity. By adopting certain dress styles, *samari* distinguish themselves from others (including individuals who

---

12   Against the historical backdrop of the civilizing mission of colonial empires, the question of how anthropologists have written about mimicry and its relation to the politics of identity in Africa and elsewhere has invited criticisms and countercriticisms (see Bhabha 1994; Ferguson 2002; Gable 2002). The question falls beyond the purview of this chapter, however.

don't follow trends), but their goal is ultimately to publicize their membership in a fan club and to belong by blending in. They strive for imitation, not originality, by replicating the "maximum effect" created by their idol. Yet dressing like their idol does not lead to the "dissolution of identity," for the goal is to stand out as a celebrity lookalike. As Constantine Nakassis (2016, 177) observes in his ethnography of Indian male college students acting like film stars, the point is to signal allegiance by "agentively appropriating the hero's image" rather than dissolving into it.

In the 1990s, I met a few Michael Jackson doppelgängers (dressed in black pants, white socks, and so on) who had mastered the star's famous moonwalk. Today, Wizkid's fans pay close attention to what the star wears, does, and says. They keep track of his presence on social media, scour magazines that feature articles about him, and model their persona after his—and then they share pictures of themselves in "Wizkid style" on Instagram, Facebook, or Viber. As a Wizkid fan put it, "I try to remain in synch with his personality." *Style* here speaks to the modes of subjectivity *fadantchés* elaborate, drawing on a variety of sartorial and performative registers to realize a connection with their idol and, in the process, affirm their membership in the dispersed community of consumers that is fandom.

Through consumption, fans can be said to enact particular competencies based on fashion sense, constructing "looks" and "outfits." Dress is essential to fashioning oneself as a fan and claiming to be part of a high-energy, self-aware, and passionate fandom. In other words, it is through dress that fans construe their relationship with public figures and engage in "para-social interactions" (Horton and Wohl 1956) with them.[13] "He is my brother. I dress like him," is how a Wizkid fan described his connection to the Afropop phenom. Thanks to social media, the distinction between private citizen and public persona is often blurred. Fans who follow their idols online can entertain the illusion that they know them and are close to them. Publicizing one's devotion to a public figure by dressing *en style* affirms that closeness. Occasionally, such affirmation of closeness relies on fetishization rather than strict emulation. "Obama is my man. He is one of us," Sani, a school dropout, told me. Unable to secure permanent employment, the young man took odd jobs and frequently relied on his parents for subsistence. He had

---

13   Mass media, Donald Horton and Richard Wohl (1956) observed, give spectators the illusion of face-to-face relationships with performers. The intimacy at a distance that radio, television, and other modes of communication—including newer media—produce is what they call "parasocial interaction."

recently purchased an expensive pair of sandals he could not really afford simply because the name Obama was plastered on them. He confided that he became emotional when he heard Barak Obama (who was the US president at the time) speak. Consumerism, the Wizkid and Obama cases suggest, is driven by and sustains affect.

Fashion and clothing function as outward markers of fandom for both insiders and outsiders. Audiences at home and abroad are connected through their participation in a technologically mediated musical culture that often relies on the image of self-made black performers. Wizkid, who grew up in a Lagos slum and is now one of the richest musicians on the continent, speaks to—and for—struggling youths looking for aspirational models. Everything he says and wears becomes part of the spirit of entrepreneurship he embodies. In other words, his brand singularizes the most ordinary product, giving it a touch of glamor. After Wizkid appeared dressed in black with red high-tops, his Nigerien fans adopted a similar look. Two young musicians from Dogondoutchi took to wearing black outfits with red high-tops during performances.

Fans told me they often did not find the items they needed to complement the Wizkid "look." Nevertheless, any shirt in the market that bore the Starboy label or looked like something the star had worn was immediately snatched up by fans who engaged in what John Fiske (1992) calls "enunciative productivity," the shared and spoken meanings through which fans perform their identity. *Fadas* have been an important platform for the circulation and reproduction of "styled" performances. It is where young men test out new styles and new identities, where they learn to "orient themselves to the material and semiotic forms that . . . they bring into being (Nakassis 2016, 8). As an emulative performance, *style* is as much about self-enhancement as about sociality. In sum, it is critical to the making of youthful "communities of taste" (Martin 1995, 2).

The Pull of Fashion

On a cool December evening in 2015, twenty-one-year-old Oumarou was sitting on a narrow bench he shared with three friends, all members of Galaxy, a *fada* known for its embrace of reggae culture. While pouring tea into a tiny serving glass he would be passing around and refilling for the dozen *fadantchés* (*fada* members) assembled there, he described to me what fashion-conscious *samari* wore that year:

Figure 11.2. Style is a source of conceptual and pictorial inspiration for a number of *fadas*.

Baguis [baggy pants] and *deux-places*, that's over. Those MC things [hip-hop fashion], we've ditched all that. We call these things "baglo." If you wear that, people are gonna laugh at you. Now the trend is Ivoirian fashion, tight pants, tank tops. If you don't have those, you can't go out. We still wear chains, you know, we like bling bling. Because Molars [a *coupé-décalé* artist] and the others wear chains. It's MC dress that's no longer in fashion.

Something that is "in fashion" one moment will be "out of fashion" the next. The "now" of fashion is a moving target, not identifiable by any kind of time-measuring device. It is better understood as that "ungraspable threshold between 'not yet' and 'no more'" (Agamben 2009, 48). Achieving a fashionable identity built on consumer goods means having to constantly redefine and replenish it through new purchases. For Oumarou, a school dropout who left his rural village in search of a better life in the capital, fashion not only dictated what young men should wear but also exerted tyranny over them, forcing them to keep up with new styles if they wished to avoid being ridiculed by their peers. Oumarou had grown up in a strict polygynous household headed by his father, a Muslim scholar who denounced hip-hop and other musical cultures as immoral. He had hoped to find freedom and improve his prospects in Niamey, but he struggled financially. His comments about people who "laugh at you" are a reminder that while the *fada* constitutes a refuge from social conventions, paradoxically, it is also a hive of peer pressure and competition. To be sure, the *fada* is where economically marginalized young men escape the strains they frequently face. "At the *fada* you need not worry about hiding your poverty under layers of clothes," a member of Galaxy who made a living smuggling gasoline across the Nigerien border with Nigeria, explained. Relationships are built on closeness, loyalty, and reciprocity. Mock fights, playful banter, and humor routinely animate conversations, further contributing to "cultural intimacy" (Herzfeld 2005) and the bundle of practices which *fadantchés* might deny engaging in even as they guiltily enjoy them. Yet because peer-group activities are the primary outlet for the performance of masculinity, rivalry routinely infects the *fada*'s carefully cultivated climate of amity. The burden of having to compete sartorially with more prosperous peers for female attention, for instance, can be overwhelming for some.

In a conversation about the kind of clothes young people liked, a high school student told me that youth wore "the latest" because they "like novelty. [They] don't want to wear an old thing." The young man received an allowance from his father to replenish his wardrobe with basics. He supplemented it by running errands for a shopkeeper during holidays so he could acquire Adidas sneakers (his favorite brand) and fancy "European" clothes. When I pressed him to elaborate on young people's fixation with novelty, he said: "We are new so we only like new things." Following trends is something that youth do well by virtue of their structural position. Youngsters have been described as more likely to experiment and more inclined to embrace change than other segments of society (Mannheim 1952). Though people of all ages exhibit care in the way they dress, especially when they attend celebrations and public events, many would nevertheless agree that fashion is associated with youth.

Wizkid himself is said to like fresh, crisp clothes that show no sign of wear. "It's hard for me to wear the same thing twice," the young musician reportedly admitted (Frank 2016). Such admission underscores not only his fondness for novelty by also his newfound financial status (as a child, the artist often had to buy secondhand clothes). New clothes are a sign of prosperity.

Individuals wishing to flaunt their wealth may choose to have their clothes sewn out of *bazin VIP* (damask fabric), a pricy fabric that reportedly cannot be washed. A woman purchasing *bazin VIP* signals she is rich enough not to wear her outfits more than once or twice. Being fashionable here hinges on not only taste and the ability to navigate the consumer market but also spending power, which can be calculated swiftly by scrutinizing someone's clothes and evaluating their cost. The crispness of a fabric, its sheen, and the novelty of a style all enter into judgments of "pecuniary standing" (Veblen 1994, 16). They reveal something about the frequency of one's vestimentary purchases: a moneyed individual's wardrobe retains the aura of newness. Faded, worn garments, on the other hand, signal destitution, or at the very least, an inability to translate social connections into access to cash and cloth. Urban *samari* have access to a wide selection of dress styles whether they commission outfits from local tailors, buy cast-off imports from secondhand merchants, or acquire knockoffs known as *qualité*. Many keep up with fashion by buying clothes of foreign provenance. While *qualité* garments (thought to come from China) reportedly cannot stand much wear, making it hard for owners to maintain a neat appearance, the challenge consumers of secondhand clothes frequently face is that their purchases may look worn from the beginning.

Fashion insists on "pure contemporaneity" (Simmel 1971, 296) and constant movement. To be fashionable is to embody contemporaneity. Consider Salissou, alias Milleboy, a member of Dragon Show, the *fada* he founded with classmates while they were in tenth grade. The young man, whose father worked for the ministry of transport, sported an HBA tank top tucked in a belted denim cut-off when I first met him. He rarely took off his aviator sunglasses, consulted his phone obsessively, and routinely posted fancy pictures of himself on social media, using a filter that created a mirror image effect. He updated his wardrobe as soon as he got wind of an emerging trend, supplementing the dress allowance he received from his father with cash he received from his older sister, a schoolteacher whose husband had a prosperous business. "You see," he explained, "the point of the *fada* is to attract girls. You compete with other *fadas*. This is why *fadantchés* dress well: the aim is to make their *fada* look 'fun' for girls who are checking them out." Known as a trendsetter in his Niamey neighborhood, Milleboy carefully cultivated his image as a *gayou* (savvy urbanite in Nouchi, Ivoirian argot) to enhance his and his *fada*'s reputation. Though he did not engage in *gaspillage*, the practice of impressing everyone at a local bar by showing

Figure 11.3. A young fan of Wizkid wearing a knockoff HBA tank top and cut-off jeans.

up elegantly attired and spending your money on alcohol, he knew neighborhood youths admired him.

Thanks to the spin Wizkid puts on foreign brands, these pick up a distinctive Afro-chic luster. To Milleboy, the HBA T-shirt he wore was not just any branded attire, but *the* brand popularized by Wizkid. Aside from signifying aspirations to simultaneity with cosmopolitan worldliness, the item spoke of Milleboy's empathic connection to the Afrobeats star. When the young man and the other members of Dragon Show sported their Wizkid uniform, the HBA logo shirts acquired a double layering of valuation. To the extent that fashion is a stand-in for the good life *samari* aspire to, the *fada* is "the place where the superfluidity of objects is converted into a value in and of itself" (Mbembe 2004, 404).

The Labor of Dressing

Although Wizkid occasionally channels the spirit of Michael Jackson by showing up in glitzy embroidered jackets topped with fedoras, it is through his adoption of a wide range of styles that he has made his mark on the fashionscape. He helped popularize locally tailored outfits made of African textile by claiming that they were "the in-thing." In Nigeria, young men wear traditional dress—or "trad" as they call it—whether they are going to work, attending a wedding, or hanging out at a nightclub (Frank 2016). People have commented on social media and in private conversations that Wizkid is as comfortable parading in richly embroidered Gucci suits as he is in ripped jeans bought in Lagos. *Samari* also select from a range of different sartorial styles depending on whether they wish to put the accent on their Muslim identity, their youth, or their professional aspirations.[14] Although on the surface their cultivation of *style* may look intuitive and unrehearsed, it actually requires considerable skill and labor.

---

14 Youth make visible their membership in the Ummah, the Muslim community, by donning a locally tailored tunic with matching drawstring pants during religious holidays and family celebrations, such as naming ceremonies. By wearing the skin-tight attire of the *coupeur-décaleur* or dressing as Wizkid, they present themselves as urban youth. To project themselves as educated, aspiring professionals, they may go for the *responsable* look (buttoned-down shirt, pleated pants accessorized with a leather belt, and closed leather shoes) or the *jeune cadre* (executive) look that calls for the locally tailored, multipocketed shirt and matching pants worn by civil servants.

Wizkid's ability to frequently refresh his image as a hipster dandy is what reportedly keeps him at the vanguard of Afropop fashion trends. "His choices of dress and accessories inspire so many of our youths, regardless of how he dresses," a friend told me. "You can't say there's *one* Wizkid style. In fact, that's what young people like, they can imitate him without sticking to a style." All the same, he has so successfully "branded" certain items that *samari* associate these with Wizkid. The Wizkid fashion "starter pack" usually includes cropped jeans, a T-shirt or hoody with funky graphics, a baseball cap, and a pair of dark shades. Apparel companies are eager to capitalize on the appeal of an A-lister with a huge following: Wizkid has successfully collaborated with big brands like Nike. He also sells clothes—anything from T-shirts to hats to socks—under his own Starboy brand. Announcements of the release of a Starboy product send fans on a frenzied quest for the (usually costly) item: "Wizkid's fans, they'll go to any lengths to get one of his T-shirts. You see poor boys who try to buy a shirt that costs what they earn in a month," I was told.

Though they are frequently accused of being unproductive, *samari* typically invest significant labor in their sartorial projects. In contexts where many of them are scrambling to get by, they have learned to buy with an eye to maximizing their purchasing power—even if that implies pressuring a parent for money, pinching cash from the parental purse, or pestering kin for a loan. Acquiring the right item of clothing for the right price takes skill, especially when the item in question is in short supply—as was the case for heavy neck chains when the rapper look was popular. Buying new clothes is best— the sheen of new garments is a sign that the wearer has money to spend—but it is not always feasible. "I dress like Ivoirian artists, like Bebi Philip[15]: *tuyau* [literally "hose"; tight] jeans, tank tops, high tops. Sunglasses, no caps. I wear my hair like Nasri's [a French soccer star], you know, with the sides shaved and the top cropped," Tahirou, a jobless university graduate, who hoped to secure employment with a development agency, told me. "I used to buy new clothes, when my father took care of me, but now he is retired. Except for the shoes, now I often get *bosho* [lit., from Boston; secondhand]. I also buy jeans from a guy who regularly goes to Benin." Buying the right clothes, Tahirou suggested, requires savvy, effort, and dedication.

In addition to demanding hard work, dressing well when one is short on cash entails what Karen Hansen calls "clothing competence" (2013, 416), namely the set of skills that participate in the work of consumption.

---

15   Bebi Philip is a *coupé-décalé* artist from the Côte d'Ivoire.

Specifically, such competence includes the ability to select the right items from a vast array of clothes, taking into account quality and value, and assemble these items smartly so as to produce a certain "look." As Tahirou noted, "It takes time [to find good secondhand garments], you have to sift through piles of clothes." The "look" further hinges on garment care. One must reserve the clean and fresh appearance of these items to stretch their "lifespan." Young men take pains to rotate their garments. They avoid wearing their good clothes too often,[16] reserving them for select occasions: to attend the Friday prayer, pay one's respect to local customary authorities, go to a wedding, and so on.

The labor involved in dressing well entails producing the illusion that one is flush with cash even in the most strained of circumstances. Like the *bluffeurs* of Abidjan who spend without restraint on pricy brands and nightlife entertainment to impress others, many *samari*'s reputations hinge not on financial stability so much as on the "display of potential" (Newell 2012, 1). These young men are expert at managing impression. Their performance may gather praise, but just as often it may be dismissed as *farotage* ("show off" in Nouchi) to stress its "too much" quality. The clothes these *samari* wear, the accessories they use are calculated to create an appearance of wealth and success regardless of whether they have actually achieved prosperity. When you ask, however, you find out that the shirt they are wearing belongs to their brother, the motorbike they are driving is borrowed from a friend, and the fancy cell phone they flaunt they are about to trade in for a cheaper model because they desperately need cash (cell phones are frequently used as money reserves).

Finally, the work of dressing encompasses mastering a set of bodily techniques that bring dress and body together and thus participate in the successful enactment of *style*. As Wendy Parkins (2002, 5) notes, the body is "never simply a neutral clothes horse." How a person wears their clothes so as to produce a certain embodied identity is generally the outcome of a training process during which they learn to inhabit their clothes (Entwistle and Wilson 2001). One does not instinctively know how to walk in high heels. Similarly, a person wrapped tightly in several yards of fabric moves across space differently than when wearing an untailored, flowing gown. The capacity to translate dress into bodily presentation requires the cultivation of a dress habitus. Young men wearing low riders to emulate their favorite

---

16 Clothes are laundered using strong detergents containing bleach, and they are hung up (or laid out) to dry in the sun. Consequently, the colors fade rapidly.

coupé-décalé artists may walk around nonchalantly, but their moves are, in fact, quite practiced—otherwise their pants would likely slide down their thighs. Wizkid fans who aspire to be "like him" do so through a joint performance of dress and body—a "fleshy mise-en-scène" (Sylvanus 2013, 40) that is initially rehearsed but eventually becomes second nature. The clothes they wear afford them confidence, but it is ultimately by learning to inhabit them that they truly impersonate the dashing, trendsetting artist. In sum, dress as practice and as emulation requires labor: it is a form of production as well as an affectively and economically demanding form of investment.

Fandom and Fun

According to Roland Barthes, being fashionable provides an illusion that one has control over one's immediate circumstances. Fashion, Barthes argued, creates a "dream of wholeness" in which one can be "everything at once, without having to choose" (1983, 255). By enabling a person to be at once "herself and another" (Barthes 1983, 256), fashion calls upon the self to multiply itself in a single being. Barthes's approach has been criticized for defining clothes as inert texts lending themselves to straightforward reading. Yet it rightfully points to the centrality of dress in processes of self-enhancement. By focusing on *style* as a performance in whose various manifestations some *samari* enhance themselves, I have examined how the "dream of wholeness" operates in Niger's fan culture. Dressing *en style*, I have argued, requires effort, dedication, and skill. The point is to be noticed. As a young man put it, "Samari [who dress *en style*] want other youths to look at them, they want to be admired." Importantly, it is a performance associated with youth. By adopting garments whose distinctive designs participate in a patently "modern" aesthetics, *samari* effectively distinguish themselves from elders while taking advantage of the freedom their claims to being youth entitles them to. Dress thus provides a useful lens through which to consider *samari*'s practices of self-making at a time when traditional mechanisms of social mobility are compromised, and consumption has become a critical mode of identity production.

Claiming youth is political act (Durham 2004). It enables individuals to enjoy the resources and claim the privileges associated with such a status. Youth have few obligations and responsibilities. They have the right to engage in provisional, transient, and inconsequential activities. "As a youth, you can act irresponsibly. You can dance, you can wear fashionable clothes, it doesn't matter," is how one twenty-two-year-old man, who sold cleaning products in the street, put it. In short, youth are allowed to have fun. In a general sense, fun signals a departure from rules and conventions. It typifies spur-of-the-moment, inconsistent, free-form expressions and activities. The recent craze for *coupé-décalé* among West African youth underscores Asef Bayat's (2007, 434) point that youngsters are the main practitioners of fun. The goal of *coupé-décalé* is not to raise social consciousness. Quite the contrary, it aims to reassure by projecting an idealized future. It does so by producing joy, excess, pomp, and lightheartedness.

The most successful ambassador of *coupé-décalé* was undoubtedly DJ Arafat who profitably drew on social media to export his music worldwide. Aside from enjoying a huge following in Francophone Africa, the Ivoirian musician was a master at branding. He called his fanbase *la Chine* (China) and nicknamed himself *le Président de la Chine* (The president of China) to signal the extent of his influence. His accidental death on August 12, 2019, at age thirty-three, spurred a giant outpouring of emotion in Niger where many of his fans had named themselves or their *fadas* after him. Often dubbed the "king" of *coupé-décalé*, DJ Arafat personified the spirit of a musical culture that celebrated the resilience of young migrants who returned home wealthy from the scams they engaged in abroad. Like other artists who took advantage of the lowered barriers of distribution for pop music, he amassed millions of fans who followed his every move on social media. In Niger, young men who copied his flashy style "from his hairdo to his pants, belts, shoes, everything!" (as a friend put it) felt part of the broad, Ivoirian-based movement orchestrated by digital media. The massive grief his death provoked is a testament to the success of media technologies and informal networks of cultural production in shaping national publics.

Like the previous generation of hip-hop aficionados or current consumers of Afrobeats, *coupé-décalé* fans seek to distinguish themselves from an adult order of masculinity. The brand names embroidered in large letters on their garments; the ripped, dyed, roughened, patched, or pleated texture of their jeans; and their loud, unconventional construction (extra pockets, zippers, buttons and so on) function as "excessive supplements" (Nakassis 2016, 45) that, by distancing their wearers from their more soberly attired elders, identify them as youth. Adopting this aesthetics of excess allows them to constantly test the terms of inclusion in the world of *style*. As much as *samari* bemoan their status as social cadets, it is precisely because they are not yet adults that they are able to transgress boundaries and experiment with a range of identities before settling into mature social roles. By dressing *en style*, young men bracket the here and now of youth—marked by inventiveness, irreverence, and impulsiveness—from the then and there of adulthood, marked by responsibility, propriety, and convention. Through media consumption and fan fashion, *samari* thus define themselves as youth and draw on the dispensations and privileges that youth affords them. As a form of productive labor requiring that youth make the most of their resources in conditions of scarcity and uncertainty, *style* is best summed up as a "semiotic of difference and deferral cast in material form" (Nakassis 2016, 5).

Bibliography

Agamben, Giorgio. 2009. "What Is the Contemporary?" In *What Is an Apparatus? and Other Essays*. Translated by David Kishik and Stefan Pedatella, 39–54. Stanford, CA: Stanford University Press.

Allman, Jean, ed. 2004a. *Fashioning Africa: Power and the Politics of Dress*. Bloomington: Indiana University Press.

———. 2004b. "Fashioning Africa: Power and the Politics of Dress." In *Fashioning Africa: Power and the Politics of Dress*, edited by Jean Allman, 1–10. Bloomington: Indiana University Press.

Appadurai, Arjun. 1986. "Introduction: Commodities and the Politics of Value." In *The Social Life of Things: Commodities in Cultural Perspective*, edited by Arjun Appadurai, 3–63. New York: Cambridge University Press.

Barber, Karin.1995. "Money, Self-Realization, and the Person in Yorùbá Texts." In *Money Matters: Instability, Values, and Social Payments in the Modern History of West African Communities*, edited by Jane I. Guyer, 205–24. Portsmouth, NH: Heinemann.

Barthes, Roland. 1983. *The Fashion System*. Translated by Matthew Ward and Richard Howard. Berkeley: University of California Press.

Bastian, Misty L. 2013. "Dressing for Success: The Politically Performative Quality of an Igbo Woman's Attire." In *African Dress: Fashion, Agency, Performance*, edited by Karen Tranberg Hansen and D. Soyini Madison, 15–29. New York: Bloomsbury.

Bayat, Asef. 2007. "Islamism and the Politics of Fun." *Public Culture* 19, no. 3: 433–59.

Bhabha, Homi. 1994. *The Location of Culture*. London: Routledge.

Clark, Gracia. 2005. "The Permanent Transition in Africa." *Voices* 7, no. 1: 6–9.

Certeau, Michel de. 1984. *The Practice of Everyday Life*. Translated by Steven F. Randall. Berkeley: University of California Press.

Durham, Deborah. 2004. "Disappearing Youth: Youth as a Social Shifter in Botswana." *American Ethnologist* 31, no. 4: 589–605.

Entwistle, Joanne, and Elizabeth B. Wilson, eds. 2001. *Body Dressing*. London: Bloomsbury.

Fanon, Frantz. 2008. *Black Skin, White Masks*. Translated by Richard Philcox. New York: Grove.

Ferguson, James. 2002. "Of Mimicry and Membership: Africans and the 'New World Society.'" *Cultural Anthropology* 17, no. 4: 551–69.

Fiske, John. 1992. "The Cultural Economy of Fandom." In *The Adoring Audience: Fan Culture and Popular Media*, edited by Lisa A. Lewis, 30–49. New York: Routledge.

Frank, Alex. 2016. "Meet Wizkid, Nigeria's Best Dressed Pop Star." *Vogue*, February 19. https://www.vogue.com/article/wizkid-interview-africa-nigeria-style.

Fuh, Divine. 2012. "The Prestige Economy: Veteran Clubs and Youngmen's Competition in Bamenda, Cameroon." *Urban Forum* 23: 501–26.

Gable, Eric. 2002. "Anthropologist's (New) Dress Code: Some Brief Comments on a Comparative Cosmopolitanism." *Cultural Anthropology* 17, no. 4: 572–79.

Gandoulou, Justin-Daniel. 1984. *Dandies à Bacongo: Le culte de l'élégance dans la société congolaise contemporaine*. Paris: L'Harmattan.

Gondola, Ch. Didier. 1999. "Dream and Drama: The Search for Elegance among Congolese Youth." *African Studies Review* 42, no. 1: 23–48.

Guyer, Jane. 1995. "Wealth in People, Wealth in Things: Introduction." *Journal of African History* 36: 83–90.

Hall, Stuart, and Tony Jefferson. 1976. *Resistance through Rituals: Youth Subcultures in Post-War Britain*. London: Hutchinson.

Hansen, Karen Tranberg. 2000. *Salaula: The World of Secondhand Clothing and Zambia*. Chicago: University of Chicago Press.

———. 2013. "Secondhand Clothing and Africa: Global Fashion Influences, Local Dress Agency, and Policy Issues." In *The Handbook of Fashion Studies*, edited by Sandy Black, Amy de la Haye, Joanne Entwistle, Regina Root, Agnès Rocamora, and Helen Thomas. New York: Bloomsbury.

———. 2010. "Secondhand Clothing and Fashion in Africa." In *Contemporary African Fashion*, edited by Suzanne Gott and Kristyne Lougran, 39–52. Bloomington: Indiana University Press.

———. 2004. "The World in Dress: Anthropological Studies of Clothing, Fashion, and Culture." *Annual Review of Anthropology* 33: 369–92.

Heath, Deborah. 1992. "Fashion, Anti-Fashion, and Heteroglossia in Urban Senegal." *American Ethnologist* 19, no. 1: 19–33.

Hebdige, Dick. 1979. *Subculture: The Meaning of Style*. New York: Methuen.

Herzfeld, Michael. 2005. *Cultural Intimacy: Social Poetics and the Nation State*. New York: Routledge.

Horton, Donald, and Richard R. Wohl. 1956. "Mass Communication and Para-Social Interaction: Observations on Intimacy at a Distance." *Psychiatry* 19, no. 3: 215–30.

Jeffrey, Craig. 2010. *Timepass: Youth, Class, and the Politics of Waiting in India*. Stanford, CA: Stanford University Press.

Liechty, Mark. 2003. *Suitably Modern: Making Middle-Class Culture in a New Consumer Society*. Princeton, NJ: Princeton University. Press.

Mannheim, Karl. 1952. *Essays on the Sociology of Knowledge*. Edited by Paul Kecskemeti. London: Routledge & Kegan Paul.

Martin, Phyllis M. 1995. *Leisure and Society in Colonial Brazzaville*. Cambridge: Cambridge University Press.

Masquelier, Adeline. 2019a. *Fada: Boredom and Belonging in Niger*. Chicago: University of Chicago Press.

———. 2007. "Negotiating Futures: Islam, Youth, and the State in Niger." In *Islam and Muslim Politics in Africa*, edited by Benjamin F. Soares and René Otayek, 243–62. New York: Palgrave.

———. 2009. *Women and Islamic Revival in a West African Town*. Bloomington: Indiana University Press.

———. 2019b. "Young Men of Leisure? Youth, Conspicuous Consumption, and the Performativity of Dress in Niger." In *Conspicuous Consumption in Africa*, edited by Deborah Posen and Ilana Van Wyk, 152–71. Johannesburg: Wits University Press.

Mbembe, Achille. 2004. "Aesthetics of Superfluidity." *Public Culture* 16, no. 3: 373–405.

Miller, Daniel. 2019. "Style and Ontology." In *The Anthropology of Dress and Fashion*, edited by Brent Luvaas and Joanne B. Eicher, 78–87. New York: Bloomsbury.

Munn, Nancy. 1986. *The Fame of Gawa: A Symbolic Study of Value Transformation in a Massim (Papua New Guinea) Society*. Durham, NC: Duke University Press.

Nakassis, Constantine V. 2016. *Doing Style: Youth and Mass Mediation in South India*. Chicago: University of Chicago Press.

Newell, Sasha. 2012. *The Modernity Bluff: Crime, Consumption, and Citizenship in Côte d'Ivoire*. Chicago: University of Chicago Press.

Nicolas, Guy. 1986. *Don rituel et échange marchand dans une société sahélienne*. Paris: Institut d'Ethnologie.

Parkins, Wendy. 2002. "Introduction: (Ad)dressing Citizens." In *Fashioning the Body Politic: Dress, Gender, Citizenship*, edited by Wendy Parkins, 1–7. New York: Berg.

Schneider, Jane. 2006. "Cloth and Clothing." In *Handbook of Material Culture*, edited by Christopher Tilley, Webb Keane, Susanne Küchler, Michael Rowlands, and Patricia Spyer, 203–19. London: SAGE.

Simmel, Georg. 1971[1904]. "Fashion." In *On Individuality and Social Forms: Selected Writings*, edited by D. N. Levine, 294–323. Chicago: University of Chicago Press.

Singerman, Diane. 2007. "The Economic Imperatives of Marriage: Emerging Practices and Identities among Youth in the Middle East." Working Paper 6, Wolfensohn Centre for Development, Washington, DC, and Dubai School of Government.

Sommers, Marc. 2012. *Stuck: Rwandan Youth and the Struggle for Adulthood*. Athens: University of Georgia Press.

Sylvanus, Nina. 2013. "Fashionability in Colonial and Postcolonial Togo." In *African Dress: Fashion, Agency, Performance*, edited by Karen Tranberg Hansen and D. Soyini Madison, 30–44. New York: Bloomsbury.

Veblen, Thorstein. 1994. *The Theory of the Leisure Class*. Mineola, NY: Dover Thrift Editions.

Weiss, Brad. 2009. *Street Dreams and Hip Hop Barbershops: Global Fantasy in Urban Tanzania*. Bloomington: Indiana University Press.

Wilson, Godfrey. 1941. *An Essay on the Economics of Detribalization in Northern Rhodesia*. Part 2. Rhodes Livingston paper 6. Manchester, UK: Manchester University Press.

Worden, Sarah. 2010. "Clothing and Identity: How Can Museum Collections of Hausa Textiles Contribute to Understanding the Notion of Hausa Identity?" In *Being and Becoming Hausa: Interdisciplinary Perspectives*, edited by Anne Haour and Benedetta Rossi, 213–34. Leiden, The Netherlands: Brill.

Chapter Twelve

The Revolution Lost

Generational Change and Urban Youth Logics in Conakry's Dance Scene

Adrienne J. Cohen

Badjibi, the octogenarian director of one of Conakry's largest private dance troupes, spoke with me about the shortcomings of the current generation of Guinean performing artists: "I want the next generation to become like us, even to surpass us," he said. "Our time has passed, so if they listen to us, they can go further. But if they don't listen, they will lose out. The day we are no longer here, maybe they'll realize, but it will be too late." The directors of dance troupes, or "ballets" in Guinea's capital city of Conakry, regularly speak in such disapproving terms about younger dancers and musicians. These elders lament that in their hurry to make it big, young performing artists play and dance too fast and aren't interested in the specific rural histories of dances they perform: hence they mix movements indiscriminately between once-discrete dances, resulting in cultural loss. Elders suggest, in contrast, that members of their own socialist generation—trained between 1958 and 1984—were loyal guardians of national culture. Badjibi's comments exemplify a broader discourse of nationhood and generation that is playing out at the level of cultural production in Conakry.

In making sense of the contestations around dance in Guinea, I employ Deborah Durham's definition of generations as "age-conscious cohorts" produced by "rapid shifts in experience."[1] Artists trained during Guinea's social-

---

[1] Durham, "Youth and the Social Imagination," 113.

ist period or "First Republic" (1958–84), who now direct most of the dance troupes in Conakry, comprise the cohort of people I refer to as *elders*. I use the term *youth* to refer to those who were trained after the death of socialist president Sékou Touré in 1984. While there are arguably multiple ways of parsing either of these cohorts, much of the generational tension expressed among Conakry's performing artists may be understood through the lens of political-economic change in Guinea, namely the shift from state-socialism to neoliberal capitalism that began in the mid-1980s.[2] Notably, while elderly artists speak of vanishing culture, dance troupes continue to emerge all over the city. Rites of passage in Conakry (including weddings, births, and circumcisions) are animated by performers who train in such troupes, and young dancers and musicians cultivate productive careers, often with international trajectories of touring and teaching. So why do elders seem to think ballet culture is endangered? In this chapter, I interpret typical accounts of cultural loss put forth by socialist-trained artists in Conakry within a broader context of generational transformation in which young people are reframing an artistic practice forged during the First Republic to make sense in the neoliberal present. In an era in which troupes operate privately, and young artists must find creative ways to support themselves financially in a global market economy, Conakry ballet artists cultivate new practices and logics that both evidence their uncertainties and celebrate their sense of global connection and potential. This chapter is based on extensive ethnographic fieldwork among dancers, musicians, and ballet directors in Guinea's capital city of Conakry, including twelve months of participant-observation and interviewing in Conakry from 2010 to 2013, three years of dance apprenticeship and language study in Conakry from 2002 to 2005, and additional fieldwork among Guinean artists in the United States from 2006 to the present.

---

2   While social mobility, or the lack thereof, can affect who classifies as *youth* or *elder* in contemporary Africa (e.g., Cole, "Jaombilo"; Mains, "Neoliberal Times"; Meiu, "'Beach-Boy Elders'"; Vigh, *Terrains of War*), the socialist/post-socialist identifications I describe here do not tend to fluctuate similarly. In other words, a dancer who has attained status beyond his or her years does not then begin to reflect the ethical or aesthetic orientations of socialist-trained elders.

Art and the Guinean Revolution

Guinea's socialist government, led by independence president Ahmed Sékou Touré, used dance as a central medium of nation building and political propaganda. Between 1959 and the late 1960s, the Guinean state developed a nationwide system of dance troupes (ballets) tasked with training dancers and musicians to perform folkloric versions of ethnic dances on stage. Ballet production was organized and regulated through a complex hierarchical national system of troupes, beginning with the village or district level, up through sectional, federal, and national levels. There were thousands of troupes nationwide[3] and regular competitions that gave artists opportunities to move up the ranks. Ballet programs were intended to promote and emblematize an egalitarian socialist nation, aligned with a broader project of Pan-African liberation.[4] Practitioners who performed in the national companies, especially the top company *Les Ballets Africains*, were considered cultural diplomats abroad and were celebrated in party media as exemplary socialist citizens. While African ballet was not invented by Guinea's socialist state, it was organized and politicized during the First Republic in a completely novel way. The Guinean playwright and poet Fodéba Keita founded a troupe called *Les Ballets Africains de Keita Fodéba* in Paris, which was transformed in 1960 into Guinea's first national ballet company, *Les Ballets Africains de la République de Guinée*.[5] While state-sponsored dance and theater troupes were a common feature of many socialist and anticolonial nationalist movements on the continent,[6] Guinea was a key progenitor of this kind of cul-

---

3   There is no consensus in the literature on the exact number of troupes in Guinea during the Touré era, but there were thousands of district committees, around two hundred sections, and thirty to forty federations (see, e.g., Rivière, *Guinea*, 97; PDG-RDA, *La Révolution,* 88; Counsel, *Mande Popular Music,* 79).
4   See, for example, Hashachar, "Guinea Unbound."
5   See Cohen, "Stages in Transition," 26. Fodéba Keita went on to serve in the new government as minister of the interior, though was imprisoned and killed by the regime in 1969, at a time when the president was becoming increasingly paranoid about potential threats to his regime and plots against him (see, e.g., Arieff and McGovern, "History is Stubborn").
6   See, for example, Askew, *Performing the Nation*; Braun "Dancing Ambiguities"; Castaldi *Choreographies*; Neveu-Kringelbach *Dance Circles*; Schauert *Staging Ghana*; Shipley *Trickster Theatre*; and Skinner "Cultural Politics."

tural diplomacy. Other emerging postcolonial nations followed the Guinean model as they developed their own cultural policies.[7]

Young people were important figures in the Guinean "revolution"—the term Guineans use to refer to the reign of Sékou Touré. Both in the years before independence and after, Sékou Touré's political party[8] contested many forms of gerontocratic authority—especially the entrenched authority of elders in initiations and secret societies, the right of older men to marry multiple (and often much younger) women, and the power of lineage or "caste" to circumscribe the future of young people.[9] The party made a calculated decision to lose the votes of powerful elderly men in exchange for the support of a broader coalition of women, young people, and underclass/lower caste persons.[10] Indeed, Mike McGovern describes Guinea's "cultural revolution"—modeled on the Chinese Cultural Revolution—as a "dictatorship of the youth (rather than the proletariat)."[11] Guinea's cultural revolution, however, which was launched in 1968, did not mark an exceptional break from the rest of the revolution but involved increased state attention to the role of artists, and especially young artists, in disseminating the party's ideological agenda.[12]

When Sékou Touré died in 1984, a military colonel named Lansana Conté took power in a bloodless coup and remained president until 2008. Conté's regime liberalized the economy and drastically reduced funding for the performing arts, effectively dismantling the nationwide cultural infrastructure for training and competition that had sustained the ballet profession during the First Republic.[13] Many practicing and retired national artists took mat-

---

7   For example, Counsel, *Mande Popular Music*, 86; Edmondson, *Performance and Politics,* 21; and Schauert, *Staging Ghana*, 15.

8   In the years before independence, Touré led the Guinean branch of the interterritorial political alliance *Rassemblement Démocratique Africain* (RDA), which turned into the *Parti Démocratique de Guinée* (PDG) after independence (see Mortimer, *France and the Africans,* 345).

9   See Dave, *Revolution's Echoes*; McGovern, *Unmasking*; and Straker, *Youth*.

10 McGovern, *Unmasking*, 170; and Schmidt, *Mobilizing the Masses*.

11 McGovern, *Unmasking*, 174–75.

12 See Counsel, "Music for a Revolution," 554; and Dave, *Revolution's Echoes*, 52–53.

13 Guinea has had three different presidents since the end of its socialist experiment in 1984: Lansana Conté (1984–2008), Moussa Dadis Camara (2008–2009), and Alpha Condé, who was the first to be elected in internationally watched democratic elections. However, the most significant break that artists—and indeed many average people in Conakry—identify is that from the

ters into their own hands, founding private troupes in Conakry. These urban ballets took over the work of training and mentoring Guinean performing artists, tasks that had previously been the responsibility of the national socialist system of troupes. In the postsocialist era, however, aggressive liberalization and privatization disrupted the connection between country and city that had been built into the socialist system, as private ballets did not have the wherewithal to recruit from the countryside. While the socialist ballet infrastructure existed nationwide, channeling the best artists from rural villages into top-tier federal and national companies through competitions, the private Conakry ballets of the postsocialist era do not have a direct connection (via recruitment or festivals) with performance practices in rural villages.

Guinean ballet has therefore increasingly become an urban genre, as dance ideas emerge and circulate within the capital with no systematic link to people or practices in other parts of the country. In contemporary Conakry, dance is learned and shared in formal troupes as well as in social ceremonies featuring improvisational dance. In troupes, young people often do as they are told, sit at the feet of their teachers, and perform what the directors ask them to perform. Young people have creative input into some of the movement in formal troupes, but the structure and decision making resides with the elders. Ceremonies, by contrast, are often organized by youth, and are spaces where they can invent and exchange new ideas without being beholden to directors. As young dancers increasingly develop novel repertoires of movements and logics governing their practice in the context of urban ceremonies, elderly artists claim that the vital national culture they worked so hard to create is being lost. These critiques, however, ignore many points of continuity and meaningful translation across generations, and they do not acknowledge an emerging urban repertoire of dance that reflects the changing contours of lived experience for young people in Conakry.

Mobilizing Narratives of Cultural Death and Redemption

Moussa Celestin Camara (henceforth "Celestin") sat with me for an interview in 2013. He was the director of Guinea's national ballet, Djoliba, at the time and a founding director of a nonprofit organization advocating for

---

First Republic under the rule of Sékou Touré to the Second Republic under the rule of Lansana Conté—a break that marked the liberalization of the economy, the end of socialism, and a sharp decline in government patronage of theater, dance, and music.

private dance and percussion companies in Conakry. Celestin spoke about how young artists are borrowing other cultures' musical and dance styles and lamented that in this process of borrowing influences from elsewhere, "What is ours will disappear . . . and if what is ours disappears, we are lost." He punctuated his comments with the adage: "A people without culture is a dying people."

Celestin's worries were echoed by many other elderly Guinean artists I spoke with in Conakry. When I asked them further about what comprises "culture"—that entity they claim is responsible for preserving social cohesion itself—they often invoked notions of "origin" and "tradition," articulated by the French loan words *originale* and *traditionnelle*. They explained that "original" dances and rhythms are those indigenous to rural villages, many of which continue to have local ritual and ceremonial functions in the countryside. The term "traditional," then, refers to dances and rhythms that were adapted and performed in socialist-era ballet productions and urban ceremonies. Elders suggest that Guinean ballet is ideally a staged version of rural "original" dances, and they presume the value of contemporary practices (on stage or in ceremonies) to derive from resemblance to rural originals. This idealized recollection of what ballet culture *is* not only ignores the dynamism of rural practices but also misremembers the many ways in which performers during the First Republic participated in revision, translation, and even violent desacralization of dance practices that had once been performed only in ethnic enclaves.

Indeed, Sékou Touré's party-state championed a competing set of ideological premises framing its political program. The party embraced a romantic notion of African authenticity and cultural coherence aligned with Pan-Africanist ideals *alongside* an ideology of Marxist modernity that emphasized linear progress and the suppression of practices deemed backward.[14] Guinea's performing arts were situated at the intersection of these ideologies. The focus on authenticity and African dignity was expressed in the idea that the stage was a forum for showcasing the country's local cultural heritage. The focus on modernization was also, however, integral to the aesthetics of ballet production. Socialist ballets signaled Guinea's modernity through a number of metacommunicative practices, including speed, accumulation, and invention. Staged dances were consistently performed much faster than their rural counterparts and ballet practitioners elaborated on existing rural movements

---

14   McGovern, *Unmasking*, 19.

in order to create vast stage repertoires with many more steps than were typically performed in the villages where the dances and rhythms came from.

The transformation that took place between the village and the stage and between the rural and the urban is consistently downplayed in elders' accounts of Guinean ballet culture. Also erased in their accounts is the violence that took place at the intersection between the competing ideologies of Marxist modernity, on one hand, and national and supranational/Pan-African authenticity,[15] on the other. The paradigmatic expression of this violent intersection was exemplified by the Guinean state's embrace of an iconoclastic "Demystification Campaign," which targeted indigenous religious and related aesthetic practices in the southeastern forest region and in the coastal region inhabited by Baga, Landuma, and Nalou ethnic groups.[16] Demystification involved the destruction of masks, the banning of ritual activities associated with initiations, and the forced exposure of dances, rhythms, and masquerades that had been considered secret or sacred.[17] The ethnically particular performance practices that were exposed as a result of demystification then became fodder for the national folklore of the socialist era, which proposed to celebrate "ethnic unity" by staging discrete indigenous dances alongside one another. Other less controversial ethnic dances and rhythms were introduced voluntarily by dancers and musicians from rural areas who performed in ballet troupes.

Demystification was rarely discussed in party media. Instead, party rhetoric and playbills for the national companies stressed the seamless conversion of ethnic dances into a national frame and the harmonious display of ethnic unity on stage. The socialist generation of high-level (national and federal) ballet artists, surrounded by all of this celebratory rhetoric, conveniently forgot—or simply failed to notice—the more violent part of the story. Even in cases where demystification was not the catalyst for bringing dance practices to the stage, the ballet version of these practices was much modified. Yet practitioners speak of a neat transposition of rural practices onto the national stage. The brief synopsis of a complex history I have provided in

---

15 Nationalist and Pan-Africanist discourses and agendas surrounding the concept of authenticity in Guinea were interconnected (see Hashachar, "Guinea Unbound").

16 See McGovern, *Unmasking*, 171; and Sarró, *Religious Change*.

17 For example, Højbjerg, *Resisting*; McGovern, *Unmasking*; Rivière, *Guinea*; and Straker, "Militant Theatre" and *Youth*.

this section offers a few points of entry for understanding how the socialist generation was trained to frame their own practice, which informs their critiques of youth.

Shifting Thresholds: Speed and Intermixing

The idealized equation between village and stage has never accurately described the ballet genre, as each generation of artists has reformulated their practice to make sense of (and situate themselves favorably in) the political economy in which they operate.[18] Yet, while Conakry's ballet elders rarely acknowledge similarities between their generation and the current one—each inventing tradition to make sense of the present—they are not wrong to suggest that young artists are making substantive changes to the frameworks within which dance is produced. In this section I will explore several examples of such changes and then return to the question of why loss remains the dominant theme in elders' accounts of generational difference.

When dance was staged in socialist-era ballets, there were certain aesthetic features that marked the new genre as part of a modern socialist platform: ballets increased the tempo and volume of dances and rhythms and added scores of invented moves to each ethnic dance to emblematize progress and modernity by enhancing what they conceptualized as the rural "original." Ethnic dances were juxtaposed in the same program, emblematizing an egalitarian nationalist ideal. Rural dancers themselves were relocated to the capital city when they were taken to the national companies, so ballet aesthetics and urban aesthetics began to converge—a process that continued apace after socialism when urban troupes could no longer recruit from the countryside. Young artists in postsocialist Conakry inherited that syncretic ballet legacy and continue to practice a version of it in the present.

In formal troupes, young people tend to follow the directions of their elders, but they do as they please in the ceremonies that take place in the afternoons and evenings after rehearsals. These ceremonies, therefore, are sites where youth display aesthetic logics that differ in important ways form the logics of the previous generation. These ceremonies may be productively conceptualized as "youth spaces"—spaces of interaction influenced by local and transnational cultural movements in an age of global capitalism.[19] In the context of ceremonies, young artists articulate collective feelings and

---

18   See Cohen, "Inalienable Performances" and *Infinite Repertoire.*
19   See Kennelly, Poyntz, and Ugor, "Youth, Cultural Politics."

understandings that are specific to the current political economy, and in so doing they provoke intergenerational tensions. Like the generation before them, young dancers in Conakry today employ increased tempo (referred to as "heat")[20] and inventive accumulation of moves to frame their work as modern. Indeed, artists describe the act of speeding and adding new movements to a dance-rhythm[21] as "modernizing" the dance (using the French verb *modernizer*). While none of this is new, young artists are developing different thresholds and framing logics that both index and help to construct major changes in the sociopolitical world they inhabit. Below I present two examples of shifts in logic, the first concerning tempo and second concerning mixing movements between discrete dance-rhythms.

Speed/Heat

In his response to an interview question about generational differences, "Grand" Aly Sylla, an experienced drummer trained during the socialist period, suggested not only that young people play too fast but that the way they play is combative or destructive.[22] Grand Aly also objected to what he perceives as a blurring of distinctions between discrete (ethnically coded) rhythms in the younger generation, resulting in cultural loss:

> You know the difference between generations from how they play drums. Our generation, we aren't used to speed ("hot things" *fe furaxi*), wurawurawura! No! . . . Everyone knows [the dance-rhythm] soli is faster than dundunba, right? Mendiani is faster than dundunba. But if you play dundunba like mendiani, will it be good? For us, to just go "walalalalalalal," no! Play normally. What you play will be sweet. . . . Drums are play things. They are not instruments of war/conflict. Play things—you *play* with them. That's the experience that [young people] don't have in their heads.

---

20   To describe the act of increasing the tempo of a dance-rhythm, Conakry artists use the Susu verb *rafurafe*, meaning to heat, or they use the same verb in French—*chauffer*. Susu or Soso is a Mande language spoken in coastal Guinea and the lingua franca of Conakry.

21   I use the term *dance-rhythm* to convey the interconnectedness between dance and percussion in Guinean dance. This hybrid English term *dance-rhythm* most closely approximates the Susu term for dance, *fare*, which is simultaneously the word for the percussive music played with dance.

22   Interview by author, Conakry, 2011. Grand Aly played in federation troupes during the socialist period and in the seminational percussion company Les Percussions de Guinea in the 1990s.

Grand Aly, like Celestin, suggests that young artists are acting in ways that could result in the erasure of Guinea's cultural diversity. Many older artists in Conakry similarly critique young people for "being in a hurry" in their lives as in their artistic practice. They suggest that young artists do not want to take the time to apprentice. In both dancing and drumming, this critique is leveled at practitioners who want to compose fancy solos without first mastering the basics—who want to be noticed and "make it" by traveling abroad before they take the time to learn. But the problem of skipping over the basics is not strictly a generational issue, as young people critique other young people for the same thing. Indeed, many young artists rehearse tirelessly and know very well the differences in tempo between one rhythm and the next. So why do elders like Aly often level this kind of critique at an entire generation?

Guinean polyrhythms often begin slow and then build to a plateau where they remain steady. That plateau is where the "core" dance moves (*pas xɔri*)[23] can be performed comfortably and with all of their embellishments. When a rhythm is played faster than this plateau, the core movements become difficult to execute, and the dancer is required to modify the step, often omitting the subtle micro-movements of the head and hands that make the dance "tasty" (*nyaxun*). While many young drummers know these rules of tempo and how to play rhythms at a speed that corresponds with core dance movements, young artists have also embraced several dance-rhythms that purposefully defy these norms. While young artists use speed to index modernity and virtuosity just as their elders did, they have also become especially interested in several dance-rhythms that actively cultivate an aesthetic of *excessive* speed, which indexes something different. In these dance-rhythms, what is qualitatively different from the typical approach to tempo is the fact that the plateau is transcended and the players and dancers begin to produce an aesthetic of frenzy in which the dance and music teeter on the brink of being out of control. The rhythm and corresponding dance solo often end when someone falters instead of with a purposeful break to stop the music. Tempo, in these dance-rhythms, can emblematize precarity, uncertainty, and a frantic sense of keeping up at a time when people are grappling with the fallout of

---

23   "Core steps" referred to in Conakry with the French-Susu term *pas xɔri*, invokes the Mande concept of essential structure through the Susu word *xɔri* meaning core, bone, seed, or kernel. There are core steps in each dance, and these movements are typically not transposed across rhythms.

neoliberal economic policies.[24] An aesthetic dimension of excess or exaggeration is not unique to ballet culture in Conakry. As several authors in this collection have shown, whether it is in relation to Afro hip-hop (Bamba, Taylor, and Kerr) or popular online media (Yeku, Kwabena, Brian, and Maringira), there is a sense in which hyperbole or overemphasis has become central to the aesthetics of popular urban youth culture on the continent.

Notably, the rhythms that best exemplify this approach to tempo as an index of precarity are performed almost exclusively in ceremonies where young people are not beholden to the choreographic directions of their elders. These dance-rhythms—the best examples of which are called *sɔkɔ chaud*, *acrobats' konkɔba*, and *sabar*—became popular in Conakry during the 1990s and have become central to the urban lexicon of improvisational dance that young artists cultivate to the dismay of many of their elders. These dances are rarely performed on stage or taught in dance classes because they are so contentious and defy the typical logics guiding the performance of Guinean ballet. Another key contrast between these three popular dance-rhythms and others is the fact that they do not have a rural "original." Sabar is a Senegalese dance, and therefore it has no equivalent in the Guinean countryside, while *sɔkɔ chaud* and acrobats' *konkɔba* are both urban creations that took on new titles and movements to mark their difference from dances derived from villages in socialist-era ballet productions. Without elaborating the details of these dances, which I describe elsewhere,[25] I suggest here that these three dances, which have become incredibly popular among young artists, exemplify tempo as an index not of mastery or command (as in past articulations of progress) but of precarity and resourcefulness. These urban dance-rhythms constitute an addition to (not a bastardization of) the repertoire of dances that Conakry artists know, yet they are understood and marked as separate by their common exclusion from staged performances and classes.

---

24 In Guinea and across the globe, neoliberal reforms have produced profound inequality and uncertainty through the privatization of public resources and the shrinking of social welfare programs (see, e.g., Campbell and Clapp "Guinea under Structural Adjustment"; Ferguson *Expectations, Global Shadows*; Ganti "Neoliberalism," 94).

25 On sabar see Cohen, "Performing Excess." On sɔkɔ chaud and acrobats' konkɔba see Cohen, *Infinite Repertoire,* chapter 4.

Mixing

One of the other main critiques leveled at youth by elderly artists in Conakry is about mixing and purity in dance. Elders think young dancers indiscriminately combine movements of diverse dance-rhythms in their solos with little regard for the dance's provenance and don't know or care about the history of the dances they perform. The socialist generation, however, also combined movements between dances in their solos and choreographed pieces, and they invented scores of dance steps in order to make rural dances more stage worthy. Youth also include cultural influences derived from elsewhere in their solos. They glean ideas from international films and music videos, from visiting migrants, and from workshops in Euro-American contemporary dance, and include them in their solos in ways that openly undermine the claim that Guinean dances are ethnically particular. Again, the previous generation engaged in similar practices of global citation but are reluctant to acknowledge similarities between what they did and what is happening now.

I suggest, then, that the main difference between generations is not about mixing per se but about the thresholds and logics guiding that mixing. Socialist-era ballet practitioners, influenced by the party's celebration of indigeneity and authenticity, conceptualized their work as a transposition of village to stage, and of the embellishments they added to each dance as adornment that produced a more modern aesthetic without losing the "original." Younger dancers do pay attention to core steps (*pas xɔri*), which exemplify an inalienable and often historically traceable element in each dance (excepting the three dances described above). However, the younger generation is moving away from ethnicity as a framing concept as they conceptualize which moves can be danced where. While both generations invented movements and traded steps across discrete dances, younger people are more liberal in the way they combine steps and are less interested the "original" as a source of value. The idea of the original implies cultural purity and singularity—ideas that are becoming less relevant for a generation of performers whose identities and cultural allegiances have been redefined by transnational encounters in the era of economic and cultural globalization.

Young dancers in neoliberal Conakry seek careers performing and teaching foreign students at home and abroad, and success in such careers depends on the ability to generate new movement. In order to be noticed by foreign students or producers, dancers must be able to distinguish themselves from others in the solo circle through personal innovations. In the context of international teaching and performing, dancers must also be able to generate steps to offer students and audiences. This interest in novelty among youth in Conakry is partly a response to foreign students' attention to individual genius and desire to learn a new set of moves in each class. Ironically, these foreign students often judge teachers simultaneously on their "authenticity" (meaning knowledge of presumably rural ethnic dances) *and* on their ability to create new steps.

With the career goals of young artists in mind, let us return to Conakry elders' critiques of youth. The claim that young people simply do not bother to learn the names of dances is partially true, but the reason for decreased interest in ethnic dances is complex. Many of the youngest dancers I spoke with in Conakry (who were in their teens and early twenties) would answer questions about which dance they were performing in ceremonies and rehearsal lines with vague waves of the hand, characterizing rhythms with a similar feel as one and the same. The dance-rhythms *tiriba* and *baho*, for example, which do not have a similar origin story, have a somewhat similar feel, so young dancers would sometimes call baho "reversed tiriba" or call tiriba "broken baho." These dancers often did not know which one was which and feigned competence by responding that they were listening to a particular rhythm "reversed" or "broken." Slightly older postsocialist dancers (in their late twenties and thirties), however, were often more familiar with the names of dance-rhythms and actively cultivated knowledge about origin stories they knew were valuable to foreign dance students with fantasies about rural authenticity. Despite the fact that some postsocialist artists know rhythm names better than others, most artists trained in the 1990s and 2000s—regardless of such knowledge—prioritize feel and time over ethnic origins as they compose solo performances. For these young artists, dance moves have use value insofar as they can be creatively interjected into solos at ceremonies, thereby boosting the value of the performer.[26] The exchange value of these moves is still entangled in discourses of authenticity and ethnic origin that guided dance in socialist-era Guinea and that continue to guide foreigners' consumption of Guinean dance.

The artists trained in the First Republic were far more loyal to ethnicity as a meaningful framing concept than are young dancers who were trained after socialism. This runs counter to the explicit state programs of each political era: the socialist state promoted an ideology of ethnic unity over ethnic particularism, while the subsequent regime of Lansana Conté (1984–2008) promoted an explicitly ethnically inflected politics that continues to inform

---

26   See Cohen, "Inalienable Performances."

Guinea's emerging democracy. One key factor informing the shift in how young artists conceptualize ethnicity is that young dancers in Conakry today are often third- or fourth-generation urbanites who are more distanced from village practices than their parents and grandparents were. These young artists therefore identify as urbanites and their approach to ethnicity reflects an experience of ethnic intermixing and co-residence that the city fosters.

Ironically, one of the guiding principles of the socialist state—the notion of erasing ethnic particularism in favor of unity—is actually being realized more fully in the current generation's approach to dance, at least in the context of ceremonies. Elders conceptualize young artists' disregard for ethnic purity in dance as "cultural loss," thereby reproducing one side of the socialist-era ideological tension between Pan-Africanist authenticity and Marxist modernity. I suggest that this disregard for ethnicity is in fact a meaningful aspect of Conakry's postrevolutionary aesthetic.

Conclusion

I have argued in this chapter that generational change among Conakry artists is far more productive than narratives about cultural loss would suggest. First, young practitioners do replicate many elements of the previous generation's approach to dance, including by engaging in heating and mixing—the very acts that their elders condemn. By revising inherited practices, young practitioners create new aesthetic experiences that meet the exigencies of the neoliberal moment. Elderly Conakry artists regularly claim, however, that young people are not protecting the cultural heritage passed down to them and characterize the actions of young artists as a form of cultural violence. Recall that Celestin suggested that youth were ushering in the "death" of their people by adopting foreign influences, and Grand Aly worried that young people were using drums not to *play* but to create conflict. Young artists themselves call attention to violent or disruptive aspects of their practice, but the violence they perform is not a vehicle of cultural destruction. Rather, it is an index of historical position. For example, when youth employ speed in ways that point to the precarious nature of an urban, postsocialist existence, they call attention to the ambient violence of neoliberal capitalism—a political-economic form that has pushed youth to work in private troupes without state patronage and to seek their futures amid vast economic uncertainty. Likewise, when artists use the vocabulary of "reversal" and "breaking" to describe how they hear dance-rhythms, they implicitly suggest that these rhythms were once straight or whole. The new logics put forth in youth performance are not aggressively countercultural or geared to undermine authority, but they stem from a situational precarity. Young people understand themselves to be reinvesting Guinean dance music with the force of a new era permeated by political and economic uncertainty and backed not by the authority of state infrastructures and ideologies but by the unofficial collective activism of a generation.

A sense of loss is persistent and insistent across elders' accounts and critiques of the present. They tend to scapegoat youth in these accounts, but the real loss, I suggest, stems from political-economic change, not from young people's failures to listen to their elders. Meaningful generational difference here is not contained in the maintenance or dissolution of forms, or even in practices such as heating or mixing (which took place in both generations) but is rather contained in shifting thresholds that signal major differences across political eras. The older generation had a stable sense of the purpose and defining logics of their practice, and they were put to the task of performing ballet for the "good of the nation." The younger generation has no such stability—no sense that they could depend on a paternalistic state—and the shifts they have embraced index that insecurity. A meaningful change in threshold reframes what a practice signals, as in the case of tempo being exaggerated until it indexes a more precarious version of modernity, or as in the case of ethnic boundaries being enfeebled until a dance's value is reframed—not by how much it conforms to an original but by its urban vitality.

More broadly, this chapter proposes that accounts of cultural loss—which are extremely common both between generational cohorts in Africa *as well as* in Africanist scholarship—must be understood in their interactional contexts and not simply as literal statements about the world.[27] Why are such

---

27 One productive thread in the recent literature on youth in Africa that engages with accounts of loss in a nuanced way explores how the category of youth is often prolonged indefinitely as young people struggle to achieve social adulthood (e.g., Hansen, "Getting Stuck"; Mains, "Neoliberal Times"; Masquelier, "Teatime"; Somners *Stuck*). The youth in question are "stuck" in limbo, waiting, "nullified" because they cannot make lives for themselves through the same avenues pursued by their parents' generation. Ethnographers often explore how this sense of generational change drives young people to pursue creative, yet risky solutions to their liminal predicament (e.g., Cole, *Sex and Salvation;* Melly, "Titanic Tales"; Vigh "Life's Trampoline"). Some other related work in anthropology describes a "crisis of social reproduction" brought about by violent conflict and the uncertainty of neoliberal economies

accounts so persistent? How might we read more meaningfully into their contexts of emergence and repetition? The criticisms elders level at youth in Conakry's performing arts scene echo accounts of cultural loss and a "crisis of transmission" in contemporary Africa that was prominent in anthropological and art-historical narratives of a bygone era. Academics and Western consumers of African art once thought of "authentic" African objects and practices as those that existed in rural areas. The culture of urban spaces and global interactions was considered to be of lesser art-historical value and ethnographic interest. Anthropologists and art historians alike have spent years undermining these tropes of authenticity and vanishing culture,[28] yet similar narratives persist in different guises in academic and popular media accounts of youth on the continent as well as on the ground in local intergenerational dynamics among Africans themselves.[29] In the introduction to the edited volume *Vanguards or Vandals: Youth, Politics, and Conflict in Africa*, for example, Jon Abbink laments the disintegration of the kind of social cohesion exemplified in monographs of single ethnic groups produced by early cultural anthropologists, solemnly stating that "only faint traces of social order and cultural integrity still exist."[30] Abbink's premise of social disintegration, which highlights experiences of violent conflict on the continent, mirrors the discourse of elderly artists in Guinea as they criticize youth for failing to reproduce the supposedly cohesive sociocultural world of the previous

---

(e.g., Abbink and Van Kessel, *Vanguard or Vandals*; Comaroff, "Occult Economies," 284, 289; DeBoeck and Plissart, *Kinshasa*; Honwana and DeBoeck, *Makers and Breakers*). DeBoeck's work on youth in Kinshasa offers a chilling account of social fragmentation in the wake of violent conflict. He asks, for example, "What happens if the very nature of the imaginary as a flexible but organized field of social practices has become disorganized and has lost, at least to some extent, its localizing force and its capacity for creating continuity, producing sociality?" (*Kinshasa*, 157). While much of this work is quite nuanced and richly ethnographic, I think it is important to ask why it is so common for scholars to suggest that African societies may not be able to reproduce themselves, while we tend not to treat other societies as existentially at risk in the same way.

28 See, for example, Barber, *African Popular Culture*; Clifford, "Histories"; Errington, "Primitive Art"; and Strother, "Secret History."
29 For example, David Berliner describes such local trends in coastal Guinea in Berliner, "'Impossible' Transmission" and "Object of Transmission."
30 Abbink, "Being Young," 2.

generation. But stories about rupture are also stories about idealized pasts and index how difficult it can be for one generation to recognize the legitimacy of novel logics in another. In Guinea, elders' narratives about cultural death call attention to something that was *actually* lost, which was the hopeful guiding force of the revolution, and the broader utopianism of global state-socialist movements that it tapped into. The discourse of loss amidst a thriving postsocialist ballet scene is a reminder of the sacrifices that elders made for a political movement that could not deliver on its promises. In contexts where generations define themselves or each other in terms of loss, what is the subtext of those claims? By exploring accounts of cultural loss within broader embodied and discursive interactional contexts, we may conceptualize these accounts not as confirmation that once-whole social entities are disintegrating but as indices of generative sociocultural transformations afoot.

Bibliography

Abbink, Jon. "Being Young in Africa: The Politics of Despair and Renewal." In *Vanguards or Vandals: Youth, Politics, and Conflict in Africa*, edited by Jon Abbink and Ineke Van Kessel, 1–34. Leiden, The Netherlands: Brill, 2005.

Abbink, Jon, and Ineke Van Kessel, eds. *Vanguard or Vandals: Youth, Politics, and Conflict in Africa*. Leiden, The Netherlands: Brill, 2005.

Arieff, Alexis, and Mike McGovern. "History is Stubborn: Talk about Truth, Justice, and National Reconciliation in the Republic of Guinea." *Comparative Studies in Society and History* 55, no.1 (2013): 198–225.

Askew, Kelly. *Performing the Nation: Swahili Music and Cultural Politics in Tanzania*. Chicago: University of Chicago Press, 2002.

Barber, Karin, ed. *Readings in African Popular Culture*. Bloomington: Indiana University Press, 1997.

Berliner, David. "An 'Impossible' Transmission: Youth Religious Memories in Guinea–Conakry." *American Ethnologist* 32, no.4 (2005): 576–92.

———. "When the Object of Transmission is Not an Object." *RES* 51 (2007): 88–97.

Braun, Lesley Nicole. "Dancing Ambiguities in the Democratic Republic of Congo." *Critical African Studies 11, no. 1* (2019): 1–18.

Campbell, Bonnie, and Jennifer Clapp. "Guinea's Economic Performance under Structural Adjustment: Importance of Mining and Agriculture." *Journal of Modern African Studies*. 33, no. 3 (1995): 425–49.

Castaldi, Francesca. *Choreographies of African Identities: Negritude, Dance, and the National Ballet of Senegal*. Urbana and Chicago: University of Illinois Press, 2006.

Clifford, James. "Histories of the Tribal and the Modern." In *The Predicament of Culture: Twentieth-Century Ethnography, Literature, and Art,* by James Clifford, 189–214. Cambridge, MA: Harvard University Press, 1988.

Cohen, Adrienne. "Inalienable Performances, Mutable Heirlooms: Dance, Cultural Inheritance, and Political Transformation in the Republic of Guinea." *American Ethnologist* 43, no.4 (2016): 650–62.

———. *Infinite Repertoire: On Dance and Urban Possibility in Postsocialist Guinea.* Chicago: University of Chicago Press, 2021.

———. "Performing Excess: Urban Ceremony and the Semiotics of Precarity in Guinea-Conakry." *Africa: Journal of the International African Institute* 89, no. 4 (2019): 718–38.

Cohen, Joshua. "Stages in Transition: Les Ballets Africains and Independence, 1959–1960." *Journal of Black Studies* 43, no.1 (2012): 11–48.

Cole, Jennifer. "The Jaombilo of Tamatave (Madagascar), 1992–2004: Reflections on Youth and Globalization." *Journal of Social History* 38, no. 4 (2005): 891–914.

———. *Sex and Salvation: Imagining the Future in Madagascar.* Chicago: University of Chicago Press, 2010.

Comaroff, Jean, and John L. Comaroff. "Occult Economies and the Violence of Abstraction: Notes from the South African Postcolony." *American Ethnologist* 26, no.2 (1999): 279–303.

Counsel, Graeme. *Mande Popular Music and Cultural Policies in West Africa: Griots and Government Policy Since Independence.* Saarbrucken, Germany: VDM Verlag, 2009.

———. "Music for a Revolution: The Sound Archives of Radio Television Guinée." In *From Dust to Digital: Ten Years of the Endangered Archives Programme,* edited by Maja Kominko, 547–86. Cambridge: Open Book, 2015.

Dave, Nomi. *The Revolution's Echoes: Music, Politics & Pleasure in Guinea.* Chicago: University of Chicago Press, 2019.

DeBoeck, Filip, and Marie Plissart. *Kinshasa: Tales of the Invisible City.* Antwerp: Ludion, 2006.

Durham, Deborah. "Youth and the Social Imagination in Africa: Introduction to Parts 1 and 2." *Anthropological Quarterly* 73, no. 3 (2000): 113–20.

Edmondson, Laura. *Performance and Politics in Tanzania: The Nation on Stage.* Bloomington: Indiana University Press, 2007.

Errington, Shelly. "What Became Authentic Primitive Art?," *Cultural Anthropology* 9 (1994): 201–26.

Ferguson, James. *Expectations of Modernity: Myths and Meanings of Urban Life on the Zambian Copperbelt.* Berkeley and Los Angeles: University of California Press, 1999.

———. *Global Shadows: Africa in the Neoliberal Economy.* Durham, NC: Duke University Press, 2006.

Ganti, Tejaswini. "Neoliberalism." *Annual Review of Anthropology* 43 (2014): 89–104.
Hansen, Karen Tranberg. "Getting Stuck in the Compound: Some Odds against Social Adulthood in Lusaka, Zambia." *Africa Today* 51, no. 4 (2005): 3–16.
Hashachar, Yair. "Guinea Unbound: Performing Pan-African Cultural Citizenship between Algiers 1969 and the Guinean National Festivals." *Interventions* 20, no. 7 (2018): 1003–21.
Højbjerg, Christian Kordt. *Resisting State Iconoclasm among the Loma of Guinea*. Durham, NC: Carolina Academic, 2006.
Honwana, Alcinda, and Filip DeBoeck, eds. *Makers and Breakers: Children and Youth in Postcolonial Africa*. Oxford: James Curry, 2005.
Kennelly, Jacqueline, Stuart Poyntz, and Paul Ugor. "Special Issue Introduction: Youth, Cultural Politics, and New Social Spaces in an Era of Globalization." *Review of Education, Pedagogy, and Cultural Studies* 31, no. 4 (2009): 255–69.
Mains, Daniel. "Neoliberal Times: Progress, Boredom, and Shame among Young Men in Urban Ethiopia." *American Ethnologist* 34, no. 4 (2007): 659–73.
Masquelier, Adeline. "Teatime: Boredom and the Temporalities of Young Men in Niger." *Africa* 83, no. 3 (2013): 470–91.
McGovern, Mike. *Unmasking the State: Making Guinea Modern*. Chicago: University of Chicago Press, 2013.
Melly, Caroline Marie. "Titanic Tales of Missing Men: Reconfigurations of National Identity and Gendered Presence in Dakar, Senegal." *American Ethnologist* 38, no. 2 (2011): 361–76.
Meiu, George Paul. "'Beach-Boy Elders' and 'Young Big-Men': Subverting the Temporalities of Ageing in Kenya's Ethno-Erotic Economies." *Ethnos* 80, no. 4 (2014): 472–96.
Mortimer, Edward. *France and the Africans 1944–1960: A Political History*. New York: Walker and Company, 1969.
Neveu-Kringelbach, Hélène. *Dance Circles: Movement, Morality and Self-Fashioning in Urban Senegal*. New York and Oxford: Berghahn, 2013.
PDG-RDA (*Parti Démocratique de Guinée- Rassemblement Démocratique Africain*) [n.d.] *La Révolution et la Culture*. Conakry no. 35.
Rivière, Claude. *Guinea: The Mobilization of a People*. Translated by Virginia Thompson and Richard Adloff. Ithaca, NY: Cornell University Press, 1977.
Sarró, Ramon. *The Politics of Religious Change on the Upper Guinea Coast: Iconoclasm Done and Undone*. Edinburgh: Edinburgh University Press, 2009.
Schauert, Paul. *Staging Ghana: Artistry and Nationalism in State Dance Ensembles*. Bloomington: Indiana University Press, 2015.
Schmidt, Elizabeth. *Mobilizing the Masses: Gender, Ethnicity, and Class in the Nationalist Movement in Guinea, 1939–1958*. Portsmouth, NH: Heinemann, 2005.
Shipley, Jesse Weaver. *Trickster Theatre: The Poetics of Freedom in Urban Africa*. Bloomington: Indiana University Press, 2015.

Skinner, Ryan Thomas. "Cultural Politics in the Post-Colony: Music, Nationalism, and Statism in Mali, 1964–75." *Africa* 82, no. 4 (2012): 511–34.

Somners, Marc. *Stuck: Rwandan Youth and the Struggle for Adulthood.* Athens: University of Georgia Press, 2012.

Straker, Jay. "Stories of Militant Theatre in the Guinean For- est: 'Demystifying' the Motives and Moralities of a Revolutionary Nation-State." *Journal of African Cultural Studies* 19, no. 2 (2007): 207–33.

———. *Youth, Nationalism, and the Guinean Revolution.* Bloomington: Indiana University Press, 2009.

Strother, Z. S. "Gabama a Gingungu and the Secret History of Twentieth-Century Art." *African Arts* 32, no.1 (1999): 18–31.

Vigh, Henrik. *Navigating Terrains of War: Youth and Soldiering in Guinea-Bissau.* New York and Oxford: Berghahn, 2006.

———. "Life's Trampoline: On Nullification and Cocaine Migration in Bissau." In *Affective Circuits: African Migrations to Europe and the Pursuit of Social Regeneration, edited by* Jennifer Cole and Christian Groes. Chicago: University of Chicago Press, 2016.

Chapter Thirteen

Culture Players and Poly-Ticks

Botswana Youth and Popular Culture Practices

Connie Rapoo

Introduction

Popular culture and the creative industries are growing areas in Botswana. This is mainly due to the change in the political will to support these areas as part of the national development agenda for economic diversification. In 2011, the Botswana government established the cultural and creative industries as one of the sectors that drives the country's economy and underscored its potential to reinforce the move away from reliance on the mining and extractives industry. While this was a commendable decision on the part of the state, it is regrettable that several years later, there is still no policy that is used to drive the growth of the sector. Several programs and projects that are especially designed for the youth such as the Youth Development Fund, the Citizenship Entrepreneurial Development Agency, and the Economic Diversification Drive are in place but remain inaccessible to many. The youth remain vulnerable to the harsh realities of poverty, unemployment, discrimination, and exclusion. The reason for this, Thulaganyo Mogobe (2015) notes, is the lack of proper planning and the unavailability of resources and infrastructure needed for the sector. The biggest challenge, however, is mismanagement of resources, and failure to implement, monitor, and evaluate such government-initiated programs and projects. Due to this weakness, many of the well-intended initiatives to support young people in Botswana continue to fail. Hence, a country that has done relatively well, at least politically and economically, for the past fifty years of independence is now struggling to stay above water.

What is happening in Gaborone, Botswana's capital, is arguably commonplace and characteristic of the African postcolonial space in general. The persistent crises in Africa have been attributed to the negative impact of neoliberal policies by the World Bank and the IMF, especially the structural adjustment policies imposed on African countries since the mid-1980s. Aggressive privatization, mass retrenchments from the public sector, and the defunding of social services have all combined to create harsh conditions for Africans, especially those in urban spaces. The socioeconomic crises in Gaborone are only a reflection of a broader continent-wide problem arising from the inequities associated with neoliberal globalization. The country is wrestling to contain a plethora of challenges, including high youth unemployment, rising crime rates, staggering death statistics from road accidents and the HIV/AIDS pandemic, gender inequality, and poor governance. Urban crises in Gaborone remain a concern especially when measured against the city's population of 231,592 and the country's total population of slightly over two million people.[1] The Statistics Report of 2017/2018 indicates that the number of people living below the poverty line in cities and urban centers is 162,233.[2] The report indicates further that 15,633 people in Gaborone and urban centers are unemployed.[3] Across the country, a total of 146,958 able-bodied people—that is, under the age of forty—are recorded as unemployed.[4] The *National Youth Policy* of 2010 acknowledges that the youth constitutes the most vulnerable group because they are the most susceptible to unemployment, exploitation, poverty, hunger, homelessness, crime, alcohol, and substance abuse. The policy thus recommends targeted education curricula, talent development for income generation, and involving the youth in sport, recreation, and creative arts in order to empower

---

1   Statistics Botswana Population and Housing Census, 3.
2   Statistics Botswana Report (2017/2018), 89.
3   Statistics Botswana Report, 91.
4   Statistics Botswana Report, 213.

them for their economic survival.[5] However, more still needs to be done to support the youth in employment and self-employment ventures such as giving them access to land, market spaces, and finance (Sechele 2016).

It is worth noting that Gaborone bears the brunt of Botswana's urban crises. The city is experiencing high population growth rates mainly due to rural-urban migration. Such migration is mainly due to unemployed youth seeking jobs in the city. Urbanization scholar Fred Kruger observes that the migration process exacerbates the growth of vulnerable groups in the city.[6] A major problem, Kruger notes, is "the unemployment situation of many young people who leave school with no prospects of finding a job in their villages, and who, therefore, move to the country's metropolitan centres to find work."[7] According to his study, the lack of employment and the high costs of accommodation in Gaborone characterize the city's vulnerable groups and the overall crises. Gwen N. Lesetedi's essay on rapid urbanization in Botswana echoes Kruger's observations. Observing that rural-urban migration is one of the factors that account for the city's population growth, Lesetedi explains that this occurs mainly due to the recurrent drought conditions that contribute to the erosion of the rural economy and the significant differences between economic opportunities in rural and urban areas.[8] The rapid urbanization that occurs as a result of migration, according to Lesetedi, leads to a number of negative consequences, including the escalation of the cost of urban development, failure to provide services and infrastructure, and the rising levels of urban poverty.[9] Thus, the social realities of the postcolonial metropolis that are characterized by conditions of precarity, poverty, and anxiety can be witnessed in Gaborone like elsewhere in the continent. In the face of unrelenting socioeconomic problems that frame the postcolonial urban experience, popular culture provides a platform for Botswana youth to comment on these harsh social realities. The creative work of urban youth thus emerges as powerful forms of social records and popular critique of the crises in Gaborone and how it impacts their lives.

Agitation for individual agency and social change permeates the creative energies of Gaborone youth popular culture performers. As social agents, they tap into local experiences, realities, and aesthetics in order to comment

---

5   *National Youth Policy*, 14–20.
6   Kruger, "Urbanization and Vulnerable Urban Groups," 287–93.
7   Kruger, 290.
8   Lesetedi, "Rapid Urbanization in Botswana," 147.
9   Lesetedi, 148.

on present contingencies. A good illustration is the act of revivifying local articulations with new meanings of hope and self-determination, as in referencing a popular folk song titled *A re chencheng* [Let's change]. Produced several decades ago by one of Botswana's much-adored traditional musicians, Ratsie Setlhako, the song has served not only to immortalize the singer but has also been used to spread messages about accountability, social progress, and the need to maintain a sense of national collectiveness. The song assembles a collage of snippets of village life and sonic political vignettes, including the singer's recollection of how they were once summoned to a communal gathering by the chief to be reminded of the need to "change," presumably to keep up with the demands of changing times. The line from the lyrics "*a re chencheng, nako di a re sia*" (let's change, the times are speeding ahead of us) points to that memory. This song has been appropriated by other users to anchor similar messages for Botswana citizens, including contemporary references to former US President Barack Obama's compelling message, "We are the change we seek." Setlhako's admonition appears to have laid a solid foundation for the use of popular performance to address current social predicaments in contemporary Botswana society. Particularly, Botswana youth involved in the production of various popular cultural forms use their creative output to reiterate similar messages that resonate with the famous cultural power of "A re chencheng." These youths are social actors who animate Botswana's popular cultural space with varied cultural repertoires but more importantly also act as formidable creative social critics whose voices have a strong bearing on ongoing processes of social change in Botswana. Like other youths elsewhere in the Continent, Gaborone youth actively "seek alternative social avenues for negotiating an illogical and contradictory Postmodernity which promises great futures in the face of an indeterminate and precarious present," to echo youth culture scholar Paul Ugor.[10] Ugor argues convincingly thus:

> The youth of the late–modern world are now seen as living under extenuating circumstances where they negotiate a set of risks that intrude on all aspects of their daily lives. Thus, globally we have begun to witness how youth are now reacting in different ways and degrees to not only the contradictions of a global late-capitalist economy that promises so much and gives very little, but also the great ironies of postmodern civilization where youth are living in a paradox, with their futures on hold or on a speedy reverse to a bottomless abyss.[11]

---

10   Ugor, "Extenuating Circumstances," 4.
11   Ugor, 3.

Thus, the youth exhibit indomitable energies through their cultural repertoires of hope, agency, and social change. The popular genres selected for interrogation in this essay underscore young people's significant role in using the power of culture and performance to document, interpret, and change the social, political, and economic challenges facing the country.

This article thus interrogates contemporary installments of popular culture and performance by Botswana artists as commentaries on what the youth in the country are wrestling with. Particularly, it explores how the youth interpret the socioeconomic predicaments that they encounter in the city of Gaborone. It reads their creative energy and output as part of the city's cultural activism, understood here as forms of cultural expression that are geared toward sociopolitical transformation. The youth are often defined by their proclivity for recalcitrance in the Botswana pop-cultural consciousness. Their creative energy is often read as disruptive "noise." Building on sociologist Deborah Durham's views, this article interrogates how young artists use popular arts to "shift" local understandings of the creative energy of young people in social activism despite their marginalized voices and positionality. Creative power subverts the construction of youth energy as recalcitrance to read it as versatility and self-assertion. The paper illustrates the creative youth as social "shifters" who draw inspiration from the Botswana collective cultural memory and conjoin it with global repertoires to create hybridized formations that address the current sociopolitical predicaments that they contend with. At the very core of my critique then is the intersection between youth cultural activism and social space, especially urban space. Specifically, I demonstrate the ways in which popular culture has become an important resource for young people to both document and critique unfavorable socioeconomic conditions shaping and impinging on their lives in urban spaces.

"A city," writes space theorist Henry Lefebvre, is "a space which is fashioned, shaped and invested by social activities during a finite historical period. . . . It is a space just as highly expressive and significant, just as unique and unified as a painting or a sculpture."[12] Lefebvre explains further that a city combines reality with ideality and embraces the practical, the symbolic, and the imaginary. The city is inscribed with collective remembrances of the past upon which the youth draw inspiration to navigate contemporary experience. This article thus reads the popular representations of Gaborone city by the youth denizens who "compose," construct, and interpret the city's

---

12   Lefebvre, *Production of Space*, 73.

social fabric through various cultural repertoires. Here, I build on Karin Barber's idea of cultural representations as "social facts." Barber argues that

> as well as being social facts, however, texts are commentaries upon, and interpretations of, social facts. They are part of social reality but they also take up an attitude of social reality. They may criticize social forms or confirm and consolidate them: in both cases they are reflexive. They are part of the apparatus by which human communities take stock of their own creations. Textual traditions can be seen as a community's ethnography of itself.[13]

The popular youth texts under investigation in this article do not only function as social accounts or records of processes of urban change; they also double as forceful agitations for the need for urgent social change, emphasizing the crucial need for collaboration and vigilance in changing the national mind-set in order to achieve sustainable communities and a viable legacy for future generations. These popular cultural forms offer important insight into how the youth deploy new cultural aesthetics to comment on the landscapes of deprivation and degeneration in Gaborone. They demonstrate the interplay of cultural memorialization and creative resistance as strategies to circumvent the crises that the youth face.

Gender, History, and the Politics of Archiving in Popular Theater

In April 2016, *A Woman of Many Firsts* premiered at the Maitisong Festival—Botswana's national theater space located in Gaborone. Written and performed by Moduduetso Lecoge and directed by Moletedi-One Ntseme, the play dramatizes the life of Dr. Gaositwe Chiepe, one of Botswana's prominent female political figures. The actor, Lecoge, who is in fact the granddaughter of Dr. Chiepe, poignantly brought to the stage the experiences of her grandmother as a young girl growing up in Serowe Village and traces her school days and political career between 1948 and 1999. This one-woman act is an example of contemporary Botswana popular theater that illustrates the role of memory and personal archives in documenting history. The play is read as a social commentary on the youth condition in Gaborone, specifically how Dr. Chiepe's experiences point to the continuing marginalization of women and girls in Botswana's patriarchal society. *A Woman of Many Firsts*

---

13   Barber, "Popular Arts in Africa," 4.

dramatizes the legacy of gendered constructs and patriarchal sensibilities that frame the gender crisis and adversely affects the citizenship experiences of female youth in the country.

The term "popular theater" is used here to refer to conscientizing theater: that is, the expressive art form that speaks and performs in a language and through an idiom that is accessible and intelligible to the people. Popular theater furthers the interests of the ordinary people by publicly displaying and communicating issues that the collective vulnerable—the silenced, marginalized, and excluded majority—have to contend with and that is not part of state or mainstream public communication. Popular theater/performance thus constitutes performative art that constructs a public audience that is united by similar sociopolitical experiences and economic challenges. As Karin Barber would have it, this is art that furthers the cause of the people by opening their eyes to their objective situation in society. It "conscientizes" them, thus preparing them to take radical and progressive action.[14] This reading of the "popular" departs from the understanding of popular performing arts as forms produced by and for the "subaltern classes," as theorized by scholars such as David Kerr.[15] Kerr's conceptualization of the "popular" places emphasis on the "authentic" indigenous sacred rituals that recall the practice of African orality, forms of masquerades, precolonial rites, and ritualistic enactments that functioned as cultural resistance to European imperialism.[16] Neither does my reading of African popular theater conform to his categorization of African theatrical forms as those premised on Africa's experience with colonialism, which, in his view, is "the 'womb' out of which a negating indigenous theatre was born."[17] His view that African popular theater and indigenous performing arts are necessarily and intrinsically linked to the experience of colonialism is flawed. I argue that while the trajectory of colonialism is an undeniable historical experience that Africa encountered, it does not suffice as the defining moment through which to understand African popular performance. The "popular" should not be confined to the prehistoric, ritualistic observances of supposedly pristine Africa that do not make use of "borrowed" Western theatrical conventions. In fact, the idea of an insulated Africa without cross-cultural contact with the wider world is erroneous since, as Karin Barber has shown, the continent has had

---

14   Barber, "Popular Arts in Africa," 7.
15   Kerr, *African Popular Theatre*, x.
16   Kerr, 15.
17   Kerr, 16.

a long history of transnational cultural interaction and borrowing from the Western world since the late nineteenth century.[18] This article thus reads popular performing arts as cultural formations that creatively conscientize a variety of audiences on a variety of topical issues—social, political, and economic—in order to attain social transformation.

I argue in this article that Botswana urban youth weave a tapestry of popular consciousness through creative public displays and dis/plays. Public displays function to "unmake" the state operations of silencing, excluding, and homogenizing the ordinary and/or marginalized majority. They help to enhance and consolidate accessibility to the urban space by promoting participation in public dialogues for social change. Public dis/plays traverse the normalized techniques of public communication; they do not perform according to the normalized sociopolitical "script." Public dis/plays perform contrary to the perceived norm, seeking to subvert, interrupt, and challenge essentialized and normalized categories and responses in order to promote urban change. This reading extends Karin Barber's reading of modern urban-oriented popular formations. She asserts that popular arts are "arts that seem to exhibit a preoccupation with social change which is in effect their determining characteristic. They do not merely allude to innovation or make use of occasional use of novelties: they derive their energies from change, are constituted out of it, and are also, often quite consciously, about it."[19] These are acts of memorialization and identity construction that use innovative strategies to instigate social change. These popular cultural repertoires are often animated by social change as they are about social transformation itself.

In that light, *A Woman of Many Firsts* is examined as a popular theater piece because of its choice in aesthetics, which is geared toward accessibility and social change. The play uses both Setswana and English languages, a technique that reflects the preponderance in the use of codeswitching by the majority of the population in metropolitan centers such as Gaborone. It brings to the urban stage concerns about gender inequality, exploitation, and discrimination, all of which reflect the priorities of the feminist agenda in the country, particularly the need to include women in top national governance and decision-making forums. Since April 2016, the play has been performed before mixed audiences in Gaborone, following its premiere at the Maitisong National Arts Festival. The aesthetic of presentational theater also establishes proximity with the audience. In the three shows that I attended,

---

18   Barber, "Orality, the Media, and New Popular Cultures in Africa," 4.
19   Barber, "Popular Arts in Africa," 13.

the audience members were mostly women, and they seemed to appreciate the themes raised in the play. It received positive reviews in local newspapers, which commended its relevance and timeliness. "Botswana needs to know a bit more about this icon," one review says, emphasizing on Lecoge's successful re-enactment of Dr. Chiepe's life.[20] "She has created a legacy by being grounded on selflessness, respect, tenacity, and hard work, characteristic of a typical Motswana matriarch."[21] The play has thus been embraced as part of the conscientization agenda about Botswana women's involvement in shaping the country's political and economic history. Arguably, the strife for feminist conscientization, the urgency to appreciate women's activism, the sense of accessibility, and the innovative ways of attracting and constructing a public urban collective justifies its reading as "popular theater."

A Woman of Many Firsts narrativizes the educational, sociopolitical, career, and emotional trajectories of Dr. Chiepe. According to Lecoge, the play traces her grandmother's "many firsts," specifically her accomplishments as Botswana's first woman to obtain a master's degree as far back as the 1950s; as the first female education officer and subsequent director of education; Botswana's first female high commissioner to the United Kingdom; and the first and only female member of cabinet and member of Parliament for several years. These pioneering accomplishments, according to Lecoge, inspired her to bring her grandmother's life to the stage. "It is a story worth sharing," she insists in an interview with the author.[22] "My grandmother's many firsts provide a legacy that should be emulated by young women in Botswana who have similar aspirations but who are facing multiple social and political barriers." By animating her grandmother's lived experiences on the Botswana stage, Lecoge embodies the family's ethnography. Her performance functions as a creative ethnographic account of family history, thereby giving the text an autobiographical slant. As an actor, she demonstrates the role of theater and popular culture in showcasing the interplay of bodily inscriptions of memory and politicized performance, that is, performed history.

Two scenes from the play corroborate this assertion. In the first scene, young Ms. Gaositwe Chiepe's uncles instruct her mother to take Gaositwe out of school, insisting that she should instead be learning how to become a woman like every other girl in the village. The mother refuses and says she will continue to pay her school fees if the uncles are not willing to help

---

20   Sekaba, "Lecoge Brings Back a Woman of Many Firsts."
21   Sekaba, "Lecoge Brings Back a Woman of Many Firsts."
22   Rapoo, interview with Lecoge, Gaborone, April 12, 2019.

educate the female children. We learn through the scene that Gaositwe's father had passed away at the time, leaving the mother to provide for her family alone. The scene ends with the mother's resolute determination to pay for her children's school fees. She asserts, "There is no law that states that girls should not receive an education. And I will educate my child with or without your help." This determination by a vulnerable widow to support the education of her girl-child is indicative of a quiet form of radical feminism by African women in both private and public African spaces that is rarely addressed in mainstream discourses of feminism. It is representative of a resolute resistance to the oppressive dynamics of patriarchy that privilege the interests of men over women. Lecoge's performance thus functions to model a quiet but radical and subversive form of indigenous feminism to the younger Botswana generation.

In another scene, Gaositwe narrates her tumultuous encounters in her career trajectory. She stresses that she climbed the ranks from being education officer to being the first Motswana female director of education but that she did not feel she got the respect she deserved. She also informs the audience that when she was an education officer, she got a lower salary than her white female counterpart. "*O ne a amogela go nkgaisa ka gore ke lekgoa* [She got a higher salary because she was white] even though she only had a diploma and I had a degree." As the play progresses, we also learn that she was the first woman from Botswana to get her driver's license and to buy a car but that there were many barriers to cross before she could get authorization to drive.

A Woman of Many Firsts thus presents Dr. Chiepe's experiences of sexism, toxic masculinity and its associated exploitations, and racism. The play is a compelling re-presentation of, and a commentary on, Botswana patriarchal sensibilities. It exposes the twin effects of a poisonous sexism trenchantly enabled by a patriarchal culture and systemic racism shamelessly sustained by a racist postcolonial system. To borrow from feminist theorist Judith Butler (2004), the play dramatizes women's vulnerabilities in the face of colonial and patriarchal forces and structures. She was exposed to social and political violence because of her identity—as a girl, as a woman, and as a black woman struggling to navigate the postcolonial, male-dominated space that was at the time highly charged with white supremacist perspectives. Lecoge's memorialization of her grandmother's life and struggles thus stages the triple yoke of womanhood, motherhood, and blackness that bell hooks (1981, 1984) so famously theorized in her work. Lecoge elaborates on the notion of black women's experience as existing on the margins of feminist theory and practice. I argue that the play demonstrates how popular culture provides a creative space for young audiences to learn from the Other's experiences of vulnerability. As Judith Butler asserts, "Each of us is constituted politically in part by virtue of the social vulnerability of our bodies—as a site of desire and physical vulnerability, as a site of a publicity at once assertive and exposed."[23] Chiepe's vulnerability is reenacted on the contemporary Botswana popular theater stage for the purpose of displaying the facts of discrimination and gendered stereotypes experienced by women. The re-enactment shows the cultural imaginary of female domesticity and the violence women incur when they dare to gain access to the public sphere. The crucial point I argue however is that the play equivocates that the experiences of Othering, discrimination, and exclusion are not reserved for the past; they permeate past and present, thus impinging on the lives of young women in contemporary Botswana. As part of popular culture, then, especially one formulated by urban youth, the play articulates the need for personal and state introspection and agitates for cultural transformation. What is crucial here is that the social and cultural re-engineering that the play advocates is one defined by young people. It addresses the youth crisis pertaining to the lasting legacies of gender discrimination and the marginalization of women and girls in the country.

As a form of popular theater, the play is also a performance repertoire that dramatizes the notion that "the personal is political." This essay reads the evocation of this philosophy in the play as a powerful social message in the larger feminist agenda of interrupting sexism in the Botswana popular and political consciousness. Lecoge's enactment of her grandmother's lived experiences elaborates on the idea that personal encounters—social and political—are commensurate with the larger sociopolitical and state machinations of patriarchy and/or misogyny. That is, the personal and the political intertwine. While many of Lecoge's grandmother's social struggles were experienced at a private/personal level, such personal battles were linked to broader sociocultural structures of power. In line with Carol Hanisch's assertion and the debates that characterized second-wave feminism, *A Woman of Many Firsts* is part of a personal-political consciousness-raising performance that calls forth the power of social actors to advance political action. To echo theorist Bertolt Brecht (1964) and his notion of the alienation effect, the play creates a space for audiences to set aside their emotions and cultural inclinations and to instead interrogate what inspires them to transform Botswana

---

23   Butler, *Precarious Life*, 20.

society. The play is thus indicative of the creative power of African popular culture to inspire political action for the transformation of social, political, and economic systems.

The play also elaborates the historicizing and archiving function of theater and popular performance, especially as cultural repertoires with strong potential for processes of memorialization. Performance theorist Diana Taylor (2003) writes about the similarities and differences between the "archive" and the "repertoire," underscoring their role in documenting history and preserving identity and memory. The *archive*, according to Taylor, is made up of elements such as texts, documents, buildings, bones, and archaeological remains; while the *repertoire* consists of forms of embodied practice/knowledge such as spoken language, dance, sports, and ritual.[24] Archival memory, she explains, works through stable signifiers that are supposedly resistant to change. By comparison, the repertoire enacts embodied memory through acts that are considered ephemeral[25] and hence fluid and open to revision and change. Most importantly, observes Taylor, "embodied and performed acts generate, record, and transmit knowledge."[26] Borrowing on Taylor's notions, the official record and memory of political figures who have contributed to the shaping of Botswana's sociopolitical history and memory are kept through state-sanctioned history books, monuments, and similar "nonephemeral" archives. However, the repertoire—through performance practices such as *A Woman of Many Firsts*—also contributes significantly to the process of capturing, storing, and transmitting history, and preserving memory. But the play does this not through a fervent replication of the narratives in formal state archives but in the ways in which it subverts and undermines mainstream history. In *Archaeology of Knowledge*, Michel Foucault notes that the archive is essentially a system of discursivity. According to Foucault, "The archive is first the law of what can be said, the system that governs the appearance of statements as unique events. But the archive is also that which determines that all these things said do not accumulate endlessly in an amorphous mass, nor are they inscribed in an unbroken linearity, nor do they disappear at the mercy of chance external accidents."[27] Which is to say, as a system of knowledge formation and a force for social change, the archive has an inbuilt system that ensures the reading

---

24   Taylor, *Archive and the Repertoire*, 19.
25   Taylor, 20.
26   Taylor, 21.
27   Foucault, *Archeology of Knowledge*, 145–46.

of its signs is consistent with its design; that is, its meanings and outcomes are already predetermined. Because of its rigged discourse, Foucault proposes a radical approach to archivization that undercuts the inbuilt discourse of linear historicity. He recommends a method of historical analysis that turns "away from vast unities like 'periods' or 'centuries' to the phenomenon of rupture, of discontinuity."[28] This alternative approach of radical and subversive epistemological work ignores or bypasses the inbuilt systems of knowledge accumulation that interrupt the smooth linearity of state-sanctioned history. Foucault expresses the need to force "it into a new time, cut it off from its empirical origin and its original motivations, cleanse it of its imaginary complicities" and directs "historical analysis away from the search for silent beginnings, and the never-ending tracing-back to the original precursor, towards the search for a new type of rationality and its various effects."[29] It is a radical approach to historiography marked by relegation and alteration, rather than continuity and consistency. In the case of *A Woman of Many Firsts*, the specificities of personalized, living memory of political development, gendered and sexist practice, as well as racist encounters that might have been omitted in official archives get recaptured and displaced through forms of popular theater/performance. This is the power of African popular culture; to open up a space for a diverse, complex, and full representation of lived experiences. *A Woman of Many Firsts* thus opens a window into what has been included or excluded in official state history. Through its techniques of displacement, the play offers a commentary on the social facts that might have previously been omitted in official archives, thus emerging as a creative product that rehistoricizes the personal experiences of Dr. Gaositwe Chiepe, consequently making it worthy of preservation.

As part of the popular culture repertoire, the play also points to the diverse ways that youth creatively contribute to the ongoing debate about attaining sustainable livelihoods in a struggling African postcolony. The African youth population has been among the hardest hit by the world economic downturn, general fiscal uncertainties, and high unemployment and crime. And the city of Gaborone has not been spared these challenges. In response, the youth as active producers of popular culture find creative means to comment on these harsh realities using inexpensive ways to re-present these urban landscapes of chronic deprivation. As I have demonstrated with the case of *A Woman of Many Firsts*, the young creators and animators of popular culture

---

28 Foucault, 4.
29 Foucault, 4–5.

select appropriate techniques and/or aesthetics to interrogate that fraught space of postcolonial want and inequity. Specifically, the play deploys minimalist aesthetics in terms of casting, costume, and scenic design to comment on the current political-economic and social issues plaguing Botswana, especially its youth generation. The production uses one actor who plays multiple roles. In line with the minimalist theater techniques that evoke Jerzy Grotowski's "poor theater," a theater anchored in the core role of the actor in displaying bodily knowledge, Ms. Lecoge reenacts the power of embodied knowledge and memory. Producing a one-woman show is also less expensive than working with numerous characters and the attendant large-cast production. As young people find themselves in precarious conditions devoid of abundant material resources or social privileges, they have resorted to modest creativities grounded in minimalism to record their daily struggles and convey their anxieties about the current culture of disenfranchisement and chronic deprivation.

Popular Soundtracks and Social Commentary

Echoes of the social facts of human vulnerability and social precariousness as well as the urgent need for transformation reverberate through other forms of popular culture in Botswana. These are perceptible through contemporary forms of popular music produced by the urban youth. Culture, religion, politics, and socioeconomic challenges provide the raw materials for the cultivation and growth of these popular culture formations. Like other countries across Africa, Botswana has had to contend with a number of socioeconomic challenges, particularly youth unemployment, crime, and poverty. The youth interrogate these challenges and use popular culture to comment on ways to address them. Popular music now represents a powerful example of the deployment of cultural aesthetics of knowledge transfer to comment on landscapes of deprivation and degeneration. The overarching theme that runs across this popular culture genre is the need to change, collaborate, and stay vigilant in becoming active agents of transformation for sustainable communities and future generations. To borrow from David Attwell, the popular forms may be read as part of the script that expresses "an air of promise" in the current historical moment of the postcolonial scene.[30]

---

30   Attwell, *Rewriting Modernity*, 6.

There is a paucity of scholarly research on the significance of contemporary music in the Botswana urban space. Research that is available is predominantly on traditional music.[31] Yet popular music in Gaborone and other urban centers is part of the growing creative arts industry and the local scene of Botswana music production and music economy. Particularly, in the current moment of globalization and rapid urbanization, youth popular music performance is ubiquitous and reverberates throughout the country. In an earlier article, I examined the significance of youth popular music styles such as hip-hop, Kwaito, Kwaito-kwasa, and re-traditionalized music and their role in constructing urban identities and landscapes (Rapoo 2011). I observe in the article the various ways through which the youth perform as creative social critics who comment on the social realities in Gaborone and note some of the possible solutions they raise through performing their repertoires. In particular, the musical genres of hip-hop and Kwaito-kwasa figure predominantly in the urban youth styles.

The development of hip-hop music in Botswana can be traced to the late 1980s and early 1990s. As other scholars of popular music in Africa have observed, hip-hop as it is currently performed on the continent can be traced to the United States, the United Kingdom, and South Africa.[32] Notably, as American hip-hop became more and more globalized, it gained local African forms; yet the genre remains distinctive. The history of hip-hop production in Botswana can be linked to artists such as Sidney Baitsile, better known as DJ Sid, and David Molosiwa, popularly known as "Dave-Ski." The two youth performers gained influence from their work as disc jockeys and music promoters in Botswana's music scene. Baitsile and Molosiwa are credited with promoting Botswana hip-hop on local radio stations together with a number of other young Botswana DJs and radio personalities.[33] The liberalization of the Botswana media through the Botswana Broadcasting Act of 1999 has also played a significant role in promoting the growth of the music industry specifically through private radio stations such as Gabz FM, YaRona FM, Duma FM, and the state-run RB2. Hip-hop music has also gained currency in Botswana through Botswana television. Radio and television programs such as *Strictly Hip Hop Live*, *Sprite Rap Activity*, and *Flava Dome*

---

31   See, for example, Denbow and Thebe, *Culture and Customs of Botswana*; and Tumedi et. al., *Lips and Pages*.
32   See Shepler, "Youth Music and Politics"; Kerr, "From the Margin"; Kerr, "Experiments in Sound"; and Nyairo, "(Re)Configuring the City."
33   Masau, "Hip Hop in Botswana."

have contributed significantly to the promotion of the genre and have given mileage to Botswana hip-hop artists as well. Increased visibility continues to be availed through music festivals and concerts, most of which are held in Gaborone. These platforms have led to growth in the number of hip-hop artists in the country, most of whom perform not only locally but also across the region and elsewhere. That a young Botswana artist named Zeus can win the Best Hip Hop Video Award at the 2009 Channel O Awards attests to the growth of the hip-hop genre in the country.

The music produced by Botswana youth demonstrates how they bring cultural and political consciousness to popular-cultural space. The songs examined here elaborate on the historicizing function of music as cultural memory and political commentary. They could also be read as palimpsestic resonances in the Botswana collective imaginary that rearticulates the notion of collective change for social transformation. Good illustrations can be seen from the *ReMmogo AllStars*, a collaboration by a number of young musicians who are part of mainstream urban music production in Botswana. The productions are part of an initiative established in 2010 by Kagiso David Morebodi called ReMmogo Youth Organization. The group consists of young Gaborone-resident music celebrities—predominantly male singers, whose music is produced by a local production company called Reign Forest in collaboration with Cross Creations and Green Hole, also locally based. The initiative has enjoyed the patronage and support of governmental and private funding organizations such as the United States Embassy in Botswana, the Botswana National Youth Council, and the Motor Vehicle Accident Fund that is administered by the Ministry of Finance and Development Planning. Music and videos from the group address topical issues such as HIV/AIDS, alcohol abuse, and road safety. ReMmogo music is an amalgam of contemporary styles, including hip-hop and rap. The group enjoys the support of followers through the local radio stations and YouTube followers. The footprints —"views" and "likes"— on Facebook and other social media indicate an appreciation for their music. See the lyrics below for the song "Tsaya Tshwetso."

ReMmogo AllStars: Tsaya Tshwetso

Stand up; get up
Let us make this world a better
  place;

Let us take charge; Re tsee mai-karabelo; Let's take responsibility
Make it your task this year
CHORUS: *Change Now!*
Make this a better world.
Make up your mind, let's go!
Another day le ReMmogo [with The AllStars musicians]
Re tseye tshwetso le boikarabelo Let's make the resolution and take responsibility

Re iphaphe; re ikgalemele Let's abstain; let's practise restraint

Re sireletse bokamoso jwa rona! Let's protect our future!

RAP: Re bua ka banana We're talking about the youth
Yellow-bone like makapi a banana [Light-skinned youth] like banana peels

Kanana ke ko re vaelang teng! Canaan is our destination
Rona Batswana; Botswana Us Botswana people
Le nna ke batla chenchi I too seek for change
Like Obama; Obama!
I know we're in a kazi We're in the ghetto
Re shapa ka mathombo; Surviving through the tubes of life support

But to be a millionaire ga se dilo tsa malungu is not just for "white people"
You gotta have vision;
You gotta have dreams
Forget about the cone
You gotta make cream!

Ke nako ya go dira se se tshwanetseng; It's time to do the right thing;
Time to walk the talk and cross the bridge;

We all know what we have to do.
E fitlhile weekend, — The weekend is here,
And dibara di tletse; — bars are packed full;
Bana, ma14, botlhe ba teng. — The youth, virgins, all are here.
Re besa dinama, plus go itewa dipina; — Enjoying barbecues and music
Tonight, I might have fun;
But I don't drink and drive.
Ke vaela gae ke le sober! — I'll go home still sober
Ke nako ya go ikgalemela, — It's time to exercise restraint,
Ke nako ya go tsaya tshwetso — It's time to make the resolution
Re kgaole chaene! — Let's cut the chain!
Repeat CHORUS

In this song, the group foregrounds the importance of taking personal and social responsibility. This admonition is made against the backdrop of the behavior of the youth in the context of the social ills prevalent in urban centers, particularly inertia, crime, and moral degeneracy. The target audience for the song is youth. The metaphors and cultural tropes used in the lyrics are compelling and resonant within the Botswana landscape. Barack Obama is an important cultural icon for the young hip-hop artists. Hip-hop artist King Freezy explains why Obama holds such an appeal for youth in Botswana:

> Obama's coming into the US presidency as the first Black President was a great change. We as young people are desperate for change ourselves; not only change in terms of governance like political parties, but also *gore diemo tsa banana di tlaa fetoga* [the circumstances and realities facing young people will change.] There will be jobs, more opportunities, and industries will change, you know; and *banana ba tlaa fiwa* attention [youth will be given attention]. He gives us hope for change. He is an icon that we look up to. In terms of what has he really done for us as *banana mo* [the youth in] Botswana; *ga a re direla sepe hela se se kalo* [he has not done much for us]; but he gave us hope. That is why when we speak about change there will always be Obama in the picture because he gives us hope that one day things will change for us.[34]

---

[34] Mmopi King Freezy Nthokana, interview with Rapoo, August 8, 2019, Gaborone.

Thus, Obama appeals to Botswana youth because he epitomizes possibilities for change; he is an embodiment of hope. His messages at the African Union[35] have also become part of the youths' popular and political consciousness. In his address, Obama emphasized that young people "embody the energy and optimism of today's Africa," that "nothing will unlock Africa's economic potential more than ending the cancer of corruption," and that there is a need to invest in young "leaders who can transform businesses, civil society and governments tomorrow."[36] Obama's messages thus resonate with young pop-culture performers who promote his vision for change throughout the continent by calling for job creation, youth participation in development dialogue, and ending corruption. "Our music is about our reality," King Freezy asserts, "and our reality can change."[37]

Similarly, the young hip-hop artists from the ReMmogo ensemble call forth Obama's political message of change, underscoring the idea that change is within everyone's grasp and is everyone's responsibility. Even though Botswana youth must contend with landscapes of deprivation, the singer asserts that affluence is not reserved for whites or expatriates in the context of Botswana. Reference to whites and expatriates here is significant because it resonates with the history of privilege and corruption in enabling access to resources in Botswana. The latest case involving British billionaire Sir Richard Branson's bid to get access to the Okavango Delta, Botswana's most prestigious and highest-earning tourist asset, entered popular consciousness amidst concerns about lack of access to land to Botswana citizens. The local newspaper *Sunday Standard* warned readers:

> If nothing else, the Okavango Delta situation attests to the Machiavellian genius of the people who have run Botswana since 1884. Soon after present-day Botswana became a British protectorate, colonial settlers gobbled up (and today still retain) the most agriculturally productive land in the country. Then, the Delta didn't have as much commercial value as it does today and was designated tribal land. When it became a high value tourist asset, intense lobbying behind the scenes produced a lease agreement whose practical effect has been to detribalise the Okavango Delta.[38]

35　Obama, "Text of President Obama's Remarks at the African Union," July 28, 2015.
36　Obama, "Text."
37　King Freezy, interview.
38　*Sunday Standard*, "If Branson Gets Okavango Delta Land."

The difficulty in getting access to land, let alone luxury safari tourism sites such as the Okavango Delta, is a social fact that Botswana indigenous populations face, especially the youth contingent. This impinges on their sustainable livelihoods because without land, they cannot access other resources such as finances for agricultural businesses or other avenues for self-employment. The music thus articulates these social conditions.

Yet the singer in the ReMmogo group asserts that anyone, including the youth from the ghetto, can be a millionaire if they focus on their dreams and visions of a future that is characterized by abundance. Besides this rather naïve assertion, the music points to the importance of self-discipline and diligence in becoming successful, albeit in the music production industry. The music deploys the metaphor of ice cream—the cone and the cream—but with a localized twist in meaning. The cone represents the idea of the hardships and challenges of living in the ghetto, while the cream concretizes the enjoyable fruits of one's labor. Alternatively, the cone is the labor, and the cream is the money that one makes from success in the music industry. These layers of metaphoric references corroborate the idea that change is inevitable if one takes personal responsibility for their lives.

Tropes of self-restraint, changes in mind-set, and discipline are recurrent throughout the lyrics. The urgency of responsible behavior is highlighted further through the imagery of the "chain" in the last line. There is a need, for example, to immediately cut the cycle of poverty and the chain of HIV/AIDS transmission and to stop the deaths resulting from drunken driving, as alluded to in the lyrics. If the youth are to reach their destination of an abundant future as encapsulated in the image of Canaan—the biblical construction of prosperity, then they must take responsibility for their actions. ReMmogo musicians thus use the space of popular culture to engage in sociocultural reengineering by urging the youth of Botswana to take charge of their lives, to be active agents in transforming their lives: that is, to be the agents of the change they seek. Agency and choice are reinforced as the core principles in acts of self-determination. More importantly, the group uses their positionality as celebrities to make comments on the role of agency in transforming the youth condition in Botswana. See the lyrics below for the song "A Re kopaneng."

ReMmogo AllStars: A Re kopaneng

A re tshwaraganeng ka matsogo	Let us hold hands
Banana le bagolo	The young and the elderly

Re ikanyeng Ramasedi;	Let us trust the Almighty
Go boloka matshelo a rona	To preserve our lives
Batsadi ba rona ba lekile gotlhe	Our parents have done their best
Go re godisa ka lerato le ka botho	To raise us in love and dignity
Maitseo le tlhomamo!	Good manners and firmness!
CHORUS: *A re kopaneng; re tshwaraganeng*	Let us unite; let us join together
Re lwantshe bolwetse bona	Let us fight this disease
Bo gapile masikale ditsala	It has seized relatives and friends
Bo gapile chaba ya rona!	It has seized our nation.
RAP:	
Ke monana, nkutlwelleng	I am a youth, listen to me!
Moono wa rona ke tshwaragano le popagano!	Our message is unity and togetherness!
I'm gonna put it down simply lie ABC	
To all masika le ditsala le baba sa nkitseng;	To all relatives and friends and those that do not know me
It's all over the radio like everything.	
HIV e re feditse;	HIV has annihilated us
Why choose to overlook	
Matlhoko a e a tsisitseng?	The pains it has brought about?
Let's all be part of the solution	
Not the problem; Ke a go kopa	I beg of you
Wise up; Motswana wetsho	My fellow Motswana[39]
A re gopoleng our brothers, our sisters	Let us remember

---

[39] Botswana is the country; "Motswana" refers to the person or national/citizen (singular); "Batswana" refers to the people (plural); and Setswana is the language.

Who fought for me and you.
Why give up so easily?
A re lwantsheng segajaja! Let us fight the pandemic
Repeat CHORUS

This song speaks to the long-lasting impacts of the HIV/AIDS pandemic in Botswana. This is one of the main causes of mortality in the country. Although the high mortality rate seems to be receding, according to the latest WHO reports, the spread of the virus, particularly among the urban youth, is still a major concern. Unity and concerted efforts are offered as techniques to curb the scourge of HIV/AIDS. The song also highlights the role of cultural memory as heritage. The lyrics point to the legacy of dignity that the youth population has inherited from the older generations. The performers thus draw attention to the notion of modernity and the urban experience in the postcolony as being commensurate with deliberate acts of self-assertion. Recalling Connell and Gibson, this song elaborates the notion that "places, and their specific socio-historical, economic and political circumstances, shape musical expression" and that "musical traditions can alter places" and act as catalysts for the construction of spatial identities."[40]

The notion of memory and re-memory, of how the past informs the present encapsulates the key thematic thrust of the song. The lyrics point to the need to reconcile the past with the present and to confront the complicity of the youth in the realities of loss experienced through the HIV/AIDS pandemic. Stylistically, the music deploys hyperbolic images of "annihilation," "seizing" (and hence disempowering), and temporary stupor to anchor the message of the song. Collective memory and unity are offered as the solution to regain a sense of consciousness. The Botswana collective cultural imaginary founded on the principle of human interdependence is conjured up as the strategy for social transformation. These include proverbial assertions such as *motho ke motho ka batho ba bangwe* [One is human because of other humans around them] and *kgetsi ya tsie e kgonwa ke go tshwaraganelwa* [A heavy load becomes lighter when more carry it]. These forms of cultural recall reinforce a cosmopolitan philosophy and a kind of "togetherness ethics" that emphasizes a sense of community. In many ways, these artists are demanding a kind of social reengineering founded on Botho/Ubuntu, the famous African philosophy that promotes empathy and compassion for

---

40   Connell and Gibson, *Sound Tracks*, 18.

others. The zone of popular culture thus reinforces the identity of the youth performers as producers of the current ideas and values that will shape future African cultural landscapes.

Conclusion

The crafting of urban identities by young people in Botswana happens at the crossroads of politics and popular culture. While the landscapes of crime, corruption, unemployment, and poverty remain a harsh reality in cities like Gaborone, the youth are reinventing contemporary African modernity through practices of popular culture. In the scenarios that have been examined in this chapter, youth desires and acts of self-determination draw inspiration from local aesthetics and global repertoires that are anchored on the notion of self-regulation as the foundation for social transformation. Barack Obama's message of social change, noting that "change will not come if we wait for some other person or some other time. We are the ones we have been waiting for. We are the change that we seek" resounded powerfully with the teeming youth population in Botswana. This message has been used alongside popular traditional musical repertoires of artists such as Ratsie Setlhako.

The youth in Botswana are using popular culture to access urban space. They creatively borrow from cultural power to recraft their identities and agitate for urban change. Urban change and social agency are predominant messages in their theatrical and musical repertoires. As Connell and Gibson (2003) observe, urban change is a product of the interaction between places and cultural forms. Urban space provides social facts for the youthful popular culture formations. There is a need, therefore, as Susan Shepler suggests, to listen to the "authentic voices" of the youth and to integrate the youth critique of the sociopolitical happenings around them. The youth in Gaborone use contemporary theater and music lyrics to comment on gendered stereotypes and to advocate for social agency and responsibility. Similar to the youth rap musicians in Dar es Salaam that David Kerr writes about in this volume and elsewhere,[41] the youth use popular culture to contest their marginality in an African postcolonial city. Kerr writes convincingly about the youth experience of exclusion from local opportunities for recognition in Dar es Salaam and how they use music to contest physical and social space. Botswana youth culture performers are performing similarly in their use of

---

41 Kerr, "From the Margins to the Mainstream," 65–80.

popular culture to simultaneously contest their marginality in accessing public space and create alternative spaces for participation in public dialogues about social transformation.

A shift in discourse is apparent in the scenarios examined here, from lamenting the historical legacies of colonization to becoming creative actors and cultural entrepreneurs, young people are finding ways to reconstruct the societies that have defined and impacted their lives in the African postcolony. Through popular culture, young producers of popular arts are claiming their space in the African metropolis, asserting their positionality as speaking subjects that seek to contribute in powerful ways to processes of social change through cultural activism. The youth performers demonstrate how popular culture enables them to gain access to the public sphere of political engagement. Their performances highlight the significance of youth participation in African modernity; that is, the need to include the youth in decision-making forums. Clearly, they are empowered to express what they feel, fear, desire, detest, and know. Their identifications as creative producers and political subjectivities draw attention to how popular culture mobilizes change in the postcolony.

Bibliography

Attwell, David. *Rewriting Modernity: Studies in Black South African Literary History.* Athens: Ohio University Press, 2005.

Barber, Karin. "Introduction: View of the Field." In *Readings in African Popular Culture*, edited by Karin Barber, 1–12. Bloomington: Indiana University Press, 1997.

———. "Orality, the Media, and New Popular Cultures in Africa." In *Media and Identity in Africa*, edited by Kimani Njogu and John Middleton, 3–18. Bloomington: Indiana University Press, 2010.

———. "Popular Arts in Africa." *African Studies Review* 30, no. 3 (1987): 1–78.

Brecht, Bertolt, and Willet, J. *Brecht on Theatre: The Development of an Aesthetic.* London: Methuen, 1964.

Butler, Judith. *Precarious Life: the Powers of Mourning and Violence.* London: Verso, 2004.

Connell, J., and Gibson, C. *Sound Tracks: Popular Music, Identity and Place.* London: Routledge.

Denbow, James, and Thebe, P. C. *Culture and Customs of Botswana.* Westport, CT: Greenwood, 2006.

Durham, Deborah. "Disappearing Youth: Youth as a Social Shifter in Botswana." *American Ethnologist* 31, no. 4 (2004): 589–605.

Foucault, Michel. *The Archaeology of Knowledge*. New York: Pantheon, 1972.
hooks, bell. *Feminist Theory: From Margin to Center*. Boston: South End, 1984.
———. *Aint I a Woman: Black Women and Feminism*. London: Pluto, 1981.
Kerr, David. *African Popular Theatre*. Oxford: James Currey, 1995.
———. "Experiments in Sound: Generating Sonic Landscapes in Online Spaces." *Journal of African Cultural Studies* 32, no. 1 (2020). 24–41: doi:10.1080/136968 15.2019.1615419.
———. "From the Margins to the Mainstream: Making and Remaking an Alternative Music Economy in Dar es Salaam. *Journal of African Cultural Studies* 30, no. 1 (2018): 65–80.
Lefebvre, Henry. *The Production of Space*. Translated by Donald Nicholson-Smith. Malden, MA: Blackwell, 1991.
Lesetedi, Gwen N. "Rapid Urbanization in Botswana: A Typical or Unique Case?" In *Issues, Challenges and Reflections on Social Development in Southern Africa*, edited by Kwaku Osei-Hwedie and B. Z. Osei-Hwedie, 37–155. Accra: Gimpa, 2010.
Masau, Problem. "Hip Hop in Botswana." *Music-in Africa* (website). https://www.musicinafrica.net/magazine/hip-hop-botswana. Accessed August 8, 2019.
McAuley, Gay. *Space in Performance: Making Meaning in the Theatre*. Ann Arbor: University of Michigan Press, 2000.
Mogobe, Thulaganyo. "Theatre Development in Botswana." *Pula: Botswana Journal of African Studies* 29, no. 2 (2015): 223–33.
National Youth Policy, Ministry of Youth, Sport and Culture. Gaborone: Government Printing and Publishing Services, 2010.
Rapoo, Connie. "Urbanised Soundtracks: Youth Popular Culture in the African City." *Social Dynamics: A Journal of African Studies* 39, no. 2 (2013): 368–83.
Sechele, Latang. "Unemployed Youth and Self-Employment in Botswana." *Mosenodi Journal* 19, no. 1 (2016): 31–44.
Sekaba, Bakgethwa. "Lecoge Brings Back a Woman of Many Firsts." *Botswana DailyNews*, April 8, 2018.
Shepler, Susan. "Youth Music and Politics in Post-war Sierra Leone." *Journal of Modern African Studies* 48, no. 4 (2010): 627–42.
Sunday Standard Reporter, "If Branson Gets Okavango Delta Land, He Could Keep It Forever." April 23, 2018. https://www.sundaystandard.info/if-branson-gets-okavango-delta-land-he-could-keep-it-forever/. Accessed August 08, 2019.
Taylor, Diana. *The Archive and the Repertoire: Performing Cultural Memory in the Americas*. Durham, NC: Duke University Press, 2003.
Tumedi, S. M., Ndada, N., and Nhlekisana, R. O. B. *Lips and Pages: Botswana Traditional Music as Socio-political Commentary*. Gaborone: Pentagon, 2010.
Ugor, Paul. "Extenuating Circumstances, African Youth, and Social Agency in a Late-Modern World." *Postcolonial Text* 8, no. 3–4 (2013): 1–12.

Chapter Fourteen

#FeesMustFall and Youth Deconstruction of South Africa's Liberation Narrative

Kristi Heather Kenyon,

Juliana Coughlin, and David Bosc[1]

Introduction

A nation's historical narrative is a text, both literally as it is printed into history books and metaphorically as it shapes wider discourse and culture.[2] This chapter interrogates the ways in which youth, through participation in the

---

1 This essay is part of a larger project examining generational shifts in protests with a focus on #FeesMustFall. It has benefited from feedback on related papers at meetings of the Successful Societies Program of the Canadian Institute for Advanced Research (CIFAR), and at the African Studies Association Conference, Canadian Association for African Studies Conference, the Canadian Political Science Association, and at the University of Saskatchewan. This paper has also been strengthened by conversations with Tshepo Madlingozi with whom Kristi Heather Kenyon is collaborating on a related project. Sincere thanks to Sarah Steidl for her assistance with notation and formatting. This project is supported by funding from the CIFAR-Azrieli Global Scholars Program and from the University of Winnipeg's Major Research Grant.

2 See Bhabha, *Nation and Narration*.

#FeesMustFall protests, are countering and rewriting a key tenet of the South African national text through the manifestation of a new generation's protest culture. We argue that in articulating their protests primarily as an expression of continuity, they challenge the premise of radical change between the apartheid and postapartheid eras, instead framing their protests as the latest iteration of a long struggle against injustice. This chapter examines youth counternarratives expressed in the #FeesMustFall protests through interviews with student participants at Pretoria universities and an analysis of online rhetoric under this hashtag. We focus on the ways in which this collaborative, participatory, and iterative movement engages in the process of rewriting South Africa's dominant national text.

Peterson contends that culture has two possible meanings; "culture as a way of life" and "culture as a range of creative and intellectual practices that are broadly called 'the arts.'"[3] In the South African context, protest continues to be a cultural practice that unites both meanings through practices such as protest dance (*toyi toyi*) and song. Within South African freedom songs Jolaosho argues, for example, that [f]ormative elements of antiphony, repetition, and rhythm constitute a musical practice that organizes protest gatherings, allows for democratic leadership, and fosters collective participation."[4] Peterson notes that "if we accept that culture is the totality of a people's self-definition, development and independence, it then follows that the struggle for freedom will express itself through culture and its social, material and creative forms."[5] This framing of culture is intimately concerned with power and contextualized within the struggle for freedom and the formation of nations and their narratives. Peterson's framing consequently highlights the ways in which narratives hold cultural power and form systems of meaning that can be interpreted as texts. This perspective aligns closely with Geertz's view that "the culture of people is an ensemble of texts," and that the real task of studying culture is to gain "access to the conceptual world in which our subjects live so that we can, in some extended sense of the term, converse with them."[6] It is this notion of culture as "webs" of signification that are

---

3   Peterson, "Youth and Student Culture: Riding Resistance and Imagining the Future," 16.
4   Jolaosho, "Singing Politics: Freedom Songs and Collective Protest in Post-Apartheid South Africa," 6.
5   Peterson, "Youth and Student Culture," 16.
6   Geertz, *The Interpretation of Cultures*, 27.

examined as an "interpretive ... search of meaning"[7] that we bring to bear on our analysis of South African youth protest culture.

In this search, Barber argues "popular culture" provides a flexible, if amorphous, form of culture that is neither necessarily traditional nor elite.[8] She insists that popular culture, while difficult to define, is a resource worthy of "serious attention" not only due to its "sheer undeniable assertive presence as social facts" but also because of its flourishing without official recognition, a persistence that, she argues, asserts popular cultures as necessary, dynamic, and sustaining forces.[9] What function then, does popular culture serve for its participants? Participation itself is a significant assertion of meaning and power. In referencing oppressive regimes, Barber notes that "meaning is communicated simply by the fact that the performance takes place at all,"[10] a statement that we argue also has meaning in democratic regimes. That people take time and risks (in this instance risks of expulsion, failing exams, physical harm, familial and social disruption) to participate is itself a powerful act of communication. It is a way to be "visible" and to insist that history is made by the people and not "only by a handful of prominent leaders."[11] Protest participation does not "merely reflect an already-constituted consciousness" but is an iterative forum through which consciousness is formed, "articulated and communicated," wherein involvement shapes the ways in which participants understand the world around them.[12] This is apparent in the #FeesMustFall protests through the ways in which participants undermine and deconstruct a powerful national liberation story and employ physical and virtual space to do so. Communication can also be a process of illuminating patterns of relationships,[13] between groups and across time. In #FeesMustFall, this is illustrated through the strategic use of elements of South Africa's cultural canon, a method that protesters use to situate themselves, to use Geertz's term, in particular webs of meaning.

In South Africa, cultural artifacts of popular protest include melodies and lyrics of songs, forms of organization and mobilization (including dance, gestures, organizational structures), and references to key people and events.

---

7   Geertz, 5.
8   Barber, "Introduction," 1.
9   Barber, 1.
10 Barber, 3.
11 Barber, 3.
12 Barber, 4.
13 Barber, 2.

#FeesMustFall protesters drew on this canon, while challenging a broader national text of liberation and reconciliation, which itself is reflected in cultural artifacts such as place names, holidays, the national anthem, and icons. The creative ways in which protesters drew on these artifacts mirror the acts of re-use, positioning, and re-creation associated with African youth cultures. Apartheid has provided ample "stock images of injustice,"[14] and many elements of antiapartheid activism are re-used in contemporary protests such as #FeesMustFall, including iconic images, historically resonant slogans, and antiapartheid songs whose rhythms and melodies continue to "leverage cultural forms and historical memory"[15] even as lyrics change to reflect current circumstances.[16] The re-use of historical protest techniques and symbols signals connection to past struggles and situates contemporary protests within that fabric of meaning. This is both a process of strategic framing, leveraging political opportunity[17] at a particular moment in history, and a habitual use of available cultural resources of protest.

As "born free" activists emerge without the direct experience of the apartheid regime and with grievances emerging from a new political and socioeconomic context, they engage re-creatively with these cultural resources of protest. They select and curate these materials in new ways, ignoring and challenging some dominant themes and resurrecting eclipsed aspects of the national historical narrative. While apartheid is by no means forgotten, the "born free" generation relates to and draws on this history in different ways,[18] making different parallels and comparisons. Some argue this generation is less politically aware[19] and less committed to democracy[20] than that of their parents. Others view them as holding unprecedented power because their allegiance to the governing African National Congress (ANC), a party whose legitimacy is largely tied to their role in the antiapartheid struggle, cannot be guaranteed.

---

14   Swidler, "Culture in Action: Symbols and Strategies," 277.
15   Jolaosho, "Singing Politics," 8.
16   Jolaosho, 191.
17   Benford and Snow, "Framing Processes and Social Movements: An Overview and Assessment," 628.
18   Mattes, "The 'Born Frees': The Prospects for Generational Change in Post-Apartheid South Africa."
19   Baines, "The Master Narrative of South Africa's Liberation Struggle: Remembering and Forgetting June 16, 1976."
20   Mattes, "The 'Born Frees,'" 133–53.

Background

The history of South Africa is one of deliberately constructed inequalities within which access to land is a central element.[21] The 1913 Land Act solidified a legal framework that limited black land rights and ensured white access to desirable terrain.[22] Following the 1948 election of the Afrikaner nationalist National Party, whose formal apartheid categorized South Africans by race (black, "colored," Indian, white), entrenched racial separation and inequality, and "removed and restricted the rights of 'non-whites' in every possible sphere."[23] Laws restricted personal relationships, political rights, and freedom of movement, and limited education and employment. Piercing in their minutiae, "petty apartheid" laws restricted access to public spaces designating, for example, park benches for "whites only."[24] Grand apartheid imposed large-scale spatial inequality assigning, through a series of laws,[25] specific areas to single racial and ethnic groups, reserving desirable lands for whites, forcibly moving black South Africans and ultimately creating artificial countries called "Bantustans" typically distant from major cities and often with limited employment options.

Throughout apartheid black South Africans protested their discriminatory reality, with youth playing an important role in this resistance.[26] The most widespread youth protest of this era is a student protest near Johannesburg now known as the Soweto Uprising. In June 1976, black students protested the introduction of Afrikaans, viewed among many black South Africans as "the language of the oppressor," as the medium of instruction.[27] More than twenty thousand students protested in the streets of Soweto, where they were met with brutal force by police. Thousands were injured, and at least 176

---

21   McKeever, "Educational Inequality in Apartheid South Africa."
22   McKeever, 117.
23   Beinart and Dubow, "Introduction: The Historiography of Segregation and Apartheid."
24   Teeger, "'Both Sides of the Story': History Education in Post-Apartheid South Africa," 1179.
25   Including the Group Areas Act of 1950, the 1959 Bantu Self Government Act, and the Black Homeland Citizenship Act of 1970.
26   Teeger, "Both Sides," 1179. Black South Africans were not alone in resisting apartheid but formed the vast majority of those participants in the domestic antiapartheid movement.
27   Ndlovu, "Soweto Uprising."

students were killed, including thirteen-year-old Hector Pieterson, whose image became an iconic example of apartheid violence. Postapartheid South Africa recognizes June 16 as a public holiday (Youth Day) in remembrance of this event.

Transition in the country began in the 1990s, and discriminatory laws were gradually repealed. ANC leader Nelson Mandela was released from prison and restrictions on political parties were lifted, culminating in 1994, with the nation's first inclusive election.[28] The 1996 Truth and Reconciliation Commission provided a forum to address past atrocities and sought to build a reconciled nation.[29] Yet many argue that truth came at the expense of justice.[30] Apartheid-era inequalities remain entrenched in many ways. Land and other forms of wealth remain concentrated in the hands of a small number of elites who are no longer exclusively white but do not reflect the country's diversity. As Hollanda notes, "The make-up of our labour market keeps this skewed picture intact" with endemic unemployment in predominantly black rural areas.[31]

The dominant change-based narrative of contemporary South Africa is a story that celebrates improvement and an escape from apartheid history, something Wilson has referred to as "discontinuous historicity."[32] In this narrative, the country was reinvented after apartheid with new cultural symbols reinforcing legal structures such as a new constitution. This national text is premised on the dramatic shift from apartheid's racial divide to the contemporary "rainbow nation" that celebrates diversity in a context of reconciliation and forward-looking optimism. It is within and in response to this new narration of equality and progress that the #FeesMustFall protests erupted, highlighting the discordance between progressive narratives and unequal lives.

---

28   Beinart and Dubow, "Introduction."
29   Hollanda, "Human Rights and Political Transition in South Africa: The Case of the Truth and Reconciliation Commission."
30   Rotberg, "Truth Commissions and the Provision of Truth, Justice, and Reconciliation."
31   Hollanda, "Human Rights," 72.
32   Wilson, "Reconciliation and Revenge in Post-Apartheid South Africa: Rethinking Legal Pluralism and Human Rights."

#FeesMustFall

The 2015–16 #FeesMustFall protests were a massive series of uprisings on South African university campuses and the first large-scale mobilization of the postapartheid generation. The roots of these protests can be traced in several ways. On the one hand, the #FMF protests came on the heels of another "must fall" movement. In March 2015, the #Rhodes Must Fall[33] movement against colonial symbols began at the University of Cape Town, resulting in the removal of a prominent statue of Cecil John Rhodes on the university campus.[34] Growing both geographically and in scope, by April mobilization broadened to include multiple facets of racism and exclusion in South African institutions of higher education.[35] #FMF can also trace its origins to ongoing fee-based protests at historically black universities.[36] The 1955 Freedom Charter and various ANC election platforms were committed to free higher education, an unhonored promise disproportionately affecting lower income and predominantly black families. The immediate trigger for the #FMF iteration of fee protests was a government announcement of a proposed fee increase of more than 10 percent in one year.[37]

By October 2015, these two strands developed into a diverse social movement at campuses across the country, including demands related to fees alongside appeals for broader university and societal change. The six long-term demands of the movement at the national level were: "free, quality, decolonised education from the cradle to the grave," "an end to outsourcing and labour brokering," "the decriminalisation of protests and protesters," "an end to debt," "reformulation of governance structures to promote participatory rather than representative democracy," and "an end to all oppressive systems including racism, exploitation, sexism, homophobia, xenophobia, and ableism, amongst others."[38]

---

33 See Jendele Hungbo's chapter in this volume.
34 Drayton, "Rhodes Must Not Fall? Statues, Postcolonial 'Heritage' and Temporality"; Evans, "Unsettled Matters, Falling Flight: Decolonial Protest and the Becoming-Material of an Imperial Statue"; Kros, "Rhodes Must Fall: Archives and Counter-Archives"; Nyamnjoh, *#RhodesMustFall: Nibbling at Resilient Colonialism in South Africa*.
35 Booysen and Bandama, "Appendix."
36 Langa, "Researching the #FeesMustFall Movement."
37 Booysen, "Two Weeks in October: Changing Governance in South Africa."
38 Naidoo, "Contemporary Student Politics in South Africa," 188.

By late October 2015, President Jacob Zuma announced there would be no increase in fees. Following the 2016 protests there was an expansion of federal grants for students, making higher education accessible without fees for a broader group of South African students. While access to education and fees were critical components of the #FeesMustFall protests, deeper grievances spoke to ongoing social inequality, a dimension that received less media attention.[39]

A growing body of literature examines diverse facets of these protests at a variety of analytical and geographical levels. The developing canon contextualizes the protests in several ways, characterizing #FeesMustFall as: a movement for sociopolitical change,[40] a form of antipoverty activism,[41] the latest iteration of South African protest culture,[42] a "decolonial" movement,[43] and as a black consciousness movement against racial inequality.[44] Examining South Africa within its continental context, scholars examine what #FeesMustFall tells us about the country's complex relationship with Africa beyond its borders, examining the treatment of noncitizens within the country[45] and within universities.[46] A cluster of research examines #FMF's impact on higher education,[47] written by academics, students, and administrators[48] and examining topics including: economic and structural impacts,

---

39 Moloi et al., "(De)Constructing the #FeesMustFall Campaign in South African Higher Education."
40 Ndlovu, *#FeesMustFall and Youth Mobilisation in South Africa*.
41 Ngidi et al., "Asijiki and the Capacity to Aspire Through Social Media."
42 Hodes, "Questioning 'Fees Must Fall'"; and Booysen, ed. *Fees Must Fall: Student Revolt, Decolonisation and Governance in South Africa*.
43 Evans, "Unsettled," 130–44.
44 Maringira and Gukurume, "Being Black' in #FeesMustFall and #FreeDecolonisedEducation: Student Protests at the University of the Western Cape"; and Molefe, "Oppression Must Fall."
45 Nyamnjoh, *#RhodesMustFall*.
46 Raghuram, Breines, and Gunter, "Beyond #FeesMustFall: International Students, Fees and Everyday Agency in the Era of Decolonisation."
47 Moloi, Makgoba and Miruka, "(De)Constructing"; Mutekwe, "Unmasking the Ramifications of the Fees-Must-Fall-Conundrum in Higher Education Institutions in South Africa."
48 Habib, *Rebels and Rage: Reflecting on #FeesMustFall*; Jansen, *As by Fire: The End of the South African University*.

neoliberalism in education,[49] and decolonizing curriculum.[50] An emerging subset of literature focuses on feminism, gender, and sexuality within the protests.[51] A significant area of focus in the current literature is the role of media in representing/misrepresenting and organizing the protests, including analyses of mainstream, student, and social media.[52] Social media, and Twitter in particular, became a critical virtual organizing space as access to physical space was restricted.[53] In some ways a freer platform, it was also a place where "truthfulness" was constructed and challenged,[54] and where virtual social exclusion and "othering" took place.[55]

Both media coverage and academic literature continue to predominantly focus on historically white English-language institutions, with a particular breadth of commentary on the University of Cape Town, University of the

---

49 Cini, "Disrupting the Neoliberal University in South Africa."
50 Costandius et al., "#FeesMustFall and Decolonising the Curriculum: Stellenbosch University Students' and Lecturers' Reactions"; and Le Grange, "Decolonising the University Curriculum."
51 Lewis and Hendricks, "Epistemic Ruptures in South African Standpoint Knowledge-Making"; Ndelu, Dlakavu, and Boswell, "Womxn's and Nonbinary Activists' Contribution to the RhodesMustFall and FeesMustFall Student Movements: 2015 and 2016"; Ndlovu, "Womxn's Bodies Reclaiming the Picket Line"; Ojakorotu and Olukayode, "FeesMustFall"; Shange, "Mappings of Feminist/Womanist Resistance within Student Movements across the African Continent"; and Xaba, "Challenging Fanon: A Black Radical Feminist Perspective on Violence and the Fees Must Fall Movement."
52 Bosch and Mutsvairo, "Pictures, Protests and Politics: Mapping Twitter Images during South Africa's Fees Must Fall Campaign"; De Jager, "Traditional News Platforms and Citizens' Reporting the News"; Kujeke, "Violence and the #FeesMustFall Movement at the University of KwaZulu-Natal," 85; and Langa, "Researching"; Ndelu et al., *#Hashtag: An Analysis of the #FeesMustFall Movement at South African Universities*.
53 Bosch, "Twitter and Participatory Citizenship"; Bosch, Luescher, and Makhubu, "Twitter and Student Leadership in South Africa"; Frassinelli, "Hashtags: #RhodesMustFall, #FeesMustFall and the Temporalities of a Meme Event"; Luescher, Loader, and Mugume, "#FeesMustFall: An Internet-Age Student Movement in South Africa and the Case of the University of the Free State"; and Ramluckan, Ally, and Van Niekerk, "Twitter Use in Student Protests."
54 Bosch and Mutsvairo. "Pictures," 71–89.
55 Mudavanhu, "Comrades, Students, Baboons and Criminals."

Witwatersrand, and Rhodes University.[56] There is less written on historically black and historically Afrikaans-language institutions. Geographically, few works of literature have focused on Pretoria-based institutions, with a few exceptions, including Paghuram et al.'s study of international students at the University of South Africa (UNISA), Nomvete and Mashayamombe's examination of the nonpartisan organizational structure of the University of Pretoria's (UP) #UPrising protests in 2015,[57] and Mavuso's personal account of protest involvement at Tshwane University of Technology (TUT).[58]

Methodology and Structure

This chapter seeks to highlight youth voices, drawing on interviews with student participants in the protests at two Pretoria universities and, more broadly, those who contributed to the critical online forum of mobilization and discourse. These two forms of data are examined with respect to the cultural creation of counternarratives with a focus on the relationship between the past and present and ideas of continuity and change. Our analysis centers on the reflections of the so-called born-free generation on the way their experiences have been depicted. We examine how they are redefining and understanding themselves in relation to the national historical narrative they have been taught which celebrates them without listening to their stories. With a focus on understudied institutions, we analyze how youth are rewriting the South African national text as a story of continuous struggle rather than liberation.

We draw on semistructured interviews conducted by Kenyon with nineteen participants in the #FeesMustFall protests who were students at Pretoria universities (UP and TUT) at the time of the protests. Contextualized by four months of fieldwork, these interviews focus on perceptions of continuity and change, experiences of exclusion and belonging, perceptions of past protests (particularly the Soweto Uprising), relationships across generations, heroes, and terminology.

---

56   Also referred to in the context of this movement as "The University Currently Known as Rhodes."
57   Nomvete and Mashayamombe, "South Africa's Fees Must Fall: The Case of #UPrising in 2015"; and Raghuram, Breines, and Gunter, "Beyond."
58   Mavuso, "My Personal Journey."

Geographically, these interviews focus on Pretoria. Sometimes referred to as the "whitest city in Africa,"[59] Pretoria is a place of multiple contestations. There is an ongoing movement to rename the city Tshwane, a name currently given to the broader metropolitan municipality. The city is physically marked by the Union Buildings, where Nelson Mandela was inaugurated and that honor him with a towering statue but also the hilltop Voortrekker monument commemorating the inland trek of Afrikaaner farmers and their battles with Zulu leaders and communities. The latter monument features a cenotaph marking the date of an Afrikaaner victory that became an apartheid-era holiday, subsequently renamed the Day of Reconciliation. The geography and social structures of the city thus provide a meaningful historical and contemporary backdrop to student protests that seek to reconcile their lives with a national rhetoric of transformation.

Within this city,[60] there is the prestigious, historically white and Afrikaans UP, and TUT, which formed from the merger of three technical institutes (technikons). UP has been described as "shaped by the reclamation of Pretoria as an Afrikaner capital" and has historically been referred to as one of the "intellectual bastions of apartheid."[61] Accounts from students in decades past have described the university as having an "authoritarian atmosphere" with pervasive racism and apartheid ideology.[62] The institution has since made considerable strides toward transformation, becoming a multiracial and, until recently, bilingual (English-Afrikaans) institution. Despite substantive and symbolic advances, the university continues to be characterized as conservative and faces significant challenges to full inclusion.[63] Regular questions are raised as to the depth and sincerity of change. Two local dimensions of the #FeesMustFall protests were language of instruction and corporatization. Concerns were raised about the ongoing teaching in Afrikaans and related marginalization and disadvantages faced by

---

59 "Tshwane has Largest Ratio of Whites in SA," South African Press Association (SAPA), January 24, 2013, https://www.iol.co.za/pretoria-news/tshwane-has-largest-ratio-of-whites-in-sa-1457957.

60 In addition to the mostly distance education of UNISA.

61 Sooryamoorthy, *Sociology in South Africa: Colonial, Apartheid and Democratic Forms*, 30.

62 Van der Waal, "Long Walk from Volkekunde to Anthropology," 20–22.

63 See, for example, one ongoing concern about accessibility of student housing: https://mg.co.za/article/2017-05-25-up-students-are-unhappy-with-racial-dynamics-in-residences/.

predominantly black non-Afrikaans-speaking students,[64] and about the increasingly corporate structure and terminology of the university.[65] UP eventually committed to ending instruction in Afrikaans as a result of the protests,[66] and, in response to students protesting, "We are not clients" reversed the renaming of the Student Centre (from Client Centre).[67]

TUT is a postapartheid, nine-campus, "mega university" that has grown to be the largest contact university in South Africa.[68] Formed in 2004 with the merger of Technikon Northern Gauteng, Technikon North-West, and Technikon Pretoria, TUT offers a range of areas of study including technical, vocational, and academic fields. The university's slogan is "We empower people" and, in contrast with UP where student protests are unusual, protests (including fee-related protests) are common.

To place the Pretoria participant interviews in a broader national context, we examine the #FeesMustFall hashtag on Twitter. After compiling a list of more than 150 protest-related hashtags, we used Hashtagify.me to determine popularity and country of origin.[69] The #FeesMustFall hashtag was selected because it was widely and overwhelmingly used in South Africa), applied to campuses throughout the country, had longevity throughout the different iterations of the protests, and was less issue- or campus-specific than other hashtags (i.e., #OutsourcingMustFall, #AfrikaansMustFall, etc.). Python[1] scripts were then coded to access Twitter's paid premium Application Programming Interface.[2] Tweets were retrieved between October 1, 2015,

---

64 See "Afrikaans Scrapped at South Africa's University of Pretoria," https://www.bbc.com/news/world-africa-47001468.
65 For example, University of Pretoria Vice-Chancellor Cheryl de la Rey's award for "businesswoman of the year" (see https://www.up.ac.za/business-management/news/post_2556244-up-vice-chancellor-is-businesswoman-of-the-year-winner-for-education), use of the term "client" instead of student, and financial-based exclusion of students.
66 "University of Pretoria: Frequently Asked Questions," University of Pretoria, accessed June 29, 2020, https://www.up.ac.za/faq.
67 Van Marle, "A 'Right' to the University."
68 "Tshwane University of Technology: About Campuses," Tshwane University of Technology, accessed June 29, 2020, https://www.tut.ac.za/other/campuses/about; "Tshwane University of Technology: Strategic Plan 2008–2012," Tshwane University of Technology, archived April 29, 2010, https://web.archive.org/web/20100429220230/http://www.tut.ac.za/About%20Us/.
69 We used this to determine geographic origin where tweets were geolocated.

and January 1, 2017.[70] Within these tweets we conducted an analysis of the ways in which the term "born free" is used and referenced with a focus on the themes outlined above.

Interviews: Telling Our Own Story

"'Born free,' it's cute. It's really cute, but it's a lie."[71]

South Africa's narrative of liberation highlights the break from an oppressive apartheid regime to an era of equality and freedom. It is premised on decisive change, and fresh, new beginnings. The "born free" generation, a label given to those born after 1994, are the first generation to have been raised in the "new" South Africa. They are meant to be the first to benefit from a nonracial system, unweighted by the country's traumatic history and living lives characterized by optimism, equality, and endless possibilities. But what is it like to be the generation that heralds a new era? To be the namesake for freedom and a better life? Do the eldest of this generation, now adults, accept the label that has been placed upon them? In interviews, #FeesMustFall participants reported a strong sense of emotional attachment to the term "born free," with several confessing that they "loved" or "used to love" it. The phrase, however, sparked conflicting emotions. Participants largely bought into the narrative of progress and optimism taught to them as children. Going to university often coincided with a coming of age characterized, in part, by disillusionment with the stories they had been told about their nation and their place within it. Students were often highly invested in this narrative of optimism, and it could be hard to give up on the dream they had been promised as children. One student, born in 1994, described her complex, evolving relationship with the term as she matured. She noted that as a child "it was so cool" and "so monumental to be born in '94" but that the glow of the label wore off as she aged.[72] She explained, "There is media coverage about your generation, 'you're different, you're different because

---

70   This is slightly broader than the timeframe of protests. The earliest retrieved tweet from this search was from October 13.
71   Interviewee 13.
72   Interviewee 14.

you're born free.' It is kind of soul crushing to have been raised on that—and then to see the cracks."[73]

Most participants rejected or disagreed with the term, describing it as a "joke," a "marketing tool," or a deliberate act of deceptive labeling. One student noted, "I think it's inherently dangerous (like 'rainbow nation') because it allows us to slap a label on something that is not even remotely close to what it is."[74] Another participant similarly described the label as "very misrepresenting" as it "created the façade of a free South Africa."[75] "Born free" was identified as "one of the phrases developed during the promotion of the rainbow democracy" acting as a "kind of a catch phrase to give a positive spin on something that isn't positive."[76] A student explained:

> When you wake up in the morning and go to class, we have to pretend sometimes that everything's okay, because someone can't be able to see in your stomach how hungry you are, what did you eat and all stuff like that. And yet, when you see on television, South Africa is portrayed as this most incredible country that has overcome racism and unity.[77]

The young participants often found it difficult to reconcile their experiences of struggle and inequality with the "positive spin" narrative showcasing the nation's progress.

Participants highlighted the contrast between political freedoms and enduring economic inequality. One student explained that while they now were free of the segregated Bantu education system, and black students were now "in the same buildings" as their white classmates, they "don't have the means to be there."[78] Similarly, another participant questioned what "freedom" was actually being celebrated, describing it as "sharing the same toilet as white people and eating in the same restaurant as them . . . or getting in the same coach, train or whatever," rather than a more substantive equality.[79] Another noted that while there was now the ability to affiliate with different political parties and structures, that this is the "only thing we're celebrating,"

---

73   Interviewee 14.
74   Interviewee 18.
75   Interviewee 16.
76   Interviewee 12.
77   Interviewee 3.
78   Interviewee 5.
79   Interviewee 4.

noting "I genuinely don't believe that we are a free."[80] The "freedom" they were told they had continued to be an experience of economic exclusion.

> You cannot really wake up and say that you are born free, you are not free. The doors are still very closed, they are shut on the face of black poor population. The doors of the economic participation are still closed and still shut for the face of the black poor and so forth. The doors of opportunities in this country and ownership and everything are still closed, the only doors that are open were the doors of the cells of Nelson Mandela and political freedom, but all other doors remains shut with a very with a key that has been thrown somewhere in Europe.[81]

"Born free" is premised on radical change that students had not experienced. As one student noted, "'born free' feels like a joke to me also because I hear these stories about apartheid and I still feel like many of them exist."[82] These voices in many ways convey the pessimism, concerns, and anxieties of a young generation designated as free, equal, and privileged by the national narrative yet confronted daily by a reality marked by old prejudices and obstacles. Unlike the crisp definition of "born free" as post-1994, students who saw nothing clear and decisive about the transition often interpreted the term with hazier boundaries, seeing similarities for those born on either side of the divide in the 1990s and, in some cases, identifying more with other generational terms such as "millennial."

Aluta Continua: *"Is This Just a Continuation or Is It the Reboot of Something?"*[83]

#FeesMustFall had an obvious historical parallel in the 1976 Soweto Uprising. The 1976 protest defined a generation, galvanized political resistance, and has been commemorated in museums and on the national calendar. Forty years later, when reflecting on the largest student protests during and after apartheid, interview participants overwhelmingly viewed their own protests as an expression of continuity in the broader black South African struggle. One participant highlighted struggle as the key and ongoing feature

---

80   Interviewee 20.
81   Interviewee 9.
82   Interview 21.
83   Interviewee 4.

of South African history, stating, "I think South Africa as we know it, some call it a nameless country, has been in protests since the sixteen hundreds, we've never stopped."[84] Students also highlighted the role of youth, noting that both were examples of "young people . . . standing up for themselves [and] demanding change."[85] Participants also spoke about the ways in which the movement built on a canon of advocacy even though the organizing space had changed markedly since 1976. One student explained:

> I do think that the way the #FeesMustFall played out is the way other historical protest movements have emerged and developed and come to the surface and come into action. We use the format that has been shown to us through history.[86]

This comment, and others like it, recognizes protest itself as an expression of continuity and as a constant across numerous social and political changes in South Africa.

Students often remarked that the protests were the same because fundamental conditions had not changed. One participant noted, "It's *still* a struggle of access to resources or access to spaces,"[87] with another adding, "It's not different. There's so many similarities."[88] They argued that while divisions of race and class were "not as clearly demarcated as before," the divisions themselves persisted in the postapartheid[89] period, and the #FeesMustFall protests must be seen against this landscape of continued oppression and viewed as "the latest manifestation" of earlier protests and "the latest in an attempt to change the system."[90] Participants noted that although students may come together across lines of race and class on campus, they may return home to vastly different realities in a still-segregated spatial landscape. One student described a "ticking time bomb" for the governing ANC, explaining, "this person is not only a student here, they are going back to Mamelodi [91] not to have water, to walk in the dusty roads."[92] Gendered differences also featured

---

84 Interviewee 15.
85 Interviewee 19.
86 Interviewee 12.
87 Interviewee 2.
88 Interviewee 20.
89 This is terminology some rejected, referring instead to "neoapartheid."
90 Interviewee 2.
91 A former township now part of the Metropolitan Municipality of Tshwane.
92 Interviewee 3.

prominently in interviews with female participants, one of whom explained the lack of access to sanitary products on campus as signaling which bodies were seen to belong in the university space.[93] These different realities shape students' experience of university and their ability to fully benefit from higher education.

Ties across time were reinforced by "archive diving"[94] done by protesters who unearthed and re-used 1994 ANC election posters emblazoned with the slogans FREE EDUCATION NOW and VOTE ANC FOR NO FEES AT THE UNIVERSITY LEVEL.[95] The commemoration of Youth Day marking the Soweto Uprising was also seen to hold potential for recognizing ongoing youth struggles. One respondent noted a need to "come together" between generations and "have one holiday where we get to commemorate and talk about it and celebrate and find a way forward and make sure that we keep that history alive."[96]

Students in the Soweto Uprising protested for access to education and specifically against the mandatory introduction of widespread instruction in Afrikaans, a language few of them or their teachers were fluent in. Afrikaans instruction was seen not only as the "language of the oppressor" but also as an educational strategy that, in the context of inadequate resources, training, and fluency, would result in worsening the already insufficient education offered to black children under apartheid. A generation or so later, #FeesMustFall protesters noted the struggle to access quality education remained and that language of instruction continued to be an issue at institutions offering courses in Afrikaans, like UP. One participant explained:

> [I]n 1976 the protest that embarked, it was on a basis of the #AfrikaansMustFall, it was on a basis of the quality of education and we're still speaking the same language even today. You know, we're still saying we want quality education. They wanted free education. We still want free education. So in a nutshell I would say . . . the premises, yes, the reasons are still the same.[97]

---

93   Gender featured prominently in interviews with female participants and was mostly peripheral among male respondents (all participants identified as either male or female). A thorough examination of these important angles is beyond the scope of this paper; see note 50 for more scholarship in this area.
94   Interviewee 4.
95   Interviewee 4.
96   Interviewee 20.
97   Interviewee 1.

Another student explained that "back then" they "were never provided the resources to actually learn in their own languages" noting, "[t]here's so many Afrikaans books, textbooks, but they were never in Zulu" or "in our own languages," noting that the #FeesMustFall protests were therefore "just a continuation"[98] as they tackled many of the same issues.[99] Students argued that they continued to face structural barriers in accessing education including funding, distance from good schools, and the lack of access to education in their first languages. The latter was a particularly contentious issue at the bilingual (English-Afrikaans) UP where white Afrikaans-speaking students had access to first-language education, but black students necessarily studied in their second or other subsequent languages.[100] Students protested against this disparity but also noted inequities in class sizes, access to instructors, and information provided between classes offered in Afrikaans and English. They argued that the quality of education for those taught in English was affected by "subsidized" Afrikaans education for a smaller group and that this linguistic division led to better education for some more than others.

While participants largely recognized similarities in conditions and in the purpose of protest, some respondents acknowledged differences in composition, organization, technique, and police response. Some respondents noted the university students participating in #FeesMustFall were, by definition, more privileged than the schoolchildren involved in the Soweto Uprising as they had managed to access a place at a university. Participants also commented on the methods of organization, including the use of social media and the scale of protests. However, the dominant observation of difference focused on the police response. Participants spoke of the greater police violence against students in 1976, with one participant stating bluntly "then they shot the student to kill them, here they just tried to disband them."[101] Respondents recognized a similar legacy, however, noting the use of "hippos" (tactical police vehicles), the passing down of protest advice from parents (i.e., bring a bandana) and shared experience of lingering trauma, commenting that participants in both protests "have sort of trauma that is still there, that they cannot stand fireworks."[102]

---

98   Interviewee 20.
99   This student does not acknowledge Bantu education under apartheid, which did use Indigenous African languages but offered markedly inferior education.
100 Afrikaans is not an exclusively white language, however, in the UP context the racial divide was reflected in the division of languages of instruction.
101 Interviewee 4.
102 Interviewee 5.

In reflecting on their own recent experiences of protest and the historically celebrated Soweto Uprising, which some saw as a critical turning point in antiapartheid activism, students overwhelmingly highlighted themes of continuity. They noted similar socioeconomic and racial divisions, similar struggles for education, similar youth activism and, at UP, an echoing of educational language politics. In both protests the struggle for education was not "just" about education but about education as the pathway to social mobility and, post-1994, the catalyst for a more equal South Africa. Thus, anything inhibiting access to full and meaningful participation in higher education was understood as inhibiting movement toward equality and protecting an unequal status quo with its roots in South Africa's history of codified racial segregation.

"My Father Was a Garden Boy, My Mother Was a Kitchen Girl": Talking about #FeesMustFall across Generations[103]

Beyond the direct comparison of the 1976 and 2015–16 protests, students highlighted similarity rather than difference through the apartheid to post-apartheid period. Repurposing "My Mother," a song of class consciousness invoked in socialist and union settings, protestors used the song to signal unity in their struggle as well as intergenerational inequality. Many noted that their "struggles don't really differ much" from those of their parents.[104] Students tried to reconcile similar struggles in a different political environment, often explaining that while their parents had fought for political freedom, students used this freedom to protest against the lack of economic freedom. One student, however, explained that without economic freedom your "political freedom increasingly becomes meaningless," describing the antiapartheid struggle as the continuing "struggle against the de-racialization of wealth in this country."[105] Others looked further back in history to trace the experiences of injustice of their families, noting that land ownership and

---

103 Paulos Lekala Marutha, "FMF 2016 Nobody Wanna See Us Together—Yamekla Gola Ft Wits Students," October 14, 2016, https://www.youtube.com/watch?v=mFmRA2U5-pQ.
104 Interviewee 13.
105 Interviewee 9.

the lack thereof is based on and perpetuates inequality, explaining "my gran can point . . . I grew up there, but that's not ours anymore."[106]

According to students, parents had a variety of reactions to their participation in protests ranging from disapproval ("Why are you wasting your education?"), concern ("Stay away, be careful") to pride ("We had our fight, this is yours"). To some extent these reactions varied according to the parents' own experiences. The small number of white students involved in the protests noted they often faced disapproval, and some were "literally on a no talking terms policy . . . because of it."[107] By contrast, black students might hear, "Yes, my child, you go back into the streets, that is what your father and I fought for 30 years ago, you continue the fight."[108] One respondent noted that the variation itself showed the ways in which the protests demonstrated a continuum from the apartheid period.

For some, mostly black students, participation was a form of intergenerational solidarity. One student explained that the reason she participated is because her parents "participated in a very similar protest."[109] Two others spoke of how their parents have said "here's the baton," and "it's on you now."[110] Several students reported their parents being proud of them for "fighting for justice"[111] and "becom[ing] politically active in [their] way."[112] The pride and continuity, however, was often couched in both fear and pain. Many families had made massive sacrifices to send their children to university, and the prospects of not graduating sparked enormous parental worry. Parents worried too about arrests, physical harm, and exhaustion. The familiarity of the struggle often brought pain for black parents:

> Especially with my dad, I hear his voice change I see eyes well up. I know he's very proud, but it just reminds him of what they had to go through. I think it hurts me too because they fought, and you know everyone believed there was going to be this big change. I think when you are fighting for something you believe in . . . you really don't expect some twenty years later for your children to be doing the same thing.[113]

---

106 Interviewee 10.
107 Interviewee 4.
108 Interviewee 4.
109 Interviewee 12.
110 Interviewees 10 and 11.
111 Interviewee 1.
112 Interviewee 12.
113 Interviewee 12.

Many students recounted significant trauma from their experiences in the protests, and this gave them insight into the experiences of their parents. There could, however, be misunderstandings between generations. One student described his grandparents' reaction:

> They said "What was the issue? I thought you guys went to school?" but they don't understand that, yes, we did go to school, but going to school had its own issues and those were the issues of money. You know, the space is not as welcoming as you guys think it is. . . . For them it's like "Go to school. Why are you guys not going to school? Why are you guys burning this?" type of a thing.[114]

Students also spoke with a sense of both responsibility, possibility, and burden of those who came before and after them. One student explained that education was considered a collective investment, "when parents send you to school they send you with the hope that one day when you complete you will come and change the situation back at home."[115] Another student explained that "our struggles as university students, it's not only based on us. It's based on the coming generations, the ones that are still in school."[116] While for some this was abstract, for many students it was both personal and concrete in the form of cousins and siblings that they wanted to follow in their footsteps with a greater sense of ease and belonging. One student noted, "I have a little sister who just turned five, so I don't want it to be that difficult for her to go to university, so it's not just about me, it's about future generations as well, those who will come after us."[117]

"iYho Solomon": New Heroes

Political and historical figures invoked in the protests contrasted with those heralded in the dominant postapartheid narrative, celebrating people such as Solomon Mahlangu, a young ANC operative whose education was interrupted by the Soweto Uprising and who was executed for murder at age twenty-two. In addition to Mahlangu, South African antiapartheid figures Steve Biko, Robert Sobukwe, and Winnie Madikizela Mandela topped the list of those referenced in interviews in a positive or inspirational context

---

114 Interviewee 2.
115 Interviewee 1.
116 Interviewee 20.
117 Interviewee 12.

alongside former president of Burkina Faso Thomas Sankara. Beyond the continent, respondents mentioned Latin American Marxists Fidel Castro and Che Guevara and American minister and activist Martin Luther King. Participants also listed writers from whom they drew an "alternative curriculum" and who informed the movement's "political schools." These included Karl Marx, *Pedagogy of the Oppressed* founder Paolo Freire, Marxist and critical theorist Franz Fanon, Pan-Africanist and civil rights scholar William Edward Burghardt Du Bois, anthropologist and politician Cheik Anta Diop, and writer, playwright and former prisoner of conscience Ngugi wa Thiong'o.[118] When citing these works, however, they "made [them] their own" seeing themselves as uniquely and appropriately capable of interpreting the meaning of literature in their own surroundings, "translating it in terms of their own understanding, what it meant to them and how it would work for them."[119]

Some students found examples closer to home, listing their peers, friends, family, and even themselves as protest heroes or inspirations. One student described her parents as her "freedom fighters" even though "their names aren't on top of buildings" adding that student leadership also provided her with peers she could both "look up to" and "relate to."[120] In both instances she noted that these were heroes she had personal relationships with. Rather than deified abstractions they were people alive during her lifetime who had a tangible impact on her life. Another participant described how they sang songs referencing struggle heroes, adding that "we even managed to use our own names,"[121] inserting themselves into the lyrics. In doing so they made a powerful claim to agency, arguing that they might be heroes, that they might have a place in an alternative national narrative and in future history books, and that they could be their own liberators.

In identifying heroes, students draw from and respond to texts of popular culture that recount and celebrate South African history in particular

---

118 Respondents also mentioned the writing of African American feminists Angela Davis and Maya Angelou, as well as local scholar Melissa Steyn, the South African national chair in critical diversity studies at the University of the Witwatersrand. Participants also made reference to prominent figures in the Western canon of political theory including Michel Foucault, Hannah Arendt, Immanuel Kant, Martin Heidegger, John Locke, and Georg Wilhelm Friedrich Hegel.
119 Interview 16.
120 Interview 16.
121 Interview 15.

ways. Students were not only, however, drawing from this collective historical canon but also situating themselves, their peers, and their parents within the contemporary evolving history of South Africa by contesting the idea that heroes needed to be well known, dead, or in the past. In doing so, they adeptly weave together diverse cultural, historical, and contemporary threads to create a new popular canon of youth protest which adapts, reinterprets, selects, rejects, and repurposes known materials and interlaces them with lived experience and known contemporaries. This act highlights text as a deliberately manufactured creation that emanates from and reflects positionality and power, both in the text rejected by student protesters and by the alternative text they are collaboratively enacting.

"Rise of the Born Frees": Creating Culture Online

While on-the-ground mobilization is the main form that the #FeesMustFall protests have taken, the voices of this generation, including those who participated in or supported these protests were also heard and circulated on social media (primarily Twitter). Although the physical manifestations of #FeesMustFall took place in concrete places, the organizing space was largely virtual. As physical space became limited and policed, Twitter became a key site through which to gather, discuss, organize, and disseminate information. As Dahlgren argues, the "web environment constitutes a key social site"[122] for young people and is not a place that they "'visit' on occasion in order to seek something special; the net and social media are increasingly part of the terrain of their daily lives."[123]

The 394 tweets that referenced the term "born free" within the #FeesMustFall hashtag, while diverse, reflected themes consistent with those in the interview data. First, the tweets often reflected an expression of continuity and frustration with the application of a celebratory label to an experience of ongoing struggle. Many of those tweeting viewed this as a label of hypocrisy. A plaintive tweet asked: "Rewind to 1994. Who would've thought 'born frees' would be going through so much two decades later?" (@asapshak, October 10, 2016). Tweeters, like the students interviewed, highlighted the contrast between political and economic freedom, stating, "We were never free, talking about 'born frees' We want economic freedom too not the bs [*sic*]

---

122 Dahlgren, "Youth Citizens and Political Participation," 11.
123 Dahlgren, "Youth," 14.

our government fed us" (@athelia_twala, October 15, 2016). (The idea of being taught or sold a story of South Africa that did not align with reality was also prominent. One person describing the "rise of the born frees" noted, "we have been sold dreams, now see us get woke" (@Mpatshi, October 5, 2016). This tweet and others like it reflect a coming of age paired with a disillusionment in the optimistic narrative they had been taught and the rose-colored aspirations ascribed to the "born free" generation. The theme of repressed or concealed topics was also highlighted. One person tweeted in 2016, "Issues that had been swept under the carpet for so long. It's not coincidental that #FeesMustFall surfaced when born frees turned 21" (February 23, 2016). This latter comment also speaks to the power of a generation coming into their own and, as adults, claiming their own priorities and narratives.

Although Twitter is a youthful medium, intergenerational dialogue, perceptions, and stereotypes also played out on this social media platform. Many, directly or indirectly identifying as belonging to an older generation, showed pride and admiration for what they saw as youth having "grown up and found their voice" (@ExploringSA, October 2, 2015) and "showing South African[s] what being free stands for " (@bububutafly, October 2015). Some parents took to Twitter to express their pride in their children, with one parent tweeting, "Pretty proud of my 'born free' child for being part of this transformation consciousness #FeesMustFall" (@ShobanaMeakhan, October 22, 2015). In describing their support for #FeesMustFall participants netizens described themselves as "pretty proud," "super proud," and flagged their tweets with the hashtag #respect. In reflecting their pride, tweeters often rejected the term "born free," stating for example, "So inspired to see born free's that aren't free fighting for free education, it's true born free's not yet born" (October 22, 2015 and "Never have I been so proud of these kids they incorrectly refer to as 'born frees'" (@ditybooks24, October 22, 2015).

Of course, social media is not only a platform for adulation, and critics also utilized Twitter to express their critiques and concerns, identifying what they saw as a different manifestation of hypocrisy. Some saw the generation as holding a "mind boggling sense of entitlement" and being "boring" and full of unreasonable complaints. These tweets often reflected a frustration with the younger generation, seeing them as unwilling to pull their weight in the capitalist economic system. For example, one tweet stated, "If I want groceries I must pay. If I want cell phone I must pay. If I want to study I must pay. Why born frees so special?" (January 13, 2016) Despite its brevity, this tweet reflects a clear position categorizing education as a commercial good, accessible through fees, alongside other goods and services. Describing "born frees" as "want[ing] it all free free free" (March 2, 2016), others stated, "wake me up when the Born Frees start with #TaxMustFall" (October 23, 2015). Reflecting a similar sentiment another person tweeted, "#FeesMustFall are not freedom-fighters, they're freebie-fighters. Born Frees want it all free! Someone else must pay" (January 13, 2016). These tweets suggest a frustration with "born frees," seeing them not as contributors to the economy and tax base but only as potential beneficiaries. Interestingly, these critiques reflect some of the socioeconomic arguments made by #FeesMustFall participants, that to be full members of society they must pay, and while they have a voice to express their grievances, they continue to lack the money required for entry.

Discussion: *"To Be Young Means to Think without Limits and Never Stop Questioning the Status Quo"*[124]

A nascent literature is starting to emerge from the so-called born free generation as they begin to formally create texts of their own and concrete cultural artifacts that can be read, circulated, and cited. In his memoir, *Born In Chains: Diary of An Angry 'Born Free,'* Chauke notes that "reflecting at the age of twenty-three may be very uncommon indeed," as "[o]ften in South Africa, it is the old and accomplished who share their stories" while "[t]he youth are left to one side."[125] He argues for the youth to tell their own stories and, in recounting his own, notes that "politically, we are free, but economically we are still far behind," calling on his "fellow young people to lift their thoughts, to question everything and be courageous."[126]

Wa Azania's *Diary of a Born Free* similarly tells her own life story and rejects the illusion of freedom. She argues that the construction of the narrative of liberation, built "as apartheid was being dismantled in South Africa" served to "distract . . . attentions from a global array of various 'new apartheids.'"[127] In the author's note to the published script of *The Fall*, a powerful play about the University of Cape Town's #RhodesMustFall and #FeesMustFall protests written and performed by protest participants, Conrad et al. explains, "Currently, colonisation continues to haunt us materially, socially and

---

124 Clinton Chauke, *Born in Chains: The Diary of an Angry Born Free*, 2.
125 Chauke, *Born*, 2.
126 Chauke, 2.
127 Azania, *Memoirs of a Born Free*, 4.

psychologically. Students, workers and academics all over South Africa are taking it upon themselves to tackle the continuing, silent, traumatic effects of oppression in South Africa."[128] As University of Cape Town scholar Leigh-Ann Naidoo argues, the #FeesMustFall protests are a powerful moment for recognition and action. She states that the "student movement has been the single most significant movement to have woken government from its growing estrangement from the demands and needs of the people," calling on government and society to "take seriously" the "voices and questions of the youth of South Africa" and "engage . . . in a manner that will allow for all us to contribute to building a better country and world."[129]

These authors, like participants in our research, argue that 1994 is not a magical moment of profound change, reflecting instead a youth narrative of disillusionment in line with Diouf's theorizing.[130] The term "born free" is ill-fitting, as it is premised on both the idea of a specific moment of transformation and of a life characterized by unprecedented freedom. As they "question everything" this generation calls attention to how their dreams have been "deferred" rather than realized[131] and demands the means to better themselves and their country. Mannheim describes generations as a "particular kind of identity location."[132] The so-called born free generation holds an identity that speaks to the timing of their birth and coming of age even as they reject the term and dispel the nation's change-based narrative in favor of an account emphasizing continued inequality and ongoing struggle. While they do not reject their generational cohort, the millennials or "born unfrees"[133] question clean lines of before and after and seek to question and reconstitute labels and categories and their meanings.

South Africa's #FeesMustFall protests draw on cultural artifacts, seeking to build a new protest culture and discourse that challenges and deconstructs South Africa's dominant narrative of progress, unity, and reconciliation in ways that claim space for conversations and action on the country's entrenched inequality. They seek, to use Peterson's words, to use culture to "liberate" themselves from the oppressive narratives of liberation to which they feel they have been disingenuously subjected. In doing so, they are

---

128 Conrad et al., *The Fall.*
129 Naidoo, "Contemporary," 189–90.
130 Diouf, "Engaging Postcolonial Cultures."
131 Mpofu, "Disruption as a Communicative Strategy."
132 Mannheim, "Problem of Generations."
133 Mabasa, "Rebellion of the Born Un-Frees."

articulating, through songs, through tweets, and through literature, a narrative of painful continuation that seeks to radically unsettle the heroic tale of change built around their generation. Through this practice they enact Barber's vision of the potential of popular culture by deconstructing and reconstructing meaning from available and created cultural artifacts and forming and communicating a new consciousness. In challenging the dominant South African national historical text, they are redefining who they are, questioning what South Africa represents, and calling for a new and more meaningful form of freedom. In creative and varied ways South Africa's youth are claiming virtual and physical space and demanding to speak for themselves and tell their own stories. As Chauke, Naidoo, and others argue, it is time for us to listen.

Bibliography

Baines, Gary. "The Master Narrative of South Africa's Liberation Struggle: Remembering and Forgetting June 16, 1976." *International Journal of African Historical Studies* 40, no. 2 (2007): 283–302.

Bandile, Bertrand Leopeng. "A Response to Habib." In *Rioting and Writing: Diaries of the Wits Fallists*, edited by Crispen Chinguno, MorwaKgoroba, Sello Mashibini, Nicolas Bafana Masilela, Boikhutso Maubane, Nhlanhla Moyo, Andile Mthombeni, and Hlengiwe Ndlovu, 89–101. Johannesburg: Society, Work, and Development Institute, University of the Witwatersrand, 2017.

Barber, Karin. "Introduction." In *Readings in African Popular Culture*, edited by Karin Barber and Tom Young, 1–11. Bloomington: Indiana University Press, 1997.

———. "Popular Arts in Africa." *African Studies Review* 30, no. 3 (1987): 1–78.

Beinart, William, and Saul Dubow. "Introduction: The Historiography of Segregation and Apartheid." In *Segregation and Apartheid in Twentieth Century South Africa*, edited by William Beinart and Saul Dubow, 1–24. London: Routledge, 2013.

Benford, Robert D., and David A. Snow. "Framing Processes and Social Movements: An Overview and Assessment." *Annual Review of Sociology* 26 (2000): 611–39.

Bhekizizwe, Peterson. "Youth and Student Culture: Riding Resistance and Imagining the Future." In *Students Must Rise: Youth Struggle in South Africa Before and Beyond Soweto '76*, edited by Anne Heffernan and Noor Nieftagodien, 16–23. Johannesburg: Wits University Press, 2016.

Booysen, Susan, ed. *Fees Must Fall: Student Revolt, Decolonisation and Governance in South Africa*. Johannesburg: Wits University Press, 2016.

Booysen, Susan. "Two Weeks in October: Changing Governance in South Africa." In *Fees Must Fall: Student Revolt, Decolonization and Governance in South Africa*, edited by Susan Booysen, 22–52. Johannesburg: Wits University Press, 2016.

Booysen, Susan, and Kuda Bandama. "Appendix." In *Fees Must Fall: Student Revolt, Decolonization and Governance in South Africa*, edited by Susan Booysen. Johannesburg: Wits University Press, 2016. 316-327.

Bosch, Tanja. "Twitter and Participatory Citizenship: #FeesMustFall in South Africa." In *Digital Activism in the Social Media Era*, edited by Bruce Mutsvairo, 159–73. London: Palgrave Macmillan, 2016.

Bosch, Tanja, and Bruce Mutsvairo. "Pictures, Protests and Politics: Mapping Twitter Images during South Africa's Fees Must Fall Campaign." *African Journalism Studies* 38, no. 2 (December 5, 2017): 71–89. https://doi.org/10.1080/23744367 0.2017.1368869.

Bosch, Tanja, Thierry M. Luescher, and Nkululeko Makhubu. "Twitter and Student Leadership in South Africa." In *Power Shift? Political Leadership and Social Media: Case Studies in Political Communication*, edited by David Taras, and Richard Davis. New York: Routledge, 2019.

British Broadcasting Corporation. "South Africa #FeesMustFall: Stories Behind the Protests." 2015. http:// www.bbc.com/news/world-africa-34592527.

Chauke, Clinton. *Born in Chains: The Diary of an Angry 'Born Free.'* Johannesburg: Jonathan Ball, 2018.

Chinguno, Crispen, Morwa Kgoroba, Sello Mashibini, Bafana Nicolas Masilela, Boikhutso Maubane, Nhlanhla Moyo, Andile Mthombeni, and Hlengiwe Ndlovu, eds. *Rioting and Writing: Diaries of the Wits Fallists*. Johannesburg: Society, Work and Development Institute, University of the Witwatersrand, 2017.

Cini, Lorenzo. "Disrupting the Neoliberal University in South Africa: The #FeesMustFall Movement in 2015." *Current Sociology* 67, no. 7 (September 12, 2019): 942–59. https://doi.org/10.1177/0011392119865766.

Cmoloi, Kholeka, Malegapuru W. Makgoba, and Collins Ogutu Miruka. "(De)Constructing the #FessMustFall Campaign in South African Higher Education." *Contemporary Education Dialogue* 14, no. 2 (2017): 211–23. https://doi.org/10.1177/0973184917716999.

Conrad, Ameera, Cleo Raatus, Kgomotso Khunoane, Orabile Ditsele, Sihle Mnqwazana, Sizwesandile Mnisi, Tankiso Mamabolo, and Thando Mangcu. *The Fall*. Cape Town: Junkets, 2017.

Costandius, E., M. Blackie, I. Nell, R. Malgas, N. Alexander, E. Setati, and M. Mckay. "#FeesMustFall and Decolonising the Curriculum: Stellenbosch University Students' and Lecturers' Reactions." *South African Journal of Higher Education* 32, no. 2 (2018): 65–85. https://doi.org/10.20853/32-2-2435.

Dahlgren, Peter. "Youth Citizens and Political Participation: Online Media and Civic Cultures." *Taiwan Journal of Democracy* 7, no. 2 (2011): 11–25.

De Jager, Tinus. "Traditional News Platforms and Citizens' Reporting the News: The Use of Social Media during the '#Feesmustfall' Campaign in South Africa." *Innovation: Journal of Appropriate Librarianship and Information Work in Southern Africa* 2016, no. 52 (June 2016): 36–50. https://journals.co.za/content/innovation/2016/52/EJC194632.

Diouf, Mamadou. "Engaging Postcolonial Cultures: The African Youth and the Public Space." *African Studies Review* 46, no. 1 (2003): 1–12.

Drayton, Richard. "Rhodes Must Not Fall? Statues, Postcolonial 'Heritage' and Temporality." *Third Text* 33, no. 4–5 (October 25, 2019): 651–66. https://doi.org/10.1080/09528822.2019.1653073.

Evans, Joanna Ruth. "Unsettled Matters, Falling Flight: Decolonial Protest and the Becoming-Material of an Imperial Statue." *TDR* 62, no. 3 (September 2018): 130–44. https://doi.org/10.1162/dram_a_00775.

Frassinelli, Pier Paolo. "Hashtags: #RhodesMustFall, #FeesMustFall and the Temporalities of a Meme Event." In *Perspectives on Political Communication in Africa*, edited by Bruce Mutsvairo and Beschara Sharlene Karam, 61–76. London: Palgrave Macmillan, 2018.

Geertz, Clifford. *The Interpretation of Cultures: Selected Essays*. New York: Basic Books, 2017.

Govinder, Kesh S., Nombuso P. Zondo, and Malegapuru W. Makgoba. *South African Journal of Science* 109, no. 11–12 (January 2013): 1–11. https://pdfs.semanticscholar.org/2479/d464cff6e9e8b2758238d49f598d89af4b2f.pdf.

Habib, Adam. *Rebels and Rage: Reflecting on #FeesMustFall*. Johannesburg: Jonathan Ball, 2019.

Hodes, Rebecca. "Questioning 'Fees Must Fall.'" *African Affairs* 116, no. 462 (January 1, 2017): 140–50. https://doi.org/10.1093/afraf/adw072.

Hollanda, Cristina Buarque de. "Human Rights and Political Transition in South Africa: The Case of the Truth and Reconciliation Commission." *Brazilian Political Science Review* 7, no. 1 (2013): 8–30. http://dx.doi.org/10.1590/S1981-38212013000100001.

Jansen, Jonathan D. *As by Fire: The End of the South African University*. Cape Town: Tafelberg, 2017.

Jolaosho, Omotayo. "Singing Politics: Freedom Songs and Collective Protest in Post-Apartheid South Africa." *African Studies Review* 62, no. 2 (June 2019): 6–29, https://doi.org/10.1017/asr.2018.16.

Kenyon, Kristi Heather. *Resilience and Contagion: Invoking Human Rights in HIV Advocacy*. Montreal: McGill-Queens University Press, 2017.

Kros, Cynthia. "Rhodes Must Fall: Archives and Counter-Archives." *Critical Arts* 29 (November 26, 2015): 150–65. https://doi.org/10.1080/02560046.2015.1102270.

Kujeke, Muneinazvo. "Violence and the #FeesMustFall Movement at the University of KwaZulu-Natal." In *#Hashtag: An Analysis of the #FeesMustFall Movement at South African Universities*, edited by Malose Langa, 83–96. Johannesburg: Centre for the Study of Violence and Reconciliation, 2017. https://csvr.org.za/pdf/An-analysis-of-the-FeesMustFall-Movement-at-South-African-universities.pdf#page=85.

Langa, Malose. "Researching the #FeesMustFall Movement." In *#Hashtag: An Analysis of the #FeesMustFall Movement at South African Universities*, edited by Malose Langa, 6–12. Johannesburg: Centre for the Study of Violence and Reconciliation, 2017. http://csvr.org.za/pdf/An-analysis-of-the-FeesMustFall-Movement-at-South-African-universities.pdf#page=8.

Le Grange, L. "Decolonising the University Curriculum." *South African Journal of Higher Education* 30, no. 2 (January 2016): 1–12. https://doi.org/10.20853/30-2-709.

Lewis, Desiree, and Cheryl Margaret Hendricks. "Epistemic Ruptures in South African Standpoint Knowledge-Making: Academic Feminism and the #FeesMustFall Movement." *Gender Questions* 4, no. 1 (November 30, 2017): 1–21. https://doi.org/10.25159/2412-8457/2920.

Luescher, Thierry M., Lacea Loader, and Taabo Mugume. "#FeesMustFall: An Internet-Age Student Movement in South Africa and the Case of the University of the Free State." *Politikon* 44, no. 2 (2017): 231–45. http://doi.org/10.1080/02589346.2016.1238644.

Mabasa, Khwezi. "The Rebellion of the Born Un-Frees: Fallism and the Neo-Colonial Corporate University." *Strategic Review for Southern Africa* 39, no. 2 (2017): 94–116. http://hdl.handle.net/2263/64982.

Maringira, Godfrey, and Simbarashe Gukurume. "Being Black in #FeesMustFall and #FreeDecolonisedEducation: Student Protests at the University of the Western Cape." In *#Hashtag: An Analysis of the #FeesMustFall Movement at South African Universities*, edited by Malose Langa, 33–48. Johannesburg: Centre for the Study of Violence and Reconciliation, 2017. https://csvr.org.za/pdf/An-analysis-of-the-FeesMustFall-Movement-at-South-African-universities.pdf#page=35.

Marutha, Paulos Lekala. "FMF 2016 Nobody Wanna See Us Together—Yamekla Gola Ft Wits Students." October 14, 2016. https://www.youtube.com/watch?v=mFmRA2U5-pQ.

Mattes, Robert. "The 'Born Frees': The Prospects for Generational Change in Post-Apartheid South Africa." *Australian Journal of Political Science* 47, no. 1 (2012): 133–53.

Mavuso, Amanda. "My Personal Journey: Being a Black Woman Student Activist on Tshwane University of Technology Soshanguve Campus." *Agenda* 31, no. 3–4 (November 2017): 5–9. https://doi.org/10.1080/10130950.2017.1392787.

McKeever, Matthew. "Educational Inequality in Apartheid South Africa." *American Behavioral Scientist* 61, no. 1 (2017): 114–31. https://doi.org/10.1177/0002764216682988.

Molefe, T. O. "Oppression Must Fall." *World Policy Journal* 33, no. 1 (2016): 30–37. https://doi.org/10.1215/07402775-3545858.

Mpofu, Shepherd. "Disruption as a Communicative Strategy: The Case of #FeesMustFall and #RhodesMustFall Students' Protests in South Africa." *Journal of African Media Studies* 9, no. 2 (June 1, 2017): 351–73. https://doi.org/10.1386/jams.9.2.351_1.

Mudavanhu, Selina Linda. "Comrades, Students, Baboons and Criminals: An Analysis of 'Othering' on Facebook in Relation to the #Rhodesmustfall/#Feesmustfall Movement at the University of Cape Town." *African Journalism Studies* 38, no. 2 (December 5, 2017): 21–48. https://doi.org/https://doi.org/10.1080/23743670.2017.1332662.

Mutekwe, Edmore. "Unmasking the Ramifications of the Fees-Must-Fall-Conundrum in Higher Education Institutions in South Africa: A Critical Perspective." *Perspectives in Education* 35, no. 2 (December 2017): 142–54. https://doi.org/10.18820/2519593x/pie.v35i2.11.

Naidoo, Leigh-Ann. "Contemporary Student Politics in South Africa: The Rise of the Black-Led Student Movements of #RhodesMustFall and #FeesMustFall in 2015." In *Students Must Rise: Youth Struggle in South Africa Before and Beyond Soweto '76*, edited by Anne Heffernan, and Noor Nieftagodien, 180–92. Johannesburg: Wits University Press, 2016.

Ndelu, Sandy, Simamkele Dlakavu, and Barbara Boswell. "Womxn's and Nonbinary Activists' Contribution to the RhodesMustFall and FeesMustFall Student Movements: 2015 and 2016." *Agenda* 31, no. 3–4 (December 2017): 1–4. https://doi.org/10.1080/10130950.2017.1394693.

Ndelu, Sandile, Yingi Edwin Musawenkosi Malabela, Marcia Vilakazi, Oliver Meth, Godfrey Maringira, Simbarasha Gukurume, and Muneinazvo Kujeke. *#Hashtag: An Analysis of the #FeesMustFall Movement at South African Universities*, edited by Malose Langa. Johannesburg: Centre for the Study of Violence and Reconciliation, 2017. http://csvr.org.za/pdf/An-analysis-of-the-FeesMustFall-Movement-at-South-African-universities.pdf#.

Ndlovu, Hlengiwe. "Womxn's Bodies Reclaiming the Picket Line: The 'Nude' Protest during #FeesMustFall." *Agenda* 31, no. 3–4 (December 2017): 68–77. https://doi.org/10.1080/10130950.2017.1391613.

Ndlovu, Musawenkosi W. *#FeesMustFall and Youth Mobilisation in South Africa: Reform or Revolution?* New York: Routledge, 2017.

Ndlovu, Sifiso Mxolisi. "The Soweto Uprising." In *The Road to Democracy in South Africa: Volume 2* (1970–1980), edited by South African Democracy Trust, 317–62. Pretoria: Unisa, 2011. http://www.sadet.co.za/docs/rtd/vol2/volume%202%20-%20chapter%207.pdf.

Ngidi, Ndumiso Daluxolo, Chumani Mtshixa, Kathleen Diga, Nduta Mbarathi, and Julian May. "Asijiki and the Capacity to Aspire Through Social Media." *Proceedings of the Eighth International Conference on Information and Communication Technologies and Development - ICTD 16* (June 2016): 1–11. https://doi.org/10.1145/2909609.2909654.

Nomvete, Sandla, and John Mashayamombe. "South Africa's Fees Must Fall: The Case of #UPrising in 2015." *South African Review of Sociology* 50, no. 3–4 (December 18, 2019): 75–90. https://doi.org/10.1080/21528586.2019.1699441.

Nyamnjoh, Francis B. *#RhodesMustFall: Nibbling at Resilient Colonialism in South Africa*. Bamenda: African Books Collective, 2016.

Ojakorotu, Victor, and Segun Eesuola Olukayode. "FeesMustFall: The 'Inner' Gender Dimensions and Implications for Political Participation in South Africa." *Gender and Behaviour* 14, no. 2 (October 2016): 7185–90. https://journals.co.za/content/journal/10520/EJC-59f3c5721.

Padayachee, Keshnee. "The Myths and Realities of Generational Cohort Theory on ICT Integration in Education: A South African Perspective." *African Journal of Information Systems* 10, no. 1 (2017): 54–84. https://digitalcommons.kennesaw.edu/ajis/vol10/iss1/4.

Raghuram, Parvati, Markus Roos Breines, and Ashley Gunter. "Beyond #FeesMustFall: International Students, Fees and Everyday Agency in the Era of Decolonisation." *Geoforum* 109 (February 2020): 95–105. https://doi.org/10.1016/j.geoforum.2020.01.002.

Ramluckan, Trishana, Sayed Enayat Sayed Ally, and Brett Van Niekerk. "Twitter Use in Student Protests." *Threat Mitigation and Detection of Cyber Warfare and Terrorism Activities Advances in Information Security, Privacy, and Ethics* (2017): 220–53. https://doi.org/10.4018/978-1-5225-1938-6.ch010.

Rotberg, Robert I. "Truth Commissions and the Provision of Truth, Justice, and Reconciliation." In *Truth v. Justice: The Morality of Truth Commissions*, edited by Robert I. Rotberg, and Dennis F. Thompson, 3–21. Princeton, NJ: Princeton University Press, 2010.

Shange, Nombulelo. "Mappings of Feminist/Womanist Resistance within Student Movements across the African Continent." *Agenda* 31, no. 3–4 (November 2017): 60–67. https://doi.org/10.1080/10130950.2017.1392155.

Sooryamoorthy, Radhamany. *Sociology in South Africa: Colonial, Apartheid and Democratic Forms*. London: Palgrave Mcmillan, 2016.

South African Press Association (SAPA). "Tshwane has Largest Ratio of Whites in SA." January 24, 2013. https://www.iol.co.za/pretoria-news/tshwane-has-largest-ratio-of-whites-in-sa-1457957.

Swidler, Ann. "Culture in Action: Symbols and Strategies." *American Sociological Review* 51, no. 2 (April 1986): 273–86. http://doi.org/10.2307/2095521.

Teeger, Chana. "'Both Sides of the Story': History Education in Post-Apartheid South Africa." *American Sociological Review* 80, no. 6 (2015): 1175–200. https://doi.org/10.1177/0003122415613078.

Thumbran, Janeke. "Separate Development and Self-Reliance at the University of Pretoria." *Kronos* 43, no. 1 (2017): 114–25. http://doi.org/10.17159/2309-9585/2017/v43a7.

Tshwane University of Technology. "Tshwane University of Technology: About Campuses." https://www.tut.ac.za/other/campuses/about. Accessed June 29, 2020.

Tshwane University of Technology. "Tshwane University of Technology: Strategic Plan 2008–2012." https://web.archive.org/web/20100429220230/http://www.tut.ac.za/About%20Us/. Archived April 29, 2010.

University of Pretoria. "University of Pretoria: Frequently Asked Questions." https://www.up.ac.za/faq. Accessed June 29, 2020.

van Marle, Karin. "A 'Right' to the University." *Acta Academia* 51, no. 1 (2019): 109–24. http://doi.org/10.18820/24150479/aa51i1.6.

Van der Waal, C. S. (Kees). 2015. "Long Walk from Volkekunde to Anthropology: Reflections on Representing the Human in South Africa." *Anthropology Southern Africa* 38, no. 3–4: 216–34.

Wa Azania, Malaika. *Memoirs of a Born Free: Reflections on the New South Africa by a Member of the Post-Apartheid Generation*. New York: Penguin Random House, 2018.

Wilson, Richard. "Reconciliation and Revenge in Post-Apartheid South Africa: Rethinking Legal Pluralism and Human Rights." *Current Anthropology* 41, no. 1 (2000): 75–98. http://doi.org/10.1086/300104.

Xaba, Wanelisa. "Challenging Fanon: A Black Radical Feminist Perspective on Violence and the Fees Must Fall Movement." *Agenda* 31, no. 3–4 (November 2017): 96–104. https://doi.org/10.1080/10130950.2017.1392786.

Afterword

Young People and the Future of African Worlds

Nadine Dolby

Africa is a continent of young people. Thus, what they do, what they think, and what they are taught matters not only to Africa but to the future of the world. As Ugor writes in the introduction to this edited collection, these young people "have exploded as powerful social actors in the continent's public domain and on the world stage."[1]

I first learned about the agency of African youth not through books and journal articles but through my own lived experiences. In the mid-1980s, the antiapartheid and divestment movement was sweeping through campuses across the United States (Martin, 2007). As an undergraduate at Boston University, I was already part of multiple activist organizations. By the spring of 1985, I was fully immersed in the protests, rallies, and sit-ins that were happening every few days on my campus and on other campuses in the Boston and New York areas. For the first time in my life, I met and became friends with my peers from South Africa and throughout the continent. These friendships expanded and deepened through the next decade, as I worked for a Boston-based antiapartheid organization, Fund for a Free South Africa, which was founded by exiled members of the African National Congress. My first trip to South Africa was in late 1991, a few months after Nelson Mandela walked out of prison and the nation entered a new era. The streets of Johannesburg pulsed with excitement, promise, and hope. On that first trip, I wandered for hours through this new city, simply absorbing the energy that surrounded me. I spent time with friends in restaurants, bars,

---

1   Ugor, "Introduction," 1.

bookstores, and community centers in Yeoville, Hillbrow, and farther afield. In the years that followed, I returned time and time again, because I could see and feel a different future on those streets.

Eventually, I landed in Durban with a Fulbright Award to do an ethnographic study of a desegregated school that was at the forefront of change. The "New South Africa" was being formed, contested, and imagined in that school—and schools like it—throughout the country. With my dissertation proposal recently defended, I arrived in South Africa in February 1996. I was ready to try to understand how young people were making sense of this new world, a tenuous leap into democracy and equality, after more than four hundred years of oppression. As a graduate student who had already made numerous trips to South Africa, I had been immersed in a world of academics and political activists. I knew and had met many leading figures in the African National Congress but had yet to meet many ordinary people in South Africa, including, especially, young people.

Within a few weeks of arrival, I was immersed in the everyday lives of multiple groups of teenagers, with all of the accompanying complexity, angst, tears, and most critically, energy. Trained as both a journalist (as an undergraduate) and an ethnographer, I knew that it was critical that I follow the story and the energy of these young people as social actors, regardless of how their priorities and realities might differ from what I had anticipated before I arrived at Fernwood (the pseudonym I have used for the school in published work; see Dolby 2001). Signs of, as Ugor writes, "resourcefulness, agency, and influence" were everywhere in this school and among these young people: I simply needed to be open to seeing them. Perhaps not surprisingly for readers of this collection, much of the agency and energy I found was expressed and engaged through the creative arts and associated sociocultural practices, particularly fashion, dress, television, and music (this was in 1996, long before the existence of social media).

As I settled into my routines at Fernwood, I drew on one particular experience in South Africa, five years earlier, to help me to begin to understand how these young people in Durban were seeing the world and living in it. As part of my first trip to South Africa in 1991, I traveled with friends (American and South African) to a rather remote part of the country, not too far from the border with Zimbabwe. We spent several days in the area surrounding Thoyandou, which was then the capital of the (soon to be abolished) Bantusan of Venda, and is now the capital of the province of Limpopo. We stayed at the Akanani Rural Development Association, which was a vibrant hub for local activists and artists. During my visit there, I met dozens of young people who lived in (what I saw) as dire economic and social circumstances, often without running water or reliable electricity, far from the urban hubs of Johannesburg, Durban, and Cape Town, and farther still from New York, London, and Paris. And yet, still, they knew (sometimes more than I did) about the world beyond. They were connected to global currents in music, art, dance, and politics. They were vibrant social actors, creating the "new" everyday: not solely the "new" South Africa but the continent, and indeed, the world. I learned from them and from that trip not solely about South Africa, and certainly not about a South Africa frozen in time and disconnected from the rest of the world. Instead, I learned about a world that was fully situated in modernity (Fabian 1983/2014).

I brought this insight from my short time in the rural areas of South Africa to my everyday work with urban youth in the core of a South African city, thus seeing the creative energy and possibility that surrounded me. I understood that the story of the "new" that I was surrounded by revolved around an engagement with popular culture. These youth were not passive receptacles for a cultural world that was imported from global centers but were active agents in both creating and disseminating these cultural worlds. The title of my dissertation, and then book, *Constructing Race* reflected this active agency. Race, like other social identities, is not a given: instead, it is a *construct* and thus actively made and remade by people as they go about their daily lives. For the urban youth in Durban whom I spent time with during the 1996 school year, race was made and remade through an engagement with popular culture. I found, repeatedly, that these high school students knew more about the world that I came from than I did. Sitting on a wall outside of Fernwood every morning before the school bell rang, they taught me about American popular culture, though they had never been there (I had been born in the United States and had lived there my entire life at that point). These students did not simply "consume" American popular culture: they sampled, cut and pasted, and made it their own, and then they taught their new American friend about it and, in the process, about the United States, South Africa, and the currents that are always already present in the in-between spaces (Dolby 2003).

As the authors in this edited collection demonstrate repeatedly, ordinary African youth are active creators, contributors, and yes, "constructors" in an increasingly globalized media and tech savvy world that moves at a dizzying pace. Whereas in the 1950s it might have taken years for popular culture to circle the globe, as Nixon (1994) demonstrates in his analysis of the connections between Hollywood, Harlem, and South African popular culture, and

David (2001) discusses in his study of the global and continental circulation of popular culture in *Drum* magazine in the 1950s, today those same circulations happen in milliseconds and through multiple, simultaneous social media platforms. So rapid is the pace that it is becoming impossible (if it ever was) to identify "origins" of any particular cultural form. Did a wildly popular African culture practice "begin" in Cape Town, Accra, Berlin, or New York? How many times did it criss-cross the globe in a matter of minutes or hours? Were the originators Cameroonians in France, children of Nigerian immigrants to the United States living in Lagos, or increasingly, Chinese youth in Africa and African youth in China? What exactly is an "origin?" Where does one "border" start and the other end? (see Dolby 2003).

All of these questions complicate our understanding of an "African" cultural practice and refocus attention on its inherent instability and fluidity, particularly as Africa develops ties to the world that go beyond the well-worn routes that lead back to colonial relationships. In a world where (in my lifetime) it was once challenging to simply fly from one region of Africa to another without a layover in an old colonial outpost somewhere in Europe, there is now immense development of new ties and flows, both within Africa and between Africa and the rest of the world. For example, Kenya was colonized and ruled by the British until independence in 1963. In 2020, Kenyan schools began to teach Mandarin, following the earlier introduction of Mandarin in schools in Uganda and South Africa. Undoubtedly, more African countries will follow, and these institutional practices will slowly begin to intersect with and rewrite concomitant cultural forms. Music, dance, film, and new media technologies both reflect and produce the larger social, economic, and political structures in which they are embedded. Of course, these ties, connections, and circulations are not new: as Nixon (1994) demonstrates in his scholarship on the ways in which the struggle against apartheid in South Africa was an inherently global one, following Gilroy's (1993) coining of the concept of the "Black Atlantic." Yet, they are faster, deeper, and not as easily plotted through the well-worn lines of former colonial relationships. Instead, these ties are indicative of the future patterns and trends that will shape the future of the African continent and the diaspora.

African youth are an intrinsic part of this decidedly global future. For example, they are at the forefront of a vibrant, worldwide movement of young people who are united in the most critical struggle that we face today as a planet: the urgent need to stop the ravages of climate change and to begin to find ways to live more harmoniously with the natural world, in a way that will ensure humanity's future survival. As the worst locust swarms in generations destroy crops, lands, and livelihoods throughout the continent, and as sea levels rise and droughts intensify, African young people are mobilizing with their peers across the globe to fundamentally change how humans inhabit the planet. In September 2019, the global climate strike swept the world, and African youth in multiple cities and countries, including Nairobi, Kampala, Cape Town, and Lagos called on their governments and the world to listen, respond, and change.

African youth have also demanded that they not be marginalized or sidelined in this global struggle. When Vanessa Nakate, a Ugandan climate activist, attended an invited youth climate science event held to coincide with the 2020 World Economic Forum in Davos, Switzerland, she stood proudly with four white female peers, including Greta Thunberg, as a recognized global leader in the fight against climate change. But when the Associated Press picture was published across the world in the days that followed, her image had been cropped out. Nakate, and the entire African continent, had been erased from this struggle. But Nakate fought back, taking on the Associate Press on Twitter and criticizing them for their decision. Eventually they apologized and the corrected photo, this time including Nakate, was recirculated and published in media outlets throughout the world.

The course of the world is neither predictable nor predetermined. We as human beings are vulnerable in ways that we often cannot imagine. But the natural world reminds us of this inevitable reality. The COVID-19 pandemic, still raging as I write this, has decimated Africa and African communities throughout the world. Yet, the instability it created also enabled the possibilities for a global Black Lives Matter movement that would have been a mere fantasy just months before. In June of 2020, the African Union condemned the brutal murder of George Floyd, and the continent of Africa exploded with Black Lives Matters protests, inspired and led by African youth.

African youth's global leadership in these two movements in just the past year—climate change and Black Lives Matters, are signs, once again, that Africa in 2020 is not a space that is acted on, but instead, it is a place and people who *act* and who make change. Within these new dynamics are possibilities for the "highly syncretic, improvisational and experimental" cultural forms that Ugor writes about in his introduction and that are evident throughout the chapters of this powerful collection. The "popular arts" are not separate from politics: instead, the arts are wholly and inextricably intertwined with the ongoing project of democracy. People act in the spaces that they can access, control, alter, and reshape; they act where they can find power. Popular culture thus becomes a powerful center of power and change (Dolby 2003).

What will come next is largely unknown. As much as the global forces of capital and neoliberalism try to control the future, ultimately, they cannot. At its core, the world is an unpredictable and capricious place, and we are all actors, creators, and constructors of its future, not simply those who have (temporary and transient) control. I know that young women and men, in what Ugor refers to as the "forgotten spaces" of Africa and parallel "forgotten spaces" across the globe can and will be the driving creative and political forces in the years ahead, in local, regional, national, continental, and global spaces. The events of the past year have laid bare that reality and reinforced that the world will have no choice but to focus on and listen to their voices, their music, their art, and how they are narrating and shaping their own lives and those across the globe. As the authors in this collection demonstrate, the continent and the diaspora are alive with the pulsing sounds, words, and ideas of African youth. Those sounds echo in my head, along with the amazing vibrancy of the African night in a tiny village outside of Thoyandou in 1991. And they give me hope.

Bibliography

David, S. M. (2001). "*Popular Culture in South Africa: The Limits of Black Identity in Drum Magazine.*" PhD diss., University of Illinois at Urbana-Champaign.

Dolby, N. (1996). *Constructing Race: Youth, Identity, and Popular Culture in South Africa*. New York: State University of New York Press.

———. (2003). "Popular Culture and Democratic Practice." *Harvard Educational Review 73*, no. 3, 258–84.

———. (2003). "A Small Place: Jamaica Kincaid and a Methodology of Connection." *Qualitative Inquiry* 9(1), 57–73.

Fabian, J. (1983/2014*). Time and the Other: How Anthropology Makes Its Object*. New York: Columbia University Press.

Gilroy, P. (1993). *The Black Atlantic: Modernity and Double Consciousness*. Cambridge, MA: Harvard University Press.

Martin, B. (2007). "'Unsightly Huts': Shanties and the Divestment Movement of the 1980s." *Peace & Change 32*, no. 3, 329–59.

Nixon, R. (1994). *Homelands, Harlem, and Hollywood: South African Culture and the World Beyond*. New York: Routledge.

Contributors

Ibrahim Bangura is a senior lecturer at the Department of Peace and Conflict Studies, Fourah Bay College, University of Sierra Leone. His research interests are in the areas of youth, gender, social protection, transnational organized crimes, and peacebuilding in Africa.

David Bosc holds a BSc (Honors) degree with a major in applied computer science from the University of Winnipeg and works in the game industry. His curiosity in this project stemmed from an interest in integrating computational methods to reinforce the arts, specifically with social media. Seeing that Twitter is a wealth of information but difficult to curate without the proper tools and background, David saw an opportunity to help bridge that gap.

Austin Bryan is a PhD student in anthropology at Northwestern University in Evanston, Illinois. At the time of fieldwork, he was a Research Fellow at Sexual Minorities Uganda in Kampala, Uganda, and a student of Africana Studies at North Carolina State University in Raleigh, North Carolina.

Adrienne Cohen is assistant professor of anthropology at Colorado State University. She has conducted extensive ethnographic fieldwork in Guinea, West Africa, on urban dance and political change and in the United States among migrant artists from Guinea. Cohen is the author of *Infinite Repertoire: On Dance and Urban Possibility in Postsocialist Guinea* (University of Chicago Press, 2021). Her work has appeared in *American Ethnologist, Journal of the Royal Anthropological Institute*, and *Africa: The Journal of the International African Institute*.

Juliana Coughlin is a recent graduate from the joint Master's program in peace and conflict studies from the University of Manitoba and the University of Winnipeg. She also holds an honors BA in political science and communication from the University of Ottawa. She has a particular interest in women's rights and has worked in this area in Ghana, Nepal, and Canada.

Nadine Dolby is professor of curriculum studies at Purdue University. She has researched and published widely in the fields of international and comparative education, qualitative inquiry, multicultural education, and animals and education. She is the author of two books: *Constructing Race: Youth, Identity, and Popular Culture in*

South Africa (SUNY Press, 2001) and *Rethinking Multicultural Education for the Next Generation: The New Empathy and Social Justice* (Routledge, 2012) and has coedited four additional books. She has published in high-impact journals in education, including *Review of Educational Research, Harvard Educational Review, Qualitative Inquiry, Anthropology & Education, Race Ethnicity and Education, Comparative Education Review, Teaching in Higher Education, Journal of College and Character, Educational Studies, Journal of Studies in International Education, The Australian Education Researcher, African Studies Review* and the *Journal of Environmental Education*. She has conducted research and lived and worked in South Africa, Australia, and the United States.

Simbarashe Gukurume is a senior lecturer at Sol Plaatje University, School of Humanities, Social Sciences Department, and a research associate at the University of Johannesburg, Anthropology & Development Studies in South Africa. He is also a junior mentor for the Harry Frank Guggenheim Young African Scholars program. He holds a PhD in sociology from the University of Cape Town, South Africa. His research interests focus more broadly on the intersections between youth, informality, and livelihoods, mobilities, social movements, displacement, and religiosities. Simbarashe's recent articles are published in the *Journal of Southern African Studies, Contemporary African Studies, Third World Thematics, African Identities, Journal of Asian and African Studies,* and *Asian Ethnicity*.

Jendele Hungbo is associate professor of journalism, communication and media studies at Bowen University Iwo and a research associate at Wits University South Africa. His research interests cut across broadcast media, new (interactive) media, postcolonial identities and representations in the media in Africa among others. He previously taught at North-West University, Mafikeng, South Africa, and has published widely in the field. A former Cadbury fellow at the Centre for West African Studies, University of Birmingham, Jendele was also a recipient of the Volkswagen Stiftung Doctoral Fellowship and has shared his research at many local and international fora.

Kristi Heather Kenyon is associate professor in the Human Rights Program at the University of Winnipeg's Global College (Canada). She previously held postdoctoral positions in the Centre for Human Rights at the University of Pretoria (South Africa) and in the Department of Political Science at Dalhousie University (Canada). Her research focuses on activism, human rights, and health with a focus on sub-Saharan Africa.

David Kerr is currently the program manager at AfOx (University of Oxford) and a research associate at the University of Johannesburg. His research interest focuses on popular culture, hip hop, masculinity, mobility, and marginality. He has published in the fields of social and cultural anthropology, cultural studies, and media studies. His first book, entitled *Migration, Memory and Masculinity: The Subculture of the Stowaway in Dar es Salaam* will be published by Mkuki na Nyota in 2021. He is currently working on a monograph that explores how street performance forms in Dar es Salaam's informal settlements act as sites of meaning making.

Godfrey Maringira is associate professor of anthropology at Sol Plaatje University, Kimberley, South Africa. He is also a research associate in the Anthropology and Development Department at University of Johannesburg, South Africa. He is a principal investigator of the International Development Research Center (IDRC) research on gang violence in South Africa. His areas of research include armed violence in Africa with a specific focus on the military in postcolonial Africa. He is the author of *Soldiers and the State in Zimbabwe* (Routledge, 2019).

Adeline Masquelier is professor of anthropology at Tulane University. A specialist in gender, religion, and health studies in Niger, she has authored three books, including *Women and Islamic Revival in a West African Town*, which was awarded the 2010 Herskovits Award and the 2012 Aidoo-Snyder Prize from the African Studies Association. Her latest book *Fada: Boredom and Belonging in Niger* was a finalist for the Best Book Prize from the African Studies Association. She (co)edited three books, including *Critical Terms for the Study of Africa* (with Gaurav Desai). She is currently working on a book about the mass possession of schoolgirls in Niger.

Bamba Ndiaye is a Mellon Postdoctoral Fellow in the Society for the Humanities and the Music Department at Cornell University. His research interests focus on historical and contemporary social movements in the Black Atlantic, Pan-Africanism, critical race theory, Black popular cultures, and digital humanities. He is the author of several peer-reviewed papers and book chapters. His current research projects include *Black Social Movement and Digital Technology*, "Mbas Mi: Fighting COVID-19 through Music in Senegal", and "#Justice for Breonna Taylor: Race, Class, Gender and the Rise of Primo-Protesters." Dr. Ndiaye is also the creator and host of *The Africanist*, an academic podcast that investigates historical and contemporary sociopolitical issues in Africa and the African Diasporas.

Kwabena Opoku-Agyemang received his PhD from West Virginia University and is currently a lecturer at the department of English at the University of Ghana. His research interests revolve around African digital creative expression, and his research has appeared in several peer reviewed journals and book collections. He has also guest edited journals such as *Journal of Gaming and Virtual Worlds* and *Hyperrhiz*.

Connie Rapoo is associate professor of theater and performing arts at the University of Botswana. Her areas of research interest include African theater, African popular culture, African American theater, and African diaspora studies. She has published in reputable international journals, including *Critical Arts, Theatre Journal, Arts and Communities,* and *Social Dynamics.*

Ty-Juana Taylor has broad interests in African and African diasporic studies. She received her PhD in ethnomusicology from the University of California, Los Angeles. Taylor's dissertation, "When the Streets Speak: Investigating Music, Memory, and Identity in the Lives of Abidjanese Street Children," uses music to investigate identity, memory, and community among Ivorian youth on the streets of Abidjan. In addition to being a scholar, Taylor is also a social worker who believes service and advocacy are crucial aspects of research. Taylor works with youth and homeless populations both in the United States and abroad, assisting in development, teaching, curriculum planning, therapy, and policymaking for children and youth, as seen in her music curricula written for Girl Scouts of Greater Los Angeles, and Smithsonian Folkways Learning Pathways (forthcoming). Taylor's work on Ivorian popular music can be found in *Ethnomusicology Review: Notes from the Field, Continuum Encyclopedia of Popular Music of the World,* and *SAGE International Encyclopedia of Music and Culture.*

Paul Ugor is associate professor in the Department of English at Illinois State University, Normal, Illinois. His research and teaching interests are in the areas of Anglophone world literatures, modern African literatures and cinema, black popular culture, African youth cultures, postcolonial studies, and cultural theory. He is the author of *Nollywood: Popular Culture and Narratives of Youth Struggles in Nigeria* (2016). He has also co-edited several collections including *African Youth Cultures in the Age of Globalization: Challenges, Agency and Resistance* (Routledge 2017/Ashgate 2015); *Postcolonial Text,* 8, nos. 3–4, 2013; and *Review of Education, Pedagogy and Cultural Studies* 31, no. 4 (2009). His scholarly publications have appeared in *Africa: The Journal of the International African Institute; African Literature Today, Canadian Journal of African Studies, Postcolonial Texts,* and several edited books.

James Yeku is assistant professor of African digital humanities in the Department of African and African American Studies at the University of Kansas where he teaches courses on social media and its intersections with African popular cultures. James studies the digital expressions of the literatures and cultures of Africa and the African diaspora, focusing on the African articulations of the digital cultural record.

Index

Illustrations are indicated by page numbers in italics.

Abacha, Sani, 37, 149, 261
Abati, Rueben, 136–39, 144–45
Abbink, Jon, 322–23
Abdulkareem, Eedris, 133, 178–79
Achebe, Chinua, 204
activism: antiapartheid, 370; antipoverty, 359; censure of, 256; collective, 321; corruption and, 126; criminalization of, 259; hip-hop and, 39–40; musical diatribe and, 44–46, 51, 54–55; music and, 37–39, 127; new forms of, 249, 268–72; power and, 167; queer, 214, 224–27; respectability and, 225; social space and, 331; temerity and, 48; youth and, 1–2, 9, 12
Adedeji, Wale, 120
Adejunmobi, Moradewun, 164
AFRC. *See* Armed Forces Revolutionary Council (AFRC) (Sierra Leone)
African National Congress (ANC), 237, 239, 355, 358, 367–68, 372
Afrikaans, 356, 361–63, 368–69
Afrobeats, 132–56, 279, 281, 298, 302
agency, 195, 385–87; authorial, 174; citizenship and, 176, 185, 248; colonization and, 102; corruption and, 129–30; fear of youth, 259; film and, 175; homophobia and, 229; of play, 169; play and, 167–71; postcolonialism and, 272; self-determination and, 346; social media and, 164–65, 182, 270–71; state, 181–82; violence and, 125; voice and, 178; "waithood" and, 270

Aidoo, Ama Ata, 200
Akpos, 166
Aldama, Frederick Luis, 190
alienation, 55, 151, 156, 286, 337
All People's Congress (APC) (Sierra Leone), 113–16, 127
Amankwah, Akua Serwaa, 191–92, 191n9, 192–98
ambianceurs, 93, 103
Amin, Idi, 261
Amkoullel L'enfant Peul (Ba), 50
ANC. *See* African National Congress (ANC)
Anti-Homosexuality Bill (Uganda), 208–10, 218
Apartheid, 153, 235–40, 242, 353, 355, 357, 362, 385–86
APC. *See* All People's Congress (APC) (Sierra Leone)
appropriation, 63, 82, 101, 138, 176–79, 255, 292, 330
Apter, Andrew, 143
Arab Spring, 39
archiving, 338–39
"A Re kopaneng" (ReMmogo), 346–48
Armed Forces Revolutionary Council (AFRC) (Sierra Leone), 114–15
Arnoldi, Mary Jo, 17
Asiedu, Adelaide, 191–92
ataya base, 117–18, 121, 127–28
Attwell, David, 340–41
autoeroticism, 151
Awadi, Didier, 56–57

Ba, Amadou Hampaté, 50

Baba Fryo, 133
Bad Black, 211, 220–26, *221, 224, 226,* 230
Badjibi, 307–8
Bah, Alhaji Bankaria, 125
Bahati, David, 208
Bailai Citoyen movement, 38, 47
Baitsile, Sidney, 341
ballet, 309–13
Bangura, Ibrahim, 113
Banky W, 144–45
Barber, Karin, 6, 18, 139–40, 164, 169–71, 173, 212, 214, 251, 263, 332–34, 354
Barthes, Roland, 301
Bataaxal (N'Dour), 55
Baw-Waw Society, 119, 121, 129
Bayat, Asef, 172
Bédié, Henrie Konan, 97
Ben Ali, Zine El Abidine, 39
Bender, Wolfgang, 137
Benin, 55, 57, 97, 299
Benson, Bobby, 137
Beynaud, Serge, 93–94
Big Brother Africa (television show), 8, 63, 70, 213
Big Fayia, 118
"big man" syndrome, 102
"Big Trouble nar Small Salone" (LAJ), 127
Biko, Steve, 372–73
Bio, Julius Maada, 115
Black Leo Entertainment, 125
Black Lives Matter, 389
Bobo Sango, 92
Boko Haram, 120
"Bongo Dar es Salaam" (Professor Jay), 69
Bongo Explosion, 70
Bongo Flava, 69, 71, 120–21
Bonnie Luv, 71
"Borbor Belleh" (Emmerson), 121

"Borbor Pain" (Emmerson), 121–22
Boro Sandji, 93
Botho, 348–49
Botswana, 327–50
Boyd, Danah, 174
Bramham, Peter, 146–47
Branson, Richard, 345
Breakin' (film), 63, 68
Brecht, Bertolt, 337
Bruijn, Esther de, 189
Bryan, Austin, 249
Buckingham, David, 17
"Bum-Bum" (Timaya), 149–50
Bunny Mack, 118
Burkina Faso, 38, 47, 57, 97, 373
Bushy, Margaret, 37
Butler, Judith, 337

Calender, Ebenezer, 118
California, 134
Camara, Moussa Celestin, 311–12
Camara, Moussa Dadis, 310n13
Canada, 219–20, 229, 279, 352
Canclini, Garcia, 23–24
capital, 106–8; cultural, 194, 211, 223, 229, 280; dance as, 104–5; music production and, 71, 73–74, 91; social, 73–75, 103, 106–8, 271, 283; transgressive, 212, 214, 219, 228–31
capitalism, 22, 134, 142, 163, 170, 213, 248, 308, 314, 320, 375. *See also* neoliberalism
Castro, Fidel, 373
CDF. *See* Civil Defence Force (CDF) (Sierra Leone)
celebrity, 23–24, 70–71, 80, 82–83, 100, 124, 150, 165, 281–82
Centre de Recherche et d'Action pour la Paix (Center of research and action for peace, CERAP), 90n3
Certeau, Michel de, 284

Chamisa, Nelson, 264
Chernoff, John Miller, 100–101
Chiepe, Gaositwe, 332–36
China, 104, 310, 388
Cikan-le message (Tata Pound), 57–58
citizenship: agency and, 176, 185, 248; consumption and, 291; culture and, 168–69, 213; gender and, 333; global, 147; hip-hop and, 45; politics, 112; race and, 236; responsive, 248–51; social media and, 176
Citizenship Entrepreneurial Development Agency, 327
"City Life" (Pupa Bajah), 121
Civil Defence Force (CDF) (Sierra Leone), 114–15
civil war: in Côte d'Ivoire, 103; in Nigeria, 142, 281; in Sierra Leone, 111–19, 128–29
Cliff, Gareth, 245
Cohen, Adrienne, 19
Cole, Olofemi Israel, 118
Colé Dieng, Amy, 40
comedy, 112, 167–68, 171–76, 179–80, 185, 259
Comic Pastor, 259
conscientization, 238, 333–35
Consumers and Citizens (Canclini), 23
consumption, 67, 102, 132, 135, 138–40, 146, 150–51, 156, 281–92
Conté, Lansana, 310n13, 319–20
Coplan, David, 5, 251
corruption, 126, 129–30; Bongo Flava and, 121; hip-hop and, 39, 48; moral critique of, 155; musical diatribe and, 46–47; in Nigeria, 150–51, 180–81, 261, 265, 285; Obama on, 345; in policing, 182; in Sierra Leone, 113–14, 121–23, 127; in Zimbabwe, 266–67
Côte d'Ivoire, 20–21, 88–109
Couldry, Nick, 178

coupé décalé, 91–96, 101–6, 281–82, 301–2
COVID-19, 165, 260, 389
critical discourse analysis, 243–44
Cross Creations, 342
cross-dressing, 183–85. *See also* transgender individuals
culture: as arts, 353; in Botswana, youth and popular, 327–50; change and, 167–68; citizenship and, 168–69, 213; discursive value of, 139–40; epistemological weight of, 139–40; globalization and, 13–16, 147; hegemonic, 168, 178; identity and popular, 112; as infrapolitics, 163–86; infrapolitics and use, 171–76; online, 374–76; "origins" of, 387–88; popular, 5–10, 12–13; as popular consciousness, 212; popular music and youth, 91–92; power and, 353–54; queer transgressions and, 212–15; remix, 170–71; signification and, 353–54; as way of life, 353

Daddy Showkey, 133
Dahlgren, Peter, 270
Daifallah, Yasmeen, 242–43
dance, 80, 90n3, 91n4, 104–5, 284, 288n11, 289, 307–23, 353. *See also coupé décalé*
Dar es Salam (Yeleen), 57
Dave-Ski, 341
Davos Forum, 389
Dawson, Emelia, 195
Dean, Joni, 163
de Block, Liesbeth, 17
Debord, Guy, 22
deconstructive consciousness, 242–43
"Dem-Mama" (Timaya), 148
Dem Mama Soldiers, 147–48

democracy, 39, 389; globalization and, 141–42; in Guinea, 310n13; music and, 55; in Nigeria, 135, 148; play and, 175; sexual minorities and, 209; social media and, 168–69, 270; in South Africa, 239–40, 249, 353–58, 386; in Zimbabwe, 264
Democratic Republic of Congo (DRC), 93–94, 212, 260–61, 281n3
De Rebirth (Timaya), 148
deregulation, 140, 142, 284–85
de Waal, Alex, 1, 4
Dieng, Bassirou, 54–55
Diop, Cheik Anta, 373
Diouf, Mamadou, 2, 151, 174, 377
DJ Arafat, 93, 98–101, 107
DJ Caloudje, 93
DJ Jacob, 93
DJ Jonathan, 93
DJ Sid, 341
D-Knob, 72
Doctor Oloh, 118
"Doe don Clean" (Jungle Leaders), 121
Dolby, Nadine, 8, 168–69
Don Bosco studio, 71
Douk Saga, 92–93, 97, 103
Dovey, Lindiwe, 138
Drake, 279
DRC. *See* Democratic Republic of Congo (DRC)
Dreyfus, Albert, 57
Du Bois, W. E. B., 373
Duncan Mighty, 133
Durham, Deborah, 331
Dzah, Daniel, 190

"E Be Like Say" (Tu-Face Idibia), 135
Ebola virus disease (EVD), 127
Economic Community of West African States (ECOWAS), 116
Economic Diversification Drive, 327

ECOWAS. *See* Economic Community of West African States (ECOWAS)
education, 178–79, 364–66; civil service and, 284–85; consumerism and, 289; jazz and, 137; masculinity and, 179; privatization and, 142; rappers and, 74, 77; representation and, 135; social movements and, 47. *See also* #FeesMustFall; #RhodesMustFall
Ekine, Sokari, 17
El General (rapper), 39
Emmerson, 118–19, 121–22, 122n20, 127, 129
Englert, Brigit, 120–21
Erastus, Fridah K., 19

Fabian, Johannes, 7, 139, 251
fadas, 280–82, 285–86, 288, 288n11, 293, 296–98
"Fallen Heroes" (Keko), 217–18
Fanon, Frantz, 283, 373
fashion: *coupé décalé* and, 94, 106; hip-hop and, 135; identity and, 291, 294, 300; LGBTQ and, 218, *224*; in Niger, 279–303
Faure, Félix, 57
#FeesMustFall, 352n1, 353–55, 357–78
Fela: This Bitch of a Life (Moore), 37–38
feminism, 213, 228, 247, 334–37, 360
film, 132, 151, 177–80
flash fiction, 189–204
Foucault, Michel, 338–39
Fredericks, Rosalind, 45
freedom: creative, 155; economic inequality and, 365; of expression, 53; of movement, 356; music and, 353; pleasure and, 156; sexual, 150; social media and, 237; in South Africa, 364–66, 374–76; structural adjustment policies and, 141; in Zimbabwe, 259

Freire, Paolo, 373
Fuchs, Christian, 241
Fugard, Athol, 153

Gaffney, David, 203
Gazar B, 79
Gbadamosi, Oladaposi, 181–82
gender, 66n2, 155, 166, 183–85, 211–19, 227, 229–30, 242, 332–40, 367–68
generative materialism, 169
Geoffrion, Karin, 184
Ghana: cross-dressing in, 184; flash fiction in, 189–204; Internet access in, 188; Pidgin English in, 193; politicization of pleasure in, 155
Gift and Grace (Timaya), 147–48
globalization, 10, 151; culture and, 147, 318; media, 263; music and, 124–25, 341; neoliberalism and, 237, 249–50, 328; Nigeria and, 140–45; South Africa and, 237; youth culture and, 13–16
Gonyeti, 259
"Good Do" (Emmerson), 127
Gordimer, Nadine, 153
Green Hole, 342
Guei, Robert, 97
Guevara, Che, 373
Guèye, Marame, 46
Guinea, 114; dance music in, 307–23; revolution in, 309–11
Guyer, Jane, 288
Gwala, Dela, 247
Gwamaka Kaihura King GK, 72
GWM, 71

Hall, Stuart, 12, 139, 147, 241
Hansen, Karen, 299–300
Hardblasters, 71
Hawkes, Gail, 152
"Head of State" (El General), 39
health care, 41–42, 135, 143, 262, 285n7
Hebdige, Dick, 284
Heeks, Richard, 252
Held, David, 147
Hendriks, Thomas, 212
heroes, 373–74
Hill, Lauryn, 47–48
hip-hop, 22–23, 39, 43–45, 120, 133–38; in Botswana, 341–49; in Nigeria, 145–52. *See also* music
Hip-Hop Headphones (Peterson), 47–48
historicity, 204, 338–39, 342, 357
HIV/AIDS, 209–10, 216, 328, 342, 348
homelessness, 91, 97, 104–5, 328
homophobia, 208–12, 216, 218–19, 229–31
Honwana, Alcinda, 270–71
hooks, bell, 336–37
Houphouët-Boigny, Felix, 96–97
"How We Do It" (Keko), 218
human rights, 90n3, 141, 180, 210–11, 258, 262
humor, 164–65, 167–68, 171–76, 179–80, 185
Hurst-Harosh, Ellen, 19

"Ice Ice Baby: King of Swahili Rap" (Jabir), 69
"I Concur" (Timaya), 150
identity: African, 108; archivization and, 338; Black, 136; consumption and, 301; in Côte d'Ivoire, 96; cultural, 103; culture and, 168; distinction, 156; fashion and, 291, 294, 300; film and, 151; gender, 184, 219; generation and, 377; global, 89; modern, 102; music and, 92, 120, 282, 292–93; notional, 97; occupational, 164; political, 44; politics, 150; popular culture and, 112;

identity (*continued*)
  social, 164; social media and, 166; in South Africa, 236, 240, 247, 249; subculture and, 74; urban, 135
India, 292
inequality, 47–48, 134, 166, 237–38, 242, 287, 328, 356, 359, 365, 370–71, 377
infrapolitics: defined, 172; humor and, 171–76; popular culture as, 163–86; youth culture and, 171–76
Innocent (artist), 119
Instagram, 163–86, *166*, *177*, *179*, *182–83*
International Monetary Fund (IMF), 142, 328
Internet: culture, 374–76; oppositional culture and, 214; signification and, 241–42. See also social media
"In the Cutting of a Drink" (Aidoo), 200
Islam, 52, 286–87, 289

Jabir, Saleh, 69
"J'Accuse" (Awadi), 56–57
Jackson, Kelly, 135
Jenkins, Henry, 239
Jenner, Caitlin, 223
Jewsiewicki, Bogumil, 7
Jungle Leaders, 119, 121, 122–23, 129

Kabbah, Ahmad Tejan, 115–16
Kallon, Foday, 118
Kamara, Abdul Rahman, 126
Kamara, Alhassan, 127–28
kampu, 78–81
Kao Denero, 128
KBC, 71
Keko, 211, 215–20, *217*, 230
Kenya, 44, 132, 189n2, 204, 214, 219, 388
Kerr, David, 151, 333, 349–50

Keur Gui Crew, 39–40, 43, 61
Kilifeu, 39–40, 48–49, 54
King, Kith, 226
King, Martin Luther, Jr., 373
King Freezy, 344
Kitwana, Bakari, 137
K-Man, 119
Kouka, Simon, 57–60
Krings, Mathias, 14, 177
Kruger, Fred, 329
K-Solo, 148
Künzler, Daniel, 55
Kuti, Fela, 37–38, 61, 279
Kwaito, 341
Kwaito-kwasa, 341
Kwanza Unit, 71

LAJ, 125, 127–28
"Lalake" (Thiat and Kilifeu), 48–49
Land Act (South Africa), 356
Lange, Noloyiso, 247
Lansana, Simche, 129
Larkin, Brian, 177–78
Lecoge, Moduduetso, 332, 335, 337
Lefebvre, Henri, 169, 331–32
leisure, 76, 132, 138, 142–43, 146–48, 152, 155–56, 287. See also play
Lesetedi, Gwen N., 329
Lettre au Président (Kouka), 57–60
Libya, 114
Lomé Peace Agreement, 116n8
Los Angeles, 134
Luambo, Franco, 38
Lyotard, Jean-François, 21

Macdonald, Sharon, 156
Machozi, Jasho na Damu (Professor Jay), 69
Maddow, Rachel, 208
Mahlangu, Solomon, 372–73
Makeba, Miriam, 38, 61
Mali, 55, 57–58, 97

"Malonogede" (Timaya), 149–50
@mamafelician.Africa, 182–84
@mamatobi, 182–84
Mancgu, Xolela, 245, *246*
Mandela, Nelson, 357, 385
Mandela, Winnie Madikizela, 372–73
marginality, 7, 66–67, 82–83, 114, 134–35, 139, 143, 155–56, 169, 172, 225, 231, 332, 337
Maringira, Godfrey, 249
Marx, Karl, 283, 373
Marxism, 281n3, 312–13, 320, 373
masculinity, 66n2, 82, 179, 183–84, 195, 218, 220, 295, 302, 336–37. *See also* patriarchy
maskani, 64, 76–78, *77*
Massaquoi, David, 125
Master J, 71
materialism: culture of, 97; generative, 169; music and, 93, 97, 108, 151
Mauritania, 55
Mawingu studio, 71
Maxwele, Chumani, 237
"May I Borrow Your Husband?" (Amankwah), 192–98
Mbaya Wao, 64–65, *65, 77, 77*
Mbembe, Achille, 171, 180–81
McClintock, Anne, 192
McGovern, Mike, 309
"Melo-Melo" (Olamide), 19
Meyer, Birgit, 155
Mhando, Linda, 14
Miles, Steven, 13
Milleboy, 296–98
Miller, Daniel, 291
Mitchell, Clyde, 8
MJ Productions, 71
Mnangagwa, Emmerson, 259–61, 265–66
Model Junction Ataya Base, 128
Mogobe, Thulaganyo, 327–28
Molare, 92–93

Molosiwa, David, 341
Monsieur le President (Noir et Blanc), 57
Monsoh, David, 93
Moore, Carlos, 37
Moore, Henrietta, 147
Morebodi, Kagiso David, 342
Movement for Democratic Change (Zimbabwe), 258
Mr II, 71
Muba, Salim, 77–78
Mugabe, Robert, 257–61
"Munku Boss Pan Matches" (Emmerson), 127
Munslow, Alun, 240, 242
music: activism and, 37–39, 127; Afrobeats, 132–56, 279, 281, 298, 302; in Botswana, 341–49; capital and, 73–74; democracy and, 55; freedom and, 353; globalization and, 124–25, 341; in Guinea, 307–23; homophobia and, 211–12; identity and, 92, 120, 282, 292–93; materialism and, 93, 97, 108, 151; politicization of, 38; protest and, 38, 44–46, 49, 51, 61, 97, 120, 145–52, 354–55; reggae, 63, 79, 133, 281, 293; in Sierra Leone, evolution of, 116–24; social activism and, 37–39; sociopolitical expression and, 112; in Uganda, 215–20, *217,* 220–26, *221, 224, 226,* 226–29, *228;* youth culture and, 91–92. *See also* rap music
musical idiom, 139
musical open letter, 44–46, 55–56
music industry, in Sierra Leone, 124–26
musicking, 91n4
Muziki, 151
"Mystery of Inequality, The" (Hill), 47–48

Naidoo, Leigh-Ann, 377
Nakassis, Constantine, 292

Nakate, Vanessa, 389
National Grand Coalition (NGC), 128
National Provisional Ruling Council (NPRC) (Sierra Leone), 115–16
ndombolo dance, 93
N'Dour, Youssou, 55
neoliberalism, 43, 141–43, 146, 170, 237, 249–50, 308, 321n27, 328. *See also* capitalism
networked publics, 164
Newell, Sasha, 100–103, 291
Newell, Stephanie, 189
New York, 134
NGC. *See* National Grand Coalition (NGC)
Niger, 279–303, *290, 294, 297*
Niger Delta Crisis, 120
Nigeria, *144;* Afrobeats in, 132–56; COVID-19 pandemic in, 165; education in, 178–79; elections in, 178; flash fiction in, 204; globalization and, 140–45; hip-hop in, 120, 133–38, 145–52; Kuti and, 37–38; Odi Massacre in, 148–49; policing in, 180–82; political narratives in, 166; precarity in, 140–45; social media in, 173–74; structural adjustment policies in, 142–43
Nketia, J. H., 91n4
Noir et Blanc (rapper), 57
Nossiter, Adam, 45
NPRC. *See* National Provisional Ruling Council (NPRC) (Sierra Leone)
Ntseme, Moletedi-One, 332
Nyamnjoh, Francis, 13–14
Nyanzi, Stella, 223, 225

Obadare, Ebenezer, 172–73
Obama, Barack, 330, 344–45
Obama, Michelle, 216
Obiechina, Emmanuel, 8
occupational identity, 164
Odi Massacre, Nigeria, 148–49
Oduro-Frimpong, Joseph, 189
@OfficerWoos, 165–66, 180–85, *182–83*
Ogola, George, 167
Olamide, 19
"One Dance" (Wizkid), 279
open letter, musical, 44–46, 55–56
Opoku-Agyemang, Kwabena, 249
ordinariness, 181–82
Ossei-Owusu, Shaun, 174
Osumare, Halifu, 124, 134
Otiono, Nduka, 258
Otu, Kwame, 208
Outtara, Alassane, 97
Owambe, 151–52

"Pack for Go" (Jungle Leaders), 121
Pan-Africanism, 309, 312–13, 320, 373
Parkins, Wendy, 300
paternalism, 117, 321
patriarchy, 15, 184, 213, 229, 332–33, 336–37. *See also* masculinity
peacebuilding, 112
Peel, Michael, 143
performative agency, 167–71
permanence, social media and, 175–76
Peterson, James Braxton, 47–48
"Petit Nouchi" (DJ Arafat), 98–99
P. Funk, 71
P Funk studio, 71
"Plantain Boy" (Timaya), 148, 150
play: agency and, 169; democracy and, 175; as pervasive, 169; power and, 171–72; regeneration of, 167–71; social media and, 176; theatrical conceptualization of, 171; Web 2.0 and, 168–69
pleasure: as aesthetics and protest, 145–52; denial of, 140–45; politicization of, 155; regulation of, 184; social media and, 256

police, 42, 45–46, 50–51, 79, 134, 154, 180–82, 227, 369
politicization, 112, 125–26, 136, 138, 152–55, 248, 261, 309, 335
Ponono, Mvuzo, 240
popular culture. *See* culture
"popular," idea of, 5–13
Posel, Deborah, 139
postcolonialism, 171, 174, 176, 180, 262–66, 339–40, 349
postmodernism, 21, 24, 146, 150, 330
precarity, 140–45, 150–51, 154–56, 196, 250, 269, 284, 289, 316–17, 320–21, 340
privatization, 140, 142, 146, 285, 311, 317n24, 328
Professor Jay, 69
Protégé, 129
protest, 356–57, 359–60, 377–78; music and, 38, 44–46, 49, 51, 61, 97, 120, 145–52, 354–55. *See also* activism; #FeesMustFall; #RhodesMustFall
Pupa Baja, 119, 121, 129
Pype, Katrien, 7

Queen Sheebah Karungi, 211
queer transgressions, 212–15

Rahim the Wizard, 127
Ranger, Terence, 251
rap music: celebrity and, 70–71; getting started in, 71–73; *kampu* and, 78–81; *maskani* and, 76–78; in Tanzania, 63–83; underground, 64–68, 73–75, 82–83; *Y en a Marre* movement and, 38, 44–46, 55–60. *See also* hip-hop; music
Red Flag Movement (RFM), 125
"Red Means Stop" (Asiedu), 199–203
reggae, 63, 79, 133, 281, 293
Reign Forest, 342

remix culture, 170–71
ReMmogo Youth Organization, 342–48
respectability, 69, 202, 213, 225, 286
responsive citizenship, 248–51
Revolutionary United Front (RUF) (Sierra Leone), 114, 116, 116n8
RFM. *See* Red Flag Movement (RFM)
Rhodes, Cecil, 237–38
#RhodesMustFall, 237–40, 242–51, 246, 358, 376
Rogie, S. E., 118
Ruddock, Andy, 12, 17
"Rude Boy" (Timaya), 150
RUF. *See* Revolutionary United Front (RUF) (Sierra Leone)
Rwanda, 56, 70n24, 219, 285

"Sagacité" (Douk Saga), 94–95
"Saï saï au Coeur," 39–43
Sall, Macky, 39–40, 43, 53–54, 58–59
@Samobaba_comedian, 165, 176–80, *177, 179*
sanctions, 209
Sankara, Thomas, 373
"Sanko" (Timaya), 150
Sankoh, Foday Saybana, 114, 116n8
Santana, Stephanie Bosch, 204
SAPE (Societe des Ambianceurs et des Personnes Elegantes [Society of tastemakers and elegant people]), 93
SAPs. *See* structural adjustment policies (SAPs)
Saucier, Khalil, 133, 137–38, 140
Scott, James, 82, 172
Senegal, 38, 317. *See also* Y en a Marre movement
Sénégal au Coeur, Le (Sall), 39–40
Senghor, Farba, 51–54
September, Jerome, 244–45
Sesay, Issa, 116n8
Seseko, Mobutu, 261
Setlhako, Ratsie, 330

sexism, 336–37. *See also* feminism; gender
sexuality: Afrobeats and, 151; and exploitation of students, 178–79; in flash fiction, 194–95; popular culture and, 112
"Sexy Ladies" (Timaya), 149–50
Shapard, Robert, 190
Shepler, Susan, 121, 349
Shipley, Jesse, 44, 124
Shivan Pavin, 211, 226–29, *228*
Sidibe, Malick, 8
Sierra Leone, 21, 111–29; civil war in, 111–16; evolution of music in, 116–24; music industry in, 124–26; youth desire for change in, 126–29
Sierra Leone People Party (SLPP), 113–14, 123, 127
signification, 76, 185, 241–42, 353–54
Simmert, Tom, 14
Singerman, Diana, 269, 271
SLPP. *See* Sierra Leone People Party (SLPP)
Small, Christopher, 91n4
Sobukwe, Robert, 372–73
social capital, 73–75, 103, 106–8, 271, 283
social identity, 164
social media, 164; citizenship and, 176; democracy and, 168–69, 270; fashion and, 292; permanence and, 175–76; in South Africa, 238–39, 244–48, 363–64, 375–76; in Zimbabwe, 255–73. *See also* Instagram
solidarity, 173, 371
Solo Beton, 92–93
Sommers, Marc, 285
Sonko, Ousmane, 42–43
Sound Sultan, 133
South Africa, 235–52, *246,* 352–78, 385–86
Soweto Uprising, 356, 366–69
Spencer, Zoe, 136–37

Ssempa, Martin, 208–9
Stevens, Siaka Probyn, 114
Strasser, Valentine Esegrabo Melvin, 115
Strehle, Susan, 192
Strong, Krystal, 174
structural adjustment policies (SAPs), 142–43
subjectivity, 81–82, 282, 292
Sylla, "Grand" Aly, 315–16, 315n22
"System, The" (Jungle Leaders), 123

Talla, Malal, 45–46
Tanzania, 21, 63–83, 120–21
Tata Pound, 57–58
Taylor, Diana, 338
television, 90n3, 341–42
10 cours à la nation (Sonko), 42–43
Teni, 153–55
Teuster-Jahn, Uta, 55
theater, 169–71, 332–40
Thiam, Mandiaye, 52–53
Thiat, 39–40, 48–55
Thing'o, Ngugi wa, 373
"This Is Me I'm Kuchu" (Shivan Pavin), 226
Thurnberg, Greta, 389
Timaya, 147–48, *148,* 148–51, 156
Toop, David, 134
Touré, Ahmed Sékou, 308–9, 312
Touré, Amadou Toumani, 57
tourism, 345–46
toxic masculinity, 195, 218, 336
transformation consciousness, 237–40
transgender individuals, 211, 216, 220–26, *221, 224, 226*
transgressive capital, 212, 214, 219, 228–31
transhumance politique, 54
Trinidad, 291
Trottier, Daniel, 241
True Story (Timaya), 147
Trump, Donald, 21

Truth and Reconciliation Commission, 236, 357
"Tsaya Tshwetso" (ReMmogo), 342–44
Tshwane University of Technology (TUT), 362–63
Tsvangirai, Morgan, 258
Tu-Face Idibia, 133, 135
Tunisia, 39
Turay, Amara Denis, 125
Turay, Ben, 127
TUT. *See* Tshwane University of Technology (TUT)
Twitter, 238–39, 241–42, 244–48, 262–66, 363–64, 375
"Two Fut Arata" (Emmerson), 121

Ubuntu, 348–49
Uganda, 21; Anti-Homosexuality Bill, 208–10; HIV/AIDS in, 209–10, 216; homophobia in, 208–12, 216, 218–19, 229–31; Mandarin schools in, 388; music in, 215–20, *217, 220–26, 221, 224, 226,* 226–29, *228;* sanctions on, 209; as youthful country, 213
Ugor, Paul, 175, 269–70, 330–31, 390
"Ukwu" (Timaya), 150
unemployment, 41, 73, 113, 127, 129, 140, 142, 213, 267, 269, 271, 285–86, 289, 327–29, 339–40, 349, 357
University of Pretoria (UP), 361–62
Unwin, Tim, 251–52
UP. *See* University of Pretoria (UP)
Upgrade (Timaya), 149–50
"Urban Guerrilla Poetry," 45–46, 49
uswahilini, 75–76

Veblen, Thorstein, 282–83, 287
Versace, Lino, 92–93
Villains, 71
Vinken, Henk, 132, 147
visibility, 38, 73, 120–21, 175, 178, 222–23, 225, 243, 257, 289, 342

Wade, Abdoulaye, 44–45, 50–51, 54, 59
Wai, Zubairu, 119
"waithood," 269–70, 285
Wamichano, Sizoh, 78
Weiss, Brad, 67, 124
Wells, Chris, 249
West Side Boys (Sierra Leone), 115
Wild Style (film), 63, 68
Wilson, Godfrey, 283
Windt, Theodore, 49–50
Wiwa, Ken Saro, 149
Wizkid, 279–80, 282, 291–93, 295–96, *297,* 298–99, 301
Woman of Many Firsts, A (play), 332–40
World Bank, 142, 328
World Economic Forum, 389
writing: flash fiction, 189–204; technology and, 188–89

Yeku, James, 151, 249
Yeleen, 57
Y en a Marre movement, 21; 2012 Senegalese election and, 45; founding of, 38; rap music and, 44, 55–60; "Saï saï au Coeur" and, 39–43; social movement diatribe and, 46–55; "Urban Guerrilla Poetry" and, 45–46, 49
Yenika-Agbaw, Vivian, 14
Yo Rap Bonanza, 69
"Your Case" (Teni), 153–55
Youth Development Fund (Botswana), 327
Yumkella, Kandeh Kolleh, 128

Ze Boy One Dar, 79
Zegeye, Adebe, 236
Zeleza, Paul, 138, 152
Zimbabwe, 255–73, 386
Zola, Emile, 57
zouglou, 94, 97, 103, 105
Zuma, Jacob, 359

Printed in the United States
by Baker & Taylor Publisher Services